D1034075

AMON

the life of Amon Carter, Sr. of Texas

For Angela — who
is a Better Interviewer
Than I am —
Best Wishes

Jerry Flemmons
Fort Worth.
March 30, 1980

Saldaña

AMON

the life of Amon Carter, Sr. of Texas

By
Jerry Flemmons

Jenkins Publishing Company
Austin, Texas
1978

Design by
Larry Smitherman

Library of Congress Catalogue No. 78-2973
I.S.B.N. 0-8363-0155-2

ALL PHOTOGRAPHS USED COURTESY OF
THE FORT WORTH *STAR-TELEGRAM*

To Christopher Scott......

This is why the kite was late

No man on this foot-stool can rise to git up and say I ever knowinly injered no man or wimmin folks, while all agree than my Show is ekalled by few and exceld by none, embracin as it does a wonderful colleckshun of livin' wild Beests of Pray, snaix in great profushun, a endliss variety of life-size wax figgers, and... the most amazin' little cuss ever introduced to a discriminatin' public.

— *Artemus Ward*

Contents

Acknowledgements

This is the way Amon Carter was. He was neither better nor worse, more nor less, but as he is shown here. He was this way, which, by any measurement, is a kind of greatness. For what he was, who he was and where he was, Amon Carter was a man of importance and distinction, and I grew to admire him. Amon Carter was a great man, and altogether a human one. I attempted to show his full personality, and if I have failed, the fault is mine, not those who recalled the Amon Carter of their lives.

He began, for me, as a master's degree thesis, and ten years passed before I set about to expand him into a book. In those years are countless people who deserve more credit than I can provide here. First and foremost, my deepest gratitude is for three frank, perceptive, gracious ladies, Nenetta Burton Carter, Ruth Carter Johnson and Katrine Deakins. They opened their memories, their files and their hearts, honestly and patiently answering hours of questions, many of which must have been painful for them. I must thank, too, Amon Carter Junior, who in many ways became more than his father, and other executives of the *Star-Telegram* who participated in the project and allowed me full access to the newspaper's files, and generously provided me with time to research and write. Jack Butler, Jack Campbell, Jack Tinsley, Phil Record, Bert Honea, Jack Douglas, Cal Sutton — all have my grateful appreciation.

Sam Kinch Junior and Paul Rowan wrote earlier master degree theses which were invaluable for basic research on the lives of Amon and Jim Record. Hettie Arleth, the newspaper's librarian, and her reference room staff, especially Charlcia Bullard, allowed me to poke through the endless mass of clippings and were unflinchingly patient and kind to all my requests. Dorothy Hooper worked many hours searching for pictures. John Moulder, Z. Joe Thornton and Caleb Pirtle assisted with research and interviews. Dr. Jack Bell, Dr. Otha Spencer and Dr. Fred Tarpley, all of East Texas University, through friendship and professional advice, guided me through the thesis and into this lengthier work.

My friends, Pat and Bill Massad, provided counsel, editing and a proper writer's garret. Gerry Barker corrected my poor spelling and untangled grammatical snarls.

None of this would have been possible without the assistance of the men and women of the *Star-Telegram*, all of whom are excellent story tellers. In no particular order, they are: Bert Griffith, George Dolan, Irv Farman, Pauline Naylor, Elston Brooks, Jim Trinkle, W. L. Redus, Ida Belle Hicks, C. L. Richhart, Leroy Menzing, Bess Stephenson, Charles Boatner, Mack Williams, Flem Hall, Alf Evans, Jim Vachule, Lou Hudson, E. D. Alexander, Al Panzera, George Smith, James Byron,

DeWitt Reddick, Walter Claer, Claire Eyrich, Leonard Sanders, Ed Capers, Frank Mills, Bascom Timmons, Dean Blanton, Janice Williams and Jon McConal. Mary Crutcher, Jack Gordon, Delbert Willis and Willard Barr remembered their encounters with Amon Carter while working for the Fort Worth *Press.* Others who deserve credit are Congressman Jim Wright, J. Frank Norris Junior, Stanley Marcus, C. R. Smith, James Farley, Bill Loursey, Lon Evans, Davy O'Brien, Aaron Priest, Jimmy Durante, Bob Hope, Chester Shaw, Andy Fournier, Lawrence Wood, Don Woodard, Reverend Gaston Foote, and my wife, Martha, who endured the emotional upheavals inherent in a project of this size.

Probably I have missed someone who deserves credit for real or implied assistance given me, and if I have, I apologize.

Errors in this work, of course, are mine and mine alone and cannot be attributed to anyone else. I would welcome having the errors brought to my attention. That, however, is a useless exercise for most of you. Elston Brooks is anxiously and gleefully waiting to point out each and every mistake.

Introduction

I never knew Amon Carter. He was seven years dead when I arrived at his *Star-Telegram*. Death, however, seemed not to evict his presense. He *was* there, and, to an equivocal point, still is there, perhaps always will be. It was impossible not to be confronted by Amon, in substance if not in person. People spoke of him as though he hadn't succumbed to illness and old age but only just stepped out for a moment to give another cheer for Fort Worth. His name dropped easily and casually into conversations, and more often than not, "Mr. Carter" was uttered with a reverence and awe I could not understand. His reporters, who either revered or disliked him, retold favorite "Amon Carter" stories. He, because his name lay on so many public things of Fort Worth, continued to pop up in print. Politicians and civic leaders conjured up his memory and deeds to emphasize this and that project. Amon Carter just would not go away.

AMON

I saw him once as a dim image on a tiny Emerson television screen. He was inaugurating WBAP television. With hundreds of others come to witness that impossible invention, I crushed against windows of a hardware store in Stephenville, a small college town west of Fort Worth. I was more taken with the medium than the messenger, but in my mind Amon still appears as an indistinct Lilliputian, gray-haired and portly, whose presense on that miniscule round screen was nothing more than witchcraft.

I was then one of his boys, a *Star-Telegram* carrier, but did not associate that minikin figure with the newspaper. I did not live in West Texas. Stephenville was — is — in North Central Texas. The *Star-Telegram*, however, was dogged in its assertion that any piece of the state west of Fort Worth was West Texas. I believed the newspaper's contention and grew up thinking that I was part of that vast Canaan. I was told, and never doubted, that other regions were inferior to my, and the *Star-Telegram*'s, West Texas. From my small spot on the sandy farmland of North Central Texas the newspaper assured me nothing else on earth mattered except West Texas and West Texans.

I grew up with the *Star-Telegram*. Everybody I knew did. The *Star-Telegram* was of primacy for us long before I understood it had significance outside our small sphere of being. It came daily, as constant and comforting as our families, and was not just a newspaper but *the* newspaper, a wise theocratic companion that spoke of life beyond West Texas as a *National Geographic* explorer explained the customs of Bantus in Africa. In the *Star-Telegram*, there was nothing or no one of consequence but West Texas and West Texans (*East* Texans living in all that suffocating foliage could have been, for all we knew, a lost tribe of Israel; we felt only pity for them). When words became important to me, I wished to write them for the *Star-Telegram*. No higher journalistic standard existed.

A public education in Texas rarely was enlightening and it was several years before I knew the state had other, good newspapers or that really superior journalism was practiced elsewhere: New York, Chicago, in Washington and Los Angeles, even Kansas City and St. Louis — the national newspaper shrines. All else, I learned, was provincial, secondary. Interior American newspapers were too regional in their viewpoints, too local, to own distinction. Everybody believed that. Those beliefs, of course, were as misconceived as the *Star-Telegram*'s version of West Texas.

For its time and place, and under a pardonable sugary chauvinism, the *Star-Telegram* was not just another good regional newspaper, but a great one. By any measurement it was a better newspaper than the worst examples of Mr. Hearst, as good or better than his best. Within its wide territory and for its subject matter it was as comprehensive, as authoritative, as scrupulous as the New York *Times*, as literate as the *Star* of Kansas City, certainly as indomitable as Chicago's *Tribune*. It could also be exasperatingly dull, priggish and puritanical, boorish in its never-ending role as ringmaster for the grand circus that is Texas.

Measured against today's journalistic yardstick, the *Star-Telegram* would be short. It raked little muck, poked under few public rocks, supported too strongly the Establishment bloc, ignored almost altogether the social problems of the day. It would be considered racist, inside and out. Its boosterism voice was too strident, too constant. Newspapers, even then, reflected society around them, and, for Texas, that meant Amon Carter.

No, the early *Star-Telegram* cannot fairly be compared with today's newspapers, not even with its own modern self. It represented an historical period passed by, a time when regionalism had a purpose, when growth and progress were virtues courted by all of America.

The *Star Telegram*'s heavy journalistic sins were (1) location in Fort Worth, Texas, a side-alley city of America, and (2) a purposely myopic eyesight. While newspapers adjudged great and important were busying themselves with world and national matters, the *Star-Telegram* focused on events and people around it. It reported in meticulous detail and depth the near news, recorded and interpreted external affairs only as they related to the lives of its readers. That's why Amelia Earhart's Atlantic flight was given less attention than a new Fort Worth/Denver airmail route and how Washington political coverage largely ignored national opinion in favor of Texas bias.

In all important ways, the *Star-Telegram* honored its First Amendment franchise with complete and encompassing service to its readers. That made it a good newspaper. What made it exceptional was that it served fully and faithfully an area larger than the whole of New England, did it for so long, and for much of the time without coercion of adequate competition. Dr. DeWitt Reddick, a respected, nationally-known journalism scholar and retired head of the University of Texas School of Communication, said, "The Star-Telegram was the best illustration of a newspaper so interwoven with the birth and growth of the country around it that people accepted it as part of their lives. It was a family member. What it did was serve. I don't believe any newspaper, anywhere, at any time, ever gave so much to its area."

Stanley Walker, the almost legendary city editor of the New York *Herald-Tribune* in the 1930s, returned to his birthplace in Central Texas after World War II, sick of newspapering and big cities. He lived out his remaining years as a rancher and sometime writer. Walker correctly assessed the basic weaknesses of Texas newspapers which, in his opinion, were (1) lack of boldness — all feared controversy, and (2) the Chamber of Commerce puffery that too often passed for news. *Lone Star Merry-*

Go-Round, an anonymous pamphlet published in the mid-1930's, liked none of Texas' major newspapers, but gave grudging points to the Dallas *Morning News* editorial pages. Houston's papers, and San Antonio's, were dismissed with verbal sneers. The *Star-Telegram*, then the South's largest newspaper, was ". . . the Bible of Texas' most bigoted section," and seemed to exist for no other reason than to promote Amon Carter and his enterprises. The booklet, obviously unobjective, and Walker, were correct in that Texas newspapers spent too much time and space on civic hosannas.

In defense, however, growth was *the* story requiring on-going attention. Texas was rich in potential, poor in actuality, filled with badly educated poor people. Growth desperately was needed, and newspapers stumped for it. Because of Amon Carter, the *Star-Telegram* was superlative at the game. The *Star-Telegram* gave its readers what they wanted, and needed: hope and pride.

Readers' attitudes and needs have changed, as have those of newspapers, including the *Star-Telegram*. It was, like rumble seats and good nickel cigars, and our innocence, of another time, but of its era and its place, it was a giant. Amon Carter would have nothing less.

I have gone on too long explaining the *Star-Telegram*, but it was the most visible and viable public evidence of Amon Carter, a living extension of the frenzied zealousy with which he was stricken. It is what most people in Texas remember about him. What the newspaper was, he was.

But what he was not, was a newspaperman. He was a publisher, and publishers and journalism often are incompatible, may in fact be antagonistic to one another. He was not even a very good publisher. Amon was building West Texas and Fort Worth. He had little time for the nuts and bolts operation of any business, especially a newspaper requiring daily, even hourly, tending.

Amon did not set out to be a publisher. He never had the "calling." He fell into the newspaper business. He was a salesman who in the beginning just happened to be selling newspapers. His journalistic education came first from gentle, impractical Louis Wortham, the *Star-Telegram*'s original publisher and, later, Jimmy North, a knowing, generous man who for more than fifty years set the newspaper's unerring course and kept in harness Amon's more rash news-creating conduct. North was editor. James Record, the managing editor, made the *Star-Telegram* happen twice a day with snap and precision. Bert Honea, tall, athletic, as lean in body as in his spending habits, kept the newspaper empire solvent in spite of Amon's wheeler-dealer spending habits. Harold Hough, the circulation manager, placed the paper before readers and developed radio and television wings of Carter's publishing house. Al Shuman filled news pages with ads. Those men — "St. Amon and the five apostles," mused a cynical reporter — created a formidable sextumvirate; they built the *Star-Telegram* kingdom. They, said one observer, were "the best newspaper team in history." That is a much too liberal evaluation but doubtless they were the South's best. They proved that much.

While Amon had to be educated to the purposes of journalism, the newspaper's underlying philosophy was his alone: Sell, promote and build the city and region, and the paper will grow and prosper along with them. "When the lake rises, the boat will rise, too," was his way of explaining the newspaper's responsibilities. Amon told William Randolph Hearst in 1924, "We have never seen the good in being a nagging kind of newspaper." In 1920, syndicated columnist Claude Callen wrote, "The *Star-Telegram* is alive, clean and full of news. It works for a quarter of Texas and strives to build itself without pulling others down." A fair appraisal.

Amon, however, created a unique problem. The publisher was the newspaper's principal civic news source and news maker. That alone was trouble enough. North believed newspapermen, including publishers, should keep themselves out of print. His canon extended to families of newspapermen — Phil Record, nephew of North and James Record, won a grade school contest and an editorial board meeting was called to decide whether to publish the youngster's picture.

North ultimately gave up on Amon but the policy was in force for others, and in almost fifty years, little more than obituaries of *Star-Telegram* employees appeared in the paper. And if Amon making news was a headache for North, it was maddening for rival newspaper editors forced to provide space, often on front pages, for a competitor.

Beyond Amon's conventional newsmaking were his little antics, many of them page one stories as far away as Europe. How does an honest editor ignore a man who fires a pistol through elevator doors during a national political convention? North did, but with nagging conscience, and one almost can hear his anguished sigh rumbling out of the past. National syndicated columnists wrote regularly of Amon. Many were published in the *Star-Telegram*. More were not. The publisher's files contain scores of killed columns laid to rest by the ever-vigilant North ("This seemed a little too bullish," he scribbled on a Westbrook Pegler column.)

For the final thirty years of his life Amon Carter had more urgent interests than the newspaper but he was identified as its voice, and also as cheerleader for Fort Worth and much of Texas. He was recognized nationally as foremost exponent of the best of Texas: the joyous, expansive, unrestrained celebration of life, the genuine unfettered friendliness, the rugged individualism. And also of the worst: the doctrine that everything here is bigger and better, the loud, boisterous public displays, the practiced pretense of uncultured ignorance. Those who disliked Amon said he was an embarrassment, that he played a role no longer true of Texas. His supporters said he behaved as outsiders *thought* Texans were, so what was the harm? Not that the argument affected Amon. He did as he pleased. He did not invent Texas exaggeration but he practiced it with a zealotry and élan never seen before, or since. If you think of Texas either as a superlative state or merely a state of hyperbolic superlatives, credit/blame Amon Carter.

Amon *was* the mythical Texas. He created the modern fictional Texan portrayed in movies and books and on stage. Throughout its rather histrionic life, Texas has been a land festooned with glittering bombast. We have always been a braggy people. To hide the early misery, the ignorance, the uncomfortable circumstance in which Texans found themselves, they swaggered and boasted and overplayed their roles to a world baffled by the sound and noise rising from our Southwestern position.

It fell to Amon to arrive at a time when Texas was becoming engraved on the national mind. The 1920s and 1930s and 1940s were decades of Texanism's ascension, especially in Washington. John Nance Garner was vice president. Sam Rayburn was House speaker. Young LBJ stepped onto the American political stage. Aviation soared off the plains of Texas to commercial and military successes. The automobile became a way of life, one operating on gasoline, and Texas had the most gas and oil. In that time, too, Texans — particularly, the younger, more restless Texans — skedaddled the state. Texas was a place to get away from, wrote Stanley Walker. Texans went everywhere. They were a curious bunch. Away from the state, they were more Texan than at home. They exaggerated their nasal patois — the twangy lingua franca passing for English in West Texas, expanded their personalities into cartoon parodies, magnified themselves until outsiders came to believe the state was some kind of super factory for hyper-humanoids.

Amon Carter played the professional Texan with a perfection that would have shamed a Barrymore. "A Texan is a Texan wherever he may be," Amon was fond of saying. He invented the cowboy, the yippee-ing westerner which parodied the real thing, but which was taken out and pranced before America with a master's proficiency for living theater.

Within Texas he was a power, a force of politics, of civic boosterism, of industrial development. He was potent and important for the reason that he thrust himself into everything, partly because he was an insatiable meddler in affairs of others, partly because he could affect success when no one else could, and he knew it. He was that rarest of exceptional humans: a dreamer who made dreams come true. Because he could make success happen, Amon Carter controlled Fort Worth and West Texas, and possibly was more powerful within a city and region than any man has ever been. He ran Fort Worth. He lauded it, loved it, lavished gifts on it when it was good, punished it when it was bad. Amon was *the* Establishment of Fort Worth. To oppose him was to live a lean existence outside the city's hierarchy. He kept his power almost until the end of his life, until after World War II, when all of America changed.

West Texas, as hungry for attention and love as a flogged orphan, acceded to Amon Carter. If Haskell township needed federal funds for a new hospital, city fathers jumped into their old pickups, drove to Fort Worth, and laid their problem on his desk. A postmaster's position for Sonora? Candidates applied to Amon Carter. A state park for Monahans? New roads for Tulia? No problem. Amon Carter could do it, and did.

He succeeded because for fifty years he primed the pump of friendship with men — industry leaders and politicians — who ran the country, and because "No" was not an approved answer. "To me," Amon told Alva Johnston, who wrote about the publisher for the *Saturday Evening Post*, " 'No' is just a word in the dictionary. I don't often consult the dictionary."

Amon, the salesman, never retreated. Thirty years passed between his initial efforts to collect a General Motors assembly plant and the day first dirt was turned for construction of a Chevrolet factory. The mammoth bomber plant was lost to Tulsa but Amon pestered FDR and the military until Fort Worth got its airplane manufactory.

He was a stunning salesman who, someone said, could have sold Tupperware to Cartier's. He had the glibness of a snake oil peddler combined with the dogmatism of a saved-again evangelist and the sincerity of a first-term Congressman. The salesman was basic to Amon Carter's personality. His most primary *persona* was that of a conservative businessman. He could be an outrageous Babbitt in municipal affairs. He was a philanthropist. He was a humble country boy awed by big cities and famous people. His theatrical Texan act — the cowboy — became the best known and remembered of his characterizations, and the most useful.

All of those Amon Carters were at work and play in the first half of this century, each separate and distinct, all tempered by his considerable emotional range. He was at any and all times ebullient, gracious, intractable, articulate, pompous, argumentative, egotistical, phenomenal, mesmerizing, dictatorial and genius. "Peripatetic," *Time* called him, and perhaps that is the best one-word definition of Amon Carter. He was both a romantic and a realist, a sentimentalist of the past and a futurist. He had a mercurial anger ("He madded up sudden," remembered a contemporary), which could vanish as quickly and mysteriously as it arrived. He never forgot friends nor forgave enemies. He would be kind, magnanimous, overwhelmingly generous and altruistic one minute, petty, greedy, spiteful and selfish the next.

Philosopher Wilhelm Hegel's lament, "Only one man understood me . . . and he didn't understand me," could have been written of Amon Carter.

The publisher, also an uncomplex man, never questioned himself. He was satisfied. Excepting the period when his son was a prisoner-of-war, those who knew him best can't remember a single moment when he experienced the self-doubts peculiar to the rest of us. Qualms would have been a nuisance to him. Though he would not have understood the source or term, Amon Carter was ruled by the rationale of Nietzscheanism: aggrandizement and the will to power flowed out of him.

When he died, Fort Worth suffered a business and civic recession. Truth is, the entire country waded in the beginnings of a temporary idleness, but surely that cannot be blamed on the death of Amon Carter. Autocracy is not an innately evil form of governing if the autocrat is benevolent, and Amon most certainly was. But one-man rule doesn't provide for competitors or successors, and Amon left Fort Worth without an emperor. The city's leaders, themselves leaderless for the first time in half a century, reacted with no reaction. The missing Amon Carter caused a slack no one man could take up. By dying, someone said, Amon Carter committed his first disservice to Fort Worth. He robbed the town of his leadership for all eternity because, despite his omnipotence, he was not, as some suspected, immmortal.

He was only seventy-five.

I have called Amon Carter "important," a vastly overworked and meaningless word. He was "important," I suppose, but never so much as he and his friends believed, or now, as legends say he was. His old Democratic Party colleague, James Farley, who seemed to understand the frail control individuals have on history, told me, "Amon had an importance at the time. We all did, but not anymore." One of Carter's newsmen, Bert Griffith, said, "Texas has produced two men of greatness . . . Sam Houston and Amon Carter."

A generous overstatement. Amon had a significance for a city and region and exerted some unmeasurable influence nationally, but he was, for history's sake, just a unique man of his time and place.

This explanation of Amon Carter, this establishing of the structures which produced him, seems, in the telling, unduly forbidding and dull, and the life of Amon Carter was neither. The life and times of Amon Carter were many things: unpredictable, surprising, lively, grand and exhilarating. Alf Evans was there in the latter days and though never a part of the frenzy around Amon Carter, he nevertheless was a skillful observer and preserver of "Amon Carter stories" with an intellectual's ability for analysis.

"How Amon Carter and the newspaper are remembered in a thousand years is unimportant. Nothing will matter then anyway," said Alf. "But in the old days, everybody had fun. That's what everybody remembers about Amon Carter. They had fun."

And so they did.

Prologue

Washington. Early spring, 1939. A man leaves the White House, stepping into the twilight of a new night. Mrs. Roosevelt sees him through the door, fondly calls, "Good night, and please come again." In response, he touches the brim of his white, western-crimped hat, answering, "Thank you, I will. I've never seen him looking better. See that he takes care of himself." The door closes. The man adjusts his knee-length, bone-colored topcoat, girts the loose belt ends tightly, binding them in a square knot. He steps briskly from under the *portecochere*, strides to and through the gate, nodding politely to the guards, who call him by name with a reverence used only for important visitors.

On the street he walks quickly, as if late for an appointment, although his next meeting is not for two hours. He merely is a fast walker. Here and there he pauses to glance in shop windows, inspecting this and that article, for he is a man curious about everything, a compulsive, impulsive shopper always in search of new gadgets and knick-knacks. He smiles at Washingtonians on the street, and they smile back at the handsome, distinguished man in the white western hat. He is content, and happy, pleased with his meeting at the White House.

For an hour he and President Roosevelt had chatted as old friends comfortable with one another. They spoke of their children, especially the man's daughter, who had visited in the White House with the Roosevelts. The man told FDR a new joke. The President laughed appreciatively. Suddenly serious, the President solicited the man's opinion on the situation in Europe. The man would travel to England soon and the President asked him to report on conditions there. "I think it's already bad," said the man, "and getting worse. I don't see how we can stay out of it."

"Nor do I," answered the President.

The man continued his thoughts on war, urging FDR to move more quickly in preparing the country for yet another confrontation in Europe. The people will support you," advised the man, "I'll help. All of your friends will."

Later, the President sought the man's counsel on economy, attitudes of businessmen toward the administration, the wisdom of instituting more taxes. The man brought up the subject of a new national park he was interested in. FDR promised his support.

They spoke frankly, earnestly, for more than an hour, until interrupted by Mrs. Roosevelt. She announced dinner, and invited the man to dine with them. He declined. He had a later appointment with several military men. The President offered a limousine for the man's return to his hotel. "No, thanks," he said, "I like to walk."

Full dark. He arrives at the Mayflower Hotel, enters its lobby and surveys the solid elegance. The man always has been impressed with the hotel, his favorite in Washington. Pausing briefly, he makes a decision: He will have dinner. Uncharacteristically, he will dine alone. He dislikes eating alone, but he is suddenly hungry and his need for food overrides his antipathy for being alone. He walks quickly to the dining room, passes his hat and coat to an attendant. He is greeted enthusiastically by the maitre d', who gushes, "Welcome back to Washington. We are honored to have you with us again." He asks for a table by the window. The maitre d' suggests a drink before dinner. He declines. He only drinks in social situations. He orders dinner, and waits quietly for it, watching strollers pass in the darkness. The dining room is almost full, because Washington is an early town.

The man eats. He drinks a final cup of coffee and calls for the check. He signs his suite number, leaves a ten dollar bill on the table. At the door, the maitre d' waits with his hat and coat. He accepts them, hooks a finger inside the hat, drapes the coat over an arm. He palms a twenty for the maitre d'. The man leaves. Outside he suddenly stops, reverses himself, and returns to the dining room. He hands his hat and coat to the maitre d' and strides to the nearest table. It is occupied by an elderly couple. He smiles at them, indicating an empty chair. He asks, "May I?" They appear quizzical, but nod. He slides out the chair, and steps into it.

Above the crowd of diners, he waits. Gradually, the people notice the distinguished man standing on a chair. They stop what they are doing to stare. The room becomes silent. Good, he has their attention. He smiles, raises his hand to his mouth and shouts, "HOOOOO-RAAAAAY FOR . . . FORT WORTH . . . AND WEST TEXAAASSSSSS!"

The elderly lady drops her fork. A head is thrust out of swinging doors leading to the kitchen. Toward the back of the room, a man jumps to his feet, startled. The room is in bewildered silence. Gradually, a low conversational murmur returns. A few pieces of laughter rise above the ripple of talk. Then there is scattered applause.

The man steps from the chair, returns it under the table, thanks the elderly couple. He walks from the room, collects his hat and coat.

The maitre d' calls after him, "Good evening again, sir."

"Good night," he replies, smiling.

Chapter 1

I and they were but creatures of circumstances — the circumstances of an unfenced world.

—Anonymous Cowboy

Credo quia absurdum
I believe it because it is absurd

You may forget the singer, but don't forget the song.

—Traditional

Truth is very liable to be left-handed in history.

—Alexander Dumas

AMON

1

Lan Twohig cost his daddy six bits and a lifetime supply of syphilis. His daddy paid the one and collected the other to and from Miss Molly Hipp on a bed of corn shucks spread in an open oxen cart somewhere on the road between Indianola and San Antonio. The year was 1842, when the Texas Republic was young and healthy, and Ms. Hipp was neither. Lan Twohig's daddy surely received the disease because when Molly Hipp died a year later her death was attributed to chronic syphilis and alcoholism, and possibly the .44 caliber hole above and slightly to the left of her nose.

In later years Lan, always more jolly than he had a right to be, joshed that he and his daddy had two things in common. Neither ever saw the other and each had stayed with Molly Hipp less than twenty minutes. Ms. Hipp carried Lan the usual term, then dropped him in the rear room of a brothel beside San Pedro Creek in

San Antonio. The midwife, a rented Mexican lady, took Lan home after Molly looked on her new son and said tenderly, "Get rid of it."

Lan lived out his first year among the midwife's natural children. She passed him to pious nuns of San Juan Mission who doled him out to an Indian family within the mission compound. In his sixth year the nuns, feeling they could tolerate his wicked illegitimacy no longer, dealt him to a farming couple, Mattie Mae and John Golson, who worked 160 acres near Seguin, east of San Antonio. The Golsons were mediocre farmers, poor parents and only middling with acts of quasi-kindness toward Lan. They gave him his first real clothing, cured his cornmush-created malnutrition, presented him with a name — Enoch — and a basic education in the community log school.

John didn't last long enough for Lan to get used to him. The farmer died in the cold February of 1849. Mattie Mae became marm of the school. She was well beyond her prime, slit-mouthed, icy-eyed, a Land's-Sake and Mercy-Me woman, a living beatitude in an old print dress who tut-tutted loudly at life's crimes against her, of which there were many, but especially Lan. The nuns thoughtfully had told the Golsons of Lan's corn shuck pedigree and Mattie Mae soon came to feel the small thin boy was a special cross sent to test her faith. She alternately beat and prayed the devil out of Lan. He endured his beatings and cascades of tuts because life, he believed, was like that. From his eighth year Mattie Mae taught him the value of hard work by renting him to neighboring farmers.

In 1855, Lan Twohig *nee* Enoch Golson, thirteen, small and thin but infused with an inner toughness, again was alone. Mattie Mae tutted her last. Pneumonia. Lan did not wait for fate to pitchfork him again but gathered his few possessions, Mrs. Golson's life savings of $53, and found the nearest road which incidentally took him south.

Where Lan roamed for the next forty years or so I do not know with any certainty. He became a cowboy, a *Texas* cowboy, which was the original model. The then-new profession was being created by men who practiced severe anonymity, and whose lives were less romantic and adventuresome than John Wayne has led us to believe. The cowboy, or "cow boy," as the term was written before he began riding on Hollywood's purple celluloid landscapes, was a kind of Cossack in service of the prairie czars then inventing the American cattle industry. His forefathers were the Spanish Conquistadores, his cousins, the mountainmen who first ventured into the West. And he was, says Historian Paul Horgan, ". . . the last of the clearly traditional characters [born] from the kind of land he worked in and the kind of work he did."

He neither built not explored nor populated the West but moved ever so briefly across it, as capricious and lonely as the blowing dust. Dime novelists and penny dreadful authors scribbled magniloquent lies about the cowboy for rapt Eastern readers, but saw him only in town, often ending long cattle drives with a few desperate hours of extravagant carousal before returning to a life of social desolation. Like a cloistered monk of some distant forgotten monastery, the cowboy served his god, the rancher, and toiled at labors decidedly unglamorous. Moving often from ranch to ranch, the cowboy made few lasting friendships. He was untutored and ignorant. For endless months he lived on the range, burned in summer, frozen in winter, as punished as the cattle he attended. He slept on the ground under "hen-skin" blankets. He arose at 4 a.m., or earlier, and often was not asleep again until midnight. He was fed a constant diet of beans — "Pecos strawberries," greasy stews and Arbuckle's coffee. His aches and sprains were treated with heavy coats of axle grease, or prickly pear poultices. To stay awake during long nights of riding herd, he rubbed tobacco juice in his eyes. He lived in a society of men, and made love to the only available women, the ubiquitous "soiled doves" and "Fallen Angels," on almost a seasonal basis, like some animal in heat. He smelled of the horse he rode, of the cows he tended, and the dung of both. Miasmic as a nocturne, the cowboy was a neutered man, often profane, never profound, illiterate, itinerant — a harsh child who went crooked or stayed straight, or alternated, like an electric current. He hid his past behind such curious aliases as "Shanks" and "Pieface," "Muley," "Stormy" and "Joggy." He observed no religion but the Trinity of cow, horse and land. For his always-brief entry into towns, he exploded with drunkenness and venery, exchanging six months' wages for a few hours of release from his Trappist confinement. His was a "soulless, aimless" existence, wrote one of the few introspective cowboys who left the range world when he saw it for what it was.

No American character endured as the cowboy, though the cowboy of Hollywood and Zane Grey was nothing like the reality. The cowboy lasted little longer than *The West*, as few as twelve, perhaps as many as a score of years. Behind him came the men with hoes and plows and wives. The cowboy scorned the new arrivals, but the farmer lasted; the cowboy did not. He went away to other jobs, went away to other truths and, finally, he just went away.

So it must have been for Lan Twohig.

As many cowboys, Lan buried his past by assuming another name. His final and lasting name came, he said, from an old man, Albert Twohig, and Landers, a foreman for Shanghai Pierce. Lan said he rode with Pierce in South Texas, and immediately after the Civil War, helped the rancher move a cow herd to New Orleans. Pierce and his friend, Captain Richard King, whose ranch would become the world's largest, were a pair of those feral Caesars then composing the cattle industry. Pierce was a huge man whose voice, cowboys said, could be heard a mile distant. He became a legend with antics such as, during a late-in-life trip abroad, trying to visit His Holiness, the Pope, unannounced. Swiss guards forced him out of the Vatican with drawn bayonets.

Lan sold cattle to King and Pierce, Longhorns he had gathered, perhaps illegally, on open ranges, and Longhorns he chased and trapped in the barbarous land called the *brasada*.

Nothing ever said of the Texas Longhorn was an exaggeration. It came from where every mean and marvelous thing of Texas came, from the malignant, iniquitous brush country — the *brasada* — above the Rio Grande. It was a tortuous Eden, a natural savage wilderness without relief from the Nueces River to the Mexican Border. Every living thing inside fought for its place. There were mesquite, both brush and tree, with dirk-like thorns, and the Spanish dagger, walls of prickly pear cactus which to O. Henry seemed as ". . . large, fat hands," yellow blooming *huisache*, and the catclaw called by Mexicans "Wait-A-Minute" because it grabbed and held. Either dusted with fine gray blowing sand or, wrote Horgan, "beaten by deluges that hissed as they first struck the hot ground," the brush country was a haven for nature's angry misanthropes — the quill-backed peccary, the rattlesnake, the Longhorn. Virtually waterless and endless to a man on horseback, the *brasada* was a maze of interlocking thickets enclosing small clearings. There were wandering paths worn to dust by animals but many dead-ended and few men knew a safe route. It was for this barbarism of a land that the first cowboys, who were Mexicans, devised leather leggings called chaps. Without protection, the brush would claw a man to pieces.

In its brush country sanctuary, the Longhorn was an evil thing. Evolved from strayed Moorish cattle, the Longhorn, J. Frank Dobie wrote, was the ". . . parody of a cow." It had elk legs, could outrun a horse, was bony, high at the shoulders, low at the tail, shaggy-haired, gaunt-rumped, with a goat-limber neck holding a massive head from which grew horns curved like twin scimitars. In a wild state, cowboys claimed, the Longhorn lived on wind and gravel. An adult bull weighed twelve hundred pounds and more of muscle and bone, and a few stood as tall as a man on horseback. Angered or wounded, it feared nothing and once provoked, would attack anything, even the black bears that once roamed Texas. Should its victim escape, the Longhorn followed indefatigably with its nose to the ground sniffing the trail like a wolf. The wild Longhorn had no herd instinct, but kept a few wives for which he was a fierce champion. At sunset he called his family together for the night and his bellow, heard by cowboys camped in the *brasada*, was fearsome, chilling — the roar of a true wild beast.

The Longhorn was never civilized. It was chased down, dragged to corrals, herded, branded, conditioned to a gentler environment, but never tamed. Man and Longhorn at best held an uneasy peace. Gathered on the unfenced ranches of Southwest Texas, the Longhorns foraged on sweet grasses, multiplied, spread over Texas, and became an industry. Soon after the Civil War, when Northerners cried for meat, ranchers began driving their Longhorns to Kansas railheads. "Them Longhorns," said an Oklahoma rancher of this century, "could live on nothing, and you could drive them to market and it didn't hurt 'em because they wasn't any good to begin with." The Longhorn's meat was sinewy and gamy but it was beef and northern stomachs complained little.

The era of cattle drives lasted less than a dozen years. Railroads came to Texas. Barbed wire enclosed land. Foreign cattle, the Herefords and Angus, with fat bodies and stubby legs, were introduced. By the late 1880s, most Longhorns had been bred away, though a rancher might keep a dozen for old times' sake. In distant reaches of Texas, a few wild Longhorns survived but slowly they died or were killed by Cowboys to protect the pureblooded cows and, like the cowboys, they were no more.

Late in life, Lan Twohig was a windy man, given to bragging, so his claim of invincibility in the *brasada* perhaps was untrue. He said he was the best man ever to chase Longhorns in the brush, better even than the Mexicans who felt a mythical kinship with the wild cattle. Lan bragged he feared nothing the bush land offered. He entered with a short rope and a pistol, often afoot if the bull had come to a fighting place. He was a sure roper with the braided lariat and quick enough to escape the Longhorns' charge.

Other cowboys went in pairs, even by fours, to chase down, surround and capture the worst of the bulls. Lan went alone. He had a sense of survival, an innate grasp on the Longhorns' souls. He could track them even in the rocky stretches that left no hoofprints, intuitively following the correct trail. He knew their habits, their instincts for escape. He knew the moment they would turn and fight and he was ready with the rope or, when necessary, the pistol. Once seen, a Longhorn had no secrets from Lan. He knew how it would charge, how low or high the horns would be carried, how the animal hooked, how it turned, how desperately it would struggle against the cowboy.

Lan remembered the *brasada* and its fierce Longhorns as the best time of his life.

He sold the live cattle to ranchers, the dead ones for their hides, and occasionally worked on ranches. Mostly, Lan was just a cowboy. In 1867, he rode with one of the first cattle drives to Kansas and later accompanied four other herds before growing weary of the trail. He wandered from ranch to ranch, cowboying for the Double Moon, the G-4 near Marfa, the Rocking C in the Panhandle. Lan saw little cash money, was alone and often lonely, never married. In the late 1880s, he went beyond the Pecos to become the sole *gringo* cowboy on Moody's place. I do not know Moody's other name but he operated a ranch above the Rio Grande, probably on the eastern fringe of the Big Bend.

Lan, in those years, was an economized man in stature, manner and speech. His eyes were blue over a flattish nose. There was graying thin hair, the weather-pinched face and morning aches, but Lan was muscular, quick with his movements, hard and strong for his size.

In 1892, at fifty, Lan was too old for ranch life but he had nowhere else to go. In that year, he fought the bull. In that year, at dawn of a sunless autumn day, he stood before the green wall of a sandy gully, remembering the earlier better times, the *brasada*, the excitement of the brush and wild Longhorns.

Two days before, Lan had seen the bull Longhorn, a big blue dun with red flanks and huge flared horns. It lured three cows and a heifer from a pasture near ranch headquarters, and took them running into the bushy hills. Lan saw the bull clearly.

"Naw," said Moody, "not one of them old bulls, Lan. Ain't none of them no more."

Wild Longhorns were few but they lasted well into the Twentieth Century. As late as the 1920s one lived in a narrow canyon south of Lubbock on the high plains. A Big Bend rancher killed another in 1910. A Model T Ford encountered a wild bull in the eastern mountains of New Mexico. The Longhorn stood on a rough narrow road and the driver braked hard. The bull bellowed, pawed the ground and charged the automobile. It bashed at the car, stepped back and charged again and again. Eventually a horn pierced the radiator and the bull actually raised the machine's front wheels off the road, shook it and bounced it into a ditch.

Lan Twohig's outlaw bull Longhorn was real.

He went after it, ignoring Moody's advice to take other cowboys with him. He found prints in a sandy wash south of the ranchhouse and tracked his bull south and eastward, deeper into the brush, finally crossing Muke Water Creek. From the shadows of a cottonwood grove he saw the heifer beside a mesquite thicket.

Throughout the night, Lan watched the brushy fortress, saw the bull move the cows into a steep-sided gully. He rode around it. The gully dead-ended against a hill. The wash was filled with brush, thick with mesquite and cactus. Lan knew the bull had its nest within that thorny citadel.

And at dawn, with a thin banner of light undercoating dense clouds, Lan stood before the green wall, lightly holding his horse, Buck, listening to the silence. An aimless wind riffled the slender mesquite leaves. Lan tied on his chaps. He dropped a coiled rope over the saddle horn. He mounted. The hardness of his rifle, stuffed into a leather scabbard, pushed against his right leg.

All right, old bull, let's me and you do it.

Lan gently touched the horse's flanks. They entered the green barrier.

The path was a dark corridor, cool and dusty. Lan followed the trail straight for a dozen steps, turned sharply right, circled a mesquite trunk. Then again it was a thin line deeper into the gully. Fifty feet. He was forced to dismount as the tree ceiling lowered. He scraped cactus and the thorny catclaw clutched at him. A gray lizard hung to a mesquite limb, frightened and unmoving. On the right, the brush was thinner and Lan could see the gully's brown wall. He found fresh cow dung and once he rubbed his hand across the smoothed bark of a tree to which clung red hairs. He smiled.

The trail wandered as though aimless but, Lan knew, carefully devised. He rode when he could, walked when he could not. The coiled rope was held lightly in his right hand. He watched everywhere, his eyes never still. Above, Lan could see the beige sky.

The brush thinned. Ahead was a clearing, small, oval-shaped, twenty feet wide. He stood at its edge, shadowed by a tree. The trail led around the clearing's perimeter. Lan listened, tensed. Across the open space, he heard movement in the brush, then silence again. He sat easy on Buck for a long time, waiting. Finally, Lan impatiently urged the horse into the opening, rode slowly across and disappeared again into the green thicket. The path was broader, and he rode a hundred feet before having to dismount again beside a mound of cactus.

The cry came with suddenness, loud and fierce, frighteningly intense. Lan whirled. *Behind! The bull came out and waited for me to be trapped inside!* Ahead, he heard the cows calling to the bull. Buck skittered, his teeth grinding the bit, and Lan swung into the saddle, already pulling on the rifle, dropping the looped rope over the horn. He could hear the bull outlaw thrashing in the brush, still bellowing, charging, exploding into the clearing. Buck was at full gallop as man and horse sped into the sandy open space. The bull was in the middle, mouth agape and frothy, dripping long banners of slobber, the head bent low, horns carried right atilt, cocked like an archer's bow. Its feet beat the dust into clouds.

The suddenness of the bull startled Buck and the horse jumped to the right as horns came up in a blur, thrown like sabers. A horn struck Lan's left leg above the knee, pierced the chap's thick leather. It entered his flesh and ripped away. The horn scraped along the thick saddle and sliced a slender line on Buck's flank. Blood instantly flowed from the long wound.

Buck's momentum carried them across the clearing as Lan reined hard. The horse stumbled in the turn, its hooves punching up showers of sand. The bull was about, charging once more. Lan twisted his body and fired, then pumped the rifle again. The bullet entered along the bull's back, high on the rump. The horse was rising from its knees. Lan fired again as the Longhorn struck horse and rider.

Later Lan would remember the sound of the impact, Buck's terrified scream of agony, horns breaking through the horse's body, and he would recall the stench of the animal and the pain. He could not forget the pain.

The bull crunched against the horse. One horn ripped into the stomach, the other broke through bones in the chest and rib cage, pushed upward to lodge against the spine. The Longhorn lifted horse and rider into the air and for a long moment held them motionless before the weight became too much. They crashed to the ground, and the bloody, dusty arena was quiet. Lan was unconscious.

Much later the pain awoke him, and he screamed. He was on his right side, still in the saddle. Buck's body lay on his right leg. His left leg was pinned between the bull's head, gleaming with red blood, and the horse's heaving stomach. The horns were inside Buck. Lan's ankle was broken.

Enraged, the bull bellowed, stamped its rear feet, and butted hard against its enemy. Forced to its knees by the horse's weight and bound tightly by its horns locked into Buck's body, the bull could not disengage itself, could not rise. With each thrust of the head against Lan's leg, the cowboy cried aloud. Finally, he passed into unconsciousness. During the long day, Lan was unconscious a dozen times. The bull would not cease trying to escape its impalement and each time it thrashed at the horse, Lan was driven into pain and insensibility.

He would remember pieces of the day. Once he dimly saw the cows and heifer grazing quietly across the clearing. Sometime, he did not know when, he was aware that Buck was dead. In another moment of consciousness he remembered the rifle. He swiveled his head until he saw it behind him, two feet beyond his reach. He could not see the rope.

He awakened in dim twilight to find the bull unmoving. It breathed hoarsely, almost gasping for air, but no longer seeking escape. He could smell the blood, feel it beneath him, feel it caked on his clothing. He saw the riverlet of congealed blood leading to a blackened hole in the bull's rump. Lan's mouth was dry, his tongue swollen. His eyes were gritty with sand. He slept.

Lan awoke in the cool darkness, remembering the knife in his right pocket, beneath the awful weight of Buck. He tried to reach the knife. The bull tensed his legs, snorted once but did not move. Lan could not force his hand beneath the weight and he clawed at the ground with his fingers. He pulled away sand and earth, burrowing farther and farther underneath until he could feel the edge of the chaps, then more, and he touched the pocket. His fingers inched inside, grasped the material and pulled, slowly drawing out the pocket, dragging along the knife in its bottom. Then he had the knife between two fingers. He grabbed and held it tightly.

A pocketknife with two blades, but sharp enough. He opened the longer blade, grasp the hilt. He swung with his left hand, striking at the bull's head. The blade broke against the Longhorn's skull and, angered, the bull lunged forward. Lan screamed and the pain sent him away.

The moon, full and bright, was out, centered above the clearing. Lan awoke. The pain in his upper leg where the horn had torn through was less but his ankle throbbed. The bull was still and quiet. He cursed the animal, himself, the knifeblade's weakness. He felt again for the knife and found it near his head. He opened the remaining smaller blade. Lan had another way, one he did not like. He would release the bull. He plunged the knife into Buck's flank, and began cutting.

The bull bunched its muscles in fear but did not move.

Lan took a long time to cut away Buck's side. His hand was slippery with blood. He cut back, deeper and lower, between the horse's legs, and ran his hand into the dark cavity. He could feel the horn. The bull was pulling then, helping the man free him. Lan placed the knife blade beside the horntip to cut deeper into Buck. The Longhorn pulled. Lan heard the ripping sound, felt the horn move. The bull turned its body left, backed and the right horn tore out, free again, the blunt hard head lifted from Lan's leg. The bull shook itself, rose on its forelegs and backed away, sliding out the left horn.

It stumbled once, moving awkwardly in a circle. The bull lifted its head, swung the massive, bloody horns, limbering exhausted neck muscles. The bull stopped across the clearing and lowered its head again, staring at Lan. Lan began digging beneath Buck's body with the knife.

Lan dug twenty minutes to loosen and pull away enough dirt for a trench. Now with most of the horse's weight on the edges of the furrow, Lan cut the tiestrings and belt of his chaps, pushing hard on the saddle. His right foot slid out of its boot. He reached behind, grabbed a mesquite bush and pulled, slowly dragging himself from under the horse. He was free and lay for a moment, breathing deeply. He raised his head and looked across the clearing at the bull. The Longhorn watched Lan, studying the man with intensity.

Lan held his useless left leg and grimaced as he pivoted on his hip. He felt for the rifle, wrapped his fingers around the barrel and pulled it to him. He worked the lever and the small noise alerted the bull. It raised its head and moved right, its eyes never leaving Lan. Lan turned again on his stomach, facing the bull. He lay the rifle barrel across Buck's neck.

He could see the bull clearly in the bright moonlight, the dull, dark patches of blood, the black eyes, the horns rising from the slab head. The bull stood stiff-legged, breathing hoarsely. A muscle rippled skin across its back. It lifted a front hoof, set it hard into the dirt. Lan aimed, sighting down the barrel at the dark flat head. He tightened his finger against the trigger.

He did not shoot but held still, one eye closed, the other unblinking, staring over the gunsight. The bull waited. Lan pulled the rifle butt tighter into his shoulder, increasing the pressure. He held his eyes shut and caught his breath. His leg ached with pain. He looked again at the bull standing a dozen steps away in the thin moonlight.

He raised the rifle barrel high and fired.

And then he slept, and perhaps dreamed, for he remembered a bull crying deeply and fiercely somewhere in the brush.

Lan awoke beside Muke Water Creek, out of the bright sun. Moody knelt beside him.

"Got to wonderin' 'bout you," Moody said softly. "Came to look. I sent a hand back for the wagon."

Lan's lips were swollen, his tongue heavy and thick. His wounds had been cleaned with creek water. He hurt all over.

"It was a bull, Moody," Lan whispered hoarsely. "Like I said, old wild bull."

"You didn't get him?"

"I shot high, scared him off. Told him we'd do it agin 'nother day."

Lan smiled, and slept again.

For the remainder of his life Lan walked with a cane and never again was he an active cowboy. He stayed with Moody, working around the ranch, bossing the Mexicans. Five months after Moody found Lan in the gully, the rancher rode in with a pair of horns.

"Got somethin' for you," Moody said. "Your old outlaw's horns. Found him dead a mile above the creek."

"Sure it's him?"

"How many bull outlaws we got? It's him. Dead a month, maybe. Bones pretty well picked over but the hide's still plain. Dun with red flanks. It's your old bull."

Lan mounted the horns on polished mesquite wood and hung them above the fireplace. He often spent long evenings thinking of the bull.

Moody died in 1903. Briefly, Lan moved to San Antonio, then went north to Fort Worth where he worked in the slaughter houses and traded cattle on the side for extra money. When he had time Lan loafed with other cowmen in the Metropolitan Hotel's regal lobby. The hotel was showing its age and one day would become a part-time whorehouse but in 1905 it was the gathering place for cattlemen come to town. There Lan and his cronies drank too much, and told lies of their youth. Lan often spoke of the bull and the gully. Other cowmen professed to believe every word of Lan's tale but many did not, even when he showed the horns for proof, pointing out the thin cuts made by his broken knife.

In the fall of that year, Lan sat on the leather couch in the Metropolitan's airy lobby and told again of the bull outlaw he had fought in '92. He had an audience of old men, among them Will Drannon who, with Kit Carson, had guided Fremont to California in '45, and ancient Uncle Tuffy Thomas, one of the first cowboys up the trail to Kansas. Tuffy later would repent and become a fiery Baptist before dying but then he was a highly successful drunk around town. Others in the lobby gathered as Lan Twohig spoke of the bull.

". . . and I jus' told that old bull we'd do it 'nother day," Lan concluded. He paused dramatically to question his audience, "Do you know why I didn't kill that old bull . . .?" He ordinarily answered his own question, but that day, a voice responded loudly, "Yes!"

All heads turned to the speaker. He was a young man, almost six feet tall, built squarely. His nose and ears were prominent, but blended smoothly with the olive complexion, deep black eyes, and infectious smile.

The voice was sleek and glossy, convincing. He wore a heavy dark suit, a striped shirt partially covered by a vest, and a fluffy red bowtie, the obvious costume of a drummer.

Irritated by the interruption, Lan Twohig demanded, ''Well, s'pose you just tell us why. . . .''

The young man smiled broadly, enjoying himself.

''Because he was a mean sonofabitch, and you were a mean sonofabitch and mean sonofabitches respect each other,'' he answered.

He laughed loudly and the others, even Lan, joined in. Lan liked that answer, would appropriate it himself for future use. Still laughing, the young man left the lobby, walked quickly, very quickly, into Rusk Street, his shoulders hunched against the brisk autumn wind. He would meet Lan Twohig again, in a year or two, and the old cowboy would show him the horns. The young man, a consummate salesman, would persuade Lan to sell the horns.

That day, Lan Twohig watched the young man leave, and said curiously, ''Who's he?''

''Name's Carter,'' answered Will Drannon. ''Sells them streetcar cards.''

''Knows his sonofabitches, don't he?'' mused Tuffy.

Amon Carter was the Texas Advertising and Manufacturing Company. All of it. The A and M Company occupied a cubicle office on Fort Worth National Bank's second floor, from which Amon sold a patented indexing telephone directory. He also owned a concession for streetcar advertising cards. Business was slow but Amon Carter made a living for his wife, Zetta, and year-old daughter, Bertice.

Amon came to Fort Worth in May, 1905, from San Francisco, where he had not done well as an advertising space salesman for Barnhart & Swasey. The money, $100 a month, was too little to support his lifestyle, already grandly baroque, and a wife and child. There were debts. He was forced to send Zetta and Bertice home to her parents in nearby Bowie. At her urging Amon left San Francisco and established the Texas A and M Company in Fort Worth, but he was unhappy with the town, bored by his business. He considered a return to San Francisco. Ed Swasey offered him a $75 monthly draw and commissions in a new agency. The F. J. Cooper Advertising Company also wanted to hire him, offering a $200 monthly salary without commissions.

The streetcar concession was valuable to Amon. Barron Collier, called the "King of Streetcar Advertising," asked to purchase Amon's franchise. Collier added the incentive of a job in New York, but Amon turned him down.

That day Amon Carter returned to his office cell to keep an appointment. He was busy buying a typewriter. Amon did not type but felt the presence of a machine would impress customers. There was a narrow couch in the office and he napped on it until the typewriter salesman arrived. Amon had slept there the previous night, as he often did, against bank rules. Last evening he stayed in the White Elephant Saloon drinking and playing poker until long after midnight, and he had a mild hangover.

The salesman — a Mr. Shotts — arrived, awakened Amon, and began explaining his machine. Carter said the price was too high. The salesman, discovering that Amon did not type, wanted the machine only for ornamentation, closed the case. Mr. Shotts switched the subject to a new product he was considering. Cow chip fuel. The salesman believed oil-soaked cow manure would be a money-making item bought by thousands of folks who couldn't afford other fuels.

Cow manure was plentiful in Fort Worth. Its stockyards handled a quarter of a million head of livestock each year and were second in size and volume only to

Chicago. No one who ever experienced the aroma of downtown Fort Worth in a north wind had to be told manure was bountiful.

Amon was intrigued. Mr. Shotts said the new fuel was to be demonstrated that very day. Amon collected his hat and topcoat. The men went to look at manure.

The city's stockyards, a labyrinth of cow pens and barns, rail tracks and two new packing houses, Swift's and Armour's, lay three miles north of the courthouse in a suburban community. The men boarded a Main Street tram, crossed the Trinity River. They arrived in front of the main auction barn as the demonstration began. Reporters were there, pens poised to tell the world of burning manure. Two, A. G. Dawson, correspondent of the Dallas *Morning News*, and D. C. McCaleb, city editor of the Fort Worth *Record*, shivered behind a group of onlookers. Amon knew McCaleb slightly. He paused to say hello, introduced himself to Dawson.

The pile of cow chips was lighted ceremoniously and the audience crowded nearer to absorb the heat. Instantly all were aware of an inherent weakness in the cow chip fuel theory. Burning cow manure smells.

Amon wrinkled his nose and decided not to invest. Dawson and McCaleb repocketed their pens. They stood together, backs to the fire, trying to ignore the scented smoke. Amon was wondering why he did not return to his office when the two reporters began discussing their favorite subject — publication of a daily afternoon newspaper to compete with the Fort Worth *Telegram*. They lamented their flat wallets. Neither had business experience but knew how to write, edit and publish a newspaper.

Amon was interested. He had business experience. He could sell advertising. He had no money but thought he knew where to borrow enough. The trio became excited. A newspaper *was* possible, they agreed. Then and there they decided on a name, the *Star*, and sealed the pact with firm handshakes amidst the murky essence of smoldering cow chips.

Future social historians, take a footnote: The Fort Worth *Star*, parent of the *Star-Telegram*, which would become Texas and the South's largest, most influential publication, was the only newspaper ever conceived and founded over a pile of burning cow manure.

In hoc signo vinces.

Chapter 2

Never imagine yourself not to be otherwise than what it might appear to others that you were or might have been was not otherwise than what you had been would have appeared to them to be.

—*Lewis Carrol,* **Alice in Wonderland**

I am as bad as the worst but thank God I'm as good as the best.

—*Walt Whitman*

Could it be possible? This old saint in the forest has not heard anything of this, that God is dead.

—*Nietzche*

2

He died on a warm June evening of a slow news day, a Thursday in 1955, the twenty-third day of the month, the second day of summer. Prompt as always, he passed on deadline forty minutes in advance of the two-star edition being sent into all crannies, nooks and burgs of his West Texas empire. When death came, morning managing editor Herb Schultz was notified. Schultz told the men slouched around city desk, "He's dead."

An assistant editor turned to the ancient Royal upright, paused, then keyed out one sentence:

"Amon Giles Carter died at 8:20 p.m. Thursday."

The makeup editor collected the brusque sentence, and trudged up dingy back stairs to the fourth floor, preparing to assemble the various mechanical remains of Amon Carter's life. As was the newspaper's execrable, systematic manner, the *Star-Telegram* had killed off its boss weeks before he died. His obituary was gathered, written, inspected for accuracy, set ten-point double column, and locked into a special galley lodged against the composing room's east wall. A scrawled sign, "Do Not Remove," guarded the precious galley.

His death was not unexpected. For weeks Amon's critical illness was an acknowledged fact of coffee break conversation, and his reporters and editors had set about to make the passing as professional and dignified as possible. The master plan was to announce his demise with a scant eight hundred word story in the most immediate edition. A full page would be cleared for the complete obituary to run in subsequent issues.

The makeup editor visited the head dump frame, stooped, reached for a type case marked "72 pt. CAPS," a largish font kept in a dusty lower drawer like unsightly silverware too good to discard but used only in event of extreme urgency. The type size and style was considered gauche and tacky by the conservative *Star-Telegram* — it never cared to shout at its readers. Use of 72 pt. all-caps meant a great catastrophe, like a war, or rare, whopping notabilia such as rain in West Texas. Or for Amon Carter and the end of an era.

The editor slugged the obit "PI, 8-72 ALL-CAPS, Amon Carter . . ." He composed and counted the banner headline, AMON G. CARTER DIES AT HOME AFTER ILLNESS WHICH BEGAN IN '53." That constituted reversal of a long-standing policy. Unwritten, but strictly followed, the rule was that Amon's name was not to appear in headlines. (When he was awarded the Air Force's highest civilian honor, the story's head said merely that a "Fort Worth Man" was recognized.) The makeup editor studied the headline, ordered it set and locked on page one. He reread the brief obit.

Noting that Amon Carter was publisher of the *Star-Telegram* and board chairman of Carter Publications, Inc., owner and operator of radio/television stations WBAP, the story said he died in bed at his home, 1220

Broad Street, where he had been confined since returning late in April from the annual American Newspaper Association meeting. Carter had been ill since February 23, 1953, when struck by two heart attacks at home and a third in St. Joseph's Hospital. His final local public appearance was for the 1953 Fort Worth Exposition and Fat Stock Show, at which he introduced Texas Governor Allan Shivers to a first-night rodeo audience. Remainder of the story concerned itself with a casual inventory of Carter's many honors and interests, hardly a satisfying final word monument for Texas' best-known citizen.

An edition later and throughout Friday's PM papers, the *Star-Telegram* eulogized its late publisher in a bare bones biography spread over most of two pages. The full obituary imbued Amon with prominence and dignity, surveyed his fame, sketched his up-from-impoverishment beginnings, his major philanthropies, the showy mountaintops of his long career. It had an emotional vacancy, containing none of the verbal breast-beating we have come to expect when a newspaper loses one of its own. Decades later, one feels the awful weight of it and can empathize with the anonymous writer burdened by the task of encapsulating his boss' intemperate life with sober words, decorous phrases. The obituary is a simple, straightforward canonization of St. Amon.

At the very least, one suspects the writer itched to sneak in a final, long, loud and lingering yippee for the man who invented the cowboy. Perhaps not. Amon Carter was not very well liked by his newsmen. He was never real to them. They saw him as a phantasmagorian character, a symbiotic product of their written words built like a Ned Buntline narrative, as unauthentic as Pecos Bill or Rex the Wonder Dog. They viewed his neurotic quest for perfection as dictatorship, his eccentricities as bare egomaniacy. For them, his genius was shadowed behind sulphuric mists of anger. The pixy, gregarious man was interpreted as a foolish rich man.

His zealous, limitless promotion of Fort Worth and Texas embarrassed the newsmen. It reeked, they believed, of the smelliest kind of chamber-of-commerce journalism and was an abasement of their ethics, ideals and talents.

Why, Joseph Pulitzer, they shouted from city room soap boxes, never welcomed a smokestack industry to town with a page one banner. Horace Greeley had not published an eight-column photo of one hundred and thirty-seven visiting oil executives. The New York *Times* did not devote its upper front page to an inspiring census report the day war began in Korea. Of course not, his supporters argued, and Colonel McCormick had not mailed The World's Greatest Newspaper free to any soldier. Nor had Harry Chandler's Los Angeles *Times* printed *verbatim* trial testimony covering as many as seven full open pages, and done it for ten straight days. William Randolph Hearst, the first, perhaps had learned to turn pages of his newspapers with his bare toes, and knew eighteen Psalms by heart, but could he have driven a stagecoach down Wall Street? Yes, the Scripps and the Howards, the Copleys and the Knights, had comported themselves with dignity and regality while Amon stood on banquet tables and fired his six-shooter. But those men had only newspapers to sell — not towns, half of Texas, ideas, dreams, the future . . . glorious, magnificent, noble visions. OK, but one cannot imagine the *Times'* autocratic Mr. Ochs pronouncing New York's highest elected official a ". . . crazy sonofabitch" as Mr. Carter had for a Texas governor, and with an awed audience looking on. But, I submit to you, did not that man deserve such appraisal? Of course, but . . .

For the reporters, especially younger ones who had not endured the newspaper's downs or been exalted by its ups, Amon Carter was ignoble, never the deity to which they then compared him, and not always kindly. He was, for them, a flashy widget, molded in the *Star-Telegram* factory, folded and tossed on Fort Worth lawns or mailed by second class permit to distant hidey-holes of West Texas.

Thus, when second edition copies came into the third floor newsroom that tepid June evening, few men around the horseshoe desk gave the Carter obit more than a cursory attention. They scanned the words for accuracy, digested their meaning, noting that the photo was one taken before illness transmuted Amon Carter into a thin, sick old man.

No one knew it, but the anonymous writer blew Carter's name. Correctly, he was Giles Amon Carter. He hated "Giles" and with his first adult job had moved "Amon" out front, hiding "Giles" behind and reducing it to an initial. The despised "Giles" — it came from his maternal family branch — was further hidden when he banned even the initial from print because the *Star-Telegram* endlessly cited his name as "**Among** Carter."*

The black-bordered, three-column photograph published beside the obit was of an older, not old, Amon Carter. He appeared relaxed and unhurried, looking less than his age with unwrinkled, possibly airbrushed, face, the strong nose, prominent ears supporting white eaves of monks' fringe hair. As a *poseur* of consummate ability, the role he was playing for the photographer was of a wealthy establishmentarian, which one part of him was. He wore a conservative smile and there is in it the merest suggestion of inner relief, as though he secretly is melting a Bisodal tablet under the tongue to combat his chronic indigestion.

Picture, obituary and headline hung underneath the publisher's favorite scrap of holy writ: "Fort Worth, Texas . . . Where the West Begins." The phrase was his war whoop, his aphoristic article of faith, a mantra he chanted in all available ears. For almost fifty years the slogan rode the *Star-Telegram*'s masthead as a rallying

*Amon ultimately banished "Giles" forever. His son is Amon *Gary* Carter, Jr.

call of the faithful. It became the city's official, and highly metaphysical, credo, and the nation's best-known, most lasting municipal epigram. Mention Fort Worth in the opening half of the Twentieth Century and the audience responded by rote ". . . Where the West Begins." Amon had FDR repeating the litany in national radio speeches, Bob Hope joking with the phrase from theater stages. "Where the West Begins" appeared on crude signs beside GI foxholes in the South Pacific, and on the breast of a B-24 bombing Nazis. Will Rogers quipped to a gang of reporters, "Fort Worth . . . Where the West Begins and Dallas peters out." Even schoolboys wrote Amon Carter in care of ". . . Where the West Begins" and their letters were forwarded promptly to his Fort Worth office.

"Where the West Begins" was as effective an advertising slogan as "They Laughed When I Sat Down to Play" or "Lucky Strike Green Goes to War." Certainly, it was more durable.

There was, of course, very little truth in it.

Amon lifted the phrase from a poem and hammered it into the nation's brain until it was accepted as gospel. Wherever he went the words were rolled out, polished and spoken with great conviction for the ignorant and unknowing. Once Carter arrived in New York, emerging from Pennsylvania Station during rush hour. He sought a taxi to his suite in the Ritz-Carleton. At the curb he stood beside a middleaged English couple on holiday. All of his life Amon Carter engaged innocent strangers in idle conversation. He disliked silence, and anyone near him became an audience. The couple, as Amon, awaited an empty cab. They stood quietly for a moment. Amon opened with, "I'm from Fort Worth."

"I beg pardon?" asked the Englishman, leaning nearer.

"Fort Worth. I live in Fort Worth."

"Oh . . . oh! I see." The couple tried to look uninvolved.

"Texas! Fort Worth, Texas."

"Ah . . . Texas," said the man uncomfortably. The couple edged away.

Amon tried again, ". . . where the West Begins."

Silence. The couple shuffled, embarrassed. Amon grumped at them, "Well, gawddamnit, the west begins there."

His brow pinched with curiosity, the Englishman turned, saying, "The 'west' *what* begins there?"

Arthur Chapman was an Illinois-born reporter working for the Denver *Times* when he wrote for the ages and Amon:

> Out where the handclasp's a little stronger,
> Out where the smile dwells a little longer,
> That's where the west begins.
>
> . . . .
>
> Out where the skies are a trifle bluer,
> Out where the friendship's a little truer,
> That's where the west begins.

Chapman's imperishable, mawkish phrasing vaulted him into *Bartlett*'s and onto the *Star-Telegram* front page, even tucked within the *Congressional Record*, courtesy of Amon Carter, but he died a poor New York free lance writer, unknowing of his immortal stature.

He wrote of a West that never existed. It was a sentimental duchy of the mind. And though Amon Carter established ". . . Where the West Begins" as a bedrock truth, Fort Worth had little more claim on that geographical misdirection than Minneapolis, which briefly subscribed to the slogan. The West of Chapman and Carter always was somewhere else, perhaps farther west, or backward in time, but wherever it was, Fort Worth, Texas, definitely was not its home.

The real West, however, was near. *The West* was out there. West Texas. That was *The West*. West Texas and only West Texas was *The West*, and if there was a starting line at all it lay somewhat westernly of Fort Worth. That was not a problem for Amon. He subpoenaed *The West* and pirated it for Fort Worth as summarily as he once summoned a reporter and commanded the man to steal a train. He by God wanted *The West* in Fort Worth and to Fort Worth it came, servile as a boot-kicked pup.

As health claims on breakfast cereal boxes, newspaper slogans must be read with some degree of myopia. "All the News That's Fit to Print" often gets away from the New York *Times*. The Chicago *Tribune* wasn't always "The World's Greatest Newspaper." In early years as the *Star*, "Always for Fort Worth" was the masthead shout. Later, the paper experimented with "All the News While It is News" and "Just A Good Newspaper." Those prosaic canards were scrapped when Amon stumbled across Chapman's *ars poetica* and nailed it to the paper's masthead with the imperiality of Luther issuing his theses. The Chamber of Commerce quickly accepted the phrase as the city's civic sloganeering, partially because the philosophy was attractive but mostly because Amon demanded it be done.

More than other newspaper, the *Star-Telegram*'s apothegm was believed by its readers. They believed because the newspaper was *the word* in West Texas. It was a *Biblia pauperum* out there, at least for those folks who could read. The *Star-Telegram*, like beef and beans, was daily fare on kitchen tables as no other publication anywhere. It, a rival newsman once said, and only half in jest, was in more West Texas outhouses than Sears Roebuck. The real Bible and its surrogate, the *Star-Telegram* — both interpreted literally — were the two journals seen most often in West Texas homes. The newspaper in fact acquired an inside title, given as much for its Victorian moral view as its unquestioned acceptance in West Texas. Reporters called it "The Great Religious Daily."

AMON

For most of fifty years, the *Star-Telegram* was West Texas' newspaper. It educated the people, amused them, informed, protected, scolded, boosted, boasted and gave pride to the region and its *indigenes*. The newspaper fought for and won roads and universities, two national parks, monuments, industries, called on new immigrants, told farmers when and where to sell for better prices, gave Mama new cake recipes and Junior instructions for building his own crystal set. It nursed people and communities through sicknesses and calamities, lauded them in prosperity, consoled them in times of sorrow. The *Star-Telegram* kept West Texas in running order in a way not possible for newspapers in a more urban location.

With as many as thirteen editions through a twenty-four hour operation, the *Star-Telegram* was circulated to an area from the border of Colorado to the Rio Grande, and westward to El Paso. *Three hundred and seventy-five thousand square miles.* By train, and later, bus, truck and train, the newspaper went west daily on a delivery schedule composed with some ingenuity. In 1907 while still the *Star*, it was in one instance delivered to a postmaster in Hale Center, a village in the Panhandle. The postmaster added it to other pieces of mail, placed all in a rusty tin bucket. Driver of the Stant Rhea Stagecoach collected the bucket and hauled it fifteen miles to an abandoned dugout on the plains, where he hooked the bucket bail over a fence post. *Star* customers rode in from their prairie homes to take delivery from the rusty pail. When American Airlines established its first Fort Worth-to-Los Angeles route, the Ford Tri-Motors detoured once a week to fly low over a ranch near Guadalupe Peak, Texas's highest mountain. The pilot lowered his window and shoved out a bulky package of mail and *Star-Telegrams* for a rancher who lived merely forty miles from the closest driveable road, sixty miles to the nearest town.

And sometimes the *Star-Telegram* did not arrive at all. West Texas, being a place of natural catastrophes, storms of rain, dust or wind, and sometimes all three at once, caused delivery to be delayed or halted altogether.

In the early 1920s there was a rash of intense public attention for "The Gumps" comic strip. Bim Gump somehow allowed himself to be trapped into marriage to the fortune-hunting Widder Zander. Coming to his senses in time, Bim reneged. Widder Zander sued for breach of promise and everybody, including *Star-Telegram* readers, went to court. It was a legal war of epic dimensions and West Texans followed each day's episode with rapt attention. Suddenly: Storm in West Texas. Days passed. A pleading telegram arrived at the *Star-Telegram:*

> "Area flooded. No mail for ten days. Please wire at our expense verdict Zander vs. Gump.
> (Signed) Seminole Chamber of Commerce."

Because no reader problem was too insignificant, the *Star-Telegram* rolled into action. The newspaper immediately telegraphed the verdict (Bim was vindicated). It dramatized the strips and broadcast them on its radio station, WBAP. And when waters subsided around Seminole, Texas, one of the first travelers slopping through the mud was a *Star-Telegram* man hauling a load of back-issue newspapers just in case anybody in town had failed to learn the verdict.

West Texas repaid such consideration to their needs by being a devoted constituency. They made the *Star-Telegram* the largest and most influential newspaper in Texas, with the largest circulation in the southern half of the United States (generally on a line below Washington, D.C., St. Louis and Denver, from the Atlantic to Los Angeles' eastern city limits). The *Star-Telegram* was beside the New York *Times* for daily perusal in the White House and could be bought at a score of newsstands as far away as Chicago, where interest in Fort

Worth was less than fervent. It, or certain pertinent clippings, regularly went to as many as five hundred of America's most important businessmen, politicians and columnists. It wandered everywhere, causing a Dublin, Ireland, publisher to inquire just how a newspaper could have a circulation equal to a population of its town — did every man, woman and child subscribe? And — God only knows how this occurred — a peasant of Samarkand, Uzbekistan, in central Asia, was inspired to mail the equivalent of twenty-one cents, his donation for funds to erect a mule memorial in Muleshoe, Texas.

The *Star-Telegram* was the most famous reading habit of West Texans and because it was, they, like the faithful performing a compulsory *hajj* to Mohammed's birthplace, made pilgrimages to the source of all that printed wonder. Especially in the early days, a trip to Fort Worth was long and hard and perhaps was done but once in a lifetime, surely no more than once a year for common folks. In Fort Worth, West Texans made three necessary stops. One was at the boxy behemoth headquarters of Montgomery Ward — colloquially: "Monkey Wards." Second was the jumbled basement of Leonard Bros. Department Store, where counters overflowed with bargain merchandise and aisles teemed with more humanity than back alleys of Calcutta. And they visited the *Star-Telegram.*

Almost daily, old flivvers and rattling trucks arrived at the newspaper's front door on Seventh Street, unloading tribes of dusty *hajjis* come to pay homage. They climbed the steps, passing into the elegant lobby where they stood hushed and huddled, kids grasping Mama's dress hem or Papa's worn overalls, surveying that monument to truth. They might reach and touch a dark mahogany column, as though it could grant them wisdom and strength, and perhaps cure their poverty. Business office employees learned to let the West Texans wander as they wished and more often than not the father, his appetite for grandeur finally sated, would approach, cough for attention and announce, "I come to re-new."

He could have resubscribed by mail or through the nearest district manager, but he was in Fort Worth with his cash crop money and chose to do business in person. Money would be passed over. Papa would tuck the precious receipt into his bib pocket, regather his brood and lead them out, and the ragged Joads would pack again into their ancient vehicles, heading west for what might be a five hundred mile trip home, assured for another year that their lives would be daily blessed by the *Star-Telegram*.

None of this happened because Amon Carter put *The West* where it never belonged. It was, after all, his *West* and he could do with it as he pleased. He owned it. Lock, stock and barrel cacti. West Texas was his, his kingdom, his empire, his Xanadu, his gadget to tinker with. He was West Texas' Aesop of the Prairie, a fableizer whose yarns made the land west of Fort Worth seem a garden of earthly delights. In his accounts of West Texas, the sand, the heat, the brushy complexion became cardinal virtues or were ignored, and one felt it would be an honor to live in and serve such a place of beauty and grace. West Texans often were surprised at Amon and his *Star-Telegram*'s version of their homeland, wondering, as they counted their sunstroked cows and watched unwatered crops fizzle, just where that mythical, fabulous kingdom might be.

Because *The West* was his, Amon Carter felt a need to be a part of it. He molded himself as he sculpted the fictional image of it, with camouflage coloration and clothing, blending into the scenic legends.

He became a cowboy.

Now, Amon Carter, a child of the soil, had no credentials as a cowboy. He was a failed blacksmith's son. But *The West* seduced him, as it did generations of Saturday matinee children. He became its principal tubthumping agent, dressed and acted out his role as

Top Hand of the Plains, The Sage of the Sagebrush, Mouthpiece of the Southwest — as he came to be titled.

Amon adopted what eastern columnists variously called a "four-," "six-," or "ten-" gallon western hat. He donned multi-colored fancy boots, into the tops of which he stuffed the legs of his tailored trousers. He strapped on hand-tooled double holsters and packed them with twin, pearl-handled pistols. Occasionally, he added leather chaps branded "AGC," jingling silver spurs and a bandana knotted at the throat, held in place by an expensive pearl stickpin. In cooler weather, the costume was topped with an ivory-colored vicuna coat which, according to the Washington *Post*, resembled ". . . a cozy bathrobe." For very special events of his later life, the cowboy rode a golden palomino, seated on a silvered $5,000 saddle, a diamond stickpin stabbed into his silken bandana. Fully assembled, the Amon Carter cowboy looked like Friar Tuck playing Hoot Gibson.

Amon learned to yell "Yippee" and "Whoopee" without a shred of shame. He could bellow ridiculously, "Hoooo-e-e-e-e! Round 'em up! Head off that lit'le dogie yonder!" for a New Orleans parade crowd, and tell a New York *American* reporter that the 1923 World Series "Ought to be a right smart set-to." He spoke such prattle without blushing because above all else the cowboy enjoyed himself. He had fun. You and I were forced to give up our childish games at manhood. Amon Carter, who had no childhood, got to play cowboy all his life.

In action, the cowboy swaggered for his audience, jingling his spurs, drawling in a put-on West Texas accent, punctuating the comic dialogue by firing his pistols in the air and yipee-ing joyously. The cowboy was a caricature, not a characterization, of the western Texan, but many outsiders never knew that. They thought he was art imitating life. The New York *Tribune* actually called Amon Carter ". . . the father of the ten-gallon hat idea." Bob Considine, who should have known better, wrote that the cowboy was "a rootin', tootin', sixgun shootin' . . . lusty, gusty . . . westerner."

The cowboy, however illusionary, was very memorable.

In the beginning, Amon invented his cowboy because the swaggering cliche of a Texan was necessary. As an impetuous, exultant man, the cowboy was the release for Amon's pretentious nature. It also masked his fragile fifth grade education, his early thin sophistication. The cowboy could be as ignorant and graceless as Amon Carter wished to make him without people suspecting all was not an act. Once begun, however, he could not stop. People came to expect and demand the cowboy and Carter groused privately that he was unknown and unremembered as anything else.

For whatever other reasons Amon invented the cowboy for a fundamental purpose of salesmanship. He was a master salesman. No one who met the Texan doubted he was an extraordinary salesman, for himself, for the *Star-Telegram*, but especially for Fort Worth and West Texas. He was a walking, incessantly talking, fancy advertisement for his city, a rodomontade without peer among hawkers of municipal chauvinism. Whether stalking an oil company headquarters, a government contract or just the casual mention of Fort Worth by a syndicated columnist, the cowboy went after his quarry with the zeal of a fanatic. He sold a lifestyle, a frothy reverie Americans had come to believe was The Real West. He boosted a city, a region, and did it with personified showmanship. "As a producer, you will pardon me if I envy you," Billy Rose once told Amon. "I build shows. Christ! You built a city."

Amon *did* build a city. At his death, fully half of Fort Worth's population worked for companies he had lured into the city.

The cowboy of Amon Carter made him and Fort Worth famous. He played cowboy everywhere. Once he interrupted a Giants-Yankees World Series game by excitedly shooting his pistols in the air. His friend, John McGraw, left the Giants dugout, strolled to Amon's box along the first base line, and asked him not to do that again, please. The pistols fired starting shots for six-day bicycle races in Madison Square Garden, and signaled for the downbeat of Paul Whiteman's baton or just banged off indiscriminately for the pure hell of it.

The London *Times* thought the cowboy "picturesque" and displayed him with an English bobby. The *Evening News* of London described the cowboy as ". . . an intimate friend of Will Rogers [and] a middle-aged Texan with a drawling western accent." While in London, the cowboy was invited to dine at the home of Britain's press titan, Lord Beaverbrook. He was met at the door by a butler, who surveyed the cowboy's costume suspiciously. The butler left Amon outside while he verified the invitation of His Lordship. The butler returned, accepted the cowboy's calling card, and, never moving his eyes from the purple and white boots, stammered to other guests, "Mr. Amon Carter . . . Fort Worth, Texas . . . Where the West Begins."

In Rome, the cowboy yippeed and fired his pistols from a Ritz Hotel balcony. Management and police promptly suggested that the cowboy stop his playful act.

The cowboy attended championship prize fights, formal dinners, night clubs, groundbreakings, football games, most anything drawing a crowd. He led bands in parades, talked on national radio networks, attended rodeos. The cowboy had various styles, being soft and gentle for women, rough and rowdy for men. Often the cowboy was farcical.

In the early 1920s, Amon one day appeared at his office in the cowboy uniform. He had a similar outfit for Louis Wortham, then the *Star-Telegram* publisher. That day, the cowboys had a mission. A special train was bringing twenty railroad executives to Fort Worth. They were to discuss building a new terminal, badly needed by the city.

The pair of bogus cowboys set out for the Oklahoma line, where they flagged down and boarded the train. The railroad men were captivated by the pair, believing them to be true specimens of western Texas. In the club car the cowboys began a poker game with three of the Yankees. A dozen others crowded around to watch.

For an hour the men played high stakes poker. Amon was winning. Colonel Wortham was losing. Outside Fort Worth, Wortham suddenly turned surly. He accused Amon of cheating. Carter denied it. Both men jumped up, kicked back their chairs, drew pistols and began blazing away. Wortham grabbed his chest, gasped and slumped over the table.

Carter looked around. He and Wortham were alone in the club car. The two cowboys laughed all the way into the station.

Amon's cowboy assembled all necessary props for his role — collections of old western guns, steer horns, cigar store Indians, an ancient stagecoach, horseshoes, just anything to provide him with the sense and feel of frontier days in Texas. He nicknamed his son "Cowboy." He became a serious collector of western art by Frederick Remington and Charles Russell.

"Did he die with his boots on?" questioned a cynical reporter when told of the publisher's death. He did not. Amon disliked boots. They hurt his feet. He preferred the $150 slippers handcrafted for him by a New York shoemaker. The spur rowels caught on furniture and ladies' long dresses and were a nuisance. He wrote friends, among them William Randolph Hearst, telling of his new palomino and noting that it was the first horse he had actually ridden in forty years. Amon was never unhappy to put away the cowboy and return to his more conventional self, the conservative, hardheaded businessman.

Kindly old J. C. Penney was more correct than he knew when he said, "Fort Worth is not Where the West Begins. The West begins wherever Amon Carter is."

The cowboy was unselfish. He allowed his friends to play with him. He outfitted them in hats and boots, showed them how to swagger about his Shady Oak ranchhouse like cattle drovers come to Dodge City on Saturday night. Playing cowboy with Amon became a craze for many of the nation's most celebrated personalities, among them industry moguls and politicians who were tickled silly with their impersonations. If a person of fame or influence passed near Fort Worth, he was pulled in to be entertained by Amon. Many never intended to stop in the cowtown west of cultured Dallas.

Jimmy Walker, New York's dandified mayor, meant to slide through Fort Worth en route to the 1928 Democratic Convention in Houston. His private rail car, the Roamer, halted in the city to be switched to another train. Amon, who had spies everywhere, heard Walker was in town. He and Will Rogers, who was resting in Fort Worth before going on to the convention, went to the private car in the early morning. They awoke Walker, had him dress and leave the car. Carter asked the mayor to stay the day in Fort Worth. Walker declined politely but firmly. Meanwhile, back on board, a porter bribed by Amon was quickly packing Walker's luggage. The bags were removed from the train and sent to Amon's suite in the Fort Worth Club. Walker was angry when Carter told him what had been done. Trapped, the mayor agreed to stay the night.

The acerbic H. L. Mencken and Baltimore *Sun* publisher Paul Patterson also were guests of Amon, and the Texan arranged a full schedule for the men. He took them to his Shady Oak Farm where, as Rogers wrote in his column, "[With] the champion host of the world, Amon Carter, we held a preliminary convention last night at Shady Oaks [*sic*]. It looks like a dry vice president." Amon had the men speak over a remote

WBAP broadcast from the farm. Walker fished in the well-stocked bass pond. Next day, Amon took Walker to a civic luncheon where a glee club sang his song, "Will You Love Me in December as You Do in May?" The mayor became the luncheon's principal speaker. He told of the farm, "I got bites while fishing. Chiggers. Chiggers, you know, unlike many friends, stick close to one. Some of them are deep-seated."

Before leaving, Carter gifted Walker and the others with western hats, liquor and belts. For the happy mayor, the publisher had a special present. Lan Twobig's old scarred steer horns.

Doubtless Amon told the mayor of Lan's classic battle with the outlaw Longhorn, and of buying the horns from the old cowboy. A *Star-Telegram* photographer snapped Jimmy Walker standing stiffly in front of Amon's Shady Oak saloon. He wore brightly striped trousers and an enormous black hat. The steer horns — the *Star-Telegram* grandly claimed they were eight feet long, but they were not — stood on one tip, towering over the mayor.

That evening, Walker continued to Houston. As the train pulled away he stood on a rear platform, waving. He said something lost in the hiss of steam.

"What?" called Rogers.

Walker cupped his hands to his mouth, yelling, "I said, 'Hoooooooo-raaay for Fort Worth and Amon Carter!"

Another convert for the cowboy.

Chapter 3

We are what we pretend to be.

Kurt Vonnegut, Jr.

It is the perogative of great men only to have great defects.

—La Rochefoucauld

There is no harm done to saints if their faults are shown as well as their virtues.

Saint Frances de Sales

Amon wasn't born. He was invented a little bit at a time and largely with his own recipe.

—Alf Evans, Star-Telegram

3

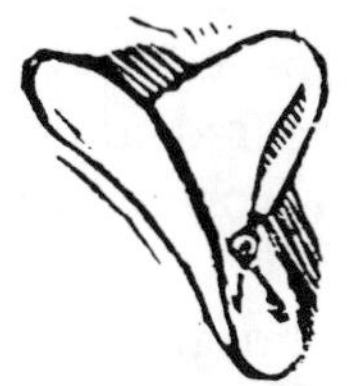

The dominating, perhaps even domineering, figure of Eighteenth Century Virginia was a king named Carter. As America's first dynastic aristocrat, Robert Carter, by force of personality and wealth, controlled the colony's society, industry, government and destiny and, coincidentally, sired a bloodline prominent even today. Kingliness begets kingliness.

A biographer admits the title could have been derisive but "King Carter" nevertheless reigned over three thousand acres, two thousand cattle and forty-four tobacco plantations. He was massa to a thousand slaves, master of a shipping armada, regal overlord of a conglomerated mercantile empire.

By various contemporary accounts Robert Carter absorbed himself in endless figuring over pounds and pense and in assuring personal responsibility within government. He cherished the "play of power in politics.'' He was deeply occupied by his family but also was a ''regular drinker of wines and a good companion in taverns.'' His home always was open to guests and he ''provided handsome quarters and a fine table.'' He passionately sought quality in everything and whatever he touched had to be the best.

Struck by the uncanny similarities of King Carter and the Texas Carter, I searched out a picture of the Virginia monarch. King Carter's portrait in Richmond's Sabine Hall shows him bewigged and haughty with a stalwart chin, distinguished nose and black trenchant eyes. Under that powdered and pompadoured wig sat Amon Carter. He and Robert Carter could have passed for brothers.

Amon was not a lineal descendant of the Virginia Carter but he was in all ways kinfolk to Robert. In life-style, business, politics, even physically, the pair of Carters were, if nothing else, soul mates. Spiritual siblings, those two. Except perhaps in the field of cussing. Biographers of Robert do not tell us whether he had any cussing skill.

Amon had a superb fluency of cussing. What Verdi reached for in arias and Nijinsky in entrechats, Amon achieved and mastered in cussing. Lyrical poetry. Peerless, magnificent, multiloquent cussing of illimitable range and sensibility. In a stateful of effusive cussers, Amon Carter was pre-eminent, I suspect, because of the emotional latitude he brought to the art. Amon was above the piddling curfish level of ordinary men lacking his passion of expression.

He was never a general all-purpose cusser — Amon in fact expressed contempt for the courser idioms — but a specialist in ''goddam'' and ''son-of-a-bitch,'' and his variations on those themes soared and rang with artistry. But, being a man with what we now term affectionately as ''old-fashioned ideas,'' Amon mostly hid away his cussing from women and children, and though outrageously profane never practiced vulgarity or obscenities.

He made "goddam" — he spoke it as "gawddam" — seem as virtuous as "golly-gee," as irreprehensible as "amen," or he could warp trees with the vexed intensity of it. "Gawddam" from Amon's lips was gentle, humorous, sympathetic, stinging or venomous. Once he strolled through his editorial offices late at night flipping off lights. A reporter working in a corner protested, "Mr. Carter, I can't see to type!" Amon turned a cool eye on the man and said evenly, "Well, you can gawddam sure squint, can't you?"

Told of the death of one of his newsmen, he cried out sorrowfully, "oh, gawddam. . ."

Gawddam was staccato punctuation or punishing lashes on a victim of his anger, or spat in disgust. Unannounced one dawn he appeared at the home of *Star-Telegram* oil editor, John Naylor, punching the bell impatiently. He woke Naylor's wife, Pauline, a parttime society writer for the newspaper. She asked Amon to wait while she roused John. Amon at first was astonished that Naylor was still in bed at that pre-sunup hour, then became angry because the editor was taking too long to dress.

Pauline returned to the living room. Amon was pacing rapidly, muttering over and over, "Gawddam, gawddam, gawddam, gawddam, gawddam, gawddam. . . ."

O. O. McIntire, the New York columnist, wondered if the "G" of Carter's name meant "goddam" and referred to the publisher as "Amon Goddam Carter."

Amon's enraged voice was as the taste of hemlock made audible and he did his best cussing when infuriated. Portly, humorless Ross Sterling was elected governor in 1932 with Amon's support on the assumption anyone was preferable to Ma Ferguson, the other major candidate and a Carter antagonist. Shopping around for a governorly deed, Sterling espied East Texas' oil fields where producers were siphoning off the black stuff at a suspiciously high rate. The governor hustled in national guard troops to enforce Texas' prorating laws and halt illegal production.

Sterling's act, concentrated in East Texas, a foreign country, was unimportant to Amon, and the *Star-Telegram*, in fact, editorially applauded. Heady with his success in the piney woods, Sterling turned his troops loose on the Panhandle plains, on Borger, a virtually lawless oil boom town. That was meddling in Amon's West Texas. The Associated Press issued a bulletin announcing Sterling's foolish sortie into Amon's world.

The publisher did not often come onto his newspaper's third floor and into its editorial offices but when he did he came like Caesar entering Rome. That day he burst out of the elevator clutching the AP dispatch, mouth drawn to a bloodless cleft, eyes awash with fury. He marched to the telephone switchboard, commanding, "Get me the governor!" and spun toward the city desk. As he whirred by reporters, all work stopped. City deskmen froze. Jim Record popped up from his managing editor's tilt-back chair, hurrumphing to attention. Carter drummed fingers on a desk, waiting. The telephone rang. Amon seized it by the throat and shouted, "Sterling?"

All editorial eyes were on Carter.

"You crazy sonofabitch," he bawled into the microphone. "What in the gawddam hell do you think you're doing in Borger?"

All was silence. The staff was awestruck.

Amon listened, then snapped, "Well, gawddamnit, I'll think of something." He jammed the receiver into its cradle and stalked from the third floor. Reporters stared at the retreating mass of wrath, then at one another in disbelief. Twenty minutes later AP clattered out an Amon-dictated pronouncement that national guard troops certainly would not march on Borger.

Governor Sterling blamed the whole mess on the guard commander who, the story said, acted without authority.

Star-Telegram reporters and editors were benumbed by the raw power of Amon's language and that he dared speak that way to Texas' most important elected official. Ever blunt and impetuous, Amon, however, was a man honest to his emotions and convictions. He spoke his mind to anybody.

Elliott Roosevelt lived in Fort Worth when he divorced a wife to marry Ruth Googins, a pretty young socialite. It was a minor scandal and reporters followed Elliott to Nevada for the divorce and then descended on Fort Worth when rumors said the President's son would marry a Texas girl. One early morning FDR telephoned Amon at home, interrupting the publisher's thrice-weekly osteopathic treatment. The President asked of the girl newspapers were linking with his son. ''Ruth Googins' only scandal is being mixed up with the Roosevelts,'' Amon bluntly told the President of the United States.

Later, Eleanor, accompanied by American Airlines president C. R. Smith, came to Fort Worth to meet privately with Googins at Amon's Shady Oak Farm on Lake Worth. Newsmen learned of the intended meeting and Amon whisked the First Lady on to Los Angeles where she and her future daughter-in-law could talk without interruption. Amon had to loan Elliott money to marry the Fort Worth girl.

Carter's reporters knew none of that, knew in fact little of the private Carter, and their memories of him grew from infrequent contact at the newspaper or public functions or on front pages of other publications.

Amon Carter was a complex man with uncomplex ways. Once the formula was understood his every reaction to any situation could be predicted. He was impulsive but rarely surprising, compulsive but always within the borders of his highly anomalous personality.

Very much of a man of his time and place, Amon was never out of character.

Amon, remembered those who knew him best, was compassionate, gentle, indulgent, honest to a fault, intensely loyal to his friends, devoted to his children, unforgiving of his enemies. He was, recalled Nenetta, his second wife, "A marvelous father, the worst husband" and she divorced him because "I got tired of being married to the Chamber of Commerce." In her divorce petition, Zetta, the first wife, charged Amon ". . . traveled much . . . sought public esteem and personal adulation, grew censorious of plaintiff and her . . . humble methods of living."

In turn, Amon was more attentive to his ex-wives than when he was married to each. Nenetta was included on guest lists of his parties, introduced to his famous friends as "the mother of my children, Amon and Ruth." After the divorce, Zetta moved to Chicago where, with little income, she sold magazines door-to-door. Amon and Nenetta's father jointly drilled a successful oil well in the early 1920s. It paid out about one hundred thousand dollars and without legal obligation Amon gave Zetta half his share. A relative borrowed Zetta's money and lost it to a bad investment. Amon gave her more money. She owned a small piece of land willed by her father. Carter had it drilled for gas. The well was successful and Zetta had an income for life.

His children, Amon Junior and Ruth, and the older Bertice, were his special passions. Amon Junior was born in St. Anne's Hall of St. Joseph Hospital. The proud publisher mounted an engraved plaque above the door: "Amon Carter Junior was born in this room, December 23, 1919." That piece of *paterfamilias* hung in place until the building was razed in the early 1950s.

Amon could not abide pain and suffering, in himself or others, and paled at the sight of blood. Ruth was born prematurely while Carter was in New York, and hers was a forceps delivery. The instrument cut her face.

Amon rushed to Fort Worth. When he saw the wound he stood beside his new daughter's crib, sobbing loudly, anguishingly questioning whether Ruth "ever will be OK?" He told little Amon "the old stork dropped Ruth and cut her" and lectured the four-year-old in a stern voice, "You will have to stand up now, you have a sister." His children's illnesses distressed him and even the minor events of their tonsilectomies incited an extreme anxiety. In his office, he paced the floor and wrung his hands, tears flowing over his cheeks, telephoning Nenetta every few minutes, "Is it over yet?"

He called Amon Junior "Cowboy" and Ruth "Sugar Pie," pampered and spoiled both, but was a "little hard" on the son. "He would give Ruthy twenty dollars to take a dose of medicine and Little Amon a lickin' if he didn't," said Nenetta. A consummate sentimentalist, Amon saved his children's first report cards and their Baptist Sunday School quarterlies. Among his office papers is a yellowed envelope inscribed: "Change from Amon Junior's first newspaper sale" — two now-tarnished pennies. He was given a flower by Ruth when she was three. He pressed the petals and entombed them forever in his files. Amon printed the children's baby pictures on *Star-Telegram* bonus checks at Christmas and named new presses bought in 1920 for Bertice and young Amon.

Of his children, Bertice was most like him. Brilliant, with a decisive, penetrating mind and forceful manner, Bertice lived with her mother in Illinois and Amon knew her least of all. He visited with her irregularly, sent an allowance in her younger years, later gave her stock in the publishing company. In return, she worshipped her father, but the fawning attention embarrassed him. A big-boned heavy woman, twice married, Bertice became a broadcaster for WFAA in Dallas. She died in 1952 of alcoholism-related kidney failure in Dallas' Parkland Hospital as Amon sat beside the bed, holding her hand throughout a long night, sorrowing deeply for the tragedy of his first born child.

Amon Carter, who played the coarse, blustering cowboy frontiersman for outlanders, loved flowers, especially heavy-scented hyacinths, lillies and red tulips. The boy who slept on towsacks and wore cast-off clothing grew into the man who treasured luxuries, silk monogrammed pajamas and sheets, tailored suits and handsome shoes. The child who lived in log cabins and drafty rooming houses without plumbing, who emptied bedpans for nickels and dimes, became the multimillionaire with meticulous personal habits. He daily scrubbed the lavatory after shaving, the tub after a bath, on hands and knees, scouring the porcelain basins like a common skullery maid.

He bathed in a Machabelli oil costing twelve dollars a bottle and, afterwards, doused himself in cologne, both of which he bought by the case and which, said Nenetta, he felt ''if a little bit is good, a lot is better.''

''You could smell him comin' and goin',' ' she recalled.

Star-Telegram newsmen knew when he had been in the elevator because Amon's heavy mush permeated the tiny cubicle. Roscoe Brown, the black elevator operator, joked of the saccharine aroma, ''You know 'Evening in Paris,' well, this is 'Night in Fort Worth.' ''

An effetist in creature comforts, Amon nevertheless owned a base streak of Texas good-ole-boyism. He craved plain foods. Meat and potatoes, nothing fancy. Fried chicken and corn cooked in bacon grease, black-eyed peas and cornbread. Barbecued beef and beans. He ventured into turtle soup and Nenetta shamed him into sampling cucumbers and a national columnist marveled that he ate Roquefort dressing on grapefruit, but mostly exotic foods confounded him. O. O. McIntire repeated many times in his syndicated column the tale of Amon's first meeting with a potato souffle at Ciro's in Paris.

Amon shoved away the dish, vowing, "I won't eat that 'til I know who blew it up."

He ate as he did almost everything, too quickly, gulping his food, and by middleage was pained with chronic indigestion. He eased his discomfort by constantly eating Bisodal tablets.

When no guests were in the house he ate at the simple kitchen table, forsaking the larger one in the formal dining room, and usually with the radio for companionship, chuckling at Amos 'n Andy, Fibber McGee and his old friends, Edgar Bergen and Charley McCarthy. And, to Nenetta's endless consternation, he brought Ike and Lindbergh, J. C. Penney, FDR and Sam Rayburn into his home through the servants' rear entrance, as though they were yardmen coming for their vittles and pay. Often after supper he rushed his children off to a movie where, being Amon, he demanded that they sit where he wished to sit, always half-way down on the right side where screen images moved irritatingly aslant. Not surprisingly, Amon favored westerns.

He was blatantly non-intellectual. He rarely attended theater or ballet or opera and, said daughter Ruth, "if he ever set foot in a museum, I don't know about it." But he was, especially in later years, Fort Worth's largest contributor to the arts merely because he thought them necessary for his town's completeness. In all of his life, reported *Time*, Amon never read more than a dozen books.

Amon collected anything and everything: people, memorabilia of his childhood, autographs of famous friends, menus, letters. His cache grew so large that much of it was moved to a warehouse. He never discarded anything. Once American Airlines retired a DC-3 passenger plane and officials organized a brief ceremony. As the company's chief stockholder, and a connoisseur of public rituals, Amon was present. A short pole flying the company flag was mounted on the plane and public relations manager Buck Marriott was in charge of raising and lowering the airplane standard with a thin string. Following the ceremony, Amon approached Marriott.

"May I have the flag, Buck?" Amon asked.

"Certainly, Mr. Carter," answered Marriott. Amon turned to leave, then paused.

". . .uh. . .Buck?"

"Yes, sir?"

"Can I have the string, too?"

He assembled large stores of string, crammed into desk drawers both at home and his office and when the drawers overflowed, Nenetta and his secretary, Katrine Deakins, simply threw away the precious hoard. Amon never missed his string, but began again gathering the valuable discards.

He lay by mounds of paper bags and rubber bands, old odds and ends, scraps of paper with indecipherable scribblings. He subscribed to a clipping service for mentions of himself and the *Star-Telegram* in other publications and those, often as many as thirty copies of an identical wire story, were squirreled away in file cabinets. After Amon's death Katrine and Jimmy North burned thirty fifty-gallon barrelsful of his packrat treasures.

Amon was excruciatingly punctual, always five minutes early, and hostesses who invited him to their homes had to be dressed and waiting at the precise hour because he already was punching impatiently on the doorbell. And his world was ever atilt. The sight of a picture hanging crookedly or a twisted lampshade gave him the fidgits and he went through life putting the world in precise symmetrical order, even compulsively shuttling objects on tables until they had a geometric configuration.

He was "king of the doodads," said Ruth, and loved gadgets, the toys denied him as a child. He bought whatever caught his eye. After the divorce, Nenetta visited an antique shop in New York and the owner, learning her name, asked if she was related to "Amon Carter down in Texas?"

"No," she replied, "but I'm the mother of his children."

After the shopkeeper understood her answer, he made his point about Amon: "He's the answer to an auctioneer's dream. He'll buy anything."

Endlessly he bought what he believed to be priceless antiques and beautiful art objects but few ever matched any decor and Nenetta and Ruth hid them away. For months after he toured the Orient, packages arrived in Fort Worth containing Mandarin robes, rich brocades, fancy underwear and jeweled letter openers, carved ivory, jade figurines. He bought dozens of pistol-shaped cigarette lighters and in South America almost was attacked by Argentine soldiers when he attempted to present one of the flaming guns to Eva Peron.

Captured though he was by the magic of doodads, nothing mechanical ever worked correctly in his hands. He could not type. He cut his fingers on can openers. Pencil sharpeners fell apart at his touch. Amon simply could not be trusted with machinery, especially automobiles. He was an awful driver, and even his children were afraid to ride with him. He drove too fast and on whichever side of the road he chose and he regarded stop signs and signal lights as work of the devil, and other drivers' responsibilities. His home was three miles from the *Star-Telegram* building and he drove the distance twice daily, always in second gear. He was much too busy to waste his time shifting gears.

Mounted to the driver's door of all his automobiles was a leather holster packed with a gleaming six-shooter. He owned many pistols, one of which he broke in 1912 pounding for immediate service on a Baltimore bar top. Another — a Remington forty-five — given him by Nelson Rockefeller served as an impromptu gavel at Shady Oak parties. And there were the twin pistols worn with his cowboy costume and Frank

James' old cap and ball forty-five. No evidence exists Amon ever fired a live round of ammunition through any of his pistols, but there is credible testimony that he was at least uncomfortable around the real thing.

Bud Fisher, the Mutt & Jeff cartoonist, joined Amon at a baseball world series in Philadelphia. As Fisher wrote in the *Saturday Evening Post*, Amon boasted loudly about Fort Worth and Texas.

"No one is considered well dressed in Texas without a six-shooter," bragged Amon, "and I'm such a dude I wear two of them."

Later the two men returned to New York and Amon visited in Fisher's apartment, continuing to bluster about his rough Texas heritage. In defense, Fisher produced a pistol given him by "Pancho Villa after shooting the original owner."

"Look," said Fisher, "here's a pistol I have and it shoots and everything."

The cartoonist loaded one shell, took aim at a blue china cuspidor across the room and fired. Noise and acrid fumes filled the room. Amon blanched, stammered a hasty goodby and rushed out. "I didn't see Mr. Carter again for a year," Fisher wrote.

The large house at 1220 Broad Street was, by Fort Worth standards, a mansion. On the grounds were a greenhouse and open gardens where Nenetta and later Minnie, the third wife, cultivated Amon's aromatic flowers, and a garage often used for parties. Too, there was a huge vault, the steel door of which came from W. T. Waggoner's defunct bank. Amon hid away important treasures in the vault: his liquor and the children's Sunday school quarterlies.

In early years, the home was surrounded by open acres at the city's western outskirts and the family kept cows and chickens, cats, rabbits and dogs. Amon loved animals, especially a bulldog named Boomer, and Blue Boy, Fort Worth's first French Poodle — another of Amon's doodads. Blue Boy, unfortunately, was a car chaser and ultimately pursued and unexpectedly caught a mailtruck. Furious, Amon attempted to have the mailman fired for maiming the poodle but the Postmaster only transferred the carrier to a route away from Carter. The menagerie naturally had losses over the years and for the death of each pet, Amon and the children staged elaborate funerals. Invariably, Amon cried during the services.

Once he bought Nenetta a blooded kitten, Lady Jane, and paid for the animal by cutting $250 from pots of a poker game in his home. Other players complained about the kitty tax but Amon dismissed their grumblings as sour grapes.

He was a splendid gambler, at poker, at dominoes, at the hundred-dollar windows of race tracks, playing as he lived, aggressively. He "won more than he lost," admitted Bert Honea, who felt Amon spent too much time gambling. In 1931, Amon emceed an American Newspaper Publishers Association dinner in Chicago. Colonel Robert McCormick, the Chicago *Tribune* publisher, asked for a biography with which to introduce Amon. He replied, ". . .I am tall, raw-boned, thirsty and possess an excellent appetite as most newspapermen do when the dinner is free. I am married, have 2 children. Fortunately, both of them take after their mother. In addition, I neither drink, smoke, swear nor stay out nights and take no interest in feminine society. I play a little indifferent poker and some bridge, mostly by ear. . ."

Amon, especially after his marriage to Nenetta, began deteriorating, stayed more and more in Suite 10G of the Fort Worth Club where, among the sodality of men, he drank and played poker, often forty-eight hours without a pause. He was a superb womanizer and tireless carouser but gambling occupied his attention most at the club.

He ran over less bold players with his money and there was a curious strain of charity, not all of it benevolent, in his poker style. During one game in 10G, a player lost more than he could afford, and Amon, the big winner, privately returned the man's losings, with a lecture on the folly of gambling beyond one's means. In another game, Amon purposely lost money to a friend deeply in debt.

Amon turned back his winnings in other games but those generosities were influenced by his schemes to help Fort Worth and the men involved held positions in which they could assist the city. Josh Cosden, of the oil family, lost fifteen thousand dollars in a craps game and paid by check. Amon refused to cash the check. A Standard oil president lost twelve hundred dollars at poker and Amon would not accept the money. Later, he asked civic favors of both men and they paid their gambling debts, but in Amon's coin.

With a Robert Burns panatella clinched in his teeth, or waved in an expressive hand like a symphony conductor's baton, Amon was a fast talker, his crisp voice incased in a soft accent that broadened into a caricatured twang when he played cowboy or told jokes and disappeared altogether on solemn occasions. He walked fast, very fast, as though fleeing bill collectors or a posse, and his step almost was a jog-trot. Everybody complained they could not keep pace with him.

The double-time step reflected the energized Amon, a man capable of working eighteen-hour days or playing around the clock without rest. He was able to recharge himself with instant twenty-minute naps but those were rare. He mostly went through life on the run, without rest. Once friends invited him on a quail hunt in West Texas and a photograph shows him on the plains beside an old car, dressed in shirt and tie and broad-brimmed hat like a man on his way to a business luncheon. Afterwards, friends complained around the Fort Worth Club that Amon "walked down all the dogs" and kept the men awake by drinking and talking all night. Amon, too, had collected all the dead quail and taken them to Shady Oak. He was never asked to go hunting again.

His friends teased him about the bird hunt until he tired of the jokes and growled angrily at them. Everything paled before Amon's anger. Of all his personality quirks the "mad spells," as Katrine Deakins named them, most affected those around him. Amon, an overachiever in all ways, had monumental fits of anger.

He was neurotically impatient, with himself, with others, and he demanded precision of an imprecise world, thus the shortest delay or smallest error instantly brought on his furies. He would puff up, redden, shout, cuss, even stamp his feet, and those who witnessed the volatile outbursts were either mesmerized or terrified. No doubt the mad spells were a bullying influence on civilians and reporters alike and there were otherwise strong-minded businessmen in Fort Worth who would agree to anything rather than face an angry Amon Carter.

"Amon the Terrible," said a newsman, reflecting on his publisher's rages. Those bitter paroxysms probably accounted for the negative memories among Fort Worthians because in a tantrum Amon was unreasonable, intimidating and simply steamrolled over anyone who dared step in his path. Told by a secretary in New York that her boss could not see Amon, the publisher brushed her aside, burst into the man's office and demanded to know "why in the hell you're putting me off?" In the 1920s when the *Star-Telegram* building was sparkling new, Amon became enraged over a trifle. He jammed on his hat and headed for the Fort Worth Club. In the lobby, a *Press* newsboy talked with several *Star-Telegram* carriers. The boy sat on a counter kicking his heels against the shining mahogany. Amon the Angry swept into the lobby.

He saw the boy and his kicking heels, burst into the circle of carriers, grabbed the *Press* newsie by the scuff of the neck and seat of the pants. Amon hauled the kid outside and abruptly dropped him on the sidewalk, continuing without a word to the club. Within hours, Fort Worth was gossiping of how Amon Carter had attacked a small boy.

When angered, Amon demanded immediate retribution. He parked his car under a tin-roofed shed reserved for *Star-Telegram* executives, and often outsiders sneaked their autos into the handy spaces. One morning Amon found an old Ford parked in his space and immediately went into a fit. Motorcycle patrolman Lawrence Wood passed and Amon yelled for him to stop.

"Give this car a ticket!" ordered Amon.

Wood protested. "I can't, Mr. Carter. It's on private property."

"I don't care, give it one anyway. That's my parking space."

"Honest, Mr. Carter, I can't. I'd get in trouble."

Amon simmered at the Ford for long moments, then told Wood, "Ride around the block." Wood rode, circling very slowly. As he turned the final corner, there was Amon pushing the old Ford into the street, blocking traffic in both directions.

"Now it's on public property. Ticket it!", growled Amon.

As volcanic as the mad spells could be they most often vanished as suddenly and mysteriously as they appeared and Amon would be contrite and seemingly embarrassed with his behavior. In the early 1950s he was forcefeeding taxpayers on merits of a bond issue to build what would become known as the "Amon Carter International Airport." The *Star-Telegram* daily published on page one highly optimistic stories praising the proposed air facility. Jim Vachule was summoned to Carter's office to receive "facts" for the next glowing report. Amon dictated and Vachule scribbled notes.

"Read that back to me," said Amon. Vachule read.

"Where's triumphant?"

"Triumphant?"

"Yes, 'triumphant'," said Amon, irritated. "I was talking about how the airport would affect us and I said it would be a 'triumphant display of the city's future.' You left out 'triumphant'."

Vachule consulted his notes.

"It's not here," said the reporter.

"I said 'triumphant'!" yelled Amon.

"I'll write it in, but I don't think you said it, Mr. Carter."

Amon detonated.

The publisher ranted, stomped back and forth in front of his newsman, lectured Vachule on the need for accuracy. Stunned by the suddeness and force of his boss' anger, Vachule was speechless. Finally, Vachule escaped, shaken by the experience.

At one a.m., the telephone rang and the sleeping Vachule groped for the receiver.

"Jim?" said the voice. "Amon Carter." Vachule instantly was awake. "Yes, sir?"

"I've been thinking about it," said Amon, "and I don't believe I said 'triumphant' after all."

They talked for a few moments and Vachule returned to bed, puzzling over his enigmatic employer. He arrived at work the next morning and found an envelope rolled into his typewriter. Inside was a crisp one hundred dollar bill. Amon was apologizing.

For those closest to him, the mad spells were both irritating and, often, humorous. They reacted by returning the anger or teasing him into a good mood or ignoring the outbursts. Amon and Bert Honea argued endlessly while North or Katrine stood in the middle as mediators, pacifying both. Nenetta and Katrine mostly ignored him. Frank Mills, WBAP's chief announcer, once entered the *Star-Telegram* lobby and found Amon loudly berating Harold Hough. The publisher blamed Hough for an unhappy advertiser and demanded he go pacify the man at once. The tirade over, Amon marched to the elevator. "Let's go get coffee," Hough said to Mills.

"But the advertiser. . .?" said Mills. "Shouldn't you go right now? Mr. Carter was really mad."

"Naw," drawled Hough. "Amon'll forget about it in twenty minutes. He'll know I'm not going."

For almost forty years Katrine Deakins daily experienced Amon's mad spells and remained as unperturbed at the end as she was in the beginning. An earlier job ended when her boss made an indecent proposal and she hit him with an ink well. She came to work as Hough's secretary. Still another of Amon's secretaries quit and Hough asked Katrine to move into the second-floor suite. She agreed but only if she could return should Amon be too much for her.

He was not and until his death Katrine served the galvanic publisher in spite of his angers. She was as tough as he was, contending, "You had to stand up to him or he'd make a mop out of you." He fired her regularly and especially every New Year's Eve on general principles and she ignored him. Amon warned Katrine never to clean his desk or office, both of which he considered sacred ground. She waited until he left town and cleaned anyway, then patiently bore the mad spell when he returned.

In the heat of a fit, Amon often would strike out at the nearest hard object to blunt the fury. At home, he once beat his fists against a wall until blood flowed. He pounded his office desk so hard he broke a diamond ring. Curious about a loud thumping from Amon's office, Katrine peeked around the door one day to find her infuriated boss loudly and determinedly beating his head against a wall.

Amon's doctors repeatedly warned that his tantrums would kill him but he outlived both the mad spells and the doctors and happily was ranting away at this and that on his death bed.

There was an innate gruffness to Amon. Part of it was contrived but more was only the wrapping of his style. He could be, and was, kindly gruff or grouchy gruff and few could distinguish between the tones. He practiced a fine, pungent sarcasm and owned almost no tolerance at all for what Harold Hough once characterized as "Amon's aversion to social horse pooky."

Though of course he was not, Amon considered himself a country boy and held elitist pretentions in low disdain. He loved nothing better than skewering the affectations of others.

Once a culture-voiced grand dame, one diligently hiding away the cotton sack twang of her early life, telephoned Amon in the early morning, cooing, "Oh, Amon, have I awakened you?"

"No," he grumped. "You woke me up."

A Washington columnist reported Amon was toured through the baronial manor house of the capital's most ardent snob. The proud host stood Amon before a canopied bed, boasting of its pedigree back to the Seventeenth Century French court.

". . .and it cost me two hundred thousand dollars," the man bragged.

"You get the mattress and springs thrown in for that?" asked Amon.

That was Amon, ever extraordinary, never common, extravagantly human. The real Amon Carter was quite different from his flamboyant cowboy. The cowboy was what he wanted to be; Amon Carter was who he was. Amon Carter was not Lan Twohig, though he tried to be, perhaps even believed himself to be a genuine Texas cowboy.

Jimmy Walker's steer horns are gone, lost or discarded or even resting in a dusty back room of some New York museum. Lan Twohig's old steerhorns were important to Amon, the first of his large western collection, probably the first piece of his cowboy personality. Why he gave those horns to Walker, I do not know. He had many others. Perhaps by 1928 he no longer needed the realness of Lan Twohig's cowboy to support the Amon Carter cowboy. Perhaps he merely was feeling generous that day.

Wherever they are, the horns speak of a life, of a time, lost and lamented. They were of *The West*.

Chapter 4

"...this place, this rural slum, this potential Utopia, this rolling chunk of God's not-always-green footstool..."

—*Stanley Walker,* Home to Texas

West Texas is bound on the north by Colorado and Oklahoma, on the west by New Mexico, on the south by Mexico and on the east by Amon Carter.

—*Amarillo* **Globe**, *1936*

The sky is high and wide and blue
And you say to strangers, Howdy-do!

—*"Cactus Jack," a song, 1933*

I went into West Texas one year and was never heard of again.

—*A failed Texas politician*

4

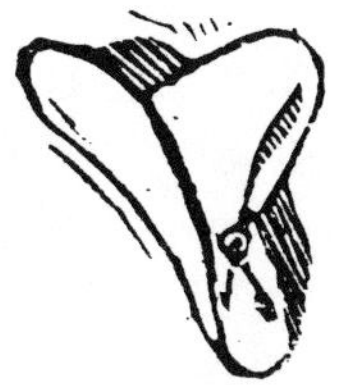

The West. Hills roll out from Fort Worth, gentle and mild and grassy, cut with seams of rocky creeks, patched by groves of oaks. No hills, logically, can be there. The Grand Prairie, the flatness beginning east of Dallas, should continue uninterrupted beyond Fort Worth, but does not. These swells of odd geography seem to billow from the Trinity westward, blending with a hundred-mile-wide band of good farming land called Cross Timbers. If there is an actual physical beginning of West Texas, it is on the soft far edge of Cross Timbers. The soil changes from rich browns and blacks to beige sands, pale red clays. Oaks disappear, succeeded by mesquite. Docile bossys of dairy farms are supplanted by fatter, less tractable beef cattle. The land no longer rolls calmly but is levelness punctuated with ragged-size knolls, sloping upward to the sun.

AMON

Out yonder beyond Cross Timbers' peach orchards, watermelon and peanut fields, is *The West* of official record, that mythical country with its straight-line horizon and flat, vacant space. It made Hollywood wealthy. Flat-bellied and lean-hipped John Waynes and Gary Coopers dwell there in boots and starched jeans, hats laid low over dark, dangerous eyes. Astride huge white stallions they race across the vastness like summer lightning. In West Texas bloom red and black and white cattle, wisps of smeared color on the gray landscape of late afternoon.

Outlanders know that Texas by heart: The boots and jeans stereotype, smells of old leather and cattle, Cadillacs and Neiman-Marcus suits for the Saturday night dance in the old corner saloon.

That's what is believed, and we Texans have gone to preposterous lengths to establish those myths. Truth is, *The West* was narrower, its lifetime briefer, its deeds less Homeric than legends imply. It had a prologue and and epilogue, but generally *The West* was written right out there in West Texas after the Civil War, when Americans began spreading toward California, filling out the continent in a fit of Manifest Destiny. *The West* ended when the first strand of barbed wire was strung between two posts. Joseph Glidden's spiked wire stopped *The West* dead in its tracks.* All after is but postscript.

The West's dimensions were about five hundred by five hundred miles, roughly what now is called West Texas, and within that austere compound evolved every blessed western thing we have come to hold sacred: The cowboy, the horse, the beef cow, the ranch, the rustler, the fruited plains, purple mountains' majesty, even "They went thataway," as spoken by a sod farmer near Amarillo to a posse chasing two rustlers

*Lewis Silphy often is credited as co-father of barbed wire, but his claim is disputed. Silphy, however, did notable work in the field of chicken wire.

("Thataway," incidentally, was northeast, toward Raton, New Mexico).

By the time Amon Carter espied *The West* and dragged its embarkation point to Fort Worth, it was little more than a sunbleached skeleton. *The West* had been romanticized into poetical fiddle faddle, entrapped by Hollywood where it would die ingloriously on the back lots of Monogram and Republic as film fodder for Saturday matinee audiences. While it lived, though, *The West* had the stuff of immortality. It grew in a harsh country settled by harsh men, and because of it and them, West Texas is a rare place.

From Cross Timbers the land rises, becomes dustier, rockier, more of a savanna. Midway between the good farming land and New Mexico's mountains is a blunt stone cliff called the Cap Rock escarpment, an eroded natural palisade rising as much as a thousand feet. Above and beyond the Cap Rock begin America's High Plains, named in West Texas, *Llano Estacado*. The Staked Plains. Indians, especially Comanches, were at home there among limitless herds of buffalo and elk. The Staked Plains was a true prairie once covered by tall grasses, level and seemingly endless as the Russian Steppes.

The Cap Rock curls south, then west, hooking into New Mexico. Below the escarpment and west of the Pecos River are Texas' only true mountains, and nub-ends of Mexico's Chihuahuan Desert. The Chihuahuan barrenness melds with the Sonoran Desert and continues west to the Pacific. That country's physiognomy is one of wilderness, of distance and space, colors washed and muted. In it are Texas' ventricous belly, the Big Bend, which sags onto Mexico, and tall, crisp peaks rising almost nine thousand feet.

West Texas held the principal components of *The West* — not only ranches and the cowboys and their tools of work and play, but the Spanish, who came searching for gold and found none, the Indians, the cavalry, the buffalo for which the plains were southern grazing grounds.

The most apparent fact of West Texas was — and still is — emptiness. Enough people could not come to fill it up. One hundred acres wouldn't support neighboring farmers or ranchers. One thousand acres could, but then they no longer were close neighbors. This dispersion of peoples caused towns and villages to be distant from one another and more than any other single reason allowed Amon Carter to become the region's landlord, the *Star-Telegram* its eyes and ears. When Carter stumbled into the newspaper business there were sections of West Texas which did not have one person every hundred miles. Amarillo, which would become a full city on the high plains, was little more than a plat of canvas tents. Roads were rudimentary. The new urban innovations of electricity, sewer systems, telephones and the like virtually were nonexistent. An old cowboy once told me of a ranch for which he worked in 1901. Headquarters were 115 miles from the nearest post office. As late as the 1920s, Frank Reeves, the *Star-Telegram*'s ranching expert, often slept under trees on the prairie because he could not move from one hotel to another, or from one ranch headquarters to the next, in a single day. Even in 1930, the north-south highway from Texline near the Colorado border to San Angelo deep within West Texas was almost five hundred miles long and had less than fifty miles of hard-top paving, almost all of it around Amarillo and Lubbock. I remember folks driving eighty miles to drink a beer or see a movie, and thinking nothing of it. Distance is endemical to West Texans.

Those conditions existed in a general way well into the 1930s when West Texans began receiving what other Americans had been enjoying for decades. While electricity and indoor plumbing did not arrive in remotest West Texas until after World War II, the region always remained behind the rest of the country in every significant way — in education, medical services, public utilities, industry, jobs, transportation. My early school years during the second World War were spent in a farmhouse without electric lights or plumbing, and a classroom holding six grades, a woodburning stove and coaloil lamps. There was no bus to school. The crude road that passed the farmhouse often was a muddy morass and, when it was, Rural Free Delivery mail and the *Star-Telegram* never arrived. My grandfather often went for months without even a small coin in his pocket. Our situation was not considered impoverished — our neighbors had the same problems — but simple Central Texas rurality. West Texas, though, was not just rural; it was primitive. We were wealthy when compared with Texans living farther west where the land fought its intruders with fury.

Politicians ignored West Texas. Industry spurned it. Those who went there, for business or visiting, got out as soon as they could. There was little middle class population. West Texans, poor and isolated and largely ignorant, hungered for attention. Amon Carter merely stepped in, assumed the mortgage on West Texas' future, and became its paladin, carrying the tattered banner to all America. *West Texas is important. Amon Carter said so. See! It's right here on the front page of the Star-Telegram!*

West Texans were prisoners in a country that punished them with heat and dust, took everything and gave little. For every cattle baron there were hundreds of beaten-down cowmen. Every rich cotton farmer had dozens of failed homesteaders to look down on. The cattle business, and farming, are cyclical ventures. Cows that bring wealth one year go begging for buyers the next. A season of rain, good grasses and abundant crops is followed by perhaps years of drought and heat and dust.

No matter what happened, though, West Texans carried on. They coped. Texas was settled by a migrational flow from the mid-South, from Tennessee and Kentucky. One historian suggested the gentler farmers and merchants remained in East Texas and the malcontents, the unsociable men with hard eyes and searching souls, continued west to do battle with that unfortunate country, untouched by civilization's ebb and tide, living anonymously with their poor choice of homestead, enduring the outrageous weather, the lonely distance. They shouldered their burden, and hoped it would all change.

Most West Texans led lives contradicting the legends. Stanley Walker wrote, "Many outsiders have the idea that the marks of Texans are buoyancy, optimism and bustling energy. The average Texan is a tired man, and has been ever since he can remember . . . a quiet defeatism is the rule. They are stoics, never excited over their petty victories, and at the same time never crushed by adversity. Most of them can take an honest blow of fate without wincing much. Let a man's beautiful daughter elope at the age of fifteen with a bum, let the grasshoppers eat his pastures, let the bugs destroy his oat fields, let anthrax lay low his herd of cattle, let the screwworms decimate his sheep, let illness ruin his bank account, if any, let Republicans reach high office in the nation — whatever happens, the Texan is not greatly astonished."

He carried on.

They had floods and famines, wolves, coyotes, rattlesnakes and tarantulas as big and black as derby hats. There were range wars and blood feuds without end, diseases and deaths, Indian raids and loneliness, always the loneliness.

Ranchers, those plains emperors like Loving and Goodnight, reigned over West Texas, supreme as emirs of Turkistan, because it was a time when a man could settle on an estate larger than many European countries and be its absolute monarch. Barbed wire came about 1875. Fatter foreign cattle were introduced to replace the Longhorns. Now, the rancher needed less land. He sold some to sod farmers. Farmers discovered something ranchers never knew. The crumbly beige soil was abundantly productive when watered. Using irrigation, large farmers made the prairie rich with crops, especially cotton. Families with smaller pieces of land could not afford irrigation and had to trust nature to water their crops; the trust largely was misplaced.

A few men, digging for water, found oil, though not all of them appreciated the greasy liquid. Old Dan Waggoner ran his considerable nerve and luck into sixty thousand cattle grazing half-a-million acres covering much of seven counties. He died in 1904. His son, W. T., dug for water, and found oil. "Dammit," legend says he shouted, "cows can't drink that stuff." W. T. plugged the wells with cedar posts. Later, Amon Carter negotiated with Pappy Waggoner for Phillips Petroleum, which wanted the old man's oil. Amon reported Pappy would not accept Phillips' offer of $50,000,000. At his death, W. T. "Pappy" Waggoner was Texas' richest man, worth perhaps a billion dollars. His children knew what to do with oil and the money it produced.

West Texas was place of origin for much of Texans' exaggerations. People dared not tell the truth about their country so they made up extravagant yarns poking fun at their predicament ("It rained in Ben Green County yesterday but I didn't have time to drive over and watch it.") Or the fables were boastful chauvinism. Amon Carter had a collection of "facts" he loosed on audiences. They were generous overstatements, and a few outright lies, written for him, I suspect, by Boyce House, a *Star-Telegram* reporter who collected all those Texas brags and published them in a dozen books.

Amon's talk began with the shout, "Texas forever! Fort Worth now and hereafter!" He told audiences:

"If Texas was chopped off loose from the United States, it would float into the ocean, as it rests on a vast subterranean sea of fresh water. . . .The chief occupation of Texans is trying to keep from making all the money in the world. . . . If a Texan's head was opened the map of Texas would be engraved on his brain, and also his heart. . . . You do not belong to society as constituted in Texas unless your front gate is 18 miles from your front door. . . . If all Texas steers were one big steer he would stand with his front feet in the Gulf of Mexico, one hind foot in Hudson Bay, the other in the Arctic Ocean and with his tail brush off the mist of the Aurora Borealis. . . . SOME STATE!"

Carter never stopped reminding other, less fortunate, Americans that Texas was a sovereign nation reduced to statehood. For serious moments he restructured the data into more palatable truths:

"West Texas is an area greater than that of New York, Massachusetts, Pennsylvania and Maryland combined, peopled with 2,000,000 thrifty folks, courageous builders, ninety percent of whom are native-born white," and "Oil produced in this area is nearly one-half of all the oil produced in the world."

Through his efforts the West Texas Chamber of Commerce grew to a membership exceeded in numbers only by the United States Chamber of Commerce, a statistic that hardly flattered the region, and one causing Sam Rayburn to shake his head and mutter, "Any town big enough to have a Chamber of Commerce is beyond saving."

Somehow the early inhabitants of West Texas survived and became a hardy, taciturn, patient people imbued with a lengthy roster of social qualities. They were warmhearted, openly friendly to travelers and passing strangers, but highly suspicious of newcomers. They were independent, individualistic, conservative, proud, frank and honest — my grandfather never locked his house when leaving; neighbors might need to borrow something while he was gone. They were deeply, fundamentally religious. Social sinning was broadly condemned — smoking and dancing Methodists were considered by Baptists to be vice-ridden. Doubtless they were racially intolerant. There were few blacks and West Texans had only Mexican-Americans — the ''meskins'' — to consider inferior. ''Two things you can't find in West Texas,'' crowed one bigot, ''are Republicans and Jews.'' Isolated by the miles, West Texans were insular, unknowing, often uncaring, of what went on beyond their communities.

West Texas was another world, and even Amon Carter went there only when he had to.

The survivors had children, then grandchildren, who got an education of sorts. Given learning and a somewhat wider view of the world, the young left home, often at a dead run. They mostly came to Fort Worth, which accounted for its twenty-fold growth in the early years of this century. That always was the essential difference between Fort Worth and Dallas. Dallas received the mercantile men, ambitiously seeking fortunes; Fort Worth got the half-grown children from West Texas, not coming to town in search of a buck, but escaping. Failed farmers and ranchers fled to Fort Worth for work in the slaughter houses and other muscle industries, and with the larger migration of the early 1940s, to man the bomber plant's assembly line.

A few wealthy families came, too, maintaining second homes in Fort Worth because the town, bragged the *Star-Telegram*, was ''The Queen City of the Plains.'' A resident once complained to his city councilman that streets around his east side home were unimproved and dingy while the west side had brick avenues and tall light poles and curbing. He was told Amon Carter wanted it that way. West Fort Worth was that part of the city seen first by arriving West Texans.

The city began in 1849 as a rough log fort on grassy bluffs along the west fork of the Trinity River, a dowdy, vermicular stream which either flooded or puddled and which, until 1913, served as a convenient garbage and sewage dump. The fort was built on a site chosen by Colonel Ripley Arnold as defensible against the frontier savagery of Indians, and as a place of refuge for settlers. Arnold wasted his and the Army's time. The first group seeking sanctuary was Indians, the Tonkawas, fleeing from other Indians, the Kiowas. The fort and its white settlers were ignored by frontier savagery. Four years later the Army abandoned its fort and rode westward to more fruitful Indian-slaughtering territory. Settlers moved into the abandoned log buildings and made themselves a village. They named it Fort Worth.

Historically, the fort was never a Fort but by official U.S. Army designation, a temporary garrison for soldiers. A "camp." First citizens called the log huts a "fort" because to them it was.

Amon sold his town's history as one of those Dodge City/Tombstone/Cheyenne shootemup, Wyattearpish, cattlific, whoopee places. It actually was. Fort Worth owned all necessary components of America's legendary penny-dreadful wild west burgs. It had everything. Except a press agent. What frontier Fort Worth needed was one of those Boswellian ballyhooers to pen immortal poetry and songs* and prose to its dirty deeds and wayward ways. What it got in our literature of western lore was a place of virtual anonymity. Even Butch Cassidy, his lawless accessory, the Sundance Kid, and various others of the Wild Bunch, used Fort Worth as a final asylum before riding into the Argentine sunset, and it took historians sixty years to track them to town.

Sam Bass, a vigorous and successful North Texas bandit and train robber, bought his criminal supplies in Fort Worth. Luke Short, a deadly fast gun and adventuristic gambler who dandified his western garb with a stovepipe hat, held financial interest in the White Elephant Saloon. Wyatt Earp's consumptive friend, Doc

*The only song of semi-prominence ever composed for Fort Worth was "Big Ball's in Cowtown," popularized by Bob Wills. It often was mistaken as a musical ode to swollen testes but actually tells of a cowboy dance.

Holliday, often was seen peering over the city's poker tables. Temple Houston, youngest son of old Sam Houston, a soft-voiced eloquent trial lawyer and lethal gunfighter, periodically rode into Fort Worth, usually wearing a rattlesnake for a hatband. Cattle trails — notably the Chisholm — passed nearby and furnished off-duty cowboys for Hell's Half Acre, Fort Worth's marvelous shopping mall of sin. Railroads in all directions and buffalo hunters, the cavalry, lynchings, redeye whiskey, wagon trains, stagecoaches west to Yuma, stampedes, wild horses, gunfights — Fort Worth had it all, just as Dodge City and Abilene and Tombstone. Cowboys enjoyed rampaging streets firing their sixguns in the air, regularly plugging one another and occasionally a private citizen who wandered into lines of fire. The Acre's whores always made news — "Another soiled dove crossed the river," revealed the *Democrat*. "Yesterday another of the demimonde, weary of the trials and tribulations of her life, took a dose of laudanum and morphine. The last suicide of such nature was about two weeks ago."

And someone nailed Sally to the door. Good Sally was a pretty Acre girl with many admirers. One morning Fort Worth awoke to find Sally's carcass nailed to an outhouse door. Sally's crucifixion aroused reformers to have a go at shuttering Hell's Half Acre. The erogenous zone closed for a while, then began again, but never with the intensity of the bad old wild west days. When Butch Cassidy arrived in 1898, the Acre was reasonably calm but the district, and Fort Worth's reputation as a "murder town," remained well into the Twentieth Century.

Fort Worth truly was a rough frontier city. Aside from a lack of on-duty chronicler, the town's largest problem was one of staying power. Boom or bust. It rose with the influx of western emigration, then fell as fewer settlers came. Good fortune came with the cattle drives, and poverty afterward. Railroads brought another period of prosperity. And the buffalo hunters. And stockyards. Between the booms, Fort Worth relapsed. Workers moved out. Failed merchants decamped to other areas of steadier prosperity. During one of those lesser periods a newspaper declared that grass actually was growing in Fort Worth streets.

Packing houses were the first industries capable of sustaining Fort Worth's economy and Amon Carter arrived as the town looked to better times.

The shootemup days were forgotton. Fort Worth had to make do with slogans — "Paris of the Plain" and "Where the West Begins" — as other middling towns (Omaha, also ignored as a wild west community, grandly called itself "The Diamond Stickpin in the Bosom of the West").

Fort Worth, though western, was never where the west began, never even a significant part of those historical bits of Western Americana. It was not even a part of West Texas, where everything western began.

The city, a cowtown to its core, managed to keep its cattle and cowboy personality because it catered to cow-conscious West Texans who, ". . . lived in the most beautiful back yard a city ever had." When Amon invented his chaw-bacon rube cowboy, he was forced to mutter shibboleths of exaggerated braggadocio because Fort Worth's real history had been forgotten.

". . . most beautiful back yard a city ever had." Perhaps he was right. There is a time out there when softness comes to the plains and mountains. Bluebonnets and Indian Paint Brush and the lavenders of Sweet William and wild verbena flow over the pastures. The pampas flatness is coated with clovers and tall buffalo grasses become golden, as in Spanish Andalusia. The air is cool and clear and clanking windmills are shadowy sentinals rising over the long landscape. The land truly is epic and grand, and *The West* undeniably still is there, as glorious and indomitable as Amon Carter always wished it would be.

Chapter 5

He said he'd have to leave his home, His Daddy'd married twice
And his new ma beat him every day or two:
So he saddled up Old Chow one night and 'lit a shuck' this way.

—*Verse 4,* Little Joe, The Wrangler

The origin of Amon G. Carter is shrouded in mystery. His discovery is a matter of record. William Randolph Hearst, strolling through his beautiful gardens one dewy morn, paused in admiration before an exceptionally large cluster of violets. Underneath was the Baby Amon . . . Since then his family silver has been marked with a shrinking violet as the Carter Coat of Arms.

—*Menu Legend, Sherry's, NYC, May 7, 1928*

5

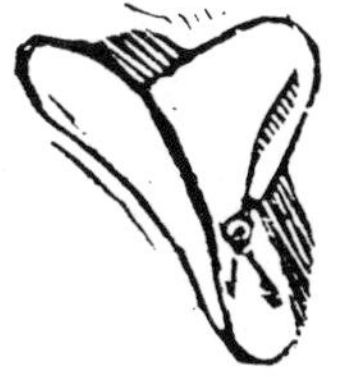

Bowie, in the mid-1890s, owned the congenital blandness of a thousand Texas hamlets, characterized by a weathered clapboard grayness and simple unornamental silence interrupted only by yawns from front porch swings and squeaky buggy wheels. Like blips on dark radar screens, fireflies provided entertainment on lukewarm summer nights, mosquitoes and chiggers went on duty after spring rains for disciplined scratching, but neither flood nor famine, cataclysm nor moral disaster, brushed Bowie. Its businesses served a thousand people from false-fronted stores. Folks gossiped, listened to a makeshift band that played badly for civic occasions and waited, often desperately, for the arrival of a Fort Worth or Denver train to salvage their prosaic lives. Those residents who escaped mostly fled to Fort Worth, a city of twenty thousand persons, sixty-five miles south by rutted road or sixty by rail. Bowie's principal street, the south finger of it, pointed toward Fort Worth. At the other end, one could strike out for Wichita Falls, although few did, and those wondered why. There were saloons enough to inspire Baptist sermons, and to satisfy men driven to drink by their humdrum ghetto. Bowie served its numbness with memories of Indians (then shuffled off the Oklahoma reservations) who had created atrocities in the 1870's by scalping settlers and burning cabins, and the adjacent Chisholm Trail, a onetime super-highway for four million cattle jammed horn to tail and driven to railhead in Kansas. The old trail in 1890 was a literal cow path. The railroad replaced cattle drives and in its way saved Bowie from absolute despair by depositing visitors at the depot and lugging farm produce to Fort Worth. And, besides, the whistle blew a dandy song for soft spring evenings.

Bowie, as tranquil as Heaven, as intolerably boring as Hell, lay on the dark sand, mesquite and scrub-oak prairies of North Texas and squeaked its porch swings and buggy wheels, marveled at the neon animation of fireflies, scratched chigger bites, ignoring and being ignored. Had Bowie but glanced to the outside world for diversion perhaps it would have taken an interest in the Great Snuff War raging all about.

Railroad Snuff and Levi P. Garrett Scotch Snuff were swinging away at one another with fiscal fierceness. Each sold snuff in square bottles of the same size and price — twenty-five cents. Railroad fired the first shot heard 'round the snuff-dipping world by cutting its price to twenty cents. Levi P. Garrett regarded the discount as crass commercialism and maintained its two-bit price, but sneaked a nickel under the cork of each bottle. Stalemated, the two great snuff generals rested their armies, plotting the next maneuver.

Snuff dippers of course were giddy over the price war. Non-snuff users generally were cognizant of neither the war nor the giddiness, but Amon Carter noticed. He was a quick-eyed boy who wore too-large clothes and roomed at Jarrott's Hotel. Amon was a recent arrival from Nocona, a half-pint settlement of even lesser appeal than Bowie. Then thirteen, young Amon was taken not by the finely ground tobacco but the knowledge that a huge, shiny nickel lay underneath the cork of each and every Garrett Snuff bottle. His youthful reverence for nickels, which he would later transfer to thousand dollar bills, was fashioned partly by a native respect for money, partly by his poverty. At the moment of the great snuff stalemate, Amon hustled to support himself. He committed miscellaneous chores, including toting buckets of drinking water into Z. T. Lowrie's wholesale grocery store. Always he detoured through the snuff department to experience the awesome presence of nickels. One early morning, Lowrie's store burned. It was a glorious blaze, more watched than fought by Bowie's bucket brigade and water wagon volunteer fire department. The flames called out most of the citizenry, who welcomed the novelty of a new conversational subject. Amon was there, but he was not thinking of the fire. His mind was on snuff.

At mid-morning, ashes smoldered. The store and its contents were little more than tangled wire and twisted tin rising out of smoking rubble. Amon approached the owner: "Mr. Lowrie, if anybody picks up anything in there, can he have it?"

"Certainly, my boy," answered Lowrie generously.

As every country boy of the period, Amon was barefooted. The ashes were hot. He searched behind S. Daube's general store where always there was a pile of discarded footware left by new shoe buyers. He selected a largish pair, bound them to his feet with baling wire and waded through ashes straight to the snuff department.

The nickels were too hot for his hands. He dug them out with a stick and dropped the coins in a number two tomato can. Amon had six dollars — the largest amount of money he had ever amassed — before other boys discovered the Garrett Snuff treasure hoard. Amon had beaten them again.

What passed for Amon's childhood was a money-making contest between him and them, the boys of Bowie. He was a born entrepreneur, a money-maker with native intelligence and sharp eye for opportunity who advanced Horatio Alger's *Pluck and Luck* plot to that of a grand design. Not that he actually enjoyed the conglomerate of enterprises he was forced to undertake. He wanted to be a cowboy. He left home at eleven, not by choice, and sneaked aboard a freight bound for what he believed was Montana and, as he later wrote, ". . . the great West where cowboys and Indians predominated." His ride was brief. A conductor halted the train and dropped Amon beside a dry stream, Salt Creek, twenty-two miles from downtown metropolitan Bowie.

"It's all right," Amon, cocky even then, called to the conductor. "I really wanted to go fishing anyway."

The trainman told him he could have all the fish he could catch in Salt Creek. Amon felt the four dimes in the pocket of his knee britches, pulled his cap lower over his eyes and trudged to Bowie where lethargy, not cowboys and Indians, predominated. He arrived at dusk, passing the friendly city limit sign warning: "Nigger, Don't Let the Sun Go Down on You in Bowie."

Amon had no idea what he would do until he remembered his father often sold peaches to a hotel/boarding house operated by Mrs. Mollie Jarrott. He walked to the hotel's rear door and rapped loudly. Mrs. Jarrott opened the door. Amon asked for work, declaring there was not anything he could not or would not do. She hired him as a handyman, chambermaid and waiter for $1.50 weekly, plus room and board. That first evening she fed the thin boy in ragged clothes and he told her of his life.

Amon's father was William Henry Carter, a sometime farmer who retreated to blacksmithing when his crops failed, which was often. The elder Carter was a small solid man, muscular, almost handsome, adorned with a drooping moustache, ignorant as the mules he shod. An early picture shows Father Carter beside a wooden board ringed by horseshoes. "W. H. Carter, Grays, Ga." is spelled out with nails on the board. Mr. Carter was at best indifferent to Amon, though at one time he tried to make a blacksmith of his son. During one of the elder Carter's retreats into the anvil business, he put his son to shoeing a goosey cow pony. The horse kicked Amon into unconsciousness, breaking three ribs. "Pa," Amon declared when awake, "I'm out of the blacksmith business."

Josephine Ream Carter, Amon's mother, was pretty with dark curly hair and esthetic features. In her childhood, she lived at La Reunion, a French commune that flourished briefly on banks of the Trinity River near Dallas. She had some musical talent and taught Amon to peck out a one-fingered piano version of "Jesus, Lover of My Soul." She encouraged his singing, which merely was awful. She spoiled little Amon. Josie wrote to a cousin, Mary Bundrad: "Willie Harkins gave Amon this dres and Gills bought Amon a dres and a yarde of red ribbon and I am going to braid it with red Flours. Tell Aunt Nancy I do reckon I have the finest boy you ever saw. He can crawl but he crawls on his belly. I can't kep him on'na palet nor hardly in the house."

Josie Carter concluded with a very telling, and prophetic, statement about Amon: "He is the worst rounder I ever saw."

William and Josie moved in the 1870's to a farm near Crafton, a wart-like collection of mismatched sod and log houses mounted on hump-backed hills in Wise County. As usual, William's farming did not go well. He cut logs and built a one-room cabin. By December 11, 1879, the hut still was unchinked. Father Carter spent the day plugging holes, attempting to stay the numbing cold of a norther that struck in the early morning. Amon arrived with the freezing gale. Josephine complained of the cold. William wrapped his wife and new son in blankets, placed both in a rocking chair, and carried them to a neighbor's warmer home.

In later years, Amon claimed his log cabin birth was a status shared by too many others to have any standing in Texas. He also said he began work early, picking 104 pounds of cotton in a single day when he was seven.

Josie died in 1892, soon after giving birth to a daughter, Addie, and Amon went to live with a grandmother in nearby Nocona, where he discovered saloons for the first time. Farmers bought half-pints of whiskey and drank them near the wagon yard, leaving the empty bottles in horse stalls. Early each morning, Amon rescued the empties and sold them to saloon keepers for twenty cents a dozen. His recycling business lasted until he decided to become a cowboy, an ambition he would pursue all of his days.

The Jarrott Hotel had eleven rooms, each containing a double bed, washstand, washbowl, pitcher and "white owl," a kind of early chamber pot. Meals were served family-style on a large oak table. Daily, Amon cleaned rooms, emptied the pots, refilled the pitchers, swept out, and served meals. He was well-liked by all the boarders except Shorty Tarpley, a sarcastic, ugly-mooded tyrant who labored in the town's livery stable. Tarpley bullied everyone, including Amon.

"Kid," he barked to Amon one morning at breakfast. "Eggs. Straight up, one over the fence and make it snappy."

Angry, Amon marched to the kitchen, selected a guinea egg, which is less than half the size of a chicken egg. He fried it hard. Cooked, the egg looked like a burned suspender button. He placed the egg in the center of a thirteen-inch steak platter and set it before Tarpley. Other boarders burst into laughter.

"Where's the other egg?" the bully demanded.

"It's over the fence," answered Amon.

This pleased the boarders so much they called the stablehand "Over-The-Fence Tarpley" until he finally moved out. Harry Bedford and Chap Loving, operators of a gambling hall, gave Amon his first suit of clothes and others collected five dollars as a reward for shutting up Tarpley.

The boarding house salary could not support Amon and he branched out to other jobs. He sold peaches. He helped a doctor. He worked in a confectionery shop, selling ice cream and candies. He took a job in a bottling works, making soda pop. Near Queen's Peak, the highest hill around Bowie, was a horse track, just two parallel paths half a mile long. Race meets were held each Saturday in the spring. Then Amon filled a fifty-gallon barrel with soda pop and set up a refreshment stand for fans. The races were matched, two ponies at a time, and betting was heavy. One Saturday, Horace Woods, a wealthy farmer, came to Amon's soda pop stand. He asked the youngster to ride his horse, Baldy, in the next race. Amon, who had never ridden anything racier than a plow horse, refused, but he was afraid of Woods, who had beaten the town's teacher for some minor insult, and he soon agreed. Woods said he would pay five dollars for the ride.

A blanket was placed on Baldy. Amon was seated on the blanket. Woods tied the boy's legs with a surcingle. He instructed Amon to let Baldy have his head out of the gate and hit the pony with a quirt one hundred yards from the finish line. Always an obedient boy, Amon let Baldy go. A hundred yards out, Amon popped Baldy's flanks. Baldy did a wheelie. The forward lunge loosened the surcingle and dislodged Amon. He slid under the horse's belly. The surcingle broke. Amon dropped to the ground and the pony sped ahead to win by two lengths.

Bruised and dirty, Amon limped in. Woods was having words with the losing horse's owner. Woods' opponent questioned whether a riderless horse could justly win a race. Woods maintained it could and, to emphasize the point, he drew a pistol. The other man said quickly, "Why, I believe you're right, Horace." Woods collected the hundred dollars and tossed Amon his riding fee. It was twenty years before the burgeoning cowboy again went near a horse.

For Amon, life in Bowie was filled with work. But occasionally he sneaked away, usually stealing rides on passing trains. He once went as far as Fort Worth because he heard a new seven-story building there featured a marvelous contraption — a platform that carried people up and down. He stepped on the elevator and rode to the top floor.

"How much do I owe you?" Amon asked the operator.

The man smiled and replied there was no charge. "Then I will ride down with you," said Amon.

He rode blind baggage to Wichita Falls to witness the hanging of Kid Lewis and Foster Crawford, a pair of cowboys who robbed the city's national bank. Texas Rangers captured the pair and stored them in the Wichita Falls jail. A railroad porter told Amon of the holdup and capture, and young Carter took the next freight north. He arrived in time to see a mob remove Lewis and Crawford from their cells. Ropes were tied to a lightpole in front of the bank and wooden boxes placed underneath. The cowboys stood on the boxes, nooses encircling their necks. Both men had worked for Captain Burk Burnett, one of North Texas' largest ranchers. Burk Burnett, feeling sympathy for his two former cowboys, asked kindly if they had any last messages for their friends and families. Gratefully, Lewis kicked the captain in the stomach. The mob pulled away the boxes.

Lewis and Crawford dangled until dawn, when their bodies were cut down and stacked in the bank's doorway. Early customers stepped over the corpses. An enterprising member of the lynch party, Amon later wrote admiringly, swapped the nooses to a bartender for a gallon of whiskey.

Amon regaled Bowieites with the hanging story. They never experienced anything so exciting. The best Bowie could offer was hi-jinks of old Dan Waggoner's cowboys. The Waggoner hands enjoyed tossing a rope loop on the legs of black train porters and swinging the terrified men upside down from store signs.

Carter met the elder Waggoner and his son, W. T., to whom he sold six-for-a-quarter cigars while working in the confectionery shop. He and W. T. — called "Pappy" — became good friends and later, in Fort Worth, Amon would consider the wealthy rancher a handy lode to mine for civic ventures needing capital. He also made friends with Will Stripling, a Bowie merchant who moved to Fort Worth, founded one of its larger department stores and became an early investor in the *Star-Telegram*. And he met the taciturn sheriff of nearby Henrietta, Dink Rickard, who one day would help Amon promote Fort Worth in a special way. Amon Carter, a saver of string and tinfoil, never wasted anything, especially friendships.

Of all young Carter's deals, the chicken and bread business seemed the most profitable. He shared the business with five other Bowie boys — John Black, Mose Johnson, Shorty Ryan, R. J. Sandefur and Tan Turner. Amon was working as roustabout in the wagon yard. The owner gave him a red wooden gun powered by a rubber plunger. It fired an eight-inch long stick. An ancient Dominique rooster lived in the wagon yard and young Amon practiced his marskmanship on the bird. One day he was too accurate and dispatched the tough old rooster with a shot to the head. An idea occurred to Amon. He asked a widow to cook the bird. She parboiled the old Dominique, trying to soften the meat, then cut up and fried the various parts.

Amon met the next train. The Fort Worth and Denver carried no dining car and passengers rushed to buy Amon's fried rooster. He was counting his profits — forty cents — as the train pulled away. Suddenly, a heavy rooster leg struck him in the head. An irate customer screamed curses at the boy for selling such a tough meal.

Dismissing the man as a grouch, Amon began thinking of train passengers and chicken. He decided chicken sandwiches would sell better than fried chicken and were, incidentally, more difficult to throw. He proposed a deal with the Widow Brodie. She would cook him one chicken daily, provide room and board, for $2.50 weekly. Amon paid two bits for each chicken. He cleared about two dollars a day. Soon, other Bowie boys took up the business and Amon gathered his five friends to form a monopoly and squeeze out competitors. The Carter cartel did well. When chickens were not available at favorable prices, the boys made late night henhouse raids, which, of course, considerably lowered the firm's overhead. If neither money nor midnight foray produced chickens, the youths substituted rabbit meat. The Chicken and Bread boys of Bowie soon became famous on the Fort Worth and Denver run through North Texas, and the nickname would follow Amon to New York.

When another of Father Carter's farms failed on him, he moved to Bowie and re-entered the blacksmithing business. Amon lived briefly with his father then, but in 1896, Papa married Ella Patterson, and in only a short time young Carter was out on his own again.

Amon never explained his troubles with the second Mrs. Carter. In 1920, five years after William Carter died, the widow wrote Amon asking for money. He told her he already was supporting a dozen relatives in addition to his immediate family and reminded her of ". . . the time you ordered me to leave my father's house, stating that I was too big to impose on him and that I should get out and make my living.'' He nevertheless sent her money — he always addressed her as ''Mrs. Carter'' — monthly until she died in Macon, Georgia. In her printed obituary, Amon was not listed among her children.

Now older and out in the world for good, Amon turned to more sophisticated means of support. He and a railroad brakeman, O. G. Hurdleston, established a knifeboard in Lindsey's saloon. The board held knives stuck in whiskey corks. Various coins were glued to each knife. Customers tried to toss wooden rings over the knives. The old carnival game seemed simple but of course was not. For one thing, the rings would not fit over the knives guarding fifty cent pieces. A deerfoot knife stabbed through a five dollar bill was turned in such a way that it was impossible to ring.

The knifeboard prospered until a part-time housepainter and pool hustler nicknamed Shadow arrived one evening. Lanky, loose-jointed and long-armed, Shadow could drop rings on any and all knives, even the five-buck deerfoot. Amon was fascinated with Shadow, partially because the man had a double row of upper teeth and smiled like twin piano keyboards. Shadow broke the knifeboard and Amon did the only honest thing. He barred Shadow from ever playing again, then hired him at five dollars a week to drop in each evening and show the suckers how to win. The knifeboard's profits increased dramatically. Shadow suggested letting the deerfoot knife pot be won regularly, so once a month, Amon turned the handle to a winning position. First winner was a farmer, Adolph Fincher. News spread quickly through Bowie: Adolph had beaten the game. Ring tossers lined up three deep that evening. A couple of weeks later, Fincher brought a bale of cotton to town. He spent all his cotton money trying to ring another knife.

Unknowing of Shadow's business arrangement, Bowie's peg-legged city marshal, Charlie Bray, offered to run the housepainter out of town. Amon declined. He had larger plans for the hustler. He financed Shadow's trip to the Dallas Fair where the housepainter beat any game the carnival folks could dream of. They split the winnings. Amon took Shadow to the pool room of Dallas' Oriental Hotel. They played like rubes until local hustlers suggested a game for money. Amon took side bets. Shadow cleaned out the Dallas pool men. The pair returned to Bowie with more than a hundred dollars.

Amon spent a portion of the pool profits on his first grownup clothes. He disembarked from the train dressed in a white suit, high-collared silk dress shirt, thin narrow red and white bowtie, black derby (Texans called derbies "chili-dippers"), and bile-green Selzswab Piccadilly shoes with tapered toes sharp-pointed as fence railings. Amon's rainbow raiment stunned Bowie. Children were frightened. Dogs growled at him. His saloon chums slapped knees and guffawed loudly. Amon put away his city duds, not really understanding why they were unacceptable.

It is of little surprise that town parents felt Amon was an inappropriate companion for their children. Hooking rides on trains, hustling farmers in saloons, the curious idea of sartorial glory — his lifestyle gave him the social standing of an itinerant spot welder. (Most of this would be forgotten sixty years later when Bowie was naming its city lake for him and bestowing other honors on its most famous son.) At eighteen, Amon was a full-grown man. He was granted the concession of Sunday dinners in the home of Mrs. Arch Turner, a widow who felt sorry for him. Several of Bowie's young people gathered each Sunday at Mrs. Turner's home and it was there presumedly that Amon met and wooed Zetta Thomas, the tall gangling daughter of a prominent family. After several years of wandering, Amon would return to marry her.

Eighteen-year-old Amon Carter was described by a contemporary biographer as "Almost six feet tall . . . of medium build. He had black eyes, rather large ears, a prominent nose, dark brown hair, and an olive complexion. His facial features were strongly formed with a pleasant, benign expression that easily showed either a lopsided grin or a broad smile. Carter greatly resembled his mother, Josephine, whose picture later hung near his desk in the *Star-Telegram*."

In 1898, having ridden elevators and worn green shoes and become a worldy young man, Amon left Bowie, itching to travel and see America. He went most of a hundred miles, north to Indian Territory and what now is Norman, Oklahoma, where the husband of a first cousin owned a grocery store. The cousin got him a job in Davis' Confectionery Shop at thirty dollars a month. He boarded at Grand Central Hotel and worked from five a.m. until almost midnight six days a week. He made friends with Bill Ince, driver of a grocer's delivery wagon, and the pair schemed to get on the road. They bought a gross of pipes and a supply of tobacco, and acquired a taffy-making machine, preparing to join a traveling circus where they would hawk smoking materials and candy.

Before they could hook on with a circus, however, Amon met a Mr. Phillips one morning at the barber shop. Mr. Phillips represented the American Copying Company of Chicago. He was hiring young men to travel and sell colored portraits. The portrait dodge, one of the plagues of early America, hardly was more legitimate than Amon's knifeboard. First, a salesman hit town and called on leading merchants, selling them frames for $1.50 each. Afterward, a crew of boys arrived and went door to door telling mothers they could have oil paintings made from their children's photographs for very little cost. The gimmick was that the paintings were odd-sized and would fit only the plaster of Paris frames sold by merchants, at prices beginning at $2.98.

Amon liked the idea. He left Ince pulling taffy, borrowed a suitcase, and hit the road. He was an instant success. He and selling were perfect for one another. The boy who could peddle inedible rooster legs and bunny sandwiches could make colored portraits seem like Rembrandts. Within a year, he was the company's top-producing salesman and by late 1901, Amon was American Copying's sales manager with a salary of $300 monthly, a magnificent sum for a young man hardly twenty-one. He traveled to every state in the union, enjoyed life on the road but understood that his future with the business was limited. During this period he also acquired Zetta as a wife. So when Ed Swasey, whom he had met in Portland — he later would rise high in the Hearst organization — offered him a job in San Francisco, Amon accepted. He went to work with Barnhart & Swasey Advertising Agency for $100 a month. Before leaving Chicago, Amon acquired from American Copying a letter of recommendation which said in part, "We believe Mr. Carter has few equals and never a superior in his representation of us."

Amon thought the statement was an underestimation of his abilities; he couldn't remember any equals.

He was almost two years away from Emerson's advice for up-and-coming dreamers: "Hitch your wagon to a *Star*."

Chapter 6

Then Hail to the Press! Chosen Guardian of Freedom! Strong Sword-arm of Justice! Bright Sunbeam of Truth!

—*Horace Greeley*, The Press

The newspaper business consists of buying newsprint at 2 cents a pound and selling it at 10 cents a pound.

—*Charles A. Dana*

There seems to be no plan because it is all plan. There seems to be no center because it is all center.

—*C. S. Lewis*

6

Perhaps there is significance in the fact that Fort Worth's second telephone, installed in the *Democrat*, a newspaper, was but a single line leading to the fourth telephone, billeted in the Club Room, a saloon two hundred feet away across Main Street. Perhaps not. Handy, yes. Editor Buckley B. Paddock wrote that he ordered a lemonade to test the new service.

Once a Confederate scout, Paddock was a leading city booster preparing to retire as active editor and make money in the real world. The portly Paddock, literate, an excellent journalist, and more than a little Victorian, earlier stood his newspaper in the path of sin, seeking to erase the cowboy's playground — Hell's Half Acre, Fort Worth's red light district where back-sore whores and card slicks serviced ranch hands with competency and perfidy.

The crusade kept cowboys out of town for awhile, thereby cutting trade at legitimate businesses. Angry merchants demanded Paddock remove his blue nose from the cribs and gambling joints. The sinful zone returned to its former busy life.

Fort Worth's first newspaper was the *Chief*, founded in 1849 by Anthony Banning Norton, who was slightly dotty. Norton was a Henry Clay supporter in the 1844 Presidential election. Clay lost to James Polk. Norton angrily treked to Texas where he vowed to neither shave nor cut his hair until Clay became President. Very soon, Norton was as hairy as a practicing hermit and Fort Worthians wearied of reading about Henry Clay.

The *Chief* and Paddock's *Democrat* withered and died as newspapers seem to have done regularly in early Fort Worth. Fully forty publications came and went before 1906 when Amon Carter and the *Star* wandered into that journalistic graveyard. Two newspapers remained at the *Star*'s conception. C. D. Reimers edited and published the *Telegram*, an afternoon daily. He was considered a good businessman and poor journalist. Clarence Ousley owned and edited the morning *Record*, which had climbed out of the coffin holding the *Register*, still another short-lived newspaper. Ousley ranks a footnote in American journalism. Early in the 1900s the Dallas *News* owned rights to national stories distributed in North Texas by the Associated Press. Fort Worth papers were blocked from publishing any AP wire news originating outside the state. Ousley began a court fight to break monopolistic control of the single news service, and won.

That boosted the *Record* and *Telegram*, both of which became AP subscribers, but effectively froze out the *Star*, leaving it victim to the Scripps-McRae service, which issued a meager five hundred words daily. W. C. Stripling, Sr., the Bowie merchant then prospering in Fort Worth, told Amon to forget the *Star*, citing the lack of AP news as reason enough for it to fail quickly. Stripling also promised Amon he would never buy even a single ad for his department store. Amon accepted the advice and ashcanned it, joining the *Star* as its only salesman, thereby becoming advertising manager.

Stripling asked Amon, "Why did you seek my advice about going to work for the Star, which I strongly advised against and which you did not accept?" Carter replied that he was like most people — they ask advice of their friends with the hope their ideas would coincide and then "went ahead to do what they originally intended to do."

When A. G. Dawson and D. C. McCaleb sniffed the manured air and spoke of their dream to begin a new afternoon newspaper, Amon had little money. His small business paid bills but could not be stretched to support his rather vigorous nightlife. He borrowed $250 from American National Bank, pledging as security a small diamond ring. That cash almost was gone, consumed mostly by a high straight held against Amon's three aces. He had no money to invest and contrary to his boast that he could borrow, knew of no one who would loan him money. Amon, however, steered Dawson and McCaleb to Paul Waples, a wealthy businessman euphemistically titled "colonel" as were half the grown men in Texas. Waples became the *Star*'s angel. The wholesale food magnate selected a few friends to finance the newspaper with fifty thousand dollars. Waples, a philanthropist and politician who became chairman of the Texas Democratic State Executive Committee, brought in Louis Wortham (yet another "colonel") as publisher/editor.

Though out of the venture Amon was offered the job of ad salesman. What followed was typical of Amon Carter. He needed the job, but it was his policy never to accept a first offer. He and Dawson bargained for weeks. Dawson offered twenty dollars a week, then twenty-five. Amon said "No" to each. Thirty dollars? Amon shunned the offer. He would work for no less than thirty-five dollars a week. Dawson replied that the *Star* could not afford Amon Carter. "I've been working for the Dallas *News* for ten years," said Dawson, "and it has never paid me more than $30 a week."

"Mr. Dawson," answered Amon, "pardon my frankness, but one of the other of you must have been imposed upon."

The *Star* was two weeks from its first issue and Amon ten days beyond the last of his borrowed $250 when Wortham arrived. Wortham summoned Carter to the office.

"How much do you want?" asked Wortham.

"Thirty-five dollars a week."

"You're hired. When can you come to work?"

"I'm working right now."

Amon's hold-out was a useless exercise. He only collected six thirty-five dollar paychecks, then voluntarily reduced his salary to twenty dollars. His lack of financial interest in the *Star* was a blessing. It never made money but mired deeper and deeper into debt. Investors lost everything.

Amon survived the failure. And Wortham. Colonel Wortham, a puckish-faced, large man with middle-parted hair, was impractical, windy, gentle, drank too much and had little notion of how to operate a daily newspaper. Amon liked him immediately. They became close friends and allies against Dawson and McCaleb, both of whom left before the newspaper's first anniversary.

The first *Star* arrived on the eve of Groundhog Day, February 1, 1906, two weeks late but with great exaltation inside the 25 x 25 foot newsroom located at Sixth and Rusk Streets, underneath the Eagle Lodge Hall and behind a saloon, the Senate Bar. Outside, no angels sang hosannas from on high. There was massive disregard by Fort Worth citizens, only forty-five hundred of whom bothered to accept free delivery for the first thirty days.

That afternoon, the *Telegram* bragged on page one of its 11,156 paid circulation.

The *Star* was a typical, typographically dull publication with seven columns, stacked headlines and few illustrations. It had sixteen pages but subsequent issues were only eight pages because the crippled flat-bed Bullock press could print no more in a single run. The ancient press was propped up on one side by an iron brace. The *Star* also owned three rickety Linotype machines and an antique stereotyping pot with a metal dipper. So crowded was the newsroom that the men stood at shelves around the walls as they worked.

Predictably, there were few local ads. The *Star*, in fact, seemed an inventory sheet for the patent medicine industry. Dr. Shoop's Rheumatic Tablets had a prominent spot, and Hostetters' Stomach Bitters, and the always popular Dr. Thurman's Lone Star Catarrah Cure ("Doubtless one of the most aggravating, disgusting and destructive diseases to which human flesh has fallen heir").

Sprinkled among the truss and hemorrhoid commercials was the day's news. Fort Worth skies were cloudy, swept by a twelve mile per hour wind. Charging "intolerable cruelty," a forty-year-old mother of twenty-seven children petitioned for dissolution of her twenty-four-year marriage. C. W. Post, a one-time Fort Worth resident, was back in town promoting his Grape Nuts as a medical cure for every known disease. Prohibitionists scorned Alice, daughter of Teddy Roosevelt, for serving wine in the White House. The Boll Weevils, a baseball team, soon would hold spring tryouts. In St. Petersburg, the Russian emperor warned peasants to stop pestering large landowners. Standard Oil was accused of stifling competition. In the West Texas town of Brownwood, Charles Hale was "terribly burned" when he struck a match to see into the innards of his new gas-powered automobile, and at nearby Abilene a pair of cowboys interrupted a ranch dance to fight with pistols and knives — "Two women were slashed right and left, inflicting severe, if not fatal, gashes on their bodies." For entertainment, there were the Edison Family Theater ("Appeals to the Masses and not to the Classes") and Greenwall's Opera House with "Mrs. Wiggs of the Cabbage Patch," featuring the original New York cast. The Majestic had live, on stage, "Don Carlos, the lion and dog trainer . . . seen in a cage with a lion which he has trained to jump from place to place and which he catches hold of and throws across the cage and in fact handles with almost as much freedom as though it were a common tame cat."

Among the few local advertisements were announcements of sales on "Ladies Dip Hip Corsets, 39 cents" and a ". . . special lot of ladies Union Suits, in gray and ecru, 25 cents." Butter was thirty cents a pound, paint seventy-five cents a gallon, valentines one cent each and Pullman train tickets to California, twenty-five dollars. F. O. "Painless" Cates charged just fifty cents per extracted tooth.

Readers got all that for two cents, or a nickle on trains and out of town.

Amon sold all ads, seventy-one column inches total, representing a $387.30 income for the fledgling paper. He in fact accepted too many ads. A front page boxed apology read:

> The response to solicitations for advertisements was so much greater than was anticipated that it was a physical impossibility for the Star to get out an issue on this date with all the advertisements that should be in the issue in it.

Presumably the absent ads ungrammatically pardoned were more anti-piles fighters and Catarrah curatives.

As a new employee, Amon's first act was to tell everybody how to run the newspaper. He laid down three rules for Colonel Wortham: One, there would be the same rates for all advertisers; two, the circulation would be guaranteed, no matter how small, and, three, the newspaper would indulge in neither contests nor premiums to secure circulation. "The advertiser must use the newspaper because it is beneficial to his business, not because the newspaper grants him special favors," lectured Amon, "and the reader must subscribe because he is interested, not because he expects to win a contest." Later, he added a fourth canon: The *Star* would sell its own national advertising, and save paying agency commissions. Those four inviolate rules would make the *Star-Telegram* the most profitable newspaper in America — "Territory considered," Amon always added when confronted with his paper's profitability.

To promote the *Star*, placards were distributed claiming the newspaper was ". . . clean, conservative, conscientious, enterprising and independent . . . with more local news than any other in the city." So what, yawned Fort Worth?

That was not an alarming reaction. Fort Worth was a somnolent town in 1906. Forty thousand people lived there, though only five thousand bothered to vote in the last election. Years earlier, a Dallas newspaper claimed Fort Worth was so lifeless a panther was seen sleeping on Main Street. Packing houses, a natural extension of the stockyards, were the largest businesses. As Amon settled into his new job, Fort Worth had a few fancy stores but far more plain ones, more dirt streets than paved boulevards, streetcars, an interurban to Dallas, innumerable saloons, more outdoor privies than indoor bathrooms, more horses than automobiles, a new eight-story skyscraper called the Wheat Building, thirty passenger trains daily and a society composed of too many families on the outer edge of poverty and below the respectability of middleclass.

Fort Worth, at age fifty-six, had a western flavor if little of the taste.

As Amon stepped down from the Texas and Pacific train to astound Bowie with green shoes, James North, who dreamed of being a lawyer, was in Sherman, in the *Democrat*'s back shop, cutting G. O. Hunter's hair out of the clanking Cottrell Press.

Hunter, and his brother, E. C., owned the newspaper and, sighed North, the old man had done it again. G. O. wore his hair pompadoured and long. When the press rolled each afternoon he stood behind the machine, reached in for papers and counted loads for his young carriers. Too often he leaned in and the gears would grab his hair, sometime jerking it out in clumps, sometime just grasping and holding tight while the press ground to a halt. Jimmy, a carrier, used shears to cut loose the *Democrat*'s co-publisher.

North was born in Jefferson, a steamboating town in East Texas. His family moved to Sherman, on the Oklahoma border, and he began delivering the *Democrat* and marveling at G. O. Hunter being snatched bald by the antagonistic press. North advanced to a kind of junior circulation manager and foreman of all carriers, then went off to the University of Texas to become a lawyer. He returned each summer to work as a reporter for the *Democrat* and had advanced to a ten-dollar-a-week salary when his family developed financial trouble. North never returned to college. In the fall of 1905 he read of a new paper to be published in Fort Worth. He applied for a reporter's job.

As Amon went on the road to peddle odd-sized kiddie portraits, James Record was a young baseball player in Paris, Texas, dreaming of becoming a lawyer. Record played leftfield for Paris' Young Men's Christian Association team. The day he left baseball forever was during a crucial game with Sulphur Springs' YMCA nine. Sulphur Springs was two runs behind. Late in the game with the bases loaded, a Sulphur Springs batter knocked a long fly ball toward Record. Catch it, and

Paris would win the Northeast Texas Championship. Miss, and Sulphur Springs had the title. A switching engine had parked in the railroad yards behind the left field fence. As the ball arrived in Record's glove, the engineer blew the train whistle. Startled, Jim dropped the ball. He walked off the field and never played baseball again, but took work as a sports writer for the Paris *Advocate*.

At seventeen, Record entered the University of Notre Dame. He was a serious scholar and won the school's medal for proficiency in Greek and Latin during his freshman year. Two years later he left Notre Dame to enter the University of Texas law school, but soon left because of illness. Recuperating in Paris, Record continued to write for the *Advocate*. One of his stories reached Jimmy North, by then city editor of the *Star*. The story told of a hot day in Paris when the temperature heated a nail until it set a fence afire. Flames jumped to a nearby barn, from which sparks ignited a house. North didn't believe a word of it, but admired the imagination.

Record decided against returning to law school. He applied unsuccessfully for a reporting position with Dallas newspapers, then approached the *Star* where North, remembering the hot nail, hired him.

In 1907, A. L. Shuman, a former traveling notions salesman who had worked in the back shop of the Marshall, Missouri, *Daily News*, stood on the steps of the Continental Bank Building enjoying the spring warmth. Amon bounded up the steps, passed Al, then called back, "Want a job?"

"Suppose so," answered Shuman.

"All right. $17.50 a week. Mine's $20 and I ought to have a little edge on you."

Shuman became ad salesman for the new paper. He joined tall, handsome, athletic Bert Honea, who came from Palestine in East Texas to be classified ad manager and bookkeeper for the struggling company. Already Honea knew he had made a mistake.

Fifth and final member of what later would become the *Star-Telegram* management team did not arrive until 1909. Harold Hough — pronounced "Huff" — had, as a teenager, combined with three friends to own a monopoly on newspaper delivery in Oklahoma City. One day he crossed tracks in a railyard and was struck by a train. His right lower leg was severed. While Hough was recovering, his three friends went on a fishing trip. Days later, the trio's bodies were found. They had been massacred. Two were scalped. The triple murder was never solved.

Hough returned to work on crutches but quit when the first man to whom he sold a paper "looked at my foot and handed me a quarter tip." He had an artificial foot fitted and learned to walk again, then joined the *Daily Oklahoman* as assistant circulation manager. Browsing through a trade publication, he read an ad. A Fort Worth newspaper needed a circulation manager. On a whim, he boarded a train for Fort Worth. He asked Amon for the job.

"What kind of circulation plans do you have for us?" questioned Amon.

"Oh, just get the papers to readers when its handy for them to read it," replied Hough.

Amon liked the answer. He hired Hough for the *Star-Telegram*.

Star-Telegram. No longer just the *Star*. The two had become one. The poor *Star* had bought the successful *Telegram*. "We were failing, so we decided to expand," was the way Amon explained the merger in later years.

From the beginning, the *Star* had no future. Without support of large local advertisers, the newspaper could not produce revenue enough to pay its bills. Soon, Amon was pawning his rings with Oscar Wells, cashier of the Fort Worth National Bank, to meet each week's payroll.

He traded part-interest in his patented telephone directory for a peach orchard near Arlington, midway between Dallas and Fort Worth. During the day he sold advertising for the *Star* and solicited orders for peaches from grocery stores. After work, he would board a streetcar to the orchard, pick and pack the peaches, and return them to Fort Worth, usually arriving about midnight. He was up again at five. a.m. to deliver the fruit before striking out on his advertising rounds.

Carter produced one early scoop for the *Star*. On the morning of April 18, 1906, he was in the Cotton Exchange. The wire operator received a flash that fire and earthquake had destroyed San Francisco. Carter copied the sparse details and rushed to the newspaper office. In his wallet Amon still carried a map of San Francisco showing circulation distribution of the *Call*. The map also displayed pictures of the Ferry Building, Palace Hotel, San Francisco *Examiner*, city hall and other structures. A cut was made of the map and printed on the *Star*'s front page beside the meager story written from Amon's notes. The *Star* published its first extra. Amon snatched a bundle and dashed into Sixth Street. Later, he hauled a load of extras to Dallas. The *Star* sold twenty-four hundred copies before the *Telegram* even learned of the disaster.

The scoop did little to rescue the *Star* and the newspaper continued to lose money. Amon, however, finally sold W. C. Stripling, Sr. an ad. He did it by pestering Stripling for twelve straight days. Each afternoon Amon met Stripling as the older man left his store. Amon began talking. He talked as they walked. He talked as they boarded the streetcar. He talked as the car took them to Stripling's home. He talked as they entered the house, talked until dinner, talked through dinner, talked until Stripling told him to leave. Next day Amon was back, talking. Stripling surrendered. He told

Amon he would give him an advertising contract if one could be sold to W. G. Burton, owner of the Burton-Peel Dry Goods Company. Amon blitzed Burton. Burton capitulated. The dry goods store contracted for three double pages, to that time the largest department store ad ever published in Texas. The $198.45 paid by Burton, and Stripling's ads, still did not rescue the *Star.*

By early 1908, the original $50,000 was gone and the newspaper was $27,000 deeper in debt. Dawson left. He and Carter never got along. Amon threatened to "knock his block off" in an argument over a proposed special edition romanticizing the West Texas cattle industry. Wortham reduced Dawson to the job of reporter, and he quit. McCaleb resigned to accept a political writing job in Austin.

And the *Telegram* was trying to hire Amon.

After the Burton ads appeared, C. D. Reimers, the *Telegram* publisher, asked Carter to become advertising manager of the larger newspaper. Reimers offered $35 weekly, then $50, and finally, $75. Amon refused the offers, saying he would not leave Waples and Wortham. Reimers said Amon was allowing sentiment to control his business sense.

"We will put you out of business," said Reimers.

Angry, Amon retorted, "Hop to it. You can't get up any earlier or stay up any later than I can, or sell any more advertising."

The *Telegram*, of course, could and did sell more advertising. By autumn, 1908, Carter and Wortham knew the *Star*'s only chance for survival was buying the *Telegram*, and the only hope of buying the larger newspaper was to pay more than it was worth. But not too much more. They went underground.

Amon enlisted the help of O. P. Thomas, secretary of the Abilene Chamber of Commerce. Thomas bid for the *Telegram*. It is generally understood that Reimers knew from the beginning who really was buying his newspaper but all parties played out the charade to the end. Thomas secured a contract-to-sell for $100,000. The terms were for $2,500 to be deposited on Monday morning, November 16, 1908, balance of $92,500 cash due in ten days. A five thousand dollar note to Goss Printing Press Company was to be assumed by the new publishers.

To obtain the $2,500, Amon went back to Oscar Wells, and left on deposit in Fort Worth National Bank vault "1 diamond ring, 3 31/32 k; 1 diamond ring, 5/8 k; 2 smaller diamond rings, one diamond and pearl scarf pin." Amon told Wells if they could not obtain the remaining $92,500 in ten days, he would give up and accept Barron Collier's New York job offer.

Amon and Wortham again approached Colonel Waples for backing. Waples at first was uninterested but Amon talked until he had the financier's promise to back the new publishing venture. And Stripling became a backer — now the store owner could see the worth of Amon running a monopoly afternoon newspaper. Among other investors were Burton and H. C. Meacham, another department store owner. Waples grandly offered corporation shares to Amon and Colonel Wortham. Each took ten percent. Waples said they could buy the balance as they wished, at cost plus six percent. Amon, of course, had no money for his ten percent. But W. B. Graham, with whom Amon worked in Chicago, had moved to Fort Worth. Amon borrowed a "piece of swamp land in Fort Meyer, Florida" from Graham and secured his ten percent. Amon was a newspaper owner.

In later years, Reimers bragged that he cheated Carter because the *Telegram* was sold for twice its worth. Amon replied that the *Telegram*'s real value was a million dollars. It would seem Carter was correct. The *Star-Telegram*, conceived over burning manure and bolstered by Florida swampland, became a hundred million dollar property.

December 31, 1908. Two o'clock in the afternoon. Editor Jimmy North and his seven reporters awaited the day's final press run. Carter strolled in. He handed an announcement to North and told him to box it on page one. North read the single paragraph. It announced the *Star*'s closing. North and the reporters were stunned.

"Boys," said Carter, "I understand that a new paper will start publication tomorrow from a plant at Eighth and Throckmorton Streets. If you show up there early enough, some of you might get jobs."

North sputtered that the *Telegram* plant was located at Eighth and Throckmorton Streets. Carter shrugged, smiled and left.

Ten minutes after the *Star* hit the streets, a horse-drawn cab arrived in front of the newspaper office. Carl Crow, assistant editor of the *Telegram*, hopped out, haughtily told the driver he would walk to his destination, the Senate Bar, twenty feet down the street. The *Telegram*, Crow lamented to North, was ceasing publication. The staff was out drinking. *Star* reporters joined them.

North later wrote that newsmen, deep into the hazy hours of New Year's Eve, deduced that the two papers were merging. Next morning, North reported early to the *Telegram* building. Carter told him he was managing editor. Given the amalgamated staffs, North had enough reporters to cover three Fort Worths, and January 1, 1909, the *Star and Telegram** became the city's only afternoon newspaper. There almost was not a second edition.

Early Saturday evening, North put his staff to work, preparing for the paper's first Sunday edition. Word came that Winfield Scott, a rancher-millionaire who settled in Fort Worth, was hosting a banquet in the Terminal Hotel at Main and Lancaster. North assigned a reporter to cover the party. In a burst of generosity, he

*Two weeks later, the "and" was removed and replaced by a hyphen.

told every other newsman within hearing to go along and help. The blanket assignment also sent a couple of off-duty *Record* reporters who were hanging around. Al Shuman opined he would just "go with the boys and supervise."

Midnight arrived. Midnight left. North had no story of the banquet. The Sunday paper lay in pieces all over the office. North was angry. Then Shuman threw open the rear door, stumbled in and passed out before North's desk. Four more reporters entered, weaved to their desks, and collapsed. North, fifty years later, recalled that "all had looked upon the wine when it was red and too often and too copiously."

Intrigued, North walked to the rear door. He found Hep Blackman, the staff cartoonist, sitting in the alley. Blackman was sobbing. Between sobs, the cartoonist claimed the greatest misfortune of his entire life had befallen him. He threw his arms around North and cried, baby-like, until the managing editor held him at arms length and demanded an explanation.

Hep cried that waiters at Scott's party were bootlegging champagne at fifteen cents a bottle, and he only had sixty cents. Life was unspeakably cruel, Hep cried. The cartoonist had empited two of his precious bottles and was half through another. North gently propped Hep against the wall and walked to the street. A second newsman was passed out at the alley's entrance. Two more sat in the street, singing. North sighed and returned to the city room.

One by one the reporters returned, all except the newsman assigned to cover the party. Scott was an important man in town. The *Star and Telegram* must have a story.

North roused Shuman, and demanded the advertising manager give him notes on the banquet. North would write the story. Shuman indignantly replied that he was a member of management of that newspaper and "not a drunken reporter." Emphasizing his lofty position, Shuman slammed a champagne bottle on North's desk, breaking the glass top. North let Shuman return to his sleep. North systematically awoke and questioned each of his newsmen. None could function well enough to help North.

Wortham arrived. The publisher asked what kind of story the paper would have on the Scott party. "None," said North, "The reporter assigned hasn't returned and those that have are too drunk to write."

"That's because you did not assign a competent reporter," snapped Wortham.

"Colonel, I did assign a competent reporter. It's not a question of competence but capacity," argued North.

"If he had been competent he would not have gotten drunk."

"Colonel, I haven't seen anybody yet come back sober from that party."

Wortham bristled and sternly informed North he was sober and could write a "hell of a good story" of the banquet. North knew Wortham was sober only because the publisher was a legislative candidate and his opponent, a prohibitionist, also attended the dinner. He asked Wortham to write the story.

"I'll see you in the bottomless pits of hell before I do it. This'll teach you next time to assign a competent reporter to cover a news event," Wortham yelled and rushed out.

North sighed and returned to his desk. The night of the fifteen-cent champagne ended. Expended reporters were found on front porches of Fort Worth's swankiest section, in gutters and along banks of the Trinity River. Hep Blackman still was sprawled in the alley at daybreak, the third empty bottle beside him. Shuman slept away the night on a city room desk. Another reporter is said to have thrown himself in front of a street car, unaware it stopped running at midnight and had not moved for hours. One newsman was arrested for swinging at a town marshal and another ran through the parlor of the city's most respected bordello, startling the madam. He was shirtless and barefooted.

The *Star and Telegram* printed a story of the Scott party on page one of its Sunday edition. Wortham changed his mind and phoned North enough facts for two sticks of type. The story appeared under a headline about a YMCA banquet. The Y story bore the Scott head. Back shop workers, it seems, learned of the fifteen cent champagne and naturally. . .

The *Star-Telegram*, corporately and hyphenetically married, survived its boozy honeymoon editions as it overcame the smoldering manured conception, and evolved into a newspaper of stature and grace and power, proving monopoly is an excellent base on which to build, provided one owns an Amon Carter.

Amon was ready to sell his newspaper, his town, his region, his state and, of course, himself.

He was ready to invent the cowboy.

And that would establish a lifestyle Damon Runyon one day would title, "Amon in Wonderland."

Chapter 7

Winning isn't everything. It's the only thing.

—Vince Lombardi

Hats off, gentleman! A genius!

—Robert Schumman's salute to young Chopin

It is quaintly interesting that when the WBAP dynamo broke down in midst of a program, Mr. Carter mounted to the roof and broadcast a speech with no other facilities than those vocal organs the good Lord had given him, and that coils were burned out in receiving sets five hundred miles away.

—Menu Legend, Sherry's, NYC, May 7, 1928

7

Harold Hough was a frump of a man, folksy, blessed with a whimsical bucolic wit, an ingratiating introvert with a studied disregard for himself. There was about him the casual physiognomy of an awkwardly assembled ragpile. He dressed with a blind man's sense of color and a new tailored suit on Hough instantly metamorphosed into a Salvation Army discard. A hat — he never removed his hat, indoor or out, and reporters suspected he even slept in it — became a deleterious thing crouched on his head, the brim casting a perpetual shadow over the little man. "He was the only person I ever saw who was rumpled all over," remembered Alf Evans. Hough was unassuming, kind, congenial and something of a promotion and circulation genius.

As unmindful of his car's appearance as his own, Hough's auto in the early years was a clanking, smoking, coughing Chevy, seemingly on its last wheels, and the very sound of it was enough to send Amon into spasms of anger. The car embarrassed the publisher and he demanded Hough replace it with a new one at company expense. The jalopy suited Hough and he refused. Amon steamed.

One day Hough's flivver was missing. He reported the theft to police but it was never seen again. Hough bought a new Chevy and Amon was happy. Years later, Amon admitted he had driven Hough's clanker to the Trinity River and sunk it in ten feet of water.

The newfangled automobile was an intrinsic piece in the early *Star-Telegram*'s pattern of success and by 1912 the newspaper, monopolistically entrenched in its afternoon position, achieved a thirty thousand circulation, almost double its press run less than three years earlier.

An excellent reporting staff had been assembled and development of a correspondents' network begun. The newspaper was spreading into West Texas with Hough offering dollar-day subscriptions and guiding public service promotions ranging from selection of Fort Worth's favorite teacher to Bibles at cost.

Many early promotions centered on the automobile, which Amon, always the futurist, predicted would transform American life. For him, the auto was a marvelous doodad and the *Star-Telegram* enthusiastically encouraged its use. Al Shuman sold the South's first full-page auto ad in 1909 to Overland Automobile Sales Company — later the Willys Jeep manufacturer — for Texas' first auto section, an extension of the state's first regular auto page.

The newspaper sponsored endurance runs to Waco, ninety miles south, led by a *Star-Telegram* car, "The Spizzerinktum Special." A Chalmers-Detroit roadster won the first run, during which, the paper reported, a driver was thrown from his car and remained "still in a somewhat critical condition" although he had "regained nearly complete consciousness."

Jim Record, who did not drive, was the newspaper's auto expert, and edited the weekly car news page. He rode with numerous professional drivers on test runs, including T. F. Abbott, who gunned a ten horsepower Maxwell up Fort Worth's courthouse steps, then bounced the auto and Jim Record back down.

In 1912 the Maxwell company proposed a race — between its car and a train, and Hough, always aware of the need to increase circulation in West Texas, proposed the speed contest be from Fort Worth to Abilene, 150 miles west, into the wilderness. Record was assigned as lookout and navigator.

The road was hypothetical, little more than buggy ruts often disappearing into the mesquite thickets or dipping into dry creek beds and Record, dressed in bug-spotted goggles and white duster, coughed and bounced and kept pointing west. There were repeated delays for repair of punctured tires or to refill the boiling radiator from cattle tanks and once to placate a startled bull. Twice, the road intersected railroad tracks and the Maxwell jumped across moments before the surging train, its engineer jeering the terrified reporter and his driver companion. Even with frequent stops the Maxwell averaged forty miles an hour and arrived in Abilene ahead of the train.

Badly unnerved, Record dismounted from the automobile, removed and neatly folded his dingy duster and returned to Fort Worth on the next east-bound train. In the office, he turned his auto editorship over to another reporter.

In 1913, James R. Record became city editor, and incidentally, "JRR," the memo signature by which he was known for sixty years. He was small, lean but sturdily built, with a resolute square face bolstered by prominent jowls which quivered when he was agitated. His carriage was one of rigid formality and he bore always the countenance of an undertaker who had just sold a five thousand dollar casket. He was exacting and obdurate with his reporters, spoke few unnecessary words and governed the editorial office with a kind of professional and Socratean style that obscured a puckish wit. No one ever saw JRR without a tie. He was eighty-seven before his wife of sixty years finally persuaded him to remove his tie when they were alone in their parlor. JRR was, to all who knew him, a decent man and a total gentleman.

Jimmy North was managing editor, Louis Wortham, publisher, Al Shuman, the advertising manager. Hough handled circulation and Bert Honea ran the business office. Amon was business manager and a company vice president. Together, in 1913, they published the fourth largest newspaper in Texas. A year earlier, the *Star-Telegram* leaped to a forty thousand circulation, up ten thousand in just twelve months.

December 15, 1912, the company celebrated its ascendancy by issuing a progress edition of two hundred and fifty pages, the largest single newspaper ever published. Amon sold seventy-four full page ads, an accomplishment he bragged was a world record, and perhaps was.

Already he was dabbling in Fort Worth's civic business as head of the Elks Club and President of the Board of Trade. He had looked westward and seen the fallow land as Utopia and the *Star-Telegram* began a slow infiltration of that poor place.

Also in 1913, William Capps, a Fort Worth attorney, purchased the *Record* from Clarence Ousley. Capps knew nothing of the newspaper business and the *Star-Telegram* simply ran away in the circulation race. The newspaper's graph line for sales and income and circulation rose dramatically in the next decade. From thirty thousand and the state's fourth position in 1912, the newspaper jumped to forty thousand and second place two years later. In another three years, circulation had reached sixty-six thousand and the *Star-Telegram* was Texas' largest newspaper, a leadership it would not relinquish until the 1950s. By 1923, Amon was able to advertise in *Newspaperdom* that his newspaper was the largest in the Southern United States with 115,000 circulation, thirty thousand more than the Dallas *News*, forty thousand ahead of the Houston *Chronicle*, twenty-five thousand above the Atlanta *Journal*.

In 1920, Amon moved the newspaper into what *Editor & Publisher* considered the "Finest Newspaper Plant in [the] Southwest." It was a "million-dollar" four-story squarish building at Seventh and Taylor streets with terra-cotta cornice work and candy-stripe window awnings. Inside were elegant marble columns and mahogany lobby counters, an employee restaurant, kitchen, three elevators and a library club with sofas and cane-backed rockers. There even was a separate "rest room for women employees" and in the basement, space "with toilets" for newsboys to remain "out of the elements." The building was air-cooled and had its own artesian well.

Six years later, in a two hundred page anniversary edition, the *Star-Telegram* boasted of its accomplishments in two decades: From 4,500 circulation to 125,000 (Sunday), $25,000 capitalization to $1,000,000, 25 employees to 343, one press to four, three linotype machines to 20, no correspondents to 600, first issue receipts of $368.04 to "considerably more."

In the new building, the business office occupied the first floor, presses were in the basement, Amon and other executives filled the second level. JRR's domain was the third floor where he worked adjacent to the city desk in an old sweater with leather sleeve patches.

Record again was afoot. In 1916, having dismissed the Maxwell nightmare from his mind, JRR learned to drive and bought an automobile. His re-entry into the troublesome world of cars was mercifully brief. JRR, witnesses said, was reasonably competent at steering but poor on braking and he very soon drove his new auto into a streetcar's path. Uninjured but shaken, Record left his crumpled machine as it lay and trudged to the office. Jimmy North had to go to the accident and oversee the removal of the wreckage. JRR never drove again.

In that decade of ascendancy, Amon Carter was busy inventing his cowboy *persona*, busy booting Fort Worth's backside to awakening as a real city, busy traveling the country servicing the *Star-Telegram*'s national accounts, busy becoming semi-famous, busy yippeeing his dithyrambic madrigal to the fecundity of his dusty Valhalla, West Texas.

Amon's artistry at grandiloquent puffery, and his genius for spreading all that bogus good news, was to haunt him. Outsiders began to believe him when he boasted Fort Worth would become a grand Paris and West Texas really was a thing of splendor. Roy Howard, his friend, listened, then offered to buy the *Star-Telegram*. Amon refused, and suddenly he had *The Press*, the newest Scripps-Howard paper, to live with. *The Press* opened in 1921 and Amon was irked because he knew Fort Worth was no more than a two-newspaper town. But there was *The Press* competing for afternoon customers while the *Record* siphoned off advertising dollars in its morning editions.

Even more alarming was the sudden arrival of William Randolph Hearst.

The Lord of San Simeon, said an observer, came to Fort Worth like a knight in rusty armor, his journalistic reputation yellowed by decades of questionable ethics and high-handed meddling into public affairs. But his newspapers were a nationwide network and a worrisome power wherever they existed, so nettling that an informal organization of competing publishers met now and then to discuss the common enemy Hearst had become.

Fort Worth was the smallest city in which Hearst ever was to publish a newspaper and he came more to punish Amon than for the rich promise of the town. Amon, Hearst discovered, did not humble easily.

As early as 1918 Hearst proffered a bid for the *Star-Telegram* as a means of buying Amon Carter. The bid was part of a five year on-going campaign to bring the Texan into the San Simeon stable. Hearst wanted the sizzle, not the steak, and the offer was refused politely. Or perhaps not so politely. Throughout the Hearst episode, Amon toyed with the regal press king. Carter liked the ego strokes of being courted by the most powerful newspaper publisher in America. He never seriously considered selling his newspaper or becoming a Hearst man but he flirted with the offers, often replying he would "think it over for a day or two." Amon was having fun.

He wrote of the Hearst hiring campaign in an autobiography he began then aborted late in life, and his correspondence files portray Hearst as a man believing he was dealing with a country hick ready to lay down his hoe and come to town. So perhaps Amon's carrot and stick act was justified.

Soon after the Hearst offer to buy the *Star-Telegram*, Joeseph Moore, the Hearst organization treasurer, asked Amon to become publisher of the Atlanta *Georgian* at $36,000 annually, plus a share of the profits. Amon scuffed his unshod rural toe in the dirt and reluctantly said, "No." Moore countered with an offer as publisher of the Chicago *Examiner*, which Amon was challenged to "put ahead of the Chicago *Tribune*." Hem and haw but no sale. Would Amon run Hearst's Baltimore paper? Aw, shucks, but, no, thank you.

January 1, 1919, Hearst wired Amon a simple message: "I wish we had you."

A month later, Moore urged the rube to ". . . cash in on your wonderful work in Fort Worth and move on in to the big tent." The rube sighed and demurred.

March 11, Moore wrote a hard-sell letter: "Mr. Hearst liked the nuts [pecans] but he would have preferred to have you present yourself in full readiness to take charge of the great big proposition . . . here in New York. [There is] really not a bigger opportunity in the newspaper business.''

Moore pled with Amon to ''take full charge of the New York American,'' the city's largest morning paper with a million Sunday circulation.

''Mr. Hearst would agree to you writing your own ticket on money and keeping your *Star-Telegram* interest and check on it four times a year,'' advised Moore. ''Forget the 'piking' amount [$75,000] we talked about the last time you were here. Stop clinging to small propositions rather than getting out into the big show.''

The hayseed considered; the hayseed declined.

The campaign cooled for a year and half. In 1921 Moore mailed Amon a fifty dollar check representing a lost world series bet between Hearst and Carter. He added a postscript:

''Mr. Hearst seems determined to get you into his organization and he brings up the matter several times a month. I have tried to explain to him just how you are situated but that doesn't quiet him at all and he comes right back again . . . that he must have you with us. Would you consider a proposition of selling Mr. Hearst your paper and coming in and establishing a chain of papers for him in Texas and the Southwest?''

Amon replied coyly, ''I am not adverse to discussing the matter with you on my next trip to NYC.'' Once there, however, Amon predictably said, ''No,'' and also refused Moore's subsequent suggestion that he become publisher of the New York *Herald-Examiner*.

Hearst wearied of playing Amon's game. Few people ever refused William Randolph Hearst anything. Amon had, and often. Just as Amon Carter could never perceive of anyone voluntarily deserting the majestic blessedness of Fort Worth and West Texas, Hearst could not understand why a man would remain intentionally in such a bobtail, ragtag place. The reason was simple:

Amon stayed in his one-horse town because he was the horse.

However baffled, Hearst set about to run Amon out of Fort Worth. Late in 1922, he bought sight unseen the Fort Worth *Record*.

Amon panicked.

The *Record* had passed through two unexceptional ownerships after William Capps bought it from Clarence Ousley and with each change declined in circulation, income and reputation. Hearst bought for his $150,000 the name and little else. Across town, J. Frank Norris, the Baptist thorn in Amon's side, chortled in his nationally-distributed fundamentalist newspaper, the *Searchlight*: "Amon has plenty of enemies in Fort Worth. The complaint is that Amon irritates quick. He has a violent dislike for some of its citizens, who return it with usury. The anti-Amonites look forward with great joy to Amon's impending ruin at the hands of the Hearst organization. The big show is on. When newspapers fall out the public always gets a square deal. One newspaper [*Star-Telegram*] owes a million dollars. The other has a hundred million dollars. It won't be long now."

The Carter/Hearst confrontation had all elemental cliches of those Saturday afternoon westerns of long ago. Amon, the white-hatted good guy, defending the town against Hearst, the yellow-hearted fast gun. Amon actually uttered that classic line so thrilling to Tom Mix and Lash LaRue fans, the precipitous words spoken before the big shootout: "The town is not big enough for the two of us."

Amon, as he explained in his incomplete autobiography, muttered those words* to Moore, and the Hearst man, following the script, needled, "If the town is so bad off as you indicate you should be glad to have a live publisher come in and revive the city."

*Throughout the Hearst incident, Amon ignored the presence of *The Press*, which, with its meager 6,000 circulation, probably merited the neglect.

Carter, deeply worried despite his brave words, made a hurried trip to New York and met with Hearst in the latter's Riverside Drive mansion. Amon asked Hearst not to come to Fort Worth.

Hearst said the protest came too late, he already had paid $10,000 for an option on the *Record*. Amon offered to buy the option. Hearst, who must have enjoyed Amon's discomfort, declined and asked once again that the *Star-Telegram* be sold to him. Angry, Amon returned to Fort Worth to oil his sixguns.

April 1, 1923, the *Record* began publishing under Hearst and that day, Amon printed on the *Star-Telegram*'s front page an editorial titled: "Welcome, Mr. Hearst." The editorial — the message was rhetorical, Hearst was in Fort Worth only spiritually, never in body — proclaimed the press king's purchase of the *Record* as "unqualified proof of the greatness of Fort Worth and the whole Southwest." Privately, he gawd-damned the whole situation and beat his fists on his desk.

The American Association of Newspaper Publishers convened in New York, in the old Waldorf. Amon met with other men whose newspapers competed with Hearst. A Colonel Blethen called the meeting to order and asked Carter what he had done when Hearst came to Fort Worth.

"We published an editorial welcoming him," answered Amon. Other publishers guffawed.

"You are a sap," said Blethen. "We have been giving him Hail Columbia and eating his fanny out."

The Carter/Hearst final shootout deserves a dramatic conclusion with the men facing off across a dusty street as the town's frightened decent folk hide behind bolted doors. There is none of that, and the fadeout is boringly unbloody. Hearst, clearly out of his league, never had a chance. What was applauded in larger, particularly northern, cities would not play in provincial Fort Worth.

Hearst published only a newspaper. The *Star-Telegram* was a life line. The *Record* stuck with a daily diet of national and international news, unaware that to West Texans, Washington, Berlin and Tokyo were not of immediate concern, and not international at all, but totally alien. The *Records*'s foreign focus could not compete with the *Star-Telegram*'s local zeal. Chinese court intrigue was not as crucial as Lubbock's mayoral election or the coronation of a 4-H sweetheart at Mineral Wells High. The Hearst paper quietly dug its own grave as Amon the Undertaker looked on, patiently waiting for the body to grow stiff and cold.

Amon, wrote Alva Johnston, "smothered the Hearst paper with kindness." Not really. It is true when Hearst sent columnist Arthur Brisbane to town in an effort to perk up reader interest and demonstrate the *Record*'s importance, Amon threw the famous newspaperman a banquet at which he honored "the world's greatest journalist." Amon did that with a smile.

And no doubt he smiled when he sent word to his merchant friends that Hearst was "an outsider" and not to be trusted. *Record* men found advertising difficult, if not impossible, to sell.

To hype its image, the *Record* resorted to several deceits. It carried on its masthead as "star reporters" the operators who handled wire machines, and daily printed thousands of extra copies — and just as quietly dumped them — to boost circulation numbers. Hearst lost $35,000 to $50,000 monthly.

May, 1924, Amon was in New York and Hearst asked to see him. Once again, the San Simeon lord offered to buy the *Star-Telegram* and hire Amon, suggesting "$500,000 cash and $100,000 a year for five years at 6½ percent interest." Amon was to remain as publisher at $100,000 a year.

Still playing with Hearst, Amon replied, "It would take $600,000 cash to satisfy my associates alone."

Plus $150,000 a year for six years, he added.

"That's at least $300,000 too much," Hearst protested.

"That's alright," countered Amon smugly, "You'll lose that amount in the next 12 months and we can make $125,000 in that time."

Almost as an afterthought, Amon said, "Sell me the *Record* for what you have in it."

Hearst accepted instantly. The *Record* was the first newspaper Hearst ever sold. Hearst's men came to Fort Worth, to room 1316 of Hotel Texas, and the *Star-Telegram* merged with the *Record* like a toad with a fly.

At the 1924 AANP convention, Amon again met Colonel Blethen, and asked, "How are you getting along eating Mr. Hearst's fanny out?"

"We're keeping it up," Blethen boasted. "How are you doing being nice?"

"Wonderful. We just ran him out of town."

Not only was Fort Worth a one-horse town, but there was just one stall for the horse.

In 1921, radio was a gadget, a funny little black box that talked. Radio intrigued Amon, the consummate gadgeteer. He wanted one of his own.

There are many versions of Amon's entry into the radio business. Credit is given alternately to Harold Hough and Amon for originating the idea. Each, in fact, credited the other. Hough's version, however, is generally accepted. In his account, Amon was warned by a New York friend that the funny little box would kill newspapers. The prediction worried him. He asked Hough, "What do you know about radio?"

"Hardly anything at all," admitted Hough.

"How much?"

"Nothing."

Amon told his circulation manager to investigate. "If this radio thing is going to be a menace to newspapers, maybe we'd better own the menace," said Amon.

He advanced Hough three hundred dollars to catapult the *Star-Telegram* into the nether world of airwaves.

What Hough knew about radio was that a friend sometime listened to a Dallas station, WRR. The friend operated an electrical supply firm. Hough asked the friend for a radio.

"How far do you want to listen?" asked the friend.

"Listen? Man, I don't want to listen. Amon wants to talk."

That was the first Hough knew talking and listening were different in radio. With that useful knowledge, he found a broadcasting unit in Dallas, a homemade rig put together by a tinkerer, W. E. Branch. Hough bought the flimsy transmitter, packed it in an old tomato crate, and transported it to the *Star-Telegram* where he installed the thing in Louis Wortham's office. Wortham was out of town. An aerial wire was strung through the window, over the street, to the roof of a nearby building. The *Star-Telegram* was on the air — illegally and poorly, but nevertheless broadcasting with the power of five homemade watts.

Almost immediately a lady in Mineral Wells, fifty miles west, wrote that she picked up the signal loud and clear. Amon read the letter and decided the gadget had promise.

Throughout the summer and fall of 1921, Hough experimented with the funny black box, spending three hundred dollars, and more, most of which came from the petty cashbox drawer. He deduced that the *Star-Telegram* needed a more powerful, professionally-constructed transmitter, and contracted with Western Electric. When the broadcast unit — the sixteenth manufactured by Western Electric and the first installed in the South — arrived, Hough applied to the Department of Commerce for a license. Herbert Hoover, then the commerce secretary, assigned the call letters, WBAP, saying they meant "We Bring A Program." May 2, 1922, with two seventy-foot tall broadcast towers rising from the *Star-Telegram* roof, WBAP became a functioning and legal radio station.

W. T. Waggoner, who lived a full two miles from the transmitter, telephoned the *Star-Telegram* to report that reception was good. He requested a song, *Wabash Blues*.

That was the pattern of early radio, including WBAP — music by local trios and orchestras, church choirs, neighborhood bands. There also were fire call reports, a little news (read by off-duty reporters), a bedtime story for kiddies, but no commercials. The station even broadcast one of the first "hillbilly" programs, featuring Confederate veteran and fiddler, Captain J. M. Bonner, backed by Fred Wagner's Hilo Five Hawaiian Orchestra.

WBAP began with ten watts of power. Within a year, it increased output to fifteen hundred watts, then ten thousand in 1928, and ten years later, became one of eight national stations with fifty thousand watts of clear channel power. Half of the station was sold in 1936 to the Dallas *Morning News*. At the same time Amon bought KGKO in Wichita Falls and moved it to Fort Worth.

Within two years of that first broadcast, Hough had moved the transmitting equipment outdoors, taking it to rodeos and football games, baseball games, groundbreaking ceremonies. By 1928, WBAP was affiliated with the National Broadcasting Company.

Hough virtually was the station's only announcer. He was dragged into the role one morning when a cub reporter failed to arrive for work. When it came time for the news to be read, only Hough was there. He remained at the mike to become the most popular broadcasting personality in the Southwest. In those days, announcers signed off with their initials. Listeners liked H. H., and wrote asking who was the man with the droll voice. His reply was, "I'm just the Hired Hand, up from the basement." Fan letters became so numerous Hough was forced to provide pictures. He posed in overalls, checked shirt, long-billed railroad cap, holding a broom and cowbell — the bell became the sound symbol of WBAP.

The Hired Hand's wry wit pleased listeners. He founded the Truth Society, for which he ran a legal, if not too serious, campaign for governor. He filed for the office pledging to campaign entirely in El Paso, Texas' westernmost city. El Paso was so far away politicians ignored it. "I just believe the people of El Paso deserve more political amusement than they get," the Hired Hand explained.

Ultimately, Hough hired "fellows with lace on their tonsils." He took himself off the air, explaining, "I'm the only announcer who ever fired himself for being no good."

In 1963, the National Association of Broadcasters, named Hough "Dean of American Broadcasters." Leroy Collins, president of the NAB and former Florida governor, called Hough the "grand old man of American broadcasting."

Throughout the prestigious award ceremony, attended by all major American broadcast executives, Harold Hough sat quietly at the head table, wearing his ubiquious rumpled hat.

Amon often talked on his radio station, emceed variety shows, manned the microphone for remote broadcasts, especially those originating from Shady Oak Farm where he featured his famous visiting friends. Radio was made for a compulsive talker like Amon, and he loved the gadgetry of it all. Television was the next logical step.

WBAP-TV went on the air in the early fall of 1948 as, crowed the *Star-Telegram*, the first television station south of St. Louis, east of Los Angeles and west of Richmond, Virginia. The initial broadcast was remote with cameras focusing on Harry Truman as he made a railroad campaign whistlestop in Fort Worth. A few days later, the station officially signed on with thirty minutes of dedicatory remarks by Amon, followed by an old movie, followed by nothing because an automobile struck a nearby power pole and knocked WBAP-TV off the air.

Planning for the station, Amon and Hough decided a grassy hillock east of downtown was perfect for the transmitter site. Amon and Hough went to inspect the property. They climbed through a barbed wire fence and began walking. A young bull was in the pasture, eyeing the men. Hough was apprehensive. Amon admonished, "Forget that gawddamned bull. He won't bother us." The bull pawed the ground irritably. Hough turned and left, saying over his shoulder, "I'm gettin' out of here. I've got a wooden leg and that bull don't know who you are." The bull charged and the men scrambled to safety through the fence.

WBAP-TV sent out its first color broadcast in 1954, as usual ahead of its time because Amon was fascinated with the new gadget. Hough had recognized the future of color television and sold Amon on investing in the expensive necessary equipment, though at the time the peacock representing NBC's Living Color seemed to most a white elephant. One bright spring day in 1954, Amon and David Sarnoff, Radio Corporation of America board chairman, jointly pulled a switch converting WBAP into a peacock subscriber. That first color broadcast lasted three hours, but it hardly mattered. In all of Fort Worth and Dallas, there were fewer than one hundred color television sets.

With the addition of television, Amon owned the full circle of communications in Fort Worth, virtually all of it beamed into the remoteness of West Texas. The propoganda monopoly's power was enormous, so much so that Alf Evans, looking back on the spoken and written word empire, commented, "Letting someone like Amon Carter have his own newspapers, radio stations and television is like letting Billy Graham have his own church; the only sermon you hear will be his."

In the very earliest years, Fort Worth newspapers had a kinship with their more cosmopolitan cousins. The papers were sold by boys and men who actually shouted "Extra!" and "Read All About It!" just as Hollywood actors in those Pat O'Brien reporter movies.

The street games generally were a motley bunch, mostly poor, life-hardened, wise and young, playing a hard-scrabble game of survival on the pavement. Those corner gladiators schemed and fought to gain, then hold, the busiest and best positions, protecting what was theirs and, without conscience, beating out a lesser boy or older man for an improved location. Territorial disputes were resolved with strong talk, fists, and at least once, clubs, and were grand forms of public entertainment, much as Europe's street acrobats. The weakest and oldest were pushed outward from downtown until, as Indians settled the problem of their infirm and elderly, they were left to die in warehouse districts and slum perimeters where newspaper street sales were as rare as hope.

All of his life, Amon Carter allied himself with the little newsboys. He saw in the often-savage corner corsairs the poverty and combativeness of his youth. He kept his office door open to them and in later years, sought out the more successful graduates to speak lovingly of the good old days. There were many alumni of those street guerrilla wars. A chief of detectives. The director of New York's cotton exchange. Merchants and millionaires. Scholars, oil men, ranchers and bums. With an enviable left jab and swung-from-the-heels right hand, a thin Ben Hogan commanded a select corner bunker before moving his skinned knuckles to the caddy lot of Glen Garden Country Club where he competed for golfing coins with another Fort Worth youngster, Byron Nelson.

For his boys, Amon staged annual dinners at which he praised their salesmanship and handed out silver dollars to each. There was a newsboy baseball team and during World War I, drill squads. The boulevard foot soldiers performed manual or arms with broomsticks and practiced other Army skills just in case America stumbled and the Kaiser's troops laid siege to the *Star-Telegram* building, Carter fondly called them the country's Second Front and often, after the forced marches, he joined the boys as they awaited another edition to peddle. Carter asked their opinions about the *Star-Telegram* — which stories sold papers, what the readers liked and disliked. Because of those talks, he instructed Harold Hough to place the comic section outside the large Sunday edition. That move made street customers instantly recognize the *Star-Telegram* among competitors and incidentally showed Texans were more interested in *Mutt and Jeff* than the Watch on the Rhine. One boy, DeWitt Reddick, told Carter of another sales gimmick. In black sections of Fort Worth, newsboys flipped the Sunday comic section to the *Jiggs and Maggie* strip, which, for unknown reasons, was a favorite of black readers.

Carter never forgot his newsboys, even when the vendor system was outdated and youngsters delivered papers to homes via bicycles. He gave each a money gift at Thanksgiving and Christmas, and provided in his will for the holiday cash to continue years after his death.

The newsboys were his pets and he forgave them any wickedness. Once he arrived at the *Star-Telegram* and a newsboy shot him in the nose with an air rifle. Possibly it was a stray shot. Probably not. Carter stumbled into his office, clutching a handkerchief to blot flowing blood and tears, bellowing, ''Gawddamnit, get that boy!''

The sniper was gone for, collared and dragged to Carter like an Aztec human sacrifice pitched on the high priest's stone altar. Carter glared at the awe-stricken boy. He began yelling, beating his fists on the desk, shouting about the mighty sin of shooting the nose of one's employer. His words fell like whip ends on the terrified youngster. The boy began sobbing, crying of how sorry he was to have shot Carter, of how he was the only support of his widowed mother. Amon sighed deeply.

"All right . . . all right," Carter said gruffly, "just don't do it again."

He handed the boy a silver dollar. The kid fled. Amon dabbed the bloody handkerchief to his wounded nose and mumbled, "Gawddamned boy. . . ."

Daily, as editions came off presses in the old *Star-Telegram* building, the news hustlers massed to fight for stacks of papers. It was like tossing chicken necks to a pack of yard dogs and reporters gathered to look on the sight in wide-eyed wonder. A mite of a lad, fatherless and the sole support of his mother and sisters, seemed the fastest and most fistic of the boys. He had an urgent punching technique, bluish-gray owl eyes, was at best semi-literate, at worst, retarded. He spoke with a slurred voice, a speech defect he later used as a valuable selling tool. His name was Monroe Odom. Time has obscured Monroe's arrival as a *Star-Telegram* newspaper hawker. Legend says he was five or ten — the story was told with both ages — when he asked Amon for a job.

Amon assayed little Monroe. "Here," said Carter, passing over twenty papers. "Sell these in an hour and you have a job." Fifteen minutes later, Monroe was tugging at Amon's coattail. His pockets hung heavy with silver dollars. Monroe had dashed to the nearest saloon. He reasoned drinkers would buy anything from a small boy with a speech impediment. For less than two-bits of newspapers, Monroe collected eleven dollars. Amon hired him instantly.

For the next fifty-three years, Monroe Odom peddled the *Star-Telegram*. At first he was a rover, then he fought and held the better corners. Ultimately, he settled at the Worth Hotel's front door where his stand was a pinewood fruit box. Carter awarded him the position. When the Worth opened in 1927, Carter selected Monroe to snip the official ribbon. And there he stayed for the rest of his life, outliving the newsvender system and outmaneuvering the soulless coin machines. Not until his death did the *Star-Telegram* place a coin-operated vending machine outside its own building because it would have encroached on Monroe's territory.

Monroe was king of the block. His stand faced Seventh Street, was within a block of four banks, a federal center complex, dozens of oil company headquarters, opposite the posh Petroleum Club, beside the even-posher Fort Worth Club, adjacent to the Worth Theater and across Taylor Street from the *Star-Telegram*. Amon could look down from his corner office and observe Monroe at his news-peddling beat.

Monroe was there, rain or shine, in cold and heat, and he claimed he was the best newspaper salesman in the world. Possibly he was. His customers included bank, oil company and college presidents. Most bought a paper daily from Monroe — and paid a sizeable tip — although they also received the *Star-Telegram* at home. Amon rarely left his office without the latest edition in his pocket, yet he bought a newspaper from Monroe each time he passed. He paid a dollar a copy.

Monroe, of course, was not a bonafide *Star-Telegram* employee. He was an independent merchant who bought wholesale and sold retail, plus tip. He rarely accepted the printed price of a nickle. If you bought from Monroe, you paid premium rates.

A new reporter once strolled into the hotel coffee shop for a late lunch. Monroe called, "Paper, mister?"

"I work for the *Star-Telegram*," the reporter explained.

"So what?" mumbled Monroe.

Weeks later, the reporter wrote of a lost boy. At lunch, Monroe came to the newsman's table, sat and began complimenting him. "Kids sell newspapers," said Monroe. "You see a copy yet?"

"No. Not yet."

Monroe handed the reporter a newspaper with the lost boy story on the front page. The reporter had no change. He gave Monroe a fifty-cent coin. Monroe shuffled out. The reporter had been "Monroed."

Most evey reporter and editor was "Monroed." It was a common and active verb meaning that Monroe once again had sold them one of their own newspapers. Editors learned to cross the street on poor news days rather than face Monroe. His judgement of story values was based on street sales. Disaster was marketable, routine was not. Editors called that "The Monroe Doctrine." Once a major Washington official was fired, and the story ran for days while a board of inquiry investigated. Monroe hooked an editor on the street.

"This Washington stir was real good the first day," he advised, "but the probe stuff is getting thin. Let's go with something else tomorrow."

As all good businessmen, Monroe changed with the times. In later years, he learned people no longer wanted news shouted at them. "Extra!" died with high paper costs and time-and-a-half wages. Monroe began mumbling the news in his indistinct, impeded voice. His peculiar style also included the right to select the story subject to be sold. A headline need not be on the front page for him to promote its message. One customer heard Monroe mumbling about "World War Three." He bought a paper, but found nothing on the front page about war. He returned and challenged Monroe. "Page 10-A," Monroe answered. There, printed under a one-column headline was a four-inch story quoting a government official that WWIII was unlikely in an age of nuclear stalemate.

Monroe tailored his pitch to fit the customer. If an oil man approached, he would pick up on a petroleum industry story. At noon, when hundreds of federal employees hit the streets, Monroe had a civil service headline ready for them. A businessman passed the hotel one day after his daughter's marriage. Monroe caught him with "Debutante Weds." In the 1930s, when the Sino-Japanese conflict was a page one item, the Japan Cotton Trading Company had offices in a nearby building. As the Japanese office staff emerged for lunch, Monroe had news from home.

Years of standing on concrete sidewalks caused him to limp badly. He spoke with that slurred voice and it became permanently hoarse. His working uniform was a canvas change apron, wrinkled khaki trousers, worn shoes too comfortable to throw away and a plastic-billed military-style cap. From his stand, he hailed his customers, or collected. Monroe gave credit.

Beeman Fisher, president of Texas Electric Service Company, began paying Monroe one dollar weekly, collectable each Friday. Each time Fisher passed, Monroe handed him a newspaper. Soon Fisher was paying two dollars, then five dollars each week.

And at Christmas, Fisher gave Monroe a yuletime bonus. Monroe was on the *Star-Telegram* Christmas bonus list, though he technically was not an employee. Incredibly, he received machine-printed Christmas bonus checks from at least three oil companies, and one bank. He became a kind of public utility to be maintained as one would a symphony orchestra or a city park.

Monroe was such a familiar presence that on days when he was ill and did not arrive for work people called the newspaper office to ask about his presence. Hotel managers came and went during the four decades without disturbing the old man with whom they shared the building. Once, a new manager spied the pine crate and

Monroe blocking the hotel entrance, and ordered a desk clerk to "get rid of that old man out there." The manager was told he would go before Monroe, and he did.

When Amon Junior was a teenager, his father decided it was time to teach the youngster the newspaper business. He put his son on the street selling newspaper's at Monroe's side. "You might as well begin at the top," said Carter. Amon Junior became publisher after his father's death. Monroe went to see his former assistant. "I just wanted you to know I plan to go on selling the *Star-Telegram*." Amon Junior knew the empire would not crumble.

Many of his customers were celebrities passing through town. Clara Bow bought one of his papers. Gary Cooper came to Fort Worth in 1940 for premiere of "The Westerner." Amon introduced the cowboy star to Monroe. At the premiere hour Cooper could not be located, and press agents were frantic. They found him in the hotel coffee shop talking to Monroe. "Don't go away," said Cooper, as the movie men were pulling him out of the restaurant. "I'll be right back."

During World War II, hoardes of stars visited Fort Worth with war bond rally troupes. Barbara Stanwyck met Monroe. "Spencer Tracy said to tell you 'Hello'," she greeted him.

Will Rogers was a favorite customer. The humorist gave Monroe twenty dollars for a newspaper, the largest single-copy price he ever received. Rogers, of course, stayed in Amon's Fort Worth Club suite. Each evening Monroe would deliver a newspaper to Rogers. Once Rogers asked Monroe to stay for dinner, and order filet mignon.

Meal finished, Monroe thanked Rogers, adding, "Wish you'd tell 'em a little more well-done next time, Will."

"OK, Monroe," laughed Rogers.

Monroe sold papers to Ike and FDR and half-a-dozen Texas governors. John Connally lived in Fort Worth before he became governor. When Connally returned as Texas' new chief official, staying in the Worth Hotel, Monroe handed him a newspaper. "First one's free, John" smiled Monroe.

Of Monroe's encounters with celebrities, his escapade with magician Harry Blackstone was most remembered. Monroe never needed a ticket to enter the Worth Theater. He just strolled in between editions. Blackstone brought his magic show to the theater. Featured was his famous escape from a wooden packing crate. At each performance, Blackstone called for volunteers on stage to nail him into the crate. Show after show, Monroe watched as audience members used the magician's hammer and nails. Blackstone always escaped on cue.

Then came the closing performance. Blackstone asked for volunteers. Monroe shuffled down the aisle. He wore a carpenter's apron bulging with spike-sized nails. He carried a heavy hammer.

Monroe beat a steady tattoo around the box. Each nail was crossed with another, virtually welded into the wood. Orchestra members heard the perplexed Blackstone muttering, "What the hell's going on?"

Monroe ended the hammering and stepped back. The curtain closed and the band struck up Blackstone's escape music. Three times the orchestra played the music. Each time the curtain opened, the box was still there. No escaped Blackstone.

On the fourth curtain pull, a standby dressed as Blackstone for such emergencies, stepped out and took a face-concealing bow. The lights dimmed quickly and the movie began.

Later, the theater manager revealed that the wooden box had to be destroyed to free Blackstone.

Monroe died one cool February evening shortly before midnight. A circulation supervisor found him on the sidewalk beside his stack of newspapers. At his funeral, the chapel was filled with businessmen, judges, *Star-Telegram* editors and publishers. Anonymously, Amon Junior insisted on paying for the funeral. Other businessmen/customers contributed to a fund for Monroe's widow. The *Star-Telegram* placed Monroe's obituary on its front page. As services were being conducted, the Texas Legislature adopted a resolution honoring "The memory of this distinguished gentleman, Monroe Odom."

At the funeral hour, a wreath was placed on the old pinewood box and a chill wind tossed the ends of the black ribbons. People wanting *Star-Telegram*s that day and forever more, fed coins to a plastic machine.

Chapter 8

I expect to look over the Parapets of Heaven and see Frank Norris frying in the bottomless pits of Hell.

—J. L. Ward, President, Decatur College

I would be willing to wager the good Lord winces every time J. Frank Norris mentions his name . . .

—Ralph McGill, Atlanta Constitution

In Fort Worth, there was an 11th Commandment: Thou Shalt Not Mess With J. Frank Norris.

—Alf Evans, Star-Telegram

8

Baptists, of course, were first in line to redeem Fort Worth souls. Blazing a trail into the wilderness, Baptists were there to preach the fledgling town's first sermon. Baptists built the first permanent church and later, in 1889, constructed a mammoth stone turreted Gothic fortress for God, who was not unpleased.

By 1909 the First Baptist Church of Fort Worth garrisoned a congregation of 334 born-again souls, all correctly water-dipped and scrubbed of sin. They were an exotic bunch of reformed sinners, socially and financially elite, conservative, unproselytic, liturgically housebroken, a tamer breed of Baptists, almost like regular Christians.

In that year their preacher passed on and God sent J. Frank Norris to tend Fort Worth's tranquil Baptist flock. Tall, gangling and gawky, slender to the brink of emaciation, Norris seemed an innocuous Ichabod Crane figure until one was transfixed by his messianic eyes. Eyes of absolutism, pale blue and painful, mesmerizing. Old Testament eyes that trespassed on other men's souls.

However arresting his appearance, Norris nevertheless was a shattered man, deeply in debt, possibly consumptive, owning faith in neither himself nor God, in his words, "pale, wan, worn, and weary." Norris' fundamentalist credentials, though, were proper. He sprang from poor Warner, a central Texas sharecropper and popular drunkard, and Mary, the severe-faced mother who loved nothing better than condemning her husband's miserable soul to hell and talking to the Lord.

Mary had visions in which God appeared before her and chatted amicably, mostly of how young Frank was to become the greatest preacher in the world. At thirteen, Frank, lean and sickly, a slender spear being honed for the Lord, was creek-dipped with Baptist salvation. At eighteen, he entered Baylor University in Waco — "Athens of the Baptist World" — to graduate seven years later valedictorian of his class. Briefly, Norris pastored a Dallas church then became editor of the Baptist *Standard,* which was to Texas Baptists as Sears catalog to a West Texas farm family, a passport to all good things.

Though moderately successful, Norris burned inside for the glorious fame promised him by God and Mary. He became despondent, neurotically depressed by the Lord's failure to act on his behalf. It was then God called him to Fort Worth and he mounted the durable First Baptist Church pulpit where he uttered untroubling sermons for the comfortable congregation. So far, so good.

For two years, Norris was a nonentity, unobtrusive, unnoticed, undisturbing to his elitist brood, a preacher accepted but unexceptional. One day an ad appeared among the hemorrhoid salve and catarrh curative notices of the *Star-Telegram.* It announced that the

Reverend J. Frank Norris would preach Sunday evening on the topic: "Why Dallas Beat Fort Worth in Baseball." A banner proclaiming the meeting and its non-Biblical message was strung over Main Street. His tame Baptists fidgeted. What was Brother Norris up to?

At 7:30 p.m. Sunday, Norris stepped into his pulpit and confronted a packed auditorium. Most in the audience were curiosity seekers. They looked on the skinny Ichabod figure who seemed weak and lifeless in the pulpit and heard his first quiet words: "Dallas beat Fort Worth because Dallas was better prepared. Boys, you had better get prepared for this game of life."

Then without warning, J. Frank Norris attacked. He shouted, wept, exhorted, pulled away his tie and celluloid collar, threw off his suit jacket, ran about the church, up and down aisles. He seared the walls with the warning of judgment, the horrors of hell and at least one witness claimed to have smelled sulphur, actually felt the heat of Hades. For two hours, Norris ranted his hardshell Baptist message, ending the performance with fists raised, shouting, "Old Devil, you think you've got these boys tonight. But, oh, Devil, you haven't!! You haven't!! These boys are going to knock a home run for Jesus Christ tonight." He sprang into an aisle, bellowing, "Come on, boys, knock a home run for Jesus!" Weeping men and women, panicked by the apparent consequences of their sinfulness, rushed forward for salvation, sliding for home. Sixty lost souls were saved that evening, not the least of which was one belonging to J. Frank Norris. The First Baptist Church never again was a calm garden of worship.

For Norris' stunned conservative congregation, the mutant metamorphosis was incredulous, even insane, and the sight of their God-inflamed *Ichabod* racing about the church hitting home runs for Jesus must have seemed the behavior of a madman. Exactly why Norris transformed himself from a staid, domesticated Baptist pastor into a hellfire and damnation revivalist, a skinny thunderbolt fired by a vengeful God, will never be known. Perhaps he grew tired of waiting for the Lord to act on his behalf. He wrote only that he decided to turn from "my . . . dead, dull, dry method" and become a "sensationalist." That summer of 1911 Norris' sensationalist preacher act became so popular services moved outside to accommodate the large audiences. As many as one hundred persons weekly joined the church, most of them the uneducated, the poor, the ignorant for whom religion was an emotional anesthetic, for whom the Heaven promised by Norris represented a happiness they would never find on earth. The socially prominent congregation looked on its new brothers and sisters in Christ, sniffed indignantly and began grumbling loudly.

Norris' messages, then and for the remainder of his career, were not from a God of love but one with a terrible swift sword for the wicked and, he warned endlessly, all of mankind is just naturally, innately sinful. His Bible was The Word, absolute bedrock Truth, each canon, comma and ampersand. He preached Salvation, Rebirth and Immortality and woe to the unbelievers and instruments of the devil. He was eloquent and loquacious and earthy, so emotional he cried at the drop of a psalm, so animated his frail arms seemed to one observer as "scythes cutting weeds for hell." By autumn the church roll numbered nine hundred members. The old congregation was a minority.

Norris openly defied his original flock. He brought in hundreds of poor people "and gave them free entertainment. Ice cream was served and they got it all over that fine heavy carpet." Next day he received the wrath of the "diamond bedecked sisters of the Ladies Aid" complaining of the pastor's use of their church. Ultimately, he "adjourned all church societies *sine die*, to meet no more" because he was asked to read their announcements in services. His board chairman suggested a sermon topic and Norris told him, "Brother Deacon, your ticket has expired, and when the train slows down at the next water tank you will have your luggage ready to get off."

"You are a damned fool," the chairman replied, according to Norris, "and this is to notify you that you are fired."

"No," said Norris, "you are the one who is fired."

"The pastor," he later wrote, suggesting he was against syntax as well as sin, "had about as much to say as to how the church should be run as a weaned yearling calf tied to a stob on the outside of a cow lot looking through the cracks of a new gate wanting to be where he is not."

Norris took the fight to the congregation and his new converts, outnumbering the old sheep, presented him with a vote of confidence. He had captured the church.

His pulpit secure, Norris looked outside, to Fort Worth and its sinful ways, to the still-burgeoning Hell's Half Acre, to the countless saloons, to the Godless Sunday picture shows, to the limitless evils of Cowtown. He looked, and smiled. Easy pickings.

J. Frank Norris is a substantial character in the South's fundamental religious history. In a region famed for snake handlers and holy rollers, the fanatical and the outrageous, Norris was for forty years the grandest show of all. He was a superb performer in the pulpit. His sermons encompassed all the passions and emotions of the highly volatile fundamentalist dogma but too they toured the whole of human experience from thumbsucking to black-eyed pea recipes, all presented with a theatrical genius. During Prohibition he raved against bootlegging, Texas' third oldest profession, and regularly dispatched agents to buy moonshine in fruit jars. He stacked the jars around his pulpit and as he spoke against the evils of booze, he smashed each jug in a galvanized tub. The gurgling noisy drama was so popular he repeated the scene many times and a local bootlegger offered to sell him liquor on a regular basis for breakage. When evolution was a topical sin among fundamentalists, Norris paraded monkeys through the church, representing them as Darwin's cousins. For money raising projects he strung rows of clothes lines throughout the church and locked the doors. He would allow the people to leave only when money was fluttering from each clothes pin. Once, for attention, he filled another number two washtub with rattlesnakes for his fascinated audience.

"Wasn't that silly?" his son asked.

"No," said Norris, "I wanted a large audience."

Norris was the most entertaining spectacle in town, better even than the two-reelers and kootch shows against which he railed, and spectators came in droves. By the early 1920s membership of the First Baptist Church reached twelve thousand and the five thousand member Sunday School was, boasted Norris, the world's largest. There was a fundamental Bible college and an association of world-wide fundamentalist churches with total membership of over three thousand. Norris published his own newspaper and established a radio station, KFQB. He became pastor of Temple Baptist Church in Detroit and kept his post in Fort Worth, proclaiming himself spiritual leader of two churches eighteen hundred miles apart.

From the mid-1930s Norris considered himself a world religious figure. He traveled extensively, staging revivals in Ireland, France, Iraq, Iran, Egypt, Scotland and Germany. He met with Churchill and Roosevelt, built churches in Israel and Shanghai.

Norris was the first Protestant minister granted private audience with a pope. He and Pius XII met and spoke of world events and afterward the Pope, through interpreters, asked permission to pray for the Baptist. Pius XII prayed, then Norris said, "Your eminence, as we say in Texas, I'd like to lay one on you, too."

The interpreters pondered and puzzled over this strange request and asked Norris to repeat his words. Finally they understood and Norris prayed loudly for Pius XII. Departing, the Pope said, "May God bless you."

Norris smiled, and replied, "May God bless you, too."

That J. Frank Norris was allowed even to enter the Vatican was a testimony to the ecumenism of a new era. For thirty years of his inflammable ministry, Catholic degradation was a favorite sermon topic and Godless popery central to Norris' Duke's Mixture of evil "isms" — Catholicism, modernism, socialism, evolutionism, communism. Sin of every stripe was very popular with Brother Norris, holding as he did the standard fundamentalist belief that anyone having a good time was ripe for hell.

Amon Carter, who always had a good time, hated J. Frank Norris and the publisher's enmity of Norris was the majority position in Fort Worth.

Amon despised the minister not for his religious views, for the publisher had few, but because Norris' notoriety damaged Carter's evangelism of boosterism for Fort Worth. He was "against the unfavorable advertising Fort Worth is receiving from Dr. Norris." Amon couldn't abide a smart aleck.

In that first summer of transformation, Norris began rummaging through Fort Worth's social sinning closets and by autumn of 1911 tar-and-feather talk was in the air. First, Norris led a fight for enforcement of a state law banning all Sunday entertainment and pressured law officials into arresting several picture show projectionists. Next he jumped on liquor and kicked around the saloons. Then he spied the venerable Hell's Half Acre and fell on that sinful eden with the enthusiasm of a prospector finding the mother lode. At Norris' insistence the ministers' association hired a private detective to investigate the Acre. The man reported eighty houses of prostitution and handed over a list of property owners. Eight of the whorehouse landlords were socially and financially prominent in Fort Worth. At least one was a church deacon. Other ministers gulped and dropped the entire matter. Norris smiled. "If a preacher is not stirring up the devil," he said, "he is dead, already sold out."

Norris poked the devil. He read the eight names from his pulpit. He frayed the men's reputation and coupled the tirade with an harangue against city officials who, he shouted, had joined in a conspiracy of sin with Acre prostitutes, thieves and bootleggers. Outside his church, the sermon was not well received.

Amon pointedly told Dr. T. L. Ray, one of Norris' new deacons, that "I wish the church would get Dr. Norris a good job somewhere else."

The controversy simmered for a month, then Norris printed in the weekly *X-Ray* a condemnation of Winfield Scott, Fort Worth's largest property owner and one of the now-infamous Acre Eight.

As winter arrived, animosity for Norris was rife. January 8, the *Star-Telegram* carried an announcement. Mayor W. B. Davis would speak Wednesday at 8 o'clock in city hall. His topic: "Liars in Capital Letters." "It is rumored," said the story, "that short and ugly terms will be applied to a number of recent utterances." No women or children admitted.

Davis stood before an overflow crowd and immediately began to verbally lash the hide off J. Frank Norris, ". . . the fanatical outcast."

Norris, opined Davis, was not "worth killing with a dollar ninety-eight cent pistol."

He concluded, "This is a time for heads of homes to act and not a time for sissy boys. If there are fifty red-blooded men in this town, a preacher will be hanging from a lamp post before daylight."

Norris survived the night, but trouble was coming. Two days afterwards, fire broke out in the First Baptist

Church auditorium. There was little damage. Firemen suspected arson. Three nights later, Norris sat alone in his church study, preparing a sermon. Two shots were fired through a window. Both missed. January 25, Norris preached on "Things That Have Happened in Fort Worth in the Last Thirty Days." Once again, he condemned corrupt city officials.

At 2:30 a.m., February 4, a freezing watchman heard an explosion, then saw flames rising from the fortress-like First Baptist Church. He fired his pistol three times as an alarm. At the same time, five blocks away at Norris' home, burning oily rags were tossed onto the back porch. By dawn, Fort Worth's most ornate church was blackened rubble. The fire at his home caused minor damage.

The following day Amon, president of the Fort Worth Board of Trade, announced that five thousand dollars "would be paid for capture of the incendiaries." The reward, he said, was "to correct reports that Fort Worth is in the hands of lawless elements."

Norris was elated by the events. He moved services to a theater and remounted his attack. His enemies' persecution of him was "an attack on righteousness," and proclaimed, "If anybody thinks a bunch of these machine . . . politicians can make a fight on my wife's husband, and I will do a flop-eared, pot-licker, suck-egg hound, when he tucks his tail between his legs and runs down tin can alley — well, they have another think comin'."

March 2, fire heavily damaged Norris' home. The family escaped by leaping from a second floor window. Ten days after the fire Norris was indicted for perjury, and a week later, he also was charged with arson.

The April trial was a sensation, its popularity undiminished even when reports had to compete with newspaper space on the *Titanic*'s sinking. Norris appeared each day with his hands folded around a worn Bible. Baptist church members crowded the courtroom while outside young boys distributed religious tracts. Church ladies held afternoon prayer sessions.

Prosecution tactics centered on two threatening notes Norris claimed had been sent him and a deacon, G. H. Connell, Norris' note warned, "You have escaped so far, but look out. The end is not yet; there is something more coming." Connell's letter was more revealing. It read, "I and others have tried to warn that damb [*sic*] preacher of yours — he continues to slander the best men in town. We have the dope on him where he was caught with a woman from Fort Worth in a St. Louis Hotel last year. How can you keep such a man when the above is known all over town? If he remains the proof will be coming." Neither note was signed.

The prosecution showed that a torn piece of stationery found in Norris' home after the February 4 fire matched the jagged edges of the note allegedly received by the pastor. Warren Andrews, a bank clerk brought in as a handwriting expert, testified that a sample of Norris' writing was the same as in both letters and, too, the minister misspelled "damn" as "damb."

That Sunday Norris spoke on martyrdom, of, as it happened, Jesus, not himself, but the analogy was clear and not lost on the largest crowd ever to hear him preach. A rumor circulated he would be shot in the pulpit and the curious came the same way people go to auto races, expecting wrecks.

April 11, the prosecution played its trump, Mrs. K. K. Taylor, former financial secretary of Norris' church. Mrs. Taylor's testimony stunned spectators. That winter, she said, Norris came to her home fretting that his congregation was "not doing enough for the Kingdom." "Unless a great calamity comes," she quoted Norris as saying, "I fear the church will never do its duty."

The pastor, she said, wanted a new five or six story church. Norris also cussed his enemies, using "that name no man wants his mother's name associated with.''

After the church burned, Norris returned to her home, sat on a sofa, slapped his knee and laughed, ''Well, I got Teddy [Roosevelt] beat. Teddy never had two extras out about him in less than 12 hours.''

Norris asked her to mail several letters for him. She refused and the pastor left. Distressed, she prayed all night, then took her story to the prosecutor.

Strong stuff. The prosecution felt confident. It should not have. A week later, the jury voted once and found Norris innocent of all charges. The courtroom exploded in Baptist joy. Men cheered, the women wept. Norris smiled. ''A black mammy,'' said the *Star-Telegram,* waved her finger in Judge Tom Simmons' face and said, ''Woe be unto you.'' Spontaneously, the crowd began singing, ''Nearer My God to Thee.'' Non-Baptists gnashed their teeth in anger.

Thus vindicated — Christianity really was on trial, he claimed — J. Frank Norris began searching for more causes with which to sensationalize his burgeoning ministry. More and more as his church grew, Norris isolated his people by preaching they and they alone were chosen by God to smite a sinful world. He, Norris lectured his flock, was a ''Saint of God'' and said his trial was like Luther in front of the Diet of Worms and ''As Paul before Agrippa.'' As a persecuted saint, Norris preached that he bore ''the cross of Christ to the reproach of the world.'' ''The Powers of Darkness'' were threatening the church, ''his'' church since Norris held deed on the new building.

Norris' enemies grew in numbers as large as his power and influence. ''The Lord must love enemies,'' said a contemporary, ''because he made so many for J. Frank Norris.'' Brother Norris was a hard man to like.

He proselyted among other churches, including Baptist, by charging their pastors had ''sold out to the forces of compromise, modernism and decay.'' ''Modernists cuckooed the Methodists and Congregationalists,'' he preached. When other pastors complained, he called them ''little two by four simian-headed sentimentalists.''

Not surprisingly, the Fort Worth ministers' association expelled him.

Unperturbed, Norris next dumped all Southern Baptist Sunday School literature as ''junk.'' He claimed Southern Baptists had made ''papal demands'' to him. When evolution became a heated topic, he found the Godless philosophy lurking in his alma mater, and preached against the ''apes and monkeys of Baylor University.'' Baylor students hanged Norris in effigy.

The Texas Baptist Convention expelled him and Southern Baptists finally shed themselves of the pesky preacher. He claimed he was in the right and they wanted to still his voice. Actually, they just wanted to shut him up.

Alone to head his own church organization, Norris began gathering other fundamentalist churches into the fold, while continuing to kick at stately Baptist kneecaps with all that he commanded — tracts, booklets, resolutions, airwaves, and lungs.

During the early 1920s, when hatred of J. Frank Norris was as popular as bootleg whiskey, Dr. L. P. Scarborough, president of the Southwestern Baptist Theological Seminary, distributed 100,000 tracts on ''Norrisism.'' And prominent Baptists bought seven consecutive nights of radio time to condemn Norris. He was called malicious, perjurer, liar, thief, scoundrel, despicable, damnable, criminal, wicked, corrupt and hellish. Norris, ever the showman, was delighted. He purchased newspaper space to advertise the attacks on him, and bought radio time immediately after each Baptist broadcast. As they signed off, he signed on. Norris asked the listening audience to forgive those ''high priests of Baptists.'' J. Frank Norris never turned the other cheek.

Amon continued to despise Norris and what he imagined the preacher's publicity was doing to Fort Worth's reputation. Sometime before 1920 Norris called on Carter in the publisher's office, and suggested the two men declare a truce. They should join forces to run Fort Worth. Amon cussed the pastor and ordered him out.

And the *Record* declared editorially: "We will not again publish the name of J. Frank Norris in these columns."

In middle age Frank Norris was a handsome man with graying hair, a firm chin, overly large ears, thin esthetic lips and those brooding eyes. His priorities shifted from Baptist-baiting to other more secular matters. His stature was such that William Jennings Bryan asked him to testify for the prosecution in the Scopes trial but the judge ruled no Biblical experts could be heard. He briefly flirted with the Ku Klux Klan as the Fort Worth chapter's official religious spokesman, then during the plague of Prohibition merrily began kicking around Catholics.

He associated the growth of bootlegging with Catholicism and preached on the topics, "Shall Catholics and Bootleggers Elect the Next U.S. Senate?" and "Shall Roman Catholics Rule Tarrant County Today?" Norris again was fishing into local political waters, defining the 1926 city administration as "morally corrupt" because Mayor H. C. Meacham was a man "with known Roman Catholic associations." That Catholic mafia syndrome occupied Norris' pulpit ideas and even when he campaigned to have Fort Worth streets and alleys cleaned of trash the versatile pastor was able to associate the garbage can crusade with papal lust. He denounced the Catholic puppet, Meacham, in his church and printed 62,000 copies of the sermon for distribution. Boys were posted around Meacham's department store to hand out the pamphlets to each customer.

Meacham was furious. He fired six employees, all members of Norris' congregation. The martyred six became a sermon topic in which Norris pled with God to punish the "dishonest" Meacham. The message was printed and Norris' boys once again surrounded the mayor's store. The preacher announced he would discuss Meacham and official graft the following Sunday.

July 17, 1926 was a scorching Saturday and the afternoon heat drove *Star-Telegram* reporters to the only logical retreat in Prohibition-dry Fort Worth — a bar hidden in an old house three blocks west of the newspaper office. The editorial department held a skeleton crew. James Record was there, and DeWitt Reddick, a part-time schoolboy reporter. They heard a noise. Both looked up.

The dignified Jimmy North was skipping down the hall, his arm raised for attention, shouting, "J. Frank Norris just shot and killed a man. . . . HOORAY!"

Without credible witnesses no one who ever knew the gentle, kindly North would believe him capable of cheering the tragedy, but his spontaneous outburst was testimony to the deeply-felt acrimony Norris created in Fort Worth. Neither North nor Record would have allowed their religious beliefs to infringe on *Star-Telegram* readers, nor would they permit any but the most correct criticism of Norris to appear in editorial columns, but both hoped the tragic shooting would be the means of at long last silencing the vitriolic Norris. Within hours most of Fort Worth shared that hope.

Norris shot D. E. Chipps, a lumber yard owner and close friend of Meacham who, according to others, was "a drunkard and a bully." In Norris' version of the shooting, Chipps telephoned him and demanded the preacher stop his crusade against Meacham. Norris said Chipps threatened to kill him. He borrowed a pistol from the church janitor and secreted it in a desk drawer. Twenty minutes later Chipps — arriving straight from

Meacham's office — burst into Norris' church study and confronted the pastor.

"I am going to kill you for what you said in your sermon, damn you," Norris quoted Chipps as yelling. Chipps moved his right hand to a back pocket. Norris opened the desk drawer, grabbed the pistol and shot Chipps three times.

Chipps was unarmed.

Eighteen days later a grand jury indicted Norris for murder and the district attorney announced he would seek the death penalty.

Norris' version was partially substantiated by L. H. Nutt, an accountant and devout member of the First Baptist Church congregation. Nutt was in the study but out of the lumberman's vision. He testified that Chipps reached for his back pocket in a threatening gesture while cursing Norris. A second witness arrived moments afterwards. Norris was rushing out of the study. "I have killed me a man," the witness said Norris boasted.

Open gossip among church members held that Meacham sent Chipps to kill Norris. The rumors were printed in Los Angeles and Chicago newspapers and Meacham threatened suit. He claimed Chipps had visited him thirty minutes before the shooting to solicit a donation for a painting of Amon Carter which was to be placed in the Fort Worth Club.

Chipps, theorized Meacham, undoubtedly was in Norris' office to ask for a donation from Norris. Chipps only was reaching into his rear pocket for a donor's list when Norris shot him without provocation.

The trial was moved to Austin, set for January, 1927, and as it opened reporters invaded the city to cover what they believed would be the end of J. Frank Norris. Every hotel and boarding house room in town was filled. The courtroom was so crowded witnesses had to enter through an open window.

The *Star-Telegram* provided an unusual service for its readers.

Jim Record, two reporters and two court stenographers were in the courtroom. The stenographers recorded every word uttered by witnesses, lawyers and the judge. Record edited the copy and it was sent via two leased wires to Fort Worth. The *verbatim* testimony, which covered as much as seven and one-half full newspaper pages and never less than four open pages, totaled almost half-a-million words.

Amon Carter said the word-for-word reporting and unusually large space devoted to the trial was a record, and perhaps it was. The approach to trial reporting was at least unique in American journalism.

Fort Worth was convinced Norris was guilty of murder, guilty of killing an unarmed man. Only the pastor's hardshelled flock seemed to believe him innocent. And the jury. The jury needed just one unanimous vote to free Norris as a man only protecting his life. "May God pity and forgive them," Norris told reporters, after the courtroom exploded into loud thankful prayers and hymn-singing. "I stand on Romans 8:28. . . ."

Later in life Norris would tell his son of the tragedy. "I shot him like I would a dog in the night who threatened my family," the pastor declared.

Immediately after the verdict of innocence, Norris went home to Fort Worth, to his church where, he later wrote, "The station was thronged with the multitudes . . . streets were lined with crowds from there to the church. Regardless of the bitter cold night . . . the great auditorium was packed to standing room and multitudes turned away."

J. Frank Norris was back in the fold, safe amid his fundamentalist Baptists who believed the infamous preacher was a true saint of God. Two years later the church was burned to the ground for the third and final time.

Norris' foes may have regretted the jury decision but what was, was, and most, even the *Star-Telegram*, accepted the fact stoically. Across town, however, the tiny voice of the *Press* was heard: ". . . while the present tragedy has come to his experience suddenly, it is not a thing unexpected by Norris of any observer . . . he would be no less service to his church if he would throw away his gun and be more continually a preacher and less a fighter."

The poor *Press* always was like that. Feisty little thing, a snippy terrier chewing on bones tossed aside by the *Star-Telegram.* Why Amon Carter did not put it out of its misery is a mystery. He had no respect for it. He believed it was a cheap claptrap piece of journalism. But he never moved to pronounce its death sentence. "In his lifetime," wrote Gary Cartwright, "Carter could have killed the Press with a flick of his finger, but he allowed it to exist, possibly because it reminded him of something out of his childhood, a disfigured monk or maybe a mangy cat."

For most of its fifty-odd years the *Press*, smallest and shakiest branch of the Scripps-Howard family tree, had the social standing of a man living in a trailer house behind a filling station. It was tossed in poor neighborhoods and rolled-up on dashboards of red-neck pickup trucks and, after it became a racy tabloid in the early 1950s, a favorite luncheon companion because it was small enough to prop up on a glass of tea. The *Press* considered itself the voice of the people, but, denied access to corporate boardrooms and society ballrooms, it was left to serve those for whom wrecks, rapes and robberies were life's only grand adventures. The *Press* worshipped the scoop and the ominous headline and the quirky angle missed or ignored by the *Star-Telegram*, and it chased fire engines and murder cases with urgent fervor.

The *Press* was born in 1921 for the same reason W. D. Hearst bought the *Record*: Amon's loud braying about the endemic future of Fort Worth and West Texas. Hearst and Roy Howard believed Amon. What he did not tell them was that he controlled the advertising purse strings in Fort Worth. After Amon bought the *Record* and turned the *Star-Telegram* into a twenty-four hour newspaper, the *Press* was the only opposition in town and from the beginning it struggled to stay alive.

Amon was ambivalent about the little newspaper across town and either ignored it or worked to siphon ad dollars from the anemic *Press.* He kept bank call advertising from the *Press* and aborted several special sections by letting his friends know he would be unhappy if they bought space in them. After a *Press* salesman solicited special advertising from Montgomery Ward, Amon wrote its president, Avery Sewell, "The *Press* has been operating here for the past 12 years. Its name has been mentioned in the *Star-Telegram* but twice — when it opened and when it moved into a new building. During this period they have devoted a big majority of their time and effort trying to run down the *Star-Telegram* or . . . embarrass its publisher." He asked Sewell not to advertise in the *Press*.

Each time the *Star-Telegram* raised its ad rates, the *Press* lost business. Advertisers who could not afford to increase their ad budgets simply cut lineage in the *Press*.

Amon confounded the *Press*. His little promotions and deals invariably became news events which the *Press* was forced to cover, and how to treat the rival publisher was a question the smaller newspaper never was able to answer. Once there was a *Press* policy to publish Amon's picture each time he appeared at a public function on the theory that people would get sick and tired of seeing him. And for a period the *Press* refused to print either his name or picture.

From its middle years, the *Press* editor/publisher was Walter Humphrey, a portly pipesmoking congenial man whose idea of a newspaper crusade, said a former reporter, was soil conservation. Amon was, at best, intolerant of Humphrey. Amon, who could introduce from memory a head table of fifty persons without stammering a name or title, called the *Press* editor "Humphreys." *Star-Telegram* reporters suspected the mispronunciation was deliberate.

In 1949, Fort Worth was flooded by the Trinity and several thousand families lost everything. The disaster proved the necessity for taming the river and a citizens' committee was formed to devise a flood control program. Amon and Humphrey were appointed to the committee. At the first meeting, Humphrey proposed that reporters be asked to attend the board's meetings.

"Hell, no," shouted Amon. "We're not going to have any gawddam reporters at any of these meetings."

Amon ranted for almost five minutes, denouncing the idea, berating Humphrey for daring to suggest such a silly thing, and finally grumbling that "Some time newspapers do more harm than good." Witnesses said Amon's denunciation of "Humphreys" was received with embarrassed silence. "Carter cut him to pieces. Walter just looked hurt," said one observer.

Amon's animosity toward Walter Humphrey perhaps was caused by more than his editorship of the ragtag *Press*. Humphrey also wrote and produced the annual Texas Gridiron Show, an evening of satire and song parady in which newsmen skewered politicians. The production brought out most state officials, many national figures and all local bigwigs. Except Amon. Uncharacteristically, Amon never attended the reporter roasts, and his newsmen believed he was too thin-skinned to watch himself portrayed as the Machiavellian power in Fort Worth. And in Walter Humphrey's Gridiron sketches, that always was Amon's role.

One skit had a reporter playing Mayor Edgar Deen. His only duty was standing on stage and listening for a loud voice to call. At the voice's first stern tones, the mayor mimicked fear and answered meekly, "Comin', Amon . . . comin', Amon . . . comin', Amon."

In one of the last shows before Carter's death, a reporter chorus sang a hymn parody, the final reverently-intoned word of which was "Aaaa-mon."

The *Press*, being poor and powerless, never made money. It was a tax write-off for the Scripps-Howard chain and by necessity, Humphrey's fiscal policy toward his small staff was stingy. Salaries were minimum, raises unique. Newsmen needing a new copy pencil had to exchange the stub of an old one. The newspaper was housed in an ancient building, dark and without air-conditioning, behind which was the New Gem Hotel, a flophouse used by black prostitutes. Often the hookers propositioned *Press* reporters on the adjacent parking lot. In the dank newsroom, black soot poured down from the floor above through an opening reporters called "the coal chute."

Despite poor pay and even poorer working conditions the *Press* surprisingly was able to maintain a hard core of very competent, loyal newsmen and editors. They fought well against the rich *Star-Telegram*, perhaps because they were the underdogs, the mom and pop grocery store clerks against the A&P. Through the years, as Cartwright recalled, the *Press*' not only nourished "honest young writers and reporters" but was "a sanctuary for freaks, for idealists, for demonologists, for outcasts, for drunks . . . and curiosity seekers."

There was Puss Ervin, a retired postman who often wrote his bowling column while wearing only his undershirt, and Sick Charley Modesette, who overcame Hodgkins Disease and regularly drank himself into such a stupor that he was forever losing his car, and Nat Lehmerman, who would doublepark his cab and rush into the *Press* to write a quick sports story, and C. L. Douglas, whose lunch often was green peas speared one at a time with a toothpick from an open can, and Jack Mosely, a good reporter who once became so excited over a murder story he fainted.

When the *Press* was good, it was very good, and if not good, it always was outlandish and startling. There was the time during its tabloid years when a deer was struck and killed by a cop car. Police butchered and barbecued the animal for their annual picnic. The *Press*, ever vigilant for the exotic angle, discovered that the deer had been a child's pet and Bud Shrake composed an immortal headline: POLICE EAT KIDS' PET.

Virtually all *Press* reporters eventually encountered Amon Carter. He went with the territory. Few of the entanglements with Amon were placid. During the 1936 Frontier Fiesta, Mary Crutcher was a pretty young girl fresh from college, and assigned to cover the centennial exposition which from start to finish was an Amon Carter production. Carter brought Vice President and Mrs. John Nance Garner to the Fiesta and Mary set out to interview Amon's guests. The publisher took Cactus Jack away to speak with *Star-Telegram* reporters. Mary began talking with Mrs. Garner. Amon returned and saw the two women. He rushed up, "jumped between us and shoved me backward," recalled Crutcher. She got off the ground, dusted herself and continued interviewing Mrs. Garner while Amon fumed.

Jack Gordon, whose black pencil moustache and slick-backed hair gave him the mien of a ladies fancy underwear salesman, was the *Press* entertainment columnist. His beat was the celebrities and all of Amon's friends were celebrities. Gordon faced off against Amon more than any other *Press* newsman. Once Amon brought Will Rogers to Fort Worth for a benefit performance. Gordon was assigned to interview the humorist for an early edition. Rogers arrived by train at mid-morning. Amon had planned a downtown parade for Rogers and the streets were lined with fans. Gordon was waiting when Rogers arrived but Amon brushed the *Press* columnist aside and ushered the humorist into a waiting open sedan.

The parade began with Rogers and Amon in the open car, followed by bands and horses and clowns. Gordon, pressed by his deadline, jumped on the sedan's running board. He began interviewing Rogers. Amon, furious, shouted, "Get the hell off!" Gordon ignored him. Amon stood, shaking his fist at Gordon as hundreds of people cheered from the sidewalks. "I said get the hell off there!" Amon yelled again.

"Aw, Amon," drawled Will, who was enjoying Carter's tirade. "Leave the boy alone. He's just trying to make a living."

Gordon stood on the running board throughout the parade to complete his interview.

Amon hosted Jeanette MacDonald for an early morning press conference in his Fort Worth Club suite. The actress asked reporters not to smoke. Gordon, a dapper, gentle man who chain-smoked black cigars, arrived late. He entered with his usual glowing stogie clutched in his hand, waving it like a baton to greet everyone. Amon ran across the room, grabbed the hand gripping the smoking cigar and pulled the bewildered columnist into the bathroom. Carter held Gordon's hand over the commode, shook it until he dropped the cigar into the water, then walked out without a word.

As a tabloid, the *Press* was bright and brassy and no one took it seriously, especially its own sports staff. Blackie Sherrod, a bear of a man and strict disciplinarian, commanded a four man staff, the antics of which confounded straight news-side reporters and editors, especially Walter Humphrey. Sherrod and his boys had reverence for nothing but good writing.

There was Jerre Todd who, as he arrived to apply for a job, raced through the door and did a baseball hook-slide into the corner of Sherrod's desk.

Sherrod glanced down at Todd and said softly, "You're hired."

Bud Shrake moved over from the news department and wrote fictional sports stories better than the real thing. Dan Jenkins became a kind of utility man and sports columnist whose best stuff, said Cartwright, "had to do with how hard it is to open a package of crackers or buy gasoline." Humphrey never understood how crackers could be the subject of a sports column. Cartwright came from the morning *Star-Telegram* police beat where conventional writing and reporting stifled his imagination.

Sherrod's boys were never ordinary. They read aloud to each other from the writings of Twain and S. J. Perelman, polished and wrote leads days in advance of a sports event, were literate and literary and wrote sports stories that never read like sports stories. They had water pistol wars and chinning contests and broad-jumping competitions, gathered often at Shanghai Jimmy's, a Mexican food cafe, to plot against the *Press* and *Star-Telegram*. One of the schemes involved Crew Slammer, a mythical sports writer they invented. Sherrod's boys promoted their Crew Slammer into the finals of a national Sports Writer of the Year contest.

When the staff broke up and scattered, as it had to, Sherrod became executive sports editor of the Dallas *Times-Herald*. Jenkins, Shrake and Cartwright became successful novelists, especially Jenkins, whose *Semi-Tough* was a national best-seller and popular movie. Jenkins and Shrake became associate editors of *Sports Illustrated*. Shrake and Cartwright wrote screenplays together. Todd opened one of Fort Worth's largest ad agencies.

By the time Sherrod's boys re-invented sports writing, the *Press* had become thoroughly limp and ineffective. Time had killed the spark. The *Press*' brightest days were the 1920s and 1930s when it competed so well the *Star-Telegram* felt obliged to kill off its rival's Pulitzer nomination.

That the lowly *Press* should have been nominated for a journalism Pultizer prize over the dominant *Star-Telegram* is not surprising, given the story's subject matter. Oil scandal. To spread Fort Worth's oil lease swindle shame before the world was, to Amon and the *Star-Telegram*, unthinkable. One did not air dirty linen in public.

Before 1917, Ranger, one hundred miles west of Fort Worth on the brink of West Texas, was a somnolent farming and ranching community, yawning and unambitious, and choking in the dust of a year-long drought. Farms were failing, cattle dying. In the fall of 1917, Texas Pacific Coal Company chanced a highly-speculative oil well near Ranger. The well was a gusher. Overnight, Ranger became the most booming oilboom town in history.

Its population rose within months to thirty thousand. Oil derricks were everywhere, on school playgrounds, in church cemetaries. Everybody was rich. Texas Pacific Coal Company refused an offer of $120,000,000 for its holdings. Failed farmers became mid-afternoon millionaires. Ranger's building permits in a single week totaled $420,000, compared to $53,000 in Houston.

As the nearest large city, Fort Worth became Ranger's oil well supply center, and a boom partner. Amon's city, at the height of the petroleum strike, gained five thousand population a month and ranked seventh in construction in the United States. Amon was ecstatic.

The Ranger strike was never the Golconda speculators believed it to be. It was a product of World War I, which needed the oil to feed its machinery, and a tub-thumping crusade by thousands of oil lease swindlers headquartered in Fort Worth. Theirs was a business of pyramiding greed, and business was good. Armed with leases on a few hundred worthless, drilled-over West Texas acres, a promoter would mail hundreds of thousands of promising letters to potential investors. Once the suckers had paid their money, the swindler would close his office, only to open again a week later under a new corporate name.

Of 2,300 known oil lease swindling firms in Texas, 2,100 were in Fort Worth.

In this maelstrom of oily greed came Dr. Frederick A. Cook, the Arctic explorer debunked by the National Geographic Society in 1909 as the North Pole claimant. The society ruled in favor of Naval Commander Robert Peary's title as the first man to reach the North Pole. Cook spent the next decade defending his story that he, not Peary, first reached the North Pole. By the early 1920s, he was in Wyoming, broke but not without inspiration. Cook spied the Ranger oil boom, and Fort Worth. He opened the Texas Eagle Oil Company of Fort Worth, Texas, spread throughout one floor of a downtown building. Within a year, he merged with 413 other companies, none, as Texas Eagle Oil, owning a single well.

Cook, opining he wanted to make all Americans rich, mailed millions of pieces of promotional letters, and let the cash flow in.

In 1921 Henry Zweifel was appointed United States attorney in Fort Worth. The *Press* began closing in on Doc Cook with a series of stories. By early 1923, Zweifel had enough evidence to prosecute the oily doctor. Prompted by the *Press*' stories, Zweifel went after all the oil lease swindlers, charging most with mail fraud. At one time he had 535 cases working at once.

Doc Cook was sentenced to fourteen years and nine months in Leavenworth.

For its part in crushing Cook and others, the *Press* was nominated for a public service Pulitzer Prize by the Associated Advertising Clubs of the World. It did not win, but only later was it and Fort Worth to learn why.

The Pulitzer Prize committee had queried the *Star-Telegram* on the *Press*' worthiness of the coveted award. Who the original inquiry went to will never be known, but it ended up in the hands of Byron Utecht, a political writer and long-time employee. Utecht promptly gutted the *Press.*

In his reply, Utecht claimed the *Press* had little to do with Cook's successful prosecution, nor any of the other oil lease swindle stories. Utecht quoted Zweifel as saying, "The *Press* had nothing to do with bringing about prosecution of Cook or the many others. . . ." The *Press*, Utecht noted in an aside to the Pulitzer jury, "has only a small street circulation." The *Press* did not win its Pulitzer Prize.

A copy of the condemning letter somehow arrived in the office of the *Press* and July 17, 1924, the paper bannered an intriguing headline: "Here's A Little 'Inside' Stuff, Folks! — It's About The Press, Pulitzer Prize, Star-Telegram and The Oil Stock Crook."

Utecht's letter was printed in full.

Sweet revenge, but momentary. For all of its feistiness, the *Press* never was a challenge to the *Star-Telegram*, never more than a minor irritant, like a bunion. The *Press* self-destructed in 1975, finally written off forever by Scripps-Howard. It had endured twenty years beyond Amon Carter who, for reasons known only to him, allowed the lesser paper to hang around. Once when he cussed the poor *Press* in one of his mad spells, someone asked him why he hated the rival newspaper.

"Because," he snapped, "their gawddamned delivery boy walks across my yard."

AMON

Amon, circa 1901.

Amon in 1903.

Amon and Calvin Coolidge.

Amon and Jack Dempsey in Amon's office after signing for the Tunney fight.

Amon and Charles Lindbergh at the Shady Oaks Ranch House.

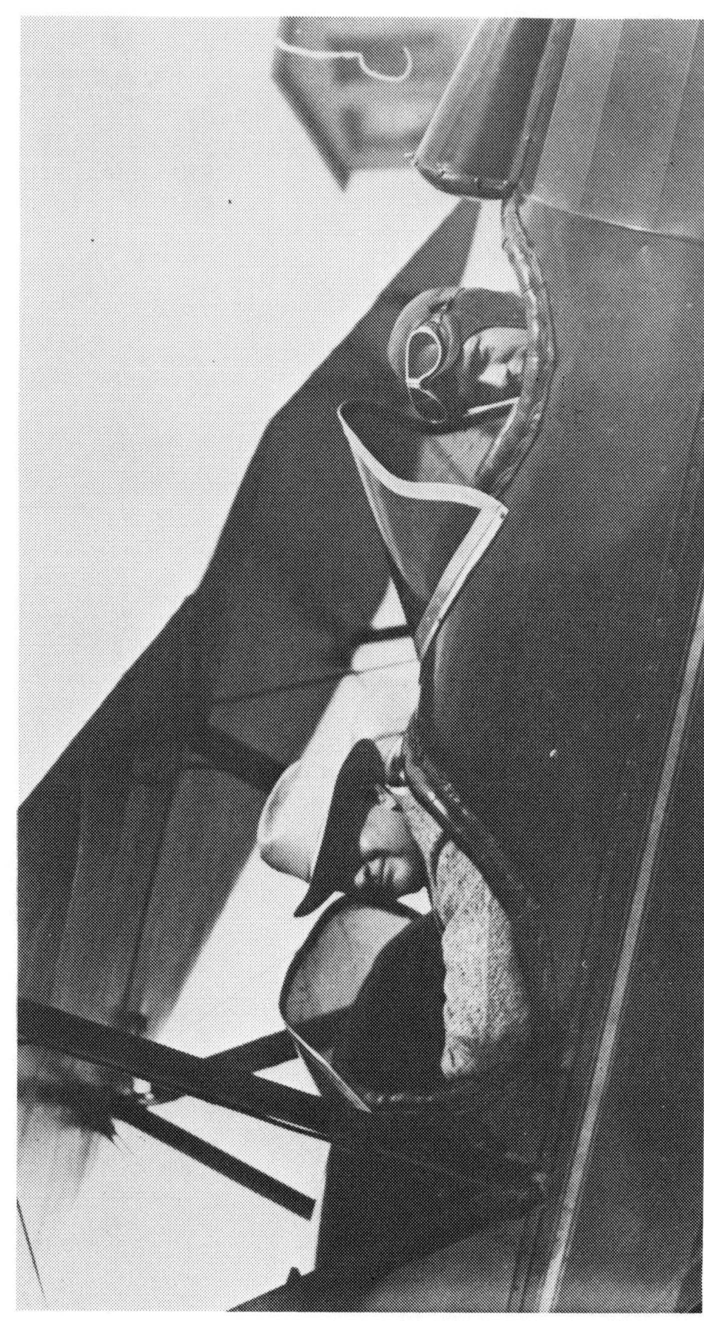

Amon and Charles Lindbergh.

AMON

Amon and John Nance Garner — 1933.

Amon and Jim Farley, Postmaster General, at FDR's 1933 inaugural.

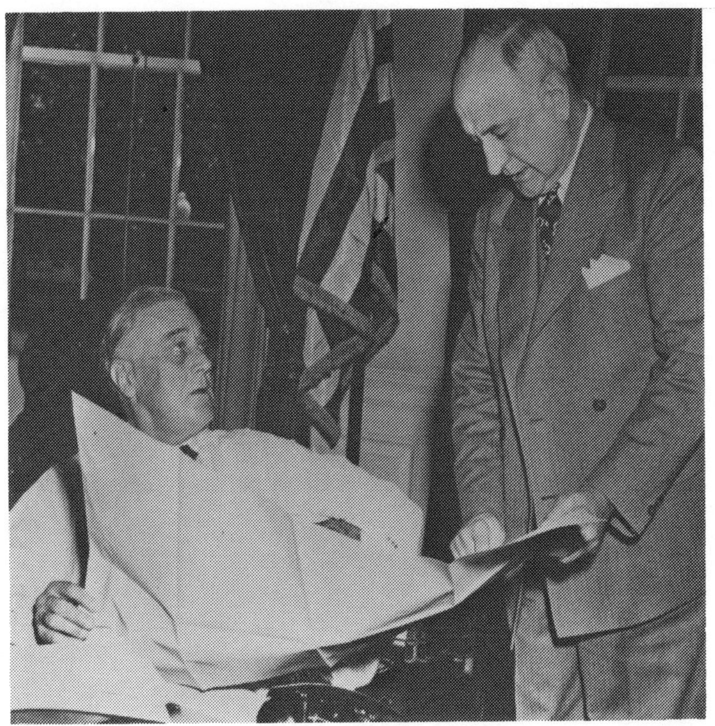

Amon delivering the Big Bend National Park papers to Franklin Roosevelt.

Amon and FDR fishing in one of Amon's Shady Oak bass ponds.

Will Rogers and Amon.

Frank Hawks, Pappy Waggoner, Will Rogers, and Amon.

Will Rogers and Amon.

Sally Rand and girls.

AMON

Early Amon Carter.

Amon on horseback.

Chapter 9

I kinda thought I'd never see
A better host than what I be
But H'elza Maxwell's just a starter
When it comes to Amon Carter.

—Elsa Maxwell, 1938

"'Dad," she asked, "what is the
'Creed of the West?"
"To treat everybody right, then make them treat you right," I replied.

—Frank Norfleet, Norfleet

You are here to please me. Nothing else on earth matters.

—Cecil B. DeMille, to his staff

9

Amon Carter, wrote Alva Johnston, loved crowds like a pickpocket.

Masses turned him on. He glowed and gloried among mobs. Kings and Presidents amused him. Washerwomen delighted him. Celebrities entertained him. He never wanted to be alone. Silence made him nervous and he talked to anyone who would listen, common strangers if friends were not near. He was a great fellow to have people in or, as a finger-breaking checkgrabber, take people out.

People were Amon Carter's fanciest doodads.

As bits of string and tinfoil, old paperclips and pencil stubs, people were collected by Amon. Especially anyone with fame.

Amon was a celebrity groupie.

Perhaps no man in American history knew so many of the high and the mighty and Amon's guest books at

Shady Oak Farm and Suite 10G in the Fort Worth Club read like Fortune's 500 list, like society's blue-blooded roster, like a political rollcall.

Duponts and Mellons and Roosevelts, the Eisenhowers, Babe Ruth and the Whitneys, Amelia Earhart and Prince Bernhardt of the Netherlands, Ken Maynard and Lady Duff Cooper, Doolittle and Rickenbacker and Firestone, Durante, Nimitz and Luce.

Charley McCarthy to Buzz Aldrin, a young lieutenant who one day would become an astronaut and the first man to urinate on the moon — nobody could escape. Anyone with a smidgen of celebrity in or near Fort Worth was Amon's guest at Shady Oak or Suite 10G. Both were bountiful watering holes for pilgrims on transcontinental crossings.

"To visit Fort Worth without meeting Amon Carter," said an English baronet, Sir William Wiseman, "is to see 'Hamlet' without the Prince of Denmark."

In Fort Worth, the famous were Amon's guests, and no arguing. "Nothin' costs nothin', either," as Jimmy Durante described the experience. Amon's hospitality, always munificent, was free, every howdy and handshake of it, and Amon was the lagniappe. He was a grand host, gracious and thoughtful and generous, or as the unbridled cowboy, wildly comic and uninhibited, whichever personality was needed.

"There's no meter on 10G," he was fond of saying when his guests tried to force payment on him. The unofficial slogan of Shady Oak was "Light, stranger, and eat." In either, guests were given bed and board, booze, entertainment and publicity, the latter a special treat for celebrities. A man with a newspaper, radio stations, access to wire services, and one with a genuine brilliance for warm conviviality, was a blessing to those with needs for ego strokings.

Everything was on the house. Amon's house. He paid for it all. No charge on public or private funds, and what must have seemed at times to Bert Honea and

Jimmy North as fiscal madness, had, to Amon, a substantive basis.

He was selling Fort Worth, and no price was too high. In Carter's files is a scrap of paper containing these words: "He who would do some great thing in this short life must apply himself to the work with such a concentration of his forces as to idle spectators who like only to amuse themselves, looks like insanity." The philosophy fit Amon, and entertaining visiting celebrities, whether Hollywood stars or Detroit automobile executives or New York bankers, benefited Fort Worth. To his thinking, whatever he paid was money well spent.

Actually, the *Star-Telegram* paid, perhaps as much as $100,000 a year. Bert Honea, for whom dollars were devine, said he didn't care to add it up. Amon just partied and the *Star-Telegram* paid the freight.

Though he partied most often in Fort Worth, Amon was not above tossing a banquet for Chicago friends or staging a boozy extravaganza in New York. Or wrestling away checks in "21" or the Stork Club or the Gay Nineties where he could order drinks for the house, then lead singalongs in his off-key baritone and recite ribald toasts: "Here's to Eve/The mother of our race/She wore fig leaves/In the proper place. Here's to Adam/The father of us all/He was Johnny on the spot/When the leaves began to fall."

Amon liked to play, and when the need to play struck him, he played, even though friends were not around. New York *World-Telelgram* columnist Frank Farrell reported Carter escorted two Ritz-Carleton room service waiters to the Stork Club "where he partied them." Lucius Beebe, in his *The Big Spenders*, wrote, "Carter's notion of showing good will, and one that was widely approved by its beneficiaries, was to arrive in New York's Waldorf-Astoria for the annual newspaper publishers' convention, take over an entire floor and throw all the keys out the windows into Park Avenue. He then kept open house like a maharaja for the duration."

That was Amon: festive, sociable, hospitable. Peddling Fort Worth. His city needed boosting. Too, his gregarious nature required an audience and his ego enjoyed the friendships. Amon was never without letters and telegrams from his renowned acquaintances. He stuffed his pockets with those communications and without provocation would loose the messages on his Fort Worth friends, bragging outrageously of his companionship with the celebrities. He bored hometown folk endlessly with accounts of escapades among the eminent.

Famous guests were all part of Amon's great conspiracy to promote Fort Worth into a national prominence. Anyone given a party in his honor, photographed and placed on page one, interviewed for the airwaves, gifted with expensive gadgets, was unlikely to forget the occasion or the city or the host. And if the celebrity owned a whit of conscience, he responded when Amon called for help.

Matthew Brush was a railroad executive. He admired aloud the blue drinking glasses at Shady Oak. Amon had paid fifteen dollars each for the crystal glasses but he nevertheless instantly presented Brush with a dozen. Amon wanted Brush in his debt. For years, Carter had been pushing for a new Fort Worth rail terminal. Earlier, he could have had one but he insisted it be larger and more costly than Dallas' terminal and Brush vetoed the deal.

Months after receiving the glasses, Brush telephoned Amon to announce, "We have just voted to build your goddamned union station. We have eleven million dollars to build the station and biggest shops and freight terminal in the Southwest. And now we are all drinking to your health with your glasses.''

''What do you think of that!'' exclaimed Brush.

''Have another drink!'' commanded Amon.

Celebrities, flattered by his attention, charmed by his courtly western manners, responded with respect and friendship. Elsa Maxwell, the legendary hostess, wrote in *Town and Country* that she had four men in her life: ''My father, Caruso, Cole Porter and Amon Carter.'' Damon Runyon also compared Amon with his father, calling Carter a ''breezy swashbuckler of a man.'' Bob Hope authored a magazine article naming Amon the most fascinating man he had ever met. Sidney Smith, the *Gumps* cartoonist, often placed Amon in the comic strip, once having Andy Gump tell Min of an approaching party, ''Amon Carter is bringing the Emperor of China. Fred Bonfils [Denver *Post* publisher] is going to hitch up his buggy for the Prince of Wales.''

As celebrity-happy as he was, Amon pretended a modesty about the whole thing. It was a personal shyness he wore well and one spawning a playful game with his *Star-Telegram* photographers. If there were famous people to be photographed — and there seemed always to be — the cameraman lined up the shot as Amon stood demurely to the side.

Invariably, one of the celebrities would call, ''Amon, come on and get in the picture.''

He had a stock answer which photographers could repeat by rote: ''No, no. Everytime I have my picture in the paper, we lose 5,000 subscribers.''

That was the photographer's cue to say, ''Mr. Carter, I believe we better have you in this picture.''

''All right,'' Amon would reply, obeying reluctantly, ''if you say so.''

Then he stood in the middle of the group where no editor could crop him out, as if one dared.

Amon's zealousy to record on film all his hosted gatherings strained the newspaper's photography department. He always furnished pictures to the guests and the *Star-Telegram* finally hired a lab man who did nothing but print Amon's photos. A common Carter photo order could number as many as seven hundred pictures.

Many of the photos landed on the newspaper's front page hogging space, editors grumbled, that could have been used for real news. For Amon, however, the *Star-Telegram* was but another gear in his Fort Worth-peddling machine. An airport advisory board of the Federal Aviaiton Agency convened in Fort Worth to discuss the city's request for a new air facility. Amon commanded that each man be photographed daily and the pictures published on page one, both morning and evening editions.

The editors howled and Amon explained, "You may think this is silly but it's necessary to get our new airport."

Very little of importance was successful in Fort Worth without Amon Carter's imprimatur. If you sold Amon, you sold the project because he would hurl his publishing forces, his energies, his money, into the enterprise and make it happen. The story of Fort Worth in the first half of this century is the story of Amon Carter hustling this and that event into national exposure. When Amon press-agented, he swept every corner. An example:

In 1941 Fort Worth golfers asked Amon to support their bid for the U.S. Open. According to Bob Considine, and surely this is an exaggeration, Amon thundered, "What the tarnation is a U.S. Open?"

He was told, agreed to help, and the prestigious tournament was held in Fort Worth, smallest city in which the Open had been held.

Amon began promoting. Considine again: "He invited President Roosevelt, all members of his cabinet, Jim Farley, heads of U.S. and Bethlehem Steel, heads of a veritable Dun & Bradstreet bookful of big firms to attend the Open. He sent them all gold badges with their names engraved on them. He chartered floors of hotels, had the city airport cleared for the arrival of private planes and told his city to open its heart to the golfers."

Additionally, Amon hosted five hundred golfers and guests at Shady Oak. Understanding that sports writers would report all that went on around the tournament, he gave each a Shady Oak hat and feted the scribes with a special barbecue. In return, the writers presented Amon with the One-Holer Award — a garishly decorated commode lid — and named him "Texas' Ace in the Hole: Prince of Hosts, Judge of Good Wines, Beautiful Women, Fine Food and Salty Song." Considine and Grantland Rice credited Amon with the tournament's unqualified success, and, incidentally, spread Fort Worth's name coast to coast through their syndicated columns, which is all Carter wanted.

The One-Holer Award plaque was duly posted at Shady Oak Farm, to join the talking steer, tiger skin, cigar store Indians and other esoterical gallimaufry Amon accumulated. He bought the 780-acre farm in 1925 from heirs of George Reynolds, a pioneer West Texas rancher. The farm, spread along shores of Lake Worth, was a landscape of blackjack and live oaks and, in season, Texas bluebonnets, Indian paintbrush and wild daisies. There was a big farm house with shaded veranda and a white picket fence festooned with running roses. Nearby were a barn and corrals and an open-fronted shed which served as a saloon for his extravaganzas, and ponds stocked with bass.

The house was a museum of Amon's curiosities: Mrs. Jarrott's huge dining room table from his boarding house days in Bowie, the china platter on which he served the bully Tarpley's guinea eggs, the furnishings of a small hardware store in keys of cities given Carter and in gilded spades and trowels, the spoils of groundbreakings and cornerstone layings. An array of mounted steer horns and several mounted heads, one stuffed buffalo head. Footballs from Texas Christian University's fighting Horned Frog teams and a baseball autographed by the Black Sox of 1919. A ten-gallon loving cup, post cards, Indian arrowheads, the church bell heard by his mother as a child, a hand-carved desk (one drawer was crammed with bits of string Amon saved for emergencies). Above the fireplace was an intricately designed wicker eagle. President Roosevelt received the bird from an artist in the 1930s. FDR gave it to General Hugh Johnson, who ordered an aide to "send that damned old thing to Amon Carter." But the mantle was dominated by the ignoble, animated head of an enormous longhorn steer. The Shady Oak steer puffed smoke from its nostrils, blinked with red sixty-watt eyes, called guests by their names — called them, in fact, bawdy, outrageous names — and sang off-color songs in a voice with a slight needle scratch. Quite often, the steer whoopeed for Fort Worth and West Texas.

Outside, real Longhorn steers grazed on the lawn, joined by a flop-eared gray mule, the latter a gift from Harold Hough who operated the Hired Hand's Mule Ranch near Decatur — "High-grade fancy mules but not too high-tone to pull a plow." A reconstructed log cabin in which Cynthia Ann Parker, mother of the last great Indian chief, Quannah Parker, lived after her rescue by Colonel Sul Ross. Travelair Monoplane Number 17, retired to the farm in 1931 by the National Air Transport Authority. It had carried Fort Worth's first bundle of airmail and bore the inscription: "To aeronautical inspectors, United States Department of Commerce, August 1, 1931. Mr. Amon Carter has retired this ship to a peaceful existence during its declining years. Its permanent station is his own 'front yard' at Shady Oak Farm. . . . He guarantees it will nevermore take the air in pursuit of pleasure, profit or diversion of any kind. It likewise has been 'retired' on the records of the department in Washington and its existing license number may remain in place until old age and remorse have taken their toll. (Signed) Clarence M. Young, Assistant Secretary of Commerce.'' Additionally, there was the plow that broke ground when Fort Worth's first railroad reached town. A forty-foot flagpole was installed by Paul Whiteman because Amon chided, ''You wouldn't know a flagpole from a fencepost.'' Amon's taste in memoribilia was anything if not novel and diverse.

His parties centered on the open-fronted saloon and through the years it, too, became a repository of miscellany. There was a stuffed horse, on the tail of which Amon sometimes mounted signs — ''Texas Horse's Ass, You've met the New York kind.'' Other signs which changed with the needs of a party: ''Dallas Passports Must Be Validated''; ''Please Do Not Sit on the Crackerbarrel, It Annoys the Cat''; ''The Customer Is Always Right Sometimes''; ''Your Wife Just Phoned,'' and ''The National Bird — Old Crow.'' Above the shed's opening was ''Howdy, Stranger'' in neon, a garish greeting sign Amon swiped from the entrance of Frontier Fiesta in 1936.

In that setting, Amon held a noisy, kaleidoscopic court. Disguised in his cowboy suit, astride the golden palomino, and astraddle the silver-mounted saddle, riding through shoulder-to-shoulder crowds, yippee-ing for Fort Worth and West Texas: Amon at home, at play, an exuberant, unforgettable man.

Shady Oak, observed Alva Johnston, was ''a sort of one-man Bohemian Grove . . . a millionaire and celebrity trap.'' It was there Johnston counted eight billion dollars bellied up to the bar one evening and there, for one large party, that the evening's bartenders were Walter Teagle, president of Standard Oil of New Jersey, Herbert Pratt, president of Standard Oil of New York and Charles Mitchell, president of National City Bank of New York. It was there Jimmy Walker pranced in his high-heeled boots and posed for photographs with old Lan Twohig's scarred horns and there H. L. Mencken, via WBAP radio, spoke of "Yokelry" and America's "Majority of Morons." It was there that young Lyndon Baines Johnson lit into a fellow Democrat, whose name is now forgotten, and was licking the man pretty good when other revelers pulled the brawlers apart, and there dignified Elsa Maxwell fired Amon's sixguns, yippeeing like a soiled dove from Hell's Half Acre. It was there FDR, seated in the rear of a Packard open sedan, cast for and caught a five-pound bass, and there one of the world's richest men, banker Otto Kahn, insisted on paying for his grub by mowing the lawn.

Amon Carter made Shady Oak an escape place where his friends could act out their western fantasies. Lord Sidney Rothermere, board chairman of the London *Daily Mail* and owner of seventy other English publications and newspapers, said of his two months in America, he remembered most the time spent at Shady Oak. The eminent British lord, aides told Amon, would not under any circumstance play cowboy with him. Within a day Amon was calling Rothermere "Sid" and had dressed him in boots and chaps and a huge, high-crowned black hat, the kind worn only by enemies of Hopalong Cassidy. While *Star-Telegram* photographers recorded the scene for posterity, Sid Rothermere, a brand new Texas good ol' boy, fastdrew his .45 caliber hogleg and "held up" a pair of passing cowboys. Amon presented the six gun to Rothermere. The English lord carried it to his castle in the Scottish Highlands where he mounted the pistol in the smoking room as a reminder of adventuring in Amon's wild, wild west.

Amon's Shady Oak soirees mostly were stag affairs where men could whoop it up without offending the womenfolk, but each New Year there was an outing, often lasting forty-eight hours, for both husbands and wives. Though more restrained than normal, the party featured gambling and drinking and invitations were sought eagerly by Fort Worth's high society set.

Other socialties were hand built for the honoree. Amon tossed a twelfth birthday party for Jim Farley's son and outfitted the kid in cowboy duds while March of Time cameras filmed the occasion for nationwide movie audiences. With Otto Kahn, there was a special mint julep in his name, business cards reading, "For Small Loans with Good Collateral and Snappy Interest, See Otto Kahn," and above the bar, a ten-foot-long sign: "Bawl Eagle Saloon, Kuhn, Loeb & Company/Financial Agents." There was a "Shindig" for Farley and Cactus Jack Garner in 1933, with mammoth "Garner for President" banners. Condé Nast, the *Vogue* publisher and Henry Luce of *Time* were inducted into the Longhorn Society of Fort Worth, a mythical organization founded by Amon.

When Amon stood on tables, fired his pistols in the air and shouted "Time to eat!", the menus offered exotic dishes. An American Petroleum Institute menu listed "Panhandle Mountain Oysters without the Fuzz [deep-fried calf testicles]," "Grilled Larded Snowbirds [white-wing doves]" and "Lubricants from the Refinery and A Bit of Tidewater." Guests received deeds to the city, gold badges naming them as Fort Worth police officers and hollow walking canes filled with bourbon [seventeen-year-old Ol Fitzgerald bottled under the Shady Oak label]. The menu for an American Airlines evening in 1945 presented more basic fare: Red beans, blackeyed peas and sowbelly, sweet potato pie, chitlins, watermelon, "light bread," and "rat trap" cheese. The party was hosted, read a card, by "The Sanitary Receptacle Company, Amon G. Carter, Secretary & Treasurer."

Seemingly without effort, Amon could bring in real cowboys and cowgirls and do an honest rodeo or erect a full-curtained stage for more formal entertainment.

Another API party in 1940 was highlighted by the "Shady Oak Follies," starring stripper Vanya Karanova and Kathryn Duffy's all-nude ensemble acting out "Satan's Dream" and "The Devil's Daughter." The acts were imported for the evening from Chicago's Chez Paree.

John Carl Kriendler, the "21" restaurant owner, honeymooned at Shady Oak with a new wife, the Baroness Luisa Dumont de Chassart, and Amon presented her with cowgirl clothes to match her husband's western wardrobe which, he told a *Star-Telegram* reporter, numbered "130 cowboy shirts, five dozen pairs of pants, three dozen western hats, three silver saddles, 26 pairs of boots [and] 20 rodeo suits." The western hat Amon gave the Baroness was swapped for her chapeau, a flowery pillbox thing, duly autographed and tossed among the other famous headgear scattered around the farmhouse.

Receiving a Shady Oak hat was a ritual of being Amon's guest and most — but not all — celebrities received one of the famous western toppers. It was a timeworn and expensive gesture by Amon. The hats cost thirty-five dollars each and Amon bought them in such numbers that *Hat Life*, an industry publication, proclaimed him the "world's greatest retail hat customer." Originally, the hats were huge, wide-brimmed, high-crowned, either black or white. Traditional western hats. Amon bought the western headgear from Borsalina Company of Italy, but when Mussolini declared war on Ethiopia, Carter sought an American manufacturer. The Stetson Company, after months of design research, began producing the Shady Oak model for Amon. He bought them through Washer Bros., a Fort Worth store. Stetson's "Open Road" Shady Oak hat was of the "silver belly shade," had a shorter crown and brim of 2 2/3 inches, looked western but could be worn in Washington or New York without ridicule.

No one knows how many hats Amon gave away, but at least thousands. The hat became his trademark, and for three decades many of America's best-known personalities wore nothing but Amon Carter Shady Oak hats. Patrick Hurley, FDR's first secretary of war, Will Rogers, Bernard Baruch and Cornelius Vanderbilt Whitney once met for lunch in Los Angeles and each was wearing a Shady Oak hat.

There was a ritual to receiving the hat. First, the donee had to exchange and autograph his own hat. "Just another bum hat trade" and "This hat is a damn sight better than I am trading for" were Will Rogers' comments on two hats he swapped. Inscribed on the new hatband was "Shady Oak Farm, Fort Worth, Texas, Where the West Begins. The Latch String Always Hangs Outside. Amon Carter." In bestowing the hat, Amon warned, "Now, don't leave this any place you shouldn't. My name's in it."

Additionally, the ceremony, said reporter Mack Williams, was adjudged by a rigid pecking order. "At the bottom of the ladder were those who received a Shady Oak hat with no mention in the *Star-Telegram*." More important visitors received a hat and a small story played inside. Next level was a hat plus a one-column picture. Biggest shots of all, remembered Williams, received their hats while standing in front of the John Nance Garner bust in Amon's office. Two column pictures of those presentations were printed on the *Star-Telegram*'s front page.

Star-Telegram reporters always were dragged into Amon's civic boosting business, and hats were a vital ingredient. Bascom Timmons, the newspaper's Washington bureau chief, had, among usual duties, the task of maintaining a file on head sizes of every important Washington official. Periodically, Amon hosted a Washington dinner and distributed hats. To avoid bruised egos, he awarded the headgear in alphabetical order.

Williams was enmeshed in a hat caper when Douglas MacArthur came to Texas. Truman fired the General and friends urged him to seek the Presidency. To test the political waters, MacArthur scheduled a series of speeches in Texas. Scripps-Howard newspapers sponsored the speaking tour. Williams and photographer John Mazziotto were assigned to follow MacArthur around the state. Newsmen from every important American paper, all wire services and many foreign journalists were in the press party and the *Star-Telegram* men were awed to be among their profession's big names.

In Houston, final stop before the general came to Fort Worth, Williams was preparing to take notes on the speech. A messenger tapped him on the shoulder. Telephone call from the office, a *Star-Telegram* editor. He told Williams, "Mr. Carter wants you to get the hat size of every out-of-town reporter covering MacArthur. He wants to give them Shady Oak hats when they get to Fort Worth."

"I can get them for you in an hour," replied Williams. "The general's speaking and I have to cover it."

"Hold on a minute," instructed the editor. He left the line.

The editor returned, and said, " . . . uh . . . Mr. Carter says to hell with the speech. Get those hat sizes now."

Williams later recorded his feelings: "So while General MacArthur spoke for the ages, and the world's best reporters scribbled busily, the only notes I made were sizes copied from hats piled on a press room bench. Mr. Carter had his own priorities."

Just why and when Amon Carter began giving away western hats has been lost to history but perhaps the tradition began as early as 1923 when he attended a London advertising conference. The delegates were invited to a morning garden party at St. James Palace. The Prince of Wales [later, Duke of Windsor] was to host the affair. Amon struck on the idea of presenting a cowboy hat to the prince. He spoke with several minions, all of whom pooh-poohed the idea, indicating that British royalty would never knowingly participate in such an undignified matter.

At 11:30 a.m., July 22, Amon arrived at the palace dressed in striped morning pants and his movie-villain-black cowboy hat which at the very least, said New York *Sun* publisher Colonel Gilbert Hodges, arrested everyone's immediate attention. Especially the Prince's aides, who attempted to head Amon off at the pass. He charged through them, to the startled prince and went into his presentation spiel. The prince was delighted, reported *Printer's Ink*, and said a western hat was exactly what he always had wanted. That even may have been the truth because in August the prince passed through New York to his Canadian ranch and was photographed by the New York *World*. The royal scion smiled broadly under Amon's cowboy hat.

Amon asked for and received the prince's autographed derby in return for the western hat, and that became the first of a large collection. FDR's Panama was there and an old felt hat of John Nance Garner's, and Doolittle's aviator cap, Bull Halsey's admiral headgear, President Truman's gray hat "worn in my senatorial campaign and the campaign for vice-president."

Truman, whom Amon did not like because of HST's anti-Texas stance on off-shore oil, was given only the standard Shady Oak hat, as were Presidents Coolidge and Hoover. There was another, very special, Stetson worn by Amon and a few of his peers, among them FDR and Churchill. It was pure beaver, embellished by ermine, and cost $150. Hornby and Freiburg, a Chicago men's store, displayed one of the fancy hats. The accompanying sign read: "This $150 Stetson is the finest hat we know of. It is a duplicate of the one worn by Amon Carter, picturesque and influential Fort Worth publisher."

Those Shady Oak hats were presented in distinctive red satin cases. His lesser hats were handed over in bunches, to whole football teams, to boards of directors, to an entire Hollywood cast attending a world premiere in Fort Worth. The record was two thousand hats given in one evening to delegates of an American Petroleum Institute convention.

Shady Oak hats became part of the Amon Carter legend and columnists often wrote of the Stetsons. Damon Runyon, after the 1936 election, told of a Republican who bet a Democratic friend that Roosevelt would not carry twenty states. The Republican promised to eat his hat if he lost. He was wearing a Shady Oak hat, and as Runyon explained, "The Indians in Texas collect Mr. Carter's discarded hats and use them for teepees. The hats are quite roomy."

The Republican, said Runyon, had bitten off more than he could chew.

A French chef was located who claimed he "once cooked a buffalo, so why not a hat?" The chef pounded it thoroughly with a sledgehammer and then broiled it over charcoal ". . . basting it constantly in its own juices."

Delicately, the chef cut Amon's hat "into thin slices and served [it] with a rich deviled sauce. The man said it tasted better than spinach. It had a fine nutty taste."

Amon's hats, bestowed by the thousands, spread throughout the United States, publicized by the *Star-Telegram**, wire services and national columnists were the most famous of his gifts, but, as a very giving

*Involved though they were with the hat conspiracies, and lust though they might for the expensive headgear, *Star-Telegram* newsmen were never considered eligible receivers. George Dolan, for example, admired the hats. He wanted one. Once he was drafted to cover a hat presentation to Harvey Firestone and other tire company executives in Suite 10G. Amon asked for the crowd to call out hat sizes, then selected the proper size for each man. Finished, Amon was aware one man — Dolan — did not have a hat. "What about you?" he asked. Delighted, but wary, Dolan replied, ". . . uh . . . Mr. Carter, I work for you." "Oh, muttered man, Carter had his cupboard overflowing with largess.

Alva Johnston catalogued the branches of Amon's Thanksgiving and Christmas doles, in order of importance, as "The Papershelled Pecan Peerage, the Pink-Meated Grapefruit Legion, the Texas Shady Oak Hat Order, the Hundred Pound Watermelon Cast and the Smoked Turkey Aristocracy."

Johnston overlooked some loot: Diamond-encrusted silver buckles and hand-tooled leather belts, flowers, copies of Amon's white vicuna coat, cigars, steer horns, steaks, silver-mounted saddles, fancy doodads he picked up here and there. Amon always was giving somebody something. Once Billy Rose gave Amon a mammoth leather chair. Carter liked it so well he bought six more for wives of his Fort Worth friends. One wife protested that the chair did not match her other furniture. Amon replied that he didn't care, the chair was hers anyway, and it was.

If the wife was miffed by a gift she didn't want, possibly she was placated the following Christmas when Amon sent her nylons and flowers. He knew the value of pillow talk and never forgot wives of hometown friends or the famous men he courted for Fort Worth. And he wooed the attention of secretaries in Washington and New York with flowers and perfumes and other feminine knicknacks to grease his entree to their important bosses. Amon, who foisted wrong-sized picture frames on the unsuspecting but always left them happy, was ever vigilant of the need to keep his fences mended.

Amon and closed the closet door on Dolan's hat. Only Jack Butler, photographers Al Panzera and John Mazziotto are known to have received a hat. Panzera and Mazziotto photographed Amon presenting hats to a TCU football team. Afterwards, he told them to select hats for themselves. Panzera, a misplaced New Yorker, wore his hat home to Brooklyn and presented it to his father. Later, the father wrote that he took the famous Shady Oak topper to a milliner, had the brim trimmed, and made a "real good hat of it." Butler was executive editor and recovering from open heart surgery when Amon Carter Junior presented him with the last official Amon Carter Shady Oak hat.

The ritual of holiday giving became, as the Shady Oak hat, a symbol of Amon Carter. America's famous, its rich high and mighty, clammered for the booty flowing from Fort Worth like street corner waifs scrambling for pocket change. And there indeed was a ranking to it all. The hat, given any time of the year, was conferred at Amon's whim but, as plastic ashtrays and post cards, was as much a souvenir of Fort Worth as emblematic of Carter. Other gifts were awarded by Amon's notion of the receiver's friendship and/or his past, present, and future importance to the city and West Texas, or the condition of his anger at the moment.

Complicated coded lists were maintained by Katrine Deakins, his secretary, and a name could appear on a master register for all holiday offerings or merely be catalogued as worthy for one item. Lists changed from year to year by the vagaries of Amon's temper. Many men, escpecially in Fort Worth, were removed from the holiday larder for transgressions, either real or imagined, unto Amon. Lyndon Johnson was lopped off all gift rosters. Governor James Allred, whom Amon never liked, was demoted from watermelons to grapefruit.

Pecans and grapefruit were minor stuff. Watermelons, turkeys, steaks and diamond-studded buckles were the big guns.

Weeks before shipping his gifts each year, Amon sent expansive letters extolling the ever-mounting virtues of Fort Worth and West Texas, noting, almost as an afterthought, that he and the Hired Hand were sending "a little something" for the holidays. The swag went out from Fort Worth, elaborately packaged and bulging with more propaganda. A letter written by the Hired Hand — Harold Hough — accompanied the gift.

Fruit and pecans were shipped through the Ben E. Keith Company and box stickers bore the message "Longhorn Brand/Grown in Texas especially for the Fort Worth *Star-Telegram*."

Amon practiced a small deceit, pretending the watermelons grew at Shady Oak. Actually, they came from sandy loam farmers in Parker County, twenty miles west of Fort Worth, and were enormous, weighing seventy pounds or more. Each was padded by straw, packed in a galvanized tub and the annual shipment filled three boxcars. In the beginning, Amon's turkeys were shipped live in wooden crates but later he switched to smoked birds prepared by Ethel Van Zandt. Each buckle was studded with at least sixteen diamonds and was designed by a jeweler of the Fair, a Fort Worth department store. The buckles cost $350.

The steaks came after the holidays. Each year Amon purchased the stock show grand champion steer, paying up to $6,000 for the prized animal. He had the steer sliced into steaks, frozen and airshipped via American Airlines to an elite list of men. In Washington, it became another of Timmon's journalistic duties to hand-deliver steaks to political bigwigs.

Amon's gift priorities were capricious but generally Presidents received the entire load, lesser men something less. Nelson Rockefeller went from grapefruit to pecans to watermelons and back to grapefruit in successive years. Mayor Fiorello LaGuardia of New York City, and Minnie Hutchinson of Bowie, Texas, a widow, were paired on the grapefruit roll. Oilman Harry Sinclair, sentenced for his part in the Teapot Dome scandal, received pecans while in prison. Paul Whiteman, columnists Bugs Baer and Damon Runyon, W. R. Hearst and golfer Bobby Jones were among the select diamond buckle crowd. Sherman Billingsley, the Stork Club owner, Otto Kahn, Rube Goldberg and a DuPont or two received steaks.

Watermelons, as many as five hundred at a time, were directed to a large catalog of celebrities, including Tris Speaker, Tex Rickard, J. C. Penney, Sam Goldwyn and Edgar A. Guest — the latter responded with a perfectly awful poem titled *A Friend in Texas*: "For once every year out of Texas, a Friend/A red-headed melon remembers to send."

Hough's letters, gems of Texas humor, were written under the aegis of "The Truth Society" ("Truth must be protected from abuse and overwork"). He always described the rigors of harvesting the foodstuff: "Your melon, originating from fancy seeds and growing in the dark, had to be killed. It grew so fast it pulled the vines all over the patch and wore out the little melons, so we killed it with an ax to protect the rest."

Once Amon declared he wanted to grow monogrammed watermelons and experimented with scratching initials on the young fruit. At maturity, however, the letters became lumpy and illegible.

Paul Whiteman had an idea. "The way to do it," advised the bandleader, "is to paste gummed letters on the melons. Get the kind of letters they paste on hatbands and paste the name on the melons. The letters will be stenciled in white under the letters."

Amon thought the idea splendid and names were pasted on five hundred melons. A week before harvest time, a farmer called to say field mice had eaten every famous name. Next year Hough suggested adhesive tape and Amon tested the idea on a few melons. Field mice did not like the taste of adhesive tape but it dried, curled and fell off most of the experimental melons. Those few successful autograph melons were sent and Hough called them "self-pronouncing." Amon abandoned his dream of personalized watermelons.

Each shipment of gifts contained drawings of Hough tending turkeys or struggling with oversized melons. One year there was a photograph of Hough dressed in overalls standing beside a tractor. Financier Otto Kahn was seated on the machine pretending that he, one of the world's richest men, was a Shady Oak stoop laborer. Another year, Amon sent pictures of every Fort Worth structure bearing his name, a conceit which would have shamed a lesser man.

Of all edible gifts, Amon's turkeys were most coveted by his friends and men with only grapefruit or pecan standing lusted in vain for the smoked gobblers.

The birds graced White House holiday tables for three decades, even before Amon was forced to give up his live turkey program. "Have expressed to you a 31-pound Texas Tom Turkey strong enough to carry a good-sized saddle and which you may ride before eating," Hough wrote to President Coolidge. Silent Cal had no problem with his live Christmas dinner. He merely turned it over to the White House chef. Those lacking Presidential prerogatives, however, were as bewildered as if they had been confronted with a Tibetan yak. Living, gobbling Texas turkeys were alien to corporate offices and city apartments.

Amon personally delivered two live toms on leashes to Mayor Jimmy Walker who graciously, if uncomfortably, posed for photos with the birds. After Amon departed, Walker, disturbed by the loud gobbling and mounting piles of turkey droppings, ordered the beasts sent to Central Park Zoo.

What to do with turkeys in the city? "The modern New York apartment is not designed with an eye to the accomodation of live turkeys," explained the New York *Sun,* describing the experience of Gilbert Hodges, its publisher. A twenty-five pound turkey, said the *Sun*, arrived by van. The driver confronted the doorman, asking for for Hodges. "I got a toikey for him," said the driver.

"You have a what, my good man?" questioned the ritzy doorman.

"Toikey, toikey! I said it plain. Don't you know English?"

"If I am supposed to understand that you are delivering a turkey to this house for Mr. Hodges, you should know enough to take it to the service entrance."

"Aw, go chase yourself 'round the block. It ain't that kind of toikey."

The crate was muscled to the sidewalk and together, doorman and van driver lugged it to the Hodges' apartment. ''Mr. and Mrs. Hodges . . . were thoroughly puzzled as to what could be done for the housing and entertainment of their startling visitor,'' reported the *Sun*. Hodges' solution was to rent an apartment across the hall where the bird was lodged and fed for more than a week while the couple sought a butcher brave enough to tackle the job of converting tom into dinner.

Geoffrey Konta, a New York attorney, had to hide his turkey in his building's basement. Bob Small, a Washington newspaperman, told of his tom. It arrived when only his children were at home. The kids released the bird. It attacked them. Later, Small chased it upstairs and down before subduing the turkey with a baseball bat. Herbert Jones, a New York advertising executive, wired, ''The Texas Tom arrived in good shape with enough fertilizer to supply requirements of my farm.'' Chicago *Tribune* Publisher Robert McCormick wrote, ''The ostrich arrived in good order. The first thing it did was to lay an egg.'' Henry Milholland, vice president of the Pittsburgh *Press*, related that his uncrated turkey ''immediately hopped up on my desk and backfired all over me and the office.'' O. R. Boyd, assistant general secretary of the American Petroleum Institute said he was home sick when the turkey was delivered to his office. Boyd's secretary sent the bird home by taxi, the cabdriver leading it like a fox terrier.

Hough described the turkeys as ''so large you only need eight to make a dozen.'' Not all recipients were subdued by their live gifts. Bud Fisher shipped his to a farm near Lake Mahopac, New York. He became friendly with it and from time to time the bird appeared in his Mutt & Jeff comic strip. The bird died of old age at the farm. Harry Sinclair wrote, ''I have taken him for a walk along Fifth Avenue, tea at the Ritz and the theater at night.''

Underwood Nazro, a Houston oilman, noted, "He was so beautiful and aristocratic that we would have liked to allow him to strut in his royal splendor but he, like many aristocrats and royalty, strutted too much and the mob turned on him, cut off his head and devoured him. Sic Transit Gloria."

Anguished wails flowing from the northeast forced Amon to quit his live dinner project. He switched to smoked birds, which necessarily limited the number of turkeys and made them all the more valuable.

Amon's gifts were manna for his friends but, too, they were shamefully blatant bribes to keep Fort Worth in the minds of men who could shape the city's destiny. Amon never denied that, but he, being a neurotically generous man, delighted in his orgy of giving.

He gave much, and often, and only once did a gift embarrass him.

After World War II, General Jonathan Wainwright, the Pacific hero and Japanese prisoner, visited Fort Worth. Naturally, Amon immediatly scheduled a dinner honoring Wainwright.

The general, an outdoors enthusiast, was given a distinctive gift. A blooded Texas hunting dog. Amon proudly presented the dog to Wainwright and passed over its leash.

As Wainwright spoke a grateful thanks, the dog stood beside the general, raised its leg and peed all over the foot that had survived the Bataan death march.

10

The main obligation is to amuse yourself.

—S. J. Perelman

I spied a dear cow boy, wrapped in white linen.
Wrapped up in white linen as cold as the day.

Verse I, Streets of Laredo

Amon Carter is returning by airplane from South America. Annexation of that continent to Fort Worth has not been announced yet.

—Dallas Journal, *1934*

They remind me of the Davis Mountains in West Texas.

—Amon's appraisal of the Andes Mountains

Chapter 10

When, in 1911, Cal Rodgers flew from the Atlantic to the Pacific and only crashed sixteen times, his feat was felt to be a kind of miracle. No one had believed a transcontinental flight was possible, not even the Wright Brothers who sold Rodgers an airplane for the insane journey. Well, *Vin Fiz*, a new soft drink, probably believed the impossible was possible. It was sponsor of the historic flight. Rodgers left from a New York racetrack and flew only a hundred miles before crashing into a chicken coop. After paying for the dead chickens and repairing his bi-plane, Daredevil Cal piloted his flying machine west along shores of the Great Lakes to Chicago, then turned Southwest to St. Louis and Oklahoma. In Mid-October, Rodgers flew into Texas, racing, he said, an eagle before settling his plane into a pasture on Fort Worth's north side. Ten thousand people cheered. Rodgers climbed out of the plane, and there was Amon Carter, first in line to shake his hand.

Amon worshipped airplanes, the rattling gimmickry of them, their adventure, the sheer thrill of being up there with those metaphorical canvas and baling wire butterflies. Airplanes were a focal point of Amon's life from the first moment he saw one, possibly as early as 1909 in New York City. He flew first about 1915, and from that experience on, said a friend, "Amon always liked to be on a plane going somewhere."

Months before Rodgers crashed his way across America, Amon promoted the first airplanes into Fort Worth. He and the *Star-Telegram* raised ten thousand dollars by public subscription to sponsor the International Aviators, a group of Frenchmen touring the United States to pique interest in the flying machine. The Frenchmen brought their airplanes — by train — to Fort Worth and demonstrated their skill at staying aloft, often for as long as five minutes. It was heady doings in Fort Worth, and Amon predicted that airplanes one day would circle the earth.

He was so taken with airplanes that he and the *Star-Telegram*'s artist conceived a fullpage futuristic drawing depicting the newspaper being delivered to homes by air.*

By 1917 Amon had lured three World War I flying fields to Fort Worth as training sites for Army aviators. His political connections brought the first airmail service to Texas in 1925. By his urging and with PWA money from his Washington friends, Fort Worth's municipal airport was expanded to accommodate early passenger planes.

He stole the Southern Division of American Airlines from Dallas and moved it to Fort Worth, but the deal was successful only because Amon took a harrow-

*Curiously, the *Star-Telegram* actually delivered one day's edition partially by airplane. In the early 1920s heavy rains flooded the Trinity River and blocked automobile traffic. That day's editions were flown over the river and dropped in large bundles. Bert Honea collected the newspapers and delivered them to westside homes.

ing flight to New York with Frank Hawks, a pioneer aviator who established several early speed records. Amon had to reach New York City to sign agreement papers for the airline headquarters move. Hawks was in Fort Worth to visit relatives. Weather was too poor for commercial airliners, but Hawks offered to fly Amon in his Lockheed. The men flew out of Fort Worth on a stormy March afternoon, bouncing through thunderstorms so violent that winds tore fabric from the plane's right wing. Over Alabama, as Hawks later told reporters, "There was a big clap of thunder and lightning and I ducked my head down. I heard the motor missing and felt the ship losing altitude." They made an emergency landing in Birmingham where Hawks tinkered with the plane's motor and Amon ate ham sandwiches. Then they swept again into the rainclouds. The eleven hour and thirty-five minute flight unnerved Amon who claimed, "Those were the worst storms I ever saw." But he was there to sign the papers. He rode the train back to Fort Worth.

At that time the regional headquarters of Southern Air Transport — which would become American Airlines — was the largest commercial system of the young industry. Earlier there was Texas Air Transport, founded by the eccentric snuff-dipping Alva Pearl Barrett. One of Barrett's idiosyncratic beliefs was in the daily singing of "My old fiddle, she's tuned up good; Best old fiddle in the neighborhood; ting-aling-aling, ting-aling-aling, tee-dee." Each morning he lined up his employees and had them sing the tune. TAT carried passengers and mail but derived the bulk of its income from selling five dollar thrill rides in Fort Worth. Amon had helped Barrett obtain financing for his small airline, and he was one of six men who invested $57,000 in TAT. The airline merged with other small commercial passenger firms to become Southern Air Transport, which then had landing rights at all important airfields from Atlanta to Los Angeles, including a convict camp near Monroe, Lousisiana. A syndicate ultimately bought up SAT and renamed it American Airlines, and Amon became a board member and largest stockholder.

It was Amon's influence that brought Carswell Air Force Base, a Strategic Air Command facility, to Fort Worth, and through the years he hosted aviation's most celebrated fliers, from Lindbergh to Amelia Earhart to Eddie Rickenbacker. There was the time when the entire American air force, led by its inventor, Benjamin Foulois, and numbering four pilots and planes, came to his city to be feted by Amon. Amon and airplanes were inseparable.

In the 1930s when American aviation was pioneering world commercial routes, Amon was there to participate in its beginnings. He was a guest on all Pan American World Airways inaugural flights, a cowboy Magellan exploring a new age.

First was the Pan Am Miami to South America flight in August-September, 1934, when the huge flying boat hopped from river to river taking its fuel from fifty-five gallon metal drums shipped ahead and stored. When he returned, Amon wrote an introduction for the diary of Ed Swasey, vice president of Hearst's *American Weekly*, titled "The Thrill of Progress." Amon published the diary over two full pages in the *Star-Telegram*, with a route map and a picture of him standing beside the Clipper floating on a Brazilian river while almost naked Indians muscled the heavy fuel drums to the plane.

In 1936, Pan American flew Amon; Roy Howard, the Scripps-Howard president; Juan Trippe, Pan Am's president; Paul Patterson, publisher of the Baltimore *Sun*; California Senator William McAdoo, and Cornelius Vanderbilt Whitney, the board chairman of Pan American, across the Pacific to Hawaii and the Philippines. Amon's name was second on the waiting list for the historic flight, placed there by his friend, Will Rogers, four years earlier when the airline began planning the route. Rogers asked that his name be placed on the roster, and added, "Put Amon Carter down, too. He wouldn't miss a chance like this."

After Rogers was killed in the Alaskan plane crash, Amon was moved up to the first position. Eleven hundred persons applied for one of six passenger spots. A movie actress, told she was number 319 on the list, offered to charter the inaugural flight to insure a seat.

In late September, Amon joined the others in Alameda, California, on San Francisco's bay, for the 2,410 mile journey to Honolulu, which was to be the world's then-longest non-stop commercial flight. As befitting the occasion, the men wore tuxedoes for the plane's departure, which was delayed when McAdoo forgot to kiss his wife goodbye. The launch ferrying the passengers to the seaplane returned to shore for the Senator to perform that neglected chore.

The plane landed safely in Honolulu, where the men spent several days resting for the next leg of their flight. A photograph showed Amon standing on the white sand beach at Waikiki, in front of the Ala Moana Hotel. He was dressed in his ice cream-white suit and the semi-cowboy rig of big hat and boots, his face almost obscured by layers of orchid leis.

The Clipper flight continued to Midway where Amon, in a longish mock ceremony, organized the first Chamber of Commerce for that isolated Pacific isle. Trippe named the publisher mayor of Midway. Then Guam where, said the Los Angeles *Times*, Amon tasted a tree oyster — a kind of fungus — and pronounced it almost edible. In Manila, Manual Quezon, the Philippines' president, hosted the men, exchanging and autographing one of his tropical hats for an Amon Carter Shady Oak Stetson.

Amon flew on to Hong Kong, where he bought thousands of dollars worth of Oriental doodads and gifts for his family, and sampled boiled shark fin for the first and last times in his life. Returning, everyone except

Amon bragged that they had read *Gone With the Wind* during the long flights. Back on Midway, Amon asked the pilot to radio an emergency call for the TCU-Texas A&M football score.

In 1939, Amon was aboard as Pan American inaugurated the last of its major routes, the flight from New York across the North Atlantic to England. He and nineteen others, including Howard and Patterson, Mrs. Ogden Reid, vice president of the New York *Herald Tribune*, and John Cowles, the Minneapolis *Star* publisher, flew from New York's seaplane basin July 8 for the nineteen hour and thirty-four minute flight to Southhampton.

Passengers passed their time playing penny-ante poker and Chinese checkers and missed the flight's drama as they slept. Midway over the Atlantic, a motor quit, and the flight engineer crawled out on a catwalk to the wing and repaired the engine.

In England, the *Times* inspected "the tall, bronzed Texas newspaper king" and pronounced him "picturesque" in his "cowboy hat, trousers tucked into ornamental blue, white and brown boots." He was, said the Associated Press, the "cynosure of all eyes. . . ."

Interviewed by the London *Evening News*, Amon bragged, "Yes, flying's a bad habit for us. When I came up from Southhampton last night, it was the first time I'd been on a train in five years. Altogether, I've been 300,000 miles by plane."

Flying back to America, the Clipper paused in Ireland, splashing down on the River Shannon near the village of Foynes, in County Limerick. A long motor-launch sped to the plane. A group of "Foynes Cowboys" unfurled a banner: "We Want Carter."

Amon stepped from the plane, waving and calling, "Top of the morning, you Irish folk."

He was handed a scroll. It read:

> I, Cornelius Aloysius Georgius Fitzgerald, of the clan, Fitzgerald, horsemen of renown, direct descendant of the

> Fitzgerald, first king of Ireland, whose ancestral home was in Foynes, do hereby extend greeting to the mighty Carter of Texas, son of the Lone Star State. I also, on behalf of the Foynes Cowboy Association, challenge the said Mighty Carter to ride an Irish Bronco. The bet — freedom of Foynes against his ten gallon hat. Greetings, son of Texas. I am finished.

In the village, Amon was led to his bronco, a twenty-year-old donkey named "Manna."

Delighted, Amon hopped aboard the donkey's back and rode it through the streets of Foynes as villagers cheered. His bet — and town — won, Amon magnanimously returned Foynes to its owners and left behind his white Stetson.

Any man who loved airplanes and flying as much as Amon had to have his own airport. As early as 1925, Amon helped the city obtain a permanent government-approved airport on Fort Worth's north side, and in 1937, the air facility was expanded and improved. Meacham Field, however, was hemmed in by development and could not be enlarged for international flights, which Amon wanted for his city. For more than a decade Amon tried to interest Dallas in a joint airport venture. The larger city, which felt about Amon the way Ahab felt about the white whale, almost acquiesced to Carter's proposal that Fort Worth and Dallas build the "biggest and best airport in the world."

In the early 1940s, the cities studied the situation and set about to plan for the airport halfway between their boundaries. An airport engineering firm suggested the terminal building be placed on a site which necessitated facing it toward Fort Worth.

Dallas Mayor Woodall Rodgers ranted in an interview that the terminal rear would point toward his city, and that positioning was highly insulting. Amon answered the mayor with a two thousand word telegram, reprinted of course in the *Star-Telegram*. He chastised

Rodgers for the mayor's narrow vision, noting that the rear-door feature "may not be as important as you think." He pointed out that the proposed airport site was one mile nearer Dallas than Fort Worth and his city was not complaining.

He added:

> Some of us in Fort Worth are just plain country folks and while we may still eat with our knife we have felt somewhat encouraged because we have learned to do it with skill . . . while you were willing always for a 50-50 deal we had found that to mean one horse and one rabbit and unfortunately we in Fort Worth had always gotten the rabbit and of late you had even been skinning the rabbit for us.

The real reason Dallas dissolved the mutual airport agreement was, naturally, Amon Carter. Dallas leaders feared he would do with the shared airport as he did with Fort Worth, as he damned well pleased. Dallas had no plans to build Amon an airport.

For five years, Amon's airport project was promoted off-stage, away from the public's eye. He continued to woo the Federal Aviation Agency and other sources of government monies, sought support from airlines, and badgered his political friends. As airplanes grew larger and faster and jet-powered, it became obvious that Meacham Field's limited facilities could never accommodate passenger planes of the future. Meanwhile, Dallas' Love Field was busier and larger and Fort Worthers, to Amon's consternation, had to go there for many flights.

Amon was determined to build Fort Worth — and himself — an airport.

First, he sold the city a 2,155-acre tract of land south of Fort Worth for $628,699. There, he would build an airport. The FAA, however, decided the area was not suitable. Moreover, there still was fragile hope that Dallas would share the new air facility, and the southern site was too far away. Midway Airport, a tiny private strip near Arlington, the hyphen between Fort Worth and Dallas, became available. Fort Worth optioned the land, bought additional adjacent acres and extended its city limits to include the new airport site.

Amon repurchased the 2,155 acres for a cash price of $685,000, providing taxpayers with a profit and badly needed funds with which to start planning for the airport.

Amon set about to sell the idea — never a very popular one — to the citizens. Editors of the period remember that the *Star-Telegram*'s coverage of the airport program and progress "was totally one-sided." "Opposition simply was not reported," said one.

Amon, while promising that the airport would be the nation's best, insisted he be consulted on every word written about the new air center.

A few months before the airport opened in 1953, Amon, Attorney Raymond Buck, and Red Mosier, an American Airlines' vice president, met in Suite 10G of the Fort Worth Club. They had drinks. Mosier had flown from New York that afternoon. He told of his conversation with the plane's pilot about Fort Worth's new airport. According to Mosier, the pilot proclaimed the new field to be the safest in the United States.

The men continued drinking. Amon, mulling over the anonymous pilot's safety opinions, concluded the public should know about such matters and summoned a *Star-Telegram* reporter. The man arrived in the suite ". . . finding Carter, Mosier and Buck partaking of liquid refreshments, of which there was an abundant quantity on a large serving table on wheels."

Carter and Mosier waxed enthusiastically about how wonderful the airport would be. Mosier related that the pilot with whom he had spoken said Fort Worth's airport would be the world's safest and fliers everywhere were falling over one another to begin using it. Carter was overjoyed by the magnified news and prodded

Mosier to provide the reporter with more details about the new airport's grandeur.

With voluminous notes, the reporter rushed to the *Star-Telegram* and wrote a seven-page story. He returned to the club for Carter's approval. Amon — his glasses were perched halfway down his nose — read the story aloud very slowly. He and Mosier dictated changes and additions, making the airport more magnificent with each pencil mark.

The reporter wrote the story again, incorporating the additional praise. Back to the suite. Carter and Mosier, recalled the newsman, were even more relaxed and enthusiastic and "the refreshments on the serving table were disappearing with jet-like speed."

Amon again read the story. Once more he and Mosier proposed alterations and improvements, each of which portrayed the new airport in ever more glowing and extravagant terms. Amon insisted, among other things, that the story contain the fact that Fort Worth's air facility would be bigger and better than the combined airports of Los Angeles and Chicago in the very near future.

One more time the story was written, and Amon finally approved the remarkable tale. He seemed, said the reporter, "extra proud of the almost fictitious story."

The airport opened in April, 1953, without Amon. He had suffered two heart attacks the previous February and was confined to a hospital bed. Young Amon stepped in for his father and read a statement from the hospital in which the publisher predicted the airport would serve two million passengers and was a "dream come true."

Irv Farman, a fine feature writer, was assigned to cover the airport dedication. He was overly-enthusiastic about the program and infused his story with pages of flowery phrases, and, additionally, editorialized praise for

Amon Carter. As usual, the story was taken to Amon for approval before publication.

In the hospital room, Amon accepted the story and read it without comment. He handed it back to Farman.

"I hope you wore a bow tie when you wrote this," grumbled the publisher.

"Why?"

"I'd hate for all this stuff to splatter off the keys and stain your tie."

The Greater Southwest International Airport was Amon's greatest failure of his life. Fort Worth never generated enough passenger business from the airlines to make a profit, and slowly service was taken from the airport and moved to Love Field. Finally, the facility was closed. The mammoth terminal building, which faced neither Fort Worth nor Dallas but in a northernly direction, became a ghostly empty building. In the 1970s the federal government forced Fort Worth and Dallas to build a joint-use airport a few miles north of Greater Southwest. When it opened it was the largest airport in the world.

Greater Southwest's second name was Amon Carter Field. C. R. Smith, American Airlines' president, tried to talk Amon out of accepting the honor of having his name placed on the airport. "He and I had a modest falling out about [it]. I said that naming it the Amon Carter Airport would certainly foreclose for a time getting Dallas participation, which was fundamentally sound and eventually came about. But it got named Amon Carter Field, nevertheless."

The complex already bore Amon's name the evening following its dedication when the first airplane landed. Three thousand spectators gathered at midnight to welcome the first scheduled commercial flight. In part, the program — featuring bands and barbeque served from a chuck wagon — was to demonstrate to Dallas just what it had missed and that Fort Worth didn't need Dallas' help to build an airport.

Flight 605 of American Airlines arrived on time. Dignitaries and half the crowd surged to the ramp, to give a real Fort Worth welcome to the first passenger alighting on Amon Carter Field.

That was Mrs. Robert I. Ross, who lived in Dallas. Second was Mrs. Frank Brandt. She, too, lived in Dallas. Third and fourth were Mr. and Mrs. E. L. Smith. Of Dallas.

There is some indisputable irony in the fact that after his airport opening, Amon flew but once more in his lifetime, to a publisher's meeting in New York. He was too sick and old, and died believing his airport was an unqualified success.

Amon and airplanes were colorful comrades. The cowboy loved aviation; it respected him. He was made an honorary member of the National Airports Advisory Committee. In 1950, Amon received the Air Force Exceptional Service Award. The honor, highest bestowed on a civilian, was given, said Stuart Symington, the Air Force Secretary, for Amon's "outstanding national service during the world wars."

That same year he was given the Frank M. Hawks Memorial Award for his contributions "to U.S. aviation." He was praised as "one of the true pioneers of American aviation." In accepting the national award, Amon recalled the stormy flight with Hawks, of the thunder and lightning, hail and wind, of his terror over Alabama.

"My greatest fear," he said, "sprang from the fact that I didn't know anybody in Birmingham."

That hot August day in Matanuska, Alaska, Will Rogers had a similar problem. The Oklahoma humorist looked into the upraised, expressionless Eskimo faces, and inquired, "Anybody here from Claremore?"

He grinned his famous grin, unknown there in the shadow of Mt. McKinley. The impassive faces stared at the grinning white man in the western-cut Shady Oak hat. His pilot, patch-eyed, crusty Wiley Post, a one-time Texas farmer who had soloed around the world, smiled at the remark and continued tinkering with his airplane, a Lockheed Orion.

Will tried again: "You see, Wiley does the flyin' and I do the talkin'. It's about a fifty-fifty job."

The Eskimoes stared.

Rogers and Post were there near the Eskimo village, waiting for the fog to dissipate, waiting to fly off to Siberia, waiting to die. For reasons unclear today, the men were near the top of the world. In June, Post told Bascom Timmons, the *Star-Telegram* Washington bureau chief, that he and Rogers wanted to inspect a possible Alaskan-Russian airmail route. A month later in Texas, Rogers told Amon that the Alaskan trip was only to "get in a little hunting." Perhaps they were there only for the adventure of it.

Rogers would have liked that, the adventure of flying into the unknown. He was an eager traveler, a million-miler in the air, a man, like Amon, always going somewhere. In 1935, William Penn Adair Rogers, of the laconic, drawling wisecrack, of the hesitant, pungent wit, was an American institution, and Amon Carter's great friend.

Of all his celebrity friends, only Will Rogers had Amon's complete admiration and love. Each had a natural attraction for the other. Both had risen from rural, folksy origins to a wealthy, widely acclaimed fame, and if Amon's fame was less than Rogers, that was acceptable to the publisher; he was willing to stand in Will Rogers' spotlight. They meshed, those two. Amon talked, Will listened. Rogers' leisurely mannerisms balanced perfectly against Amon's flamboyant exhibitionisms. "Amon never runs short on talk," Will would say when Carter's long-winded speeches seemed endless. Rogers also said admiringly, "No other city in America has anything approaching such a public citizen as Amon Carter."

Rogers wrote often of Amon in his syndicated column, poking fun of Carter's windy ways, of his constant threats "to make a speech." "Amon," Rogers once wrote, "may be depended upon to give a leather-lunged whoop for West Texas." In return, Amon laughed loudly at Will's jokes and urged him to perform free in Fort Worth.

Fort Worth was Rogers' second home and he was in and out of town — and Suite 10G — so often he kept extra clothes in the apartment. He liked the Fort Worth Club, especially its food. Chefs kept a pot of chili bubbling for him and made cornbread and fried chicken. Dr. Webb Walker's conglomerate salad was a favorite of Rogers, who once wrote of the dish: "I had dinner with him [Amon] . . . and there was an amateur doctor Walker that mixed up a batch that layed me low. The doctors called it catarral jaundice. I was the yellowest white man you ever saw. I never have heard who else died from this Carter dinner. The dish was: Open all the cans of tomatoes you have, all the cans of cove oysters, lots of sliced onions, mix 'em in a big bowl. It's sort of soup salad. It's called 'We have scraped the bottom salad'."

No one remembers when Amon and Will met. Rogers first came to Fort Worth in 1913, but did not see Amon then. Will performed his rope act — no talking — at an Elks Club smoker. Afterwards, he and Jimmy North had chili in a downtown cafe. Probably Amon and Will met in 1922 during a party at John McGraw's house in New York. From then until the humorist's death, the men were close friends. Rogers always was in Fort Worth — he called it "the Cowman's Paradise" — or Amon was visiting at Will's California ranch.

They met often in Washington, usually in their favorite capital hotel, the Mayflower. The hotel had a grand style with quiet countenance and unperturbable atmosphere. Many wealthy, elderly Washingtonians lived there, using the tranquil marble lobby for afternoon naps. Rogers once entered the Mayflower, surveyed the nodding elderly faces and solemn silence. He stood in the lobby's center, cupped his hands and yelled: "HOORAY FOR AMON CARTER, FORT WORTH AND WEST TEXAS!"

Amon's great unfulfilled dream was canalization of the Trinity River from the Texas Gulf Coast to Fort Worth. He foresaw the day when ocean liners would dock at the city's doorstep. Amon wanted Will to understand and believe in the vision. He drove the humorist to a spot where the Trinity bent around Fort Worth, and the men walked the river bank, Amon explaining the canal idea in exacting detail, Will listening in silence. Finally, Amon could stand the silence no longer.

"Well, what do you think?" he blurted.

Rogers looked at the publisher, looked at the river, then turned his eyes to the sky.

"I can see the sea gulls now," he declared.

Will carried his canal joke to his column, writing, "Fort Worth is several hundred miles from the nearest seagull but Amon wants to give Fort Worth the benefit of a tidal wave. They have had droughts, floods, boll-weevils, cattle fever, ticks and were struck by two visits of Jim Ferguson, but they have never tasted seawater. It's the only thing they haven't tasted in a bottle."

Rogers was a problem for *Star-Telegram* reporters. Each time he was in town, Amon wanted a story published. Newsmen wanted Will to utter one of his funny quips. Rogers would say little for publication. "I get paid for being funny. I can't waste my talents," he once snapped to a reporter.

When Will Rogers Junior was eighteen, the humorist asked Amon to "put my son to work on the *Star-Telegram*."

As O. O. McIntyre later wrote in the *Saturday Evening Post*, Amon agreed immediately, adding, "I'll put the boy up at the Fort Worth Club until he can get located."

Rogers warned, "Don't you do any fool thing like that! Let him hunt up a good five-dollar-a-week boarding house. Also you better ask the fire department to wake him up for awhile. That kid is a powerful sleeper."

Will, Jr., who later in his life would be owner/publisher of the Hollywood *Press*, moved into Fort Worth's YMCA and worked in the *Star-Telegram*'s advertising department. Soon, Will wired Amon, "I have a distant son that used to be in Texas somewhere. He can't write so we figured he must be on the *Star-Telegram*." Amon promised to have the son write more often.

Whenever Will was in town, Amon put aside his other business. They would sit all night in Suite 10G, Amon drinking his scotch, Will sipping an occasional beer, talking about money ("Both were trying to get all the money they could," remembered Bascom Timmons). Or Amon would hire a dozen cowboys and stage a rodeo for Will at Shady Oak. Rogers always involved himself in the rodeo, doing his lariat tricks, which often included roping a cigar from Amon's mouth.

When Fort Worth and West Texas suffered from drought and Depression, and with the *Star-Telegram* vigorously denying either was present, Amon spoke of the double blight to Will. Back in California, Rogers thought about the situation and wired Amon: "Keep this to yourself and wire me at once how it sounds. I will come to Texas towns, [and] pay all my own expenses and donate all proceeds to unemployed . . ." Amon was delighted. He offered a plane and pilot, the *Star-Telegram*, his radio station and "anything else in my power."

Rogers cancelled his scheduled appearances and toured Texas stumping for relief money. Fort Worth's contribution — $18,000 — was largest. Amon pulled most of the money from his wealthy friends, including W. T. Waggoner, which caused Rogers to write, "Why don't you do this, Mr. Waggoner? Turn over what little of your fortune Fort Worth and Amon has left you, and just let them have it, and put you on an allowance, then they wouldn't have to go through all this rigmarole."

In his Fort Worth show, Will introduced Amon — "Just say 'Hello,' and shut up, I want to talk about the Trinity."

"I been telling Amon we oughta pave it," cracked Will. It doesn't flow, it oozes. Pappy's [Waggoner] cows would drink it up."

In July, 1935, Will Rogers visited Fort Worth. He and Amon flew to West Texas, to Stamford for the Cowboy Reunion, an annual rodeo and chuckwagon gathering for ranchers and cowhands. Then Will stayed a few days in Suite 10G. He bought a new shirt and a new blue suit at Washer Brothers, left his old suit in the apartment's closet. Rogers described for Amon the planned flight to Alaska "and maybe on to Siberia."

Amon drove Rogers to the airport. The plane was late, delayed in Chicago for sacks of mail to be loaded. Will fidgeted, anxious for the plane to arrive.

You have to remember," explained Amon. "You're in the third greatest airmail center of America. They have to work all the airmail here."

"Work it or write it?" cracked Will, and soon he flew away.

That morning in Alaska, Rogers and Post waited for the fog to lift, and finally, the pilot said, "I think we can make it."

"If it's good enough for you, it's good enough for me," said Rogers, and the Lockheed lifted into the fog to fly over coastal mountains toward Point Barrow, 510 miles north. Probably Post lost his way. The plane landed at Walakpa Lagoon, sixteen miles south of Point Barrow, stayed briefly, and began to move again. It rose from the water then nosed over. Eskimoes came to the wreckage and collected the broken bodies of Post and Rogers. In their village, the Eskimoes dressed each body in long night gowns and wrapped the men in white sheets.

Almost a day passed before the world knew Will Rogers was dead.

Amon was in Washington when news came to the White House. He wept for "dear sweet Will."

Joe Crosson, a bush pilot, flew the bodies of Rogers and Post from Point Barrow to Fairbanks, where they were placed aboard a waiting Pan American World Airways plane. The plane flew on to Seattle and the waiting Amon Carter. Amon boarded the Pan Am plane and sat beside the sheet-shrouded body of his friend throughout the long night flight to Los Angeles.

The death of Will Rogers was a national tragedy. The nation mourned, and afterwards there was a clamor to create a suitable remembrance for America's most beloved man. Eddie Rickenbacker became chairman of the Will Rogers Memorial Commission, which was to raise funds to benefit, in the humorist's name, crippled and underprivileged children. Amon was Texas fund chairman.

It was an intense matter, in Fort Worth more than any other city, and especially within the *Star-Telegram* where a grieving Amon Carter dictated an editorial calling for his city and state to "lead the nation in per capita contributions." The editorial asked for "pennies, nickels and dimes" from everyone, a literal statement since Amon's fundraisers collected a five cent piece from every school child in Fort Worth. Daily, the *Star-Telegram* published county-by-county totals and inaugurated a front page box to honor "100% Companies" in which every employee gave to the campaign ("Marvin D. Evans Printing Co., 11 employees, $4.45").

Between Rogers' death and early January, 1936, the *Star-Telegram* published more than 2,000 stories about the fund drive. It printed an eighteen-part biography of Will and featured old favorite columns of his. Virtually everyone who gave money had their names published in the newspaper, even a convict who donated 25¢ and the 240 *Star-Telegram* newsboys who collected $24.

The newspaper sponsored a bi-state football game between Breckenridge, Texas, and Paul's Valley, Oklahoma, high schools. Boyce House, covering the game, exhibited the pressure on him and others, writing, "A spectacle that will form an ineffaceable picture in the minds of all who were there . . ."; it was more than just a football game.

In the end, Texas and Amon indeed raised more than any state, $256,489 of the total $1.7 million.

Still bereaved by Will's death, Amon had the humorist's portrait painted and placed in his office. It was — and is — lighted night and day.

With the arrival of 1936 and Texas' centennial celebration, Amon was able to have the PWA constructed Fiesta buildings named for Will Rogers. Still, there was more for Amon to do. He commissioned Electra Waggoner Biggs, Pappy's granddaughter, to sculpt Will seated on his favorite horse, Soapsuds (She used a New York policeman's horse as a model). Biggs finished the sculpture in 1939. For the next seven years, Amon stored the huge statue, waiting first for Amon Jr. to return from war and then the right person to come and dedicate the memorial.

In 1946, the statue finally was mounted on a grassy flatness in front of the auditorium/coliseum, and a year later Dwight Eisenhower stood on a raised platform while Margaret Truman sang, and together they formally memorialized Amon's friend, Will Rogers.

Dedication of the statue ended a year of anger for Amon.

He had placed the statue*, three thousand pounds and ten feet tall, in position, ready for unveiling, in late

*A copy of the statue, the original of which cost Amon $20,000, was placed on the campus of Texas Tech in Lubbock because Will once worked on a ranch in the Panhandle. Another poses at the entrance of the Will Rogers Memorial in Claremore, Oklahoma.

1946. All that year Will sat on Soapsuds hidden from public view. Amon had boxed up the statue. It became an object of curiosity for Fort Worthers, many of whom sneaked out "to look at old Will." What that meant was ripping the boards from the statue. Always, it was done late at night.

Amon was furious for what he believed was pure vandalism and defilement of Will's memory.

In mid-1947, Elston Brooks was a seventeen-year-old high school senior with his own radio program, and in that summer Will was unboarded twice in one week. The first midnight raid was pulled off by Amon's friends at the Fort Worth Club. The men, drinking heavily, became curious about the statue. Later in the week, Brooks and several other teenagers arrived at the newly-reboarded statue shortly before midnight. Not very artfully, they ripped off Will's fresh planks and gawked at the towering memorial.

Before 9 o'clock in the morning, Amon offered a $5,000 reward for the vandals.

In those days, the police could receive citizen rewards and officers dropped everything — murders, robberies, burglaries — to pursue the statue caper.

Brooks panicked.

He was sure they would be caught. The reward was too high. As he feared, it happened. One boy told his girl friend. The girl told her mother. The mother told the police. She asked for the $5,000. The braggart was arrested, and turned state's evidence, naming all others, including Brooks.

Brooks received a summons to police headquarters. Next day the penitent boys and their angry parents waited in a conference room. Amon burst in. He lectured the boys, told them their names would be printed in the *Star-Telegram* — a radical departure from a long-standing policy of publishing no juvenile names. He also barred them for life from the Will Rogers buildings.

His tirade finished, Amon decided he would not prefer charges against the boys.

A few months later Jim Record hired Brooks as a cub reporter. Carter often spoke with Brooks but never again mentioned the statue incident.

With the ending of the statue caper, there were numerous claims for his $5,000 reward.

The publisher finally decided no one person had a positive demand on the money. He donated it to the Fort Worth Police Benevolence Society.

Chapter 11

Not a shred of evidence exists that life is serious . . . though it is often hard and terrible.

—Branden Gill

You have only three friends in the world: God Almighty, Sears-Roebuck, and Jim Ferguson.

—Political rally speaker, 1932

Don't be misled by low-down, dirty, stinking lies being printed in the Star-Telegram.

—Farmer Jim Ferguson, 1932

Jim Ferguson mailed out pardons like Xmas cards. He once pardoned a man and the man wrote him that he hadn't been caught yet.

—Will Rogers, 1928

For kindly acts, his 'Hired Hand' he always is a-blamin',
But those who get beneath his hide all know he's dear old Amon.

—Menu, Ritz Tower, NYC, 1928

11

Prohibition in Texas was little more than a textbook theory.

Bootlegging became a profession as uplifting as the ministry, as honorable as undertaking, and more profitable than either. Every town of any size and ambition had its "Fruit Jar City," an area of camouflaged saloons from which was sold good homemade corn liquor or the real stuff sneaked across the Rio Grande from Mexico. Or understanding doctors prescribed medicinal alcohol to be collected from the nearest friendly druggist. If nothing else was available, the public could fall back on the enormous stock of patent medicines, like the soothing toddy of Lydia Pinkham's, which were as satisfying, and as intoxicating, as a good cocktail.

Star-Telegram reporters had their favorite saloon, carefully disguised as an old house, several blocks west of downtown. Jimmy North maintained a charge account there throughout Prohibition. Jim Record, whose dignity would not allow him to drink with the boys, enlisted Ned, his brother, and sports writer Flem Hall to buy bootleg whiskey and deliver it to the newspaper office.

Amon, who as most Texans felt Prohibition was an insantiy to be humored but not seriously practiced, didn't often resort to bootlegging products. Late in the game, he was forced to contract for several loads of liquor being regularly flown from Mexico into Fort Worth, but for the most part Amon had little use for bootleggers. He, after all, had stocked up for the duration. Shortly before the Eighteenth Amendment shuttered saloons and breweries, Amon purchased the entire stock of the Casey-Swasey Wholesale Liquors warehouse, providing himself and his friends with ample, and legal, drinking materials. Ever cautious for the future, Amon, too, buried ten barrels of good whiskey for unforeseen crises (the emergency cache, unfortunately, was never to be used; the barrels leaked and were empty when excavated).

Many cases of his warehouse booze were stored in the underground vault at his home. He installed a siren burglar alarm. The bankvault door was so large and heavy Amon needed two helpers to open it. Amon alone had the combination but, as Nenetta remembered, "He hid it behind every picture in the house."

Amon was settled in for a long dry spell.

By 1928, Prohibition was a generally detested practice, largely because it was unenforceable. Drys, however, still clung to their moral position, especially in the South. Harold Hough explained the situation to WBAP listeners: "The Antis have all the laws they want and the Wets have all the liquor they can drink, so everybody's happy."

Not everybody. In the South, where drinking was a religious dispute, Prohibition remained an emotional exigency. The Lord was dead set against bootlegging.

Then why did the Democratic Party allow itself to be lured into a Southern convention? It was a self-destructive decision, out of which came Al Smith, a Catholic drinker, to be paired against Herbert Hoover, the Eagle Scout GOP candidate. But into the South, to Houston, marched the Democrats, the first major party meeting below the Mason-Dixon Line since the Civil War.

Jesse Jones, the Houston capitalist, roped in the Democrats with a $200,000 check, a free, so the Democrats believed, gift to the party. The large contribution, wrote an observer, "turned out to be an extremely substantial tribute to Mr. Jones. He owned the overcrowded hotels the delegates slept in, the theaters where they sought escape from a fierce June heat, the banks where they cashed their checks, the newspapers they read, and his lumber company built the hall where Alfred E. Smith was nominated. The politicians lost their shirts in the laundry, and they lost their tempers when they learned that this man, Jones, owned the laundry, too. They eventually recovered their tempers, but not their shirts."

So, the Democrats came to Houston as Jesse Jones' well-paying guests, headquartered in the Rice Hotel. Amon arrived with cases of his warehouse liquor, Will Rogers, Paul Patterson, the Baltimore *Sun* publisher, the astringent columnist H. L. Mencken and Carl Smith, Tarrant County's sheriff and frequent traveling companion for Carter. Amon took a third-floor suite, from which he committed what Jimmy North forever more called "The Houston Incident."

It was a circus convention. As meetings began, Houston nightriders lynched an accused Negro rapist; the poor man was dangled from a bridge. J. Frank Norris, who, heavily bankrolled by Republican money, later would stump the state for Hoover, was there, preaching against the double-dose wickedness of Catholicism and liquor. There were slogans, "Smith or Suicide" and "Al for All and All for Al," countered by picket placards carrying the message, "Alcohol Is All For Al." Women prayed in nearby churches, wrote one newsman, ". . . lifting their sad tired voices in despair, invoking the power of God against Al Smith." Half a dozen fist fights broke out on the convention floor, especially around the Southern delegations. Police had to break up the melees with their nightsticks. The 1928 Democratic Convention was not a very pleasant meeting.

Amon was mad. He had come to campaign for John Nance Garner, who as a Texan and convention dark horse candidate, steadfastly maintained he did not want the nomination. Amon grumped around fringes of the convention, angry because an outsider, Smith, surely would be the nominee, angry about the drys' emotional attack on the Democrats (there was a rumored but unconfirmed report Amon confronted Norris outside the Rice Hotel and threatened to whip the Baptist preacher), but especially angry at elevators.

The Rice, too small for a national political convention, was mobbed with people. "The . . . lobby is so packed," wrote Will Rogers, "I have reached up and mopped three brows before I could find my own." He wrote of an early morning meeting of Republican ladies, "The breakfast was billed for 9 o'clock on the roof of the hotel and on account of the elevators we all arrived for a lovely luncheon."

Amon's suite, which he shared with Rogers, Patterson and Mencken, was headquarters for the *Star-Telegram*'s convention coverage. Silliman Evans, the newspaper's political reporter, manned a desk in the center of the living room. Usually, he sat there in his underwear, typing stories from notes delivered by runners from the convention floor. The bathtub was filled with bootlegged iced-down beer. Windows were wide to coax in the small breezes astir in the humid June heat.

On the convention's third day, Amon and Sheriff Smith left the suite to attend a meeting on the hotel's eleventh floor. The elevators, as usual, were packed. For two days Amon had fumed at delays caused by the elevators. That day, three upward-bound elevators passed the men despite Amon's endless impatient thumbing of the call buzzer.

Moments after the fourth elevator zipped by, Amon had a mad spell.

He snatched Smith's pistol from its holder and fired six — or perhaps four; there were differing reports — bullets through the glass elevator doors. Next time, the elevator stopped for Amon.

That is what North always testily called "The Houston Incident," and the way witnesses and Houston newspapers reported the episode — not a word of the shooting ever appeared in the *Star-Telegram*.

Amon's version was slightly different. He told Alva Johnston, who was interviewing him for a *Saturday Evening Post* story: "No shots were fired into the door of the elevator shaft."

Jimmy North wrote a more detailed explanation to Johnston: "What happened was . . . some friends phoned Carter and asked him to bring his friends up to the 11th floor . . . for a visit. Carter was on the third floor, and accompanied by . . . Carl Smith, they started out. It was in the summer and the sheriff was in his shirt sleeves and wearing a .45 Colt revolver. They pushed the elevator button time and time again. The hotel was so crowded the elevators did not stop. Carter, becoming disturbed over [the elevators] not stopping, took the Sheriff's six shooter out of the holster and hammered on the glass door of the elevator shaft with the barrel of the revolver. The door was glassed with heavy meshed wire which when hit with the . . . revolver shattered but did not fall out — thus created a shatter on the glass which looked like a cob web. The glass was not broken but gave the impression to anyone looking at it that it had been shot through. Meanwhile, the elevator stopped. . . .''

That rendition was never believed, particularly by Flem Hall, who saw the bullet holes. Hall was in Houston to cover a Fort Worth Cats' baseball game and visited the *Star-Telegram* suite. To Hall, the bullet holes in the glass elevator doors looked like bullet holes.

There is no dispute, however, over Amon's other Rice Hotel pistol shooting exhibition. He fired six shots through an open hotel window. Mencken cut out the punctured window screen and kept it as a souvenir.

''The Houston Incident'' was an Amon Carter legend that pursued him the remainder of his days. It never went away, but was trotted out by writers and story tellers anytime they wanted to regale an audience with the outrageous antics of Amon. At least once, it was used in a political campaign.

In 1932, James E. ''Farmer Jim'' Ferguson, campaigning for his wife, Miriam, in her gubernatorial race against incumbent Ross Sterling, spoke at a political rally in Arlington.

Farmer Jim warmed up on Sterling, describing the governor as ''the big fathead'' and ''big fat boy,'' then turning to Amon, ''the old cuss'' and ''consummate ass.'' Ferguson rehashed the Houston elevator episode, adding new elements. Amon, said Ferguson, was drunk and the ''elevator [was] occupied only by a little girl.'' The publisher, he said, almost shot the innocent child. Ferguson also charged that Amon, in 1928, had voted for Hoover, which in Democratic Texas was an indictment as vile as being accused of fondling kids in a bus station toilet.

One means always of breaking into the columns of the *Star-Telegram* was to attack Amon, and Ferguson's comments landed on page one, introduced by an editor's note calling Farmer Jim's attack ''a smokescreen'' because the newspaper had uncovered ''favoritism'' and ''riotous extravagance'' in Miriam's previous administration. The editor's note said Ferguson's charges were being printed, although libelous to Amon, because "the public has a sense of humor . . . a cash discount can be taken on most of Mr. Ferguson's statement."

Pa Ferguson still hadn't learned smart politicians never argue with a man who has his own newspaper in which to have the last word.

Amon and the *Star-Telegram* in 1932 once again were campaigning against Miriam Ferguson. Privately, he knew she would be elected governor, and had written to Sterling, whom he did not like, that "the times support her kind of politicking."

And Ma Ferguson did win election as governor for the second time.

Ma and Pa. Texas' political Punch and Judy. For thirty years they espoused what critics called "Fergusonism," a demogogic populist brand of earthy politics depending on the "Ferguson vest-pocket vote," which were the 150,000 poor, largely rural, Texans for whom Ma and Pa could do no wrong. For everyone else they could do wrong, and did.

Each served two terms as governor and, said a reporter, "When they didn't run Texas politicians were in a dither for fear they might."

Farmer Jim Ferguson was the son of a Central Texas minister, and a wanderer in his youth. He panned for gold in California, was a bell hop in Colorado, a pick and shovel laborer at a railroad site near Fort Worth. Finally, he settled down near Temple and married Miriam, farmed a little, read law books at night and was admitted to the bar. He also founded Temple State Bank. In 1912 he began dabbling in politics and by 1914 had parlayed himself into the governor's mansion.

Pa campaigned almost exclusively in rural areas, boondoggling tenant farmers with harangues against Texas' wealthy, educated class. Dressed in a claw hammer frock coat, fists clenched and raised to Heaven,

Pa was a splendid demagogue promising the world to work-weary sharecroppers.

By 1917 in his second term, Pa was a marked man, and impeachment charges were brought against him. Pa, as the subsequent Senate trial proved, was something of a scoundrel. He loaned himself $5,000 from public school funds. He had accepted $156,000 — in cash and in small bills; this, too, he maintained, only was a loan — from brewery lobbyists anxious to stave off Prohibition legislation. He deposited a half a million dollars of state funds in Temple State Bank — a clear conflict of interest violation — and used portions of the money to pay his own overdrafts. Pa used taxpayer money to buy his groceries, cattle feed, automobile tires, gasoline and even the chicken Ma served in the mansion. Pa Ferguson, it was revealed, bought a ukelele and paid for the instrument with state funds.

Impeached, Pa was outraged and set about to restore his good name.

Subsequently, and in open violation of law pertaining to impeachments, Pa ran again for governor. He was defeated. He was a candidate for U.S. Senate, and lost. He campaigned for President on a "Know Nothing" ticket. Meanwhile, he founded the *Ferguson Forum*, a weekly statewide newspaper pregnant with Fergusonism.

In 1923, Pa settled on a simple solution to his problem. He ran Miriam for governor. Ma, who seemed to have been a nice, uncomplicated woman deeply devoted to her husband, stumped the state for support among the vest pocket voters. She wore a poke bonnet. She was pictured baking pies and feeding chickens. Once a *Ferguson Forum* headline announced: "Ma Drops Campaign Worry to Preserve Three Gallons of Figs." Ma rarely orated but pronounced a few words of welcome then turned the platform over to Pa who in turn blistered his enemies and promised to take care of those little farmers who had supported him during all his years of persecution. He promised everybody "two governors for the price of one."

Ma Ferguson became the first woman ever elected governor of a state (she was the second to take office; Nellie Ross of Wyoming was inaugurated a few days before Ma).

Her first act was to pardon Pa for his impeachment crimes. Pa was back in business.

He took over the affairs of Texas while Ma, knitting like Madame LaFarge, performed ceremonial duties and fried chicken in the mansion. Pa became legal counsel for a group of railroads. The *Ferguson Forum* was bloated with ads by companies doing business with the state. A daughter managed a bonding business whose clientele solely were utility companies and highway contractors depending on the State of Texas. Pa sat with official commissions, boards and state agencies, issuing instructions and orders no private citizen — which he was — could legally issue. It was the best of times; it was the worst of times.

And then Ma/Pa began pardoning criminals, at which point Amon and the *Star-Telegram* stepped into the Ferguson mess.

Pa was handy for giving out pardons during his two terms but Ma emptied prisons faster than any Texas governor before or since.

Her predecessor, Pat Neff, signed 92 full pardons and 107 conditional pardons during his entire four years in office. Ma pardoned more than 2,000 criminals in her first twenty months as governor, releasing up to three hundred prisoners in a single day. During her final twenty-nine days of office, noted the *Star-Telegram*, she granted "full unconditional pardons" to thirty-three rapists, 133 murderers, 124 robbers and 127 liquor law violators.

Texas' "open door policy" was satisfactory to convicts but disturbing to the general public. There were cynical jokes ("Pardon me, Ma did" was scribbled in the dust of a Model T Ford chassis), and scurrilous asides about Ma's "cash and carry clemency administration" and rumors that all petitions for clemency first were passed through Pa's law office; nothing was ever proven.

The *Star-Telegram* began keeping score on Ma. The newspaper daily published on its front page a prominent box marked "Pardon Record" in which Ma's accumulative executive clemency totals were spread for all the state to see. "Governor Ferguson's pardon record, compiled Monday in Austin," read one, "shows that the woman governor has since her induction in office, issued up to date 2,328 clemency proclamations. Of this number 614 have been issued since April 6, this year [1925]. The classified list of proclamations follow: Conditional pardons, 771; Full pardons, 378 . . . paroles, 168 . . . reduced bonded forfeitures, 17 . . . jail and bond forfeitures remitted, 1 . . ." And so on.

Ma and Pa were indignant over the *Star-Telegram*'s publicity about their pardon and parole business. Except among the vest pocket *lumpenproletariat*, who still cherished the demagoguery of Fergusonism, Texas was irate over Ma and Pa's wholesale release policy for convicted criminals. More revelations were coming.

In mid-year, Silliman Evans uncovered the sticky asphalt topping scandal within Ma's Texas Highway Department.

Pa had been meeting with the three-member Texas Highway Commission — ". . . the commission cordially invited me to sit with them," Pa told the *Star-Telegram*, "I thought I ought to accept their kind invitation." Evans reported that suspicious contracts were given without bid or public notice to the American Road Company, a firm incorporated in Delaware with total assets of a secondhand asphalt plant and five old automobiles.

A month after American Road's incorporation, and with its new Texas highway contract, the company declared a dividend of $200,000. Sixteen days later, another dividend of \$319,000 was handed to stockholders. Within six months, American paid \$709,111.35 to fortunate stockholders. American Road never spread asphalt on any state highway. It subcontracted the contract.

A similar deal for topping was given Hoffman Construction Company. It was to be paid thirty cents per square yard. As with American Road, Hoffman sublet its contract at nine cents a square yard. In six months Hoffman was paid by Texas \$908,443.24 for work costing \$296,805.50.

The *Star-Telegram* printed it all.

Dan Moody, Texas' young red-haired attorney general (and a declared gubernatorial candidate) took Evans' research and went to court. American Road was required to return \$600,000 to the state treasury.

Tempers were short in Austin. A highway commissioner attacked and beat Evans in the lobby of the Driskill Hotel. Threats against Amon filtered into Fort Worth and he hired guards for his home and family. During the Austin trial, W. T. Montgomery told of his conversation with Frank Latham, the commission chairman.

"Montgomery," said Latham, "I had nothing more to do with letting the American Road Company contract than you had."

"Who did?"

"Jim Ferguson."

The Fergusons were furious with Amon and his *Star-Telegram*.

Back in Fort Worth, Amon chortled about the public furor he and the newspaper had caused.

Autumn arrived and with it, a favorite Carter passion — Texas football.

He dressed in his cowboy costume and with Nenetta drove to College Station for the annual Thanksgiving football game between Texas A&M and the University of Texas.

In Kyle Field, the Aggie football stadium, Amon was startled to find himself seated directly behind Ma and Pa Ferguson.

Predictably, the game enthused Amon. The Aggies, his favorite, were winning. He was up and pacing and cheering for A&M, yelling for the Aggies to pour it on. The cowboy was having a fine afternoon.

Then Amon, unexpectedly and probably spontaneously, hollered, "HOORAY FOR DAN MOODY AND THE TEXAS AGGIES!"

Ma and Pa squirmed.

The crowd applauded.

Pa whispered to an aide. The assistant told Amon he must stop yelling. Amon eyed the man.

"HOORAY FOR DAN MOODY AND THE TEXAS AGGIES!"

Ma and Pa summoned a Texas Ranger. Amon was thrown out.

Within twenty-four hours Amon's expulsion was on front pages everywhere — except the *Star-Telegram*'s. North sighed and pretended nothing was happening.

The New York *Times* devoted four columns to the football episode and ensuing uproar. O. O. McIntire wired from Paris, "You certainly busted all the front pages over here. Atta boy!" Amon's friends sent joshing telegrams. "Sic 'em," wired Frank Phillips from Oklahoma. John Willys, the auto manufacturer, offered, "If you need bail, call me."

Returning to Austin, Ma and Pa held a press conference.

"He [Amon] was as drunk as a boiled owl," declared Ma. "He was drunk and waving a cane and I know it was filled with liquor."

She claimed Amon gave away the liquor-filled canes in wholesale lots. Amon also, said Ma, gave away liquor flasks shaped like family Bibles.

Ma announced a five hundred dollar reward for arrest and conviction of persons ''worth more than $5,000'' who violated Prohibition laws. She referred to a ''North Texas publisher'' who ''dispenses pints of liquor by the dozens in public places . . . and goes scott-free, when poor and underfed men in the same city are being sent to the penitentiary yearly for carrying a thin pint.''

The Texas A&M tableau was, Amon told the Houston *Post*, evidence of Ma and Pa's public chicanery. The game had excited him, he said. He paced the grandstand, cheering the Aggie's first and second touchdowns. By the sheerest of coincidences, revealed Amon, he was beside the governor's box when he happened to insert Dan Moody's name into the cheer.

The aide asked Amon to quiet himself. Who was that man to tell him what to do? He yelled again and the Texas Ranger escorted him outside where, according to the publisher, the following conversation occurred:

AMON: Is it against the law to cheer for Texas A&M?

RANGER: No, Mr. Carter.

AMON: Is it against the law to cheer for Dan Moody?

RANGER: No, Mr. Carter.

AMON: Then what's all the shootin' about, anyway?

RANGER: Aw, forget it and let's go back inside.

Amon denied that he had been drinking — Nenetta agreed that he was not drunk.

Three days later Ma released to state newspapers a letter she had written Amon. Editors deemed it libelous and refused to print it. Amon immediately issued a statement to the Associated Press waiving the libel law. The letter went onto front pages across Texas, including even, finally, the *Star-Telegram*'s, where it was preceeded by an editor's note in which Amon stated that Ma's correspondence was being printed "as a means of getting the matter before the public and in a sense of fair play. . ."

An answer was promised the following day. Amon meant to have the last word.

It is generally believed that Ma's letter actually was written by Pa, and it is a wonderfully sardonic piece of political literature. Ma began by recounting the Aggie episode, noting that there were 25,000 people at the game, including "thousands of young boys and girls, students and friends."

"[When] you gave vent to your vociferous exclamation you were only a few feet from me," she wrote. "Your friends who know you best assure me (and I believe them) that when you are in a normal condition you are a courteous gentleman to the manner born and I attribute your seeming affront to your unusual condition and the influence under which you were laboring at the time . . . I gladly forget the apparent discourtesy to me as from my own observation I know you were not responsible at the time."

Ma turned to other matters, scolding Amon, "I am told that last year you fitted up a building owned or controlled by you (perhaps a garage building) in the old fashioned bar room way, providing a bar with the footrail, and the sawdust on the floor, and behind the bar you had a man dressed in the old fashioned bar tender, white apron style. I am also informed that at said reception given by you many became stimulated and others under the influence of an invigorating concoction and that you in company with your guests participated in the consumption of the beverage."

Ma claimed that Amon served drinks that were ". . . to say the least, stimulating, and that [you] caused to be given souvenir canes in which there was a hidden phial some thirty inches in length that contained approximately one pint of beverage."

Amon, in all ways, concluded the governor, had displayed "vices that are repugnant to the ideal of strict morality and sobriety."

She alleged that he was not fit to serve in a public position and demanded his resignation as board chairman of Texas Technological College at Lubbock, a newly opened state-supported college which Amon and the *Star-Telegram* had lobbied into reality.

The "bar room" was Amon's garage. A year earlier, he hosted executive board members of the American Petroleum Institute, which was meeting in Fort Worth. He served cases of his pre-Prohibition liquor. Each guest was given a whiskey-filled walking cane. A good time was had by all, particularly local law enforcement officials who were guests, and especially an assistant district attorney who reportedly was carried out feet first from the drinking party.

The following day, Amon headlined his reply, beginning with the classical quotation: "Whom the gods would destroy, they first make mad."

He refused to resign from the Texas Tech board*, charging Ma's statements were "malicious and without justification" and "a smokescreen to divert the real issues from the public." The governor was mad, said Amon, because the *Star-Telegram* had exposed corruption in her highway department. The publisher spoke of Pa, ". . . the real actor who like a ventriloquist behind the scenes puts his voice and his words to figures on stage."

Amon revealed that emissaries from Pa came to Fort Worth, to the publisher's office, to threaten him

*The board chairmanship, highest public office Amon ever accepted or held, was taken with great reluctance on his part. He served only because he and the *Star-Telegram* were responsible for lobbying the college into existence out there on the West Texas plains. He wanted to resign before Ma demanded that he quit the post. Then of course he could not. Amon resigned a few days after Governor Dan Moody took office. Moody beat Ma with the campaign slogan, "Hooray for Dan Moody."

and attempt to stop the newspaper's highway department stories.

As for the garage bar room, the accusation was "a farce comedy" representing "an effort to make fiction out of fact and is ancient history . . . there was no violation of the law and there could have been none. Present were city and county law enforcement officials."

He denied giving away whiskey-filled walking canes.

Turning to the Aggie incident, Amon declared his "right as one who paid his way in . . . to yell for the team of my choice, and Dan Moody for saving taxpayers' money.

"The story that I was under the influence of liquor when I cried out on the one hand for A&M and on the other for Dan Moody, is not only false in every particular but could only support the conclusion in the mind of 'Gov. Jim' that anyone who declared for Dan Moody was either drunk or crazy," concluded Amon.

Ma and Pa had no reply for Amon. The matter simmered.

Amon received more than four hundred letters from Texans supporting his public argument with the Fergusons. He and the newspaper continued gathering evidence against Ma and Pa. None was printed, probably because public sentiment had turned against the pair and Moody appeared to have enough support to win. The evidence, gathered by private detectives, was stored in Amon's files. There was a notarized deposition, stating, "That on Jan. 23, 1926, the governor called for a quart of whiskey delivered to the capital at 2:25 p.m. The governor paid $6 in the presense of Carlos Brents, U.S. Prohibition Agent." Another placed Pa in "the crap game on the 12th floor of the Texas Hotel, raided the night of March 10, 1926 . . ." And there was a picture of a still operating on Pa's ranch near Meridian in Central Texas.

The most immediate result of the stories was a demand for those whiskey-filled walking canes Amon said he never gave away. "I have established a great trade on the Dan Moody walking sticks," he wrote a New York friend. "I have just had to place an order for 50 more."

After Ma was defeated by Moody, Pa wrote Amon, "If in the heat of the campaign I have in the past said anything that I ought not to have said, I regret it." He asked Amon to reply. Amon stuffed the letter into his files and dismissed such a silly request from his mind.

But he and Texas were not free from Ma and Pa. She ran again in 1930 and was beaten by Ross Sterling. By 1932, the Depression was upon the state and demagoguery once more was fashionable. Ma was returned to office by the vest pocket vote.

A year later Eleanor Roosevelt came to Fort Worth to meet Elliott's new wife, Ruth Googins. She asked Amon to set up a meeting, which he planned for Meacham Field with a private breakfast. Reporters learned of the meeting and Amon kept Googins away. Still, there was the breakfast. Mrs. Roosevelt, Amon and other invited guests sat to eat.

Unexpectedly, the Fergusons arrived.

Ma and Pa stood around outside, waiting to be asked in. Amon ignored them. They angrily left.

"Why didn't you stay for breakfast?" called a reporter.

"Ask Amon Carter!" snapped Pa.

The reporter asked. "I arranged for the breakfast," said Amon. "I paid for it. I ordered it. I could ask who I pleased. Jim Ferguson has never given me anything."

Ma and Pa were in the area, first, to attend a charity horse race at Arlington Downs, and second, as platform guests in Dallas' Hotel Adolphus for a political banquet honoring John Nance Garner, the new vice president, and James Farley, Postmaster General and chairman of the Democratic National Committee. The men were touring Texas. Dallas snubbed Amon and did not invite him (he later would claim he had an invitation). At the time, Will Rogers and Frank Hawks were visiting Amon. The trio decided to crash the dinner and flew from Fort Worth to Dallas in Hawks' plane.

Rogers entered the banquet hall. Applause broke out as he was recognized. He ambled to the front table to speak.

"I come here only one one condition," said Rogers. "I brought a friend. If he's welcome, I'll stay. Neither of us was invited. We just butted into this party. I reckon I'd better go on back to Fort Worth with him."

Boyd Gatewood wrote in the Houston *Post*, "A thousand voices roared 'Bring him in!' In came Amon Carter."

Amon sat at the press table.

"Amon harbors no ill will toward you," cracked Rogers. "And I don't either. Amon came here with the distinct understanding that he was not to take this hotel back to Fort Worth with him. I know, Mrs. Governor and . . . er . . . er . . . , well, both of you . . . I know Amon has no ill will for you."

The audience roared.

A week later, *Time* magazine devoted a page to the Garner/Farley political blitz of Texas. The writer, captivated by the cowboy, wrote little of the politicians but devoted the article to Amon Carter.

Amon gawddamned *Time*, a fledgling publication doing everything it could to attract attention, and authored a scathing reply to the article. Amon's letter remains the longest ever published by the magazine.

Point by point, Amon disputed the story. The letter read:

> It is to be regretted that ideals once formed should be shattered and fine conceptions overturned. In the past *Time* has won its way in public favor through its accuracy in presenting current events in a crisp, snappy and concise form, and thus vitalizing its news, rather than fictitious stories, interesting because they are scurrilous.

Why you should have turned aside to make me the target for rancid legends is quite mystifying, inasmuch as I am a private citizen, holding no office and caring for none. I am not thinskinned but even the most calloused individual would resent untruths and false insinuations that drip from page 13 of your October 30th issue.

Let us take up your attack in the order in which it is made:

FIRST — You say that "Publisher Carter was reputed to have financed the Garner-Farley junket over American Airways of which he is a heavy stockholder." Permit me to say that I own no stock in the American Airways, though at one time I was the possessor of 50 shares which I disposed of.

SECOND — You also assert that I bought the *Star-Telegram* eight years ago with money made in cattle, oil and advertising. This assertion is a piece with the rest of your article. The *Star-Telegram* had its origin Feb. 1, 1906, nearly 20 years in advance of the time recorded in your story. The paper began as the Fort Worth *Star* and embraces, through succesive purchases, its two competitors of that time, the *Evening Telegram* and the *Morning Record*. My connection with it dates from the first issue of the *Star* of which I was the advertising manager — in fact, the entire advertising department — and has continued uninterrupted, throughout its development. It has always been a legitimate newspaper and its progress had nothing to do with investment on my part in cattle or oil, but its circulation of 140,000, the largest in the Southwest, was evolved from the patronage and support of the people of Texas, particularly of the West.

THIRD — You state that "Carter marshaled the Farley-Garner party out to his box at Arlington Downs to witness the rebirth of horse race betting in Texas. There an unforeseen unpleasantness occured. While Host Carter was out making a bet, Governor Miriam (Ma) Ferguson and her husband, James, popped in uninvited to chat with Postmaster General Farley." That statement is entirely erroneous and is also an injustice to the Governor and her husband. The Farley-Garner party were guests, together with Governor Ferguson and her husband, at a luncheon given in the Club House by Mr. and Mrs. W. T. Waggoner and their sons, Paul and Guy, owners of Arlington Downs. I did not attend the luncheon as I presided at another given by the combined civic clubs at the Fort Worth Club in honor of Joseph T. O'Mahoney, first assistant Postmaster General. Following this luncheon, I accompanied Mr. O'Mahoney to the races at Arlington Downs and did not in any way come in contact with Governor Ferguson and her husband, made no bets on the races nor did there occur any unpleasant event during the entire afternoon.

FOURTH — You state that "Amon Carter in 1925, full of high spirits, paraded back and forth behind the Fergusons' seats crowing in behalf of the man who succeeded Mrs. Ferguson after her first term as governor: 'Horray for Dan Moody.'" In answer to this accusation, the writer was not "full of high spirits" and was doing no crowing. Dan Moody had not succeeded Mrs. Ferguson as she was still in office. However, having been a long time admirer and rooter for A&M College, I did exclaim, "Hooray for A&M College and Dan Moody" following the touchdown by A&M against Texas. I was not concerned about the Fergusons in any way and said nothing in disparagement of them. I merely exercised my personal privilege to lift my voice for Dan Moody, the Attorney General. I thought he was entitled to recognition at the time because as Attorney General, he had sued the road contractors to recover moneys that they had procured through juicy contracts with the Highway Department during the Ferguson Administration. That I was justified in this is borne out by the fact that later Moody was instrumental in recovering from those contractors for the State of Texas something like one million dollars and was elected Governor. The story that James E. Ferguson, as you stated, offered a reward of $500,000 to any police officer that would arrest Amon Carter, is as real as Cinderalla and the glass slipper, and quite as untrue as the innuendoes in your article abound. It is doubtless true that had such a reward been offered, the rush of police officers would have been far greater than that of the A&M line.

FIFTH — You further state that "When I found that the Fergusons had horned in on a party of mine last week that I stomped away and did not return to the box until they had gone.'' This is entirely erroneous, has not a semblance of truth and is another injustice to the Governor.

SIXTH — You make the further statement to the effect that '''The lights of Shady Oak,' the comfortable country place on Lake Worth where publisher Carter and his wife do so much of their entertaining, generally burn far into the night and that he never serves beer because he dislikes it, but there is always an abundance of Texas corn and Scotch, his favorite drinks, which he usually takes neat.'' This statement is not only slanderous and false, but that you should introduce Mrs. Carter's name into such an atmosphere is proof enough that a gentleman is needed to edit your copy.

SEVENTH — You state ''Mr. Carter's generosity as a contributing Democrat is only equalled by his enthusiasm for the cause and, perhaps by his ambition to hold office.'' It is the first time the writer has ever been aware that either a man's generosity or his loyalty to his party should be subject to criticism or slander. As for my ambition to hold office, this in itself is ridiculous. I have never held public office and have repeatedly stated in the publication with which I am associated that I never expect to hold one. Therefore, it would seem that you take malicious delight in endeavoring to embarrass me with the fact that I am doing these things merely for a selfish reason — trying to acquire a public office, which I would not accept if it were tendered me. It may be that in your environment you are so accustomed to things being done for a purely selfish motive, that it is difficult for you to comprehend that there are people who do not belong to the ''Axe Grinder's Club'' and that in Texas things are done on a broader scale. Perhaps on this account, allowance should be made for your insinuation.

It is true that I have patronized baseball, football, and polo games and prize fighters; however, I do not own an airplane that will fly — merely a retired one as a souvenir at Shady Oak.

EIGHTH — You further state that ''At Houston in 1928 Carter threatened to beat up Rev. J. Frank Norris, a Protestant preacher, who opposed the Presidential Nomination of Catholic Al Smith. When Smith was nominated, Amon Carter's exuberance knew no bounds. In his exhiliration he shot his sixgun through the door of an elevator in the Rice Hotel.'' This entire statement is pure fabrication, false, slanderous, libelous and vicious.

NINTH — You state that ''last year Carter was an early passenger on the Roosevelt bandwagon, now supervises Texas patronage distribution.'' I have never climbed aboard anyone's bandwagon. As Chairman of the Garner Finance Committee, I supported Mr. Garner for President until the time Governor Roosevelt was nominated and Mr. Garner was nominated for Vice President. From that time, I naturally supported Governor Roosevelt and Speaker Garner vigorously, for which support I have no apology to make. As for controlling patronage in Texas, I have absolutely nothing to do with it. The patronage in this state is controlled by our two Senators, Vice President and our Congressmen.

TENTH — You further make a statement that the writer sends the President, at least twice a week, long telegrams and occasionally a sleepy operator is waked up or aroused with a message ''from the White House to Publisher Carter.'' This is not only false and ridiculous but it is unfair to the President as I have never received a wire of any kind from him or sent other than congratulatory messages. It is my observation that he keeps his own counsel and is perfectly able to do a wonderful job without consulting me or even you.

ELEVENTH — You state the political bickering at '' 'Shady Oak' lasted long after Vice President Garner had retired at 10 p.m.'' In the first place there was no political bickering in connection with the party. It was purely a social gathering. Vice President Garner left the farm at 10 p.m. in keeping with our promise on his acceptance of the invitation. Postmaster General Farley remained until 11:30 and the writer accompanied him to the city. It may be that some of our guests stayed later, a fact which I fail to see should be of any concern to you or even a matter of public interest.

TWELFTH — You state ''The Fergusons were placed on Postmaster General Farley's right at the Dallas banquet next night, so Amon Carter sat at the press table.'' This insinuation is entirely unwarranted. The committee in Dallas invited both Will Rogers and myself to the dinner. We flew over by plane from Fort Worth in company with Col. Frank Hawks, about 8 p.m. Rogers was called to the front by the toastmaster and asked to address the crowd. He insisted on my joining him. During the time he was talking, I occupied a vacant seat which happened to be at the Press table. My attending the party in no way conflicted with the attendance or entertainment of Governor Ferguson and her husband or the seating arrangement for the honored guests.

THIRTEENTH — In your wise crack, which is false, slanderous and vicious, you state that ''The Farley party headed back to Washington, which, thought some of Amon Carter's friends, was where Amon Carter wishes he was going on official business.'' At any time I have a desire to go to Washington on official business, I usually go.

All the foregoing statements are not only false, but like half-truths are infinitely more harmful than if they were bare-faced shameless falsehoods. They are beneath the level and dignity of any high-class journal or publication. Your gullibility in swallowing these accusations, hook, line and sinker, is unthinkable. I cannot understand how any self-respecting reporter, however careless or incompetent, could fail to ascertain the facts before putting such a story to print. It appears that this article must have been inspired from other sources, as it would be difficult to impute to your publication such a total absence of the elementary principles of decency and fair treatment.

Of the thirteen or fourteen statements supposedly setting forth facts, I find but three correct.

I was born in Crafton, Texas. I am 53 years old and as a boy I sold chicken sandwiches at the railroad station platform at Bowie. I might also add that I waited on tables at a hotel, sold soda-pop at the ball games and races on Saturday, sold newspapers, worked for a doctor for two years taking care of his horse and buggy, sweeping out his office, and in addition milked a cow — all for my board to enable me to go to school. I am not sensitive as to my age or ashamed of my early efforts to earn a living. While I have given Crafton no claim of distinction by reason of my birth, I know no cause for reproach on that score. I might add that if the editor of *Time* had been fortunate enough to have enjoyed some of my earlier experiences and hardships, the chances are he would not have been so gullible as to have swallowed a story of this nature or so lacking in the instincts of good sportsmanship.

Another statement in your article preceding your barrage of inaccuracy and fiction concerning the writer is your reference to Honorable John N. Garner, wherein you mentioned "the Farley expedition was for the purpose to rediscover little old hawk-beaked Vice President Garner." This statement in itself to fair-minded people stamps you as thoroughly lacking in the proper attitude of mind or even the respect a wayfaring man pays to the Vice President of the United States. Mr. Garner is a highly respectable, patriotic gentleman, having served his country for 30 years, brilliantly, successfully and courageously, at Washington. A good old fashioned "elm club" should be the proper rebuke for a contemptible remark of this kind.

In conclusion, come to Fort Worth, where the West begins and we will extend to you the same cordial hospitality we accord to any and all gentlemen. It is proper to add that we always give our visitors the benefit of the doubt.

If you are interested in facts or possess as much intestinal fortitude as you show gullibility, you will publish this reply in full without garbling or editing it, giving it equal prominence with the original story . . .

Chapter 12

This surpasses anything I have seen in Paris, Havana, New York and Buenos Aires.

—*Jorge Sanchez, Cuban sugar baron*

Good Heavens, Billy! It's better than your publicity. It's a goose's dream.

—*Fannie Brice, on seeing* Casa Manana

A team effort is a lot of people doing what I say.

—*Michael Winner, movie director*

Most everybody can get results when kindly encouraged but give me the man who can get there in spite of hell.

—*Epigram, in Amon's office*

12

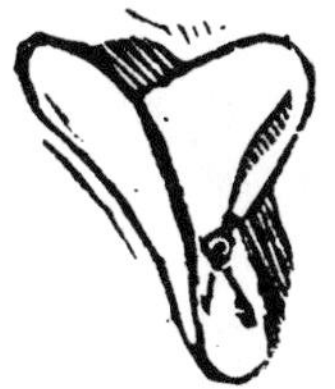

Fads, fashions and fancy ideas were forever unpunctual to Texas. The unfamiliar brought on a kneejerk suspicion and whether the interloper was hula hoops or sapiental hoopla, acceptance was grudgingly slow. Even the 1930s Depression was tardy, and most of all in Fort Worth where that dark October of 1929 and the ensuing black days was a financial mess of somewhere else, not Cowtown. Amon's city owned a bright and booming economy, lubricated by the 1917 Ranger oil strike. Petroleum runoff from a hundred miles west slid Fort Worth right into 1932 before the town became a Depression victim.

Even then, Fort Worth denied the Depression. It wasn't happening. The *Star-Telegram*, which always had a wonderful aptitude for ignoring the obvious, suggested the Depression was illusory: The Depression wasn't what everybody thought it was but only a momentary irritation, like a foot rash, and would clear up soon, probably in the next day or two. Men queued for bread and soup surely wouldn't swallow that fictional editorial theory. The illusional foot rash itched all the more.

A preview of the economical psoriasis was staged in 1930 amid the petroleum-plenty good times. Pappy Waggoner called it a money stampede while Amon Carter railed in a front page editorial of the ". . . ridiculous spectacle brought on by idle gossip, unfounded rumors and a state of hysterior [*sic*]."

It began shortly before closing time, three o'clock, February 18, a Wednesday, at First National Bank, one of Fort Worth's larger banks with stated deposits of $24,139,069.37, and cash on hand of a million bucks and change. Minutes before doors were shuttered for the day, a thousand people arrived shouting for their money. Other depositors, and still more, rushed downtown until they filled the bank lobby and clogged streets. A classic bank run.

Panicked bank officials called in Sheriff Red Wright and a posse of deputies. A single Texas Ranger, Captain Tom Hickman, arrived — there was, after all, only *one* mob. City police came (at least a dozen cops suggested *they* be given their deposited cash before the civilians became unruly). The crowd's alarm was heightened by the failure two weeks earlier of Fort Worth's Texas National Bank, which collapsed under a load of bad loans. At First National, the lawmen attempted to herd the people outside. The people refused to move, and clamored louder for their money. Reluctantly, the bank began paying out.

Amon knew none of this. He was home in bed, ill with the flu, ordered there by his friend and physician, Dr. Webb Walker. Now, Walker telephoned Amon and begged him to come to the bank. The publisher arrived at five o'clock with Pappy Waggoner. Councilman William Monnig joined them. The three men conferred with bank officials and devised strategy. Displaying joyful confidence, a bank officer announced that First National would remain open all night if necessary to serve depositors. *Cheers of relief.*

Carter stepped onto a lobby table and began talking. The *Star-Telegram* softened its publisher's role, but the *Press* issued an extra detailing Amon's involvement in the extravagant five hours. Shouting for attention, Amon began calming the depositors.

"I was in a sick bed," he declared, sniffing, "and I couldn't believe this thing when I first heard it, and then I got up and here I am. This is the safest bank in the world and you'll soon find it out. It is paying off every dollar as fast as you are passing in your checks and for every dollar it is paying you it is taking in six more. Why, right now $2,500,000 is coming from the Federal Reserve Bank in Dallas."

As though hailed from the wings — *OK, cue the money* — a convoy of heavily-armed men swept into the lobby and forced an aisle through the masses. The guards carried large United States paper currency pouches and smaller coin bags.

"See there!" shouted Amon. "What did I tell you! You can't take your money out as fast as they can bring it in. Let's boost for our city. Let's not go mad like this. Let's go home and in the morning your money will be right here for you. The organization I represent has a hundred thousand dollars here and I expect to leave it here."

Carter called on the laconic Waggoner. Pappy was about to deliver his first public speech. The rancher explained his views in terms he understood:

"I have been a cowman . . . and have swung onto many a cow's tail in a stampede, but this is the first stampede like this I ever saw . . . (Amon urged him to speak louder) . . . I am here to tell you this stampede is worse than cattle stampeding, and I want you to stop it and go on home. This bank has been in business for fifty years and will be in business long after we are gone."

Pappy raised his right hand, vowing, "I hereby pledge to you every cent I own and possess in this world that you shall not lose a single dollar in this bank. I will sell every cow and every oil well if necessary to pay for any money you lose here. Go home, I tell you, go on home."

Hesitant applause.

Pappy, whose assets were ten times those of the bank, repeated his promise. *Light cheering.* The *Press* reported that Waggoner's talk began "to turn the tide." The rancher personally escorted an elderly widow back to a cashier and redeposited her five thousand dollars.

Monnig spoke, and businessman W. P. McLean, and several bank officers, all playing a theme of heavy confidence. Amon remounted the high table, over and over urging reasoned thought and action. He lectured on Fort Worth's economic stability, its limitless financial future, how one day it would be a rich behemoth city of consequence. *Just think*, he shouted, *Fort Worth already was the nation's third-ranking air mail center*!

Many depositors who early collected their cash had rushed to the U.S. Savings Department of the Post Office. Postmaster Billy Moore arrived with all the money — $21,000 — and redeposited it with First National which demonstrated, he said, that the United States of America was not worried a single whit about the bank's stability.

Amon's pleadings, Pappy's pledge, the bank officials' confidence — all slowed withdrawals. However abated, the bank run continued. At 6:30 Amon sent out for cheese sandwiches and hot dogs. He fed the multitudes. Two orchestras arrived from the nearby Hotel Texas. The musicians set up at opposite ends of the lobby and began playing, "Singing in the Rain" and "Hail, Hail, the Gang's All Here." A few couples danced. Others sang along. Flasks of bootleg whiskey were passed around and lawmen nipped from the booze cans along with the crowd. Amon announced that depositors could use their bank passbooks for free admission into the Majestic Theater, and two hundred people rushed off to see William Boyd in Pathe's all-talking "Officer O'Brien."

Soon after, reported the *Star-Telegram*, Lynn Talley, governor of the Federal Reserve Bank, spoke, telling depositors that $6,750,000 had been transferred from Dallas to bolster First National's reserves. "This bank will not fail," he promised. The newspaper said the bank run settled into a "sort of jollification" as people digested Talley's words.

At eight o'clock, the bands played "Home, Sweet Home" to an almost empty bank. Amon returned himself and his flu to bed. The bank remained open all night. Next morning, it announced that more cash was on deposit than before the bank run. A grand jury investigated the panic but reached no firm decision, although many people were convinced that Red anarchists were behind the bank run. Amon messaged his famous and influential friends that the aborted bank run proved Fort Worth was "financially able to take care of itself." No sir, Fort Worth was above such silly ideas as bank failures and Depressions.

The money stampede that became a block party soon was forgotten and the city's oil-slick economy slipped on for another two years.

The Depression did not suddenly pounce on Fort Worth. It *sideled* in. The *Star-Telegram* was forced to cut its payroll, but the family held on. No employee was dismissed or laid off. Everyone making more than twenty dollars weekly took a ten-percent salary reduction.

Amon was concerned. At home he announced that he and Nenetta and the children would reduce their living style. They would keep the servants and cars, but discontinue all luxuries, he declared. Bad financial times affected Amon very little. As usual, he was broke and in debt, even several months' behind on the family's grocery bills, just as he was during the 1920s' money boom. During the summer of 1934, he decided his home needed new window screens. Amon asked Bert Honea for a salary advance. The penurious treasurer advised Amon to repair the screens. Amon grumbled to Nenetta that "Bert Honea is the stingiest ole sonovabitch in the world," but he patched the screens.

For the *Star-Telegram*, the Depression was semantical: Fort Worth absolutely had no Depression, and if it gets any worse, something will have to be done. It got worse. The city petitioned for federal help.

Nineteen hundred and thirty-six was Texas' centennial and the state was obliged to commemorate its one hundred years of greatness. Two years earlier, the legislature appointed a committee of civic stewards to determine how Texas would solemnize that century of well-being. The committee's answer was an exposition, a statewide spectacular, heavy with products and farm produce and all good things of Texas, well-larded by educational displays and cultural events. Amon was appointed to the elite body but did not participate in its debates, except to ask for funds with which to expose West Texas' role in the state's fortunes. A board of historians, created to advise the Centennial Commission how and where to spend three million dollars, rejected the claim on grounds West Texas ". . . contains no history to commemorate."

No history!, shrieked the indignant *Star-Telegram*, ticking off the region's contributions to Texana . . . fourteen major Spanish explorations . . . Isleta, oldest town in the state . . . oil, ranches, railroads, cowboys, cattle. The editorial even excavated the skeleton of a giant bison found in Pleistocene gravel of the Panhandle to demonstrate prehistoric importance to the state. JRR dispatched reporters into the un-desert of West Texas to begin a weekly series of stories on history out there. The series continued for more than a year.

Being ignored by historians was insult enough but piddling beside the committee's next pronouncement: Dallas would be the site of the exposition.

Amon had not pushed Fort Worth on the commission. As most everyone, he believed San Antonio or Houston, both directly involved in the state's independence battle of 1936, were logical cities for the centennial celebration. Dallas, which didn't even exist a century earlier, had no more claim on the birthday party than Fort Worth. Dallas, however, had cash. The city proposed to invest more seed money, and that, in the Depression, was incentive enough. Told of Dallas' centennial coup, Amon set a record for consecutive gawddamns.

In June, 1935, a furious Amon Carter gathered his close friends to decide what must be done with Dallas. They agreed on a scheme of retribution in which Fort Worth would show its neighbor city "how the cow ate the cabbage" — Fort Worth would produce its own separate, unofficial centennial exposition! Amon always credited William Monnig with the original idea, but the impetus creating the Fort Worth exposition, and its final form, clearly was the publisher's. No one else would have dared try it. Besides, Amon found Billy Rose.

Earlier, Fort Worth, with its depressive non-Depression, solicited and received some federal assistance, but more was needed. The planned bogus centennial created a new demand and Will Rogers' death in summer, 1935, provided an acceptable approach. Fort Worth asked for a Public Works Administration grant to construct a combination coliseum and auditorium (with an unessential but impressive adjoined tower). After Rogers' death, Amon decided the complex would be named for his humorist pal, an idea causing the terrible-tongued Harold Ickes, FDR's interior secretary and PWA director, to snap, "I can't understand why a memorial to Will Rogers should be built in Fort Worth just because he was Carter's friend."

Amon's coliseum/auditorium enterprise had a secondary purpose. It, and adjacent buildings, would house the annual livestock show after the centennial celebration. The Southwestern Exposition, Fat Stock Show and Rodeo grew out of the north Fort Worth stockyards, and since before 1900 had been a true state-wide event. Site of the proposed centennial complex was a flat-topped, graveled hillock west of downtown across the Trinity River. Once the area was Camp Bowie, a World War I training facility. Earlier, it had been a horse ranch, and afterwards, a grandiose residential development that failed in the panic of '93. The Chisholm Trail passed nearby. The 135-acre tract, bought by the city for $150,050, had a pair of period deed restrictions — no cemetery could be settled on the property and it could not be sold to Negroes. In 1935, the hill was bare of everything but scrub oaks and ebony-eyed sunflowers.

Amon flew to Washington to solicit PWA money for his project, which became known as "Amon's Cowshed."

Ickes, unimpressed, turned down Carter's request. The acerbic Ickes wrote Amon of the denial, pointing out that he had approved a school building and a tuberculosis sanitarium for Fort Worth, both of which "clearly outranked a livestock pavilion as socially-desirable projects." Amon fired a wire at Ickes, claiming. "You have knocked us in the creek for good." Naturally, he went over Ickes' head to the White House.

Back in Washington, the publisher outlined Fort Worth's program to Postmaster General James Farley. Farley presented Amon's plan to FDR. He asked Carter to wait, and purposely left the door ajar.

Farley spoke loudly to the President, "Amon wants to build a cowshed."

"Cowshed!" exclaimed Roosevelt.

The eavesdropping Carter rushed in, shouting, "Now, gawddamnit, it's not a cowshed, it's . . ."

Roosevelt and Farley convulsed in laughter.

Fort Worth officially resubmitted the project and Farley ultimately wired, "Your proposal received. Was always in favor of large cowsheds." Early November, 1935, Jesse Jones, director of the Reconstruction Finance Corporation, wrote Carter, "Your cowshed has been approved by the administration."

Amon telegraphed his thanks to FDR: "The cowshed has arrived."

Fort Worth's outlaw exposition moved along, planned for a thirty-eight acre site adjacent to the PWA coliseum/auditorium, and largely in the inexperienced hands of the town's women. They set out to create an enlightened production heavy with religion and haute culture, a show with all the excited theatrics of an elementary school pageant.

In the ladies' defense, they knew no better, being amateurs at revenge on Dallas, and having very little with which to work. Dallas would immortalize the state with an exposition of empyreanic refinement, of artsy craftsy, even fustian, enlightenment. The pricetag was fifteen million dollars. The ladies, with a few thousand dollars, began to fashion a ragamuffin reprint of Dallas' show, a religio-historic extravaganza replete with homemade parts — Boy Scouts painted as fierce Indians, a reproduction of frontier Fort Worth, jelly and baking competitions, food booths and a museum, the city symphony for uplifting musicales and an amphitheater in which to present a dramatic gala featuring alternating church choirs.

Amon gawddamned the dullness of it all, and determined to find a remedy.

In late drinking hours at the Fort Worth Club, the men pledged to hire a consultant for the ladies. Soon after the women mailed Valentines promoting the celebration ("Prairie schooner to limousine, Sunbonnet to *crepe de chine*; Texas history, watch it grow, at Fort Worth's Centennial show"), Amon contacted Rufus

LeMaire, MGM's casting director and a former Fort Worthian. By coincidence, LeMaire knew of a producer in need of a project. *Billy Rose.*

William Samuel Rosenberg was thirty-seven — but fibbed and claimed only thirty-five — when he went to work for Fort Worth. He was an extraordinary figure in American theater life, ranking somewhere beneath the Barnums and Ziegfelds he emulated but affecting the style of the stage as no other man between the middle 1930s and post-war years. Quality was not Rose's genius; bigness was. As DeMille of the movies, Rose created glossy, oversized pageantry as eye-stunning as it was mediocre. Billy Rose had a brilliance for overwhelming the senses of a popcorn and lemonade audience and the shows he devised for Fort Worth in 1936 were perfect for their time and place. In 1936, Rose was not a theater immortal, was in fact little known beyond a few blocks of Broadway where bystanders sniggerly called him "Mr. Brice," referring to his famous wife, Fannie, the Ziegfeld musical comedy star. He had been a world shorthand champion and Bernard Baruch's secretary and was a song writer of minor acclaim. He produced the thinly plotted but entertaining *Jumbo* for Broadway, a circus opus starring Jimmy Durante. His Casino de Paree and Music Hall, a pair of New York cabarets, briefly were popular. As the year began, Rose was desperate, even neurotic, to shed the "Mr. Brice" title, and in Fort Worth, he moved out of his wife's shadow.

Thirty years after the centennial, Rose wrote, "I don't know what would have happened to my ragtag career if Amon Carter hadn't offered me the job . . . but it's a cinch the pattern would have been plenty different." *Casa Manana*, the centennial's largest show, was, he wrote, "by all odds the best I've ever had my name on." A *Star-Telegram* editorial described *Casa Manana*: "No attraction of its size and lavishness has been produced in the history of American theater." For once, the newspaper's hometowning rhetoric was not exaggerated. *Casa Manana* seems to have been a benchmark of musical spectacle. For the first time there was lavishness and dramatic grandeur beyond Broadway. Billy restaged *Casa Manana*, with only thinly-disguised differences, for the remainder of his theatrical life.

In retrospect, the unauthorized centennial was the consequence of timing and personalities: Rose's desperation to become something other than Fannie Brice's husband; Amon Carter, sizzling with a classic snit against Dallas; John Murray Anderson, peaking in his abilities as a director; Albert Johnson and Raoul Pene Du Bois, still in their twenties, reaching for perfection and fame in stage design and costuming; Dana Suesse, only twenty-one, rising to be one of the few successful female songwriters; Paul Whiteman, establishing himself as a legendary mixer of symphony and jazz, and shrewd, petite and naked Sally Rand, who would make feather fans and rubber bubbles the standard for staged nudism. As those components gathered, James Reston, an Associated Press columnist, reported, "Never has Broadway been so interested in a project outside of New York."

Early 1936, Billy Rose was in Hollywood, attempting to catch on in moving pictures, which were unimpressed with Mr. Brice. He still was hanging around the studios when Amon telephoned LeMaire.

Billy came to Fort Worth. He listened. He inspected the site, learned of the Boy Scout Indians and religious undercurrent and the trivial budget. Shaking his head, as much in disbelief as refusal, Rose reboarded an American Airlines flight to New York. Amon Carter boarded the plane with Rose, and began talking. When the airplane landed in New York, Billy was sold into becoming director general of Fort Worth's Frontier Centennial. It was a question of who sold whom; Billy's salary was one thousand dollars a day for one hundred days.

The show's finance committee hiccoughed with shock.

Billy's wages was a gewgaw beside Amon's next pronouncement. Fort Worth must assemble a million bucks. Amon chaired the fund drive, and the money hustle began. First, he emptied his and his friends' pockets, then committed the *Star-Telegram* for sixty-five thousand dollars, which infuriated Bert Honea. Selling bonds at fifty dollars each, the Chamber of Commerce gouged another $250,000 from its members. Amon begged from the Texas Centennial Commission. Somehow, he wrangled a quarter of a million dollars from the United States Centennial Commission. He put the PWA, and Ickes, under siege. Elliott Roosevelt, then a Fort Worth radio station owner, messaged his father for more government cash. And Amon dogged American industry, the companies run by men he had gifted with hats and smoked turkeys and diamond-studded belts. The corporations already were committed heavily to Dallas' official centennial; few responded to Amon's first call. General Motors turned him down six times, each refusal being less and less polite. He refused their refusals, and his files reveal a full range of approaches, from overt wheedling to outright groveling. Ultimately, General Motors handed over twenty-five thousand dollars as sponsor of the showground's public address system. Most companies eventually contributed, albeit token amounts. It was hush money to stop Amon's telephone calls and telegrams.

Ground was broken March 7 and the *Star-Telegram* crowed editorially, "Faces which a few months ago were sobered . . . are tanned and smiling, for there are jobs again."

Rose returned to announce his plans, a rather remarkable revelation since he had plans at all, a situation which would have troubled a lesser man. His first press conference was pure stream of consciousness press agentry, held, incidentally, atop a gargantuan white stallion, from which Rose gleefully posed for newsreel pictures. He shouted to the crowd:

"You people stick with me and I'll make a big state out of Texas."

"Will you miss Broadway?" a reporter asked.

"Hell, I am Broadway!" admonished Billy.

Once tapped, the wellspring of puffery flooded onto the newsmen:

"I'm going to put on a show the like of which has never been seen by the human eye. This Fort Worth show will bring 5,000,000 visitors down here. It should gross $2,000,000 . . . No, No . . . it'll be a five million dollar show. We'll give them a bold ball of fire. Let Dallas, at the central centennial, educate the people. We'll entertain them in Fort Worth. We'll have a 'Lonely Hearts Ball' weekly where all lonesome women can come and find a partner in a drawing. In years to come there'll be kids telling one another that their grandma and grandpa were thrown together by fate and fell in love at the Fort Worth Frontier Centennial. I'll get Shirley Temple, Mae West, Guy Lombardo, Jack Benny. I'll get 1,000 beautiful girls for the Frontier Follies. I'll have a Texas Pageant to be called 'The Fall of the Frontier' . . . 'The Battle of San Jacinto' . . . or some other Texas name [starring, one reporter presumed, a resurrected Santa Anna leading the entire Mexican Army]. I'll have 2,000 Indians and 1,000 cowboys, and guess who wins? I'll have a chorus line of 500 pretty girls. I'll have an open-air dance floor for 3,000 dancers, and singing waiters. Dallas has all that historical stuff so we don't have to worry about that. We can just show the people a good time. I plan to drive Dallas nuts. Every time Dallas says something about its exposition, I'll give 'em Shirley Temple. This is the biggest thing I've ever done. This'll make 'Jumbo' look like a peep show."

Rose promised to import *Jumbo*, utilizing "900 extras and truckloads of circus animals." He announced a theater-restaurant seating forty-five hundred persons and a faithful recreation of an old-time saloon with a dozen two-hundred-pound beauties dancing atop a splendorful bar.

Reporters decided what they had on their hands was a fat little raving madman.

Standing a pot-bellied five-foot-two, Rose looked like a tall overweight urchin (John Nance Garner, the vice-president, called Billy a "pursley-gutted little feller"). He had sudden, excited movements, with a hopscotching kind of walk and flinging hands, smoked endlessly — though never buying cigarettes; he merely reached into the pocket of the nearest smoker and filched his tobacco needs. Within days, he was addicted to Dr Pepper, then only a Texas-based soft drink, and one with a reputation for solving constipation because everyone believed its secret formula began with prune juice (it didn't). Rose's nighttime lifestyle had given him the complexion of a fungus. He looked sickly, reporters thought, until they tried to match his twenty-hour days and field the ideas popping from his eight-story mind.

Billy scrapped the ladies' centennial program (he said their museum would have looked like "hell and a bunch of spinach"), and relegated them to positions as treeplanters, greeters and scrapbook keepers. Within days, he was auditioning girls for chorus line positions. One aspiring dancer, far under the minimum height, tapdanced for Rose. Rose advised the girl — Mary Martin from nearby Weatherford — to go home and get married and forget show business.

A week after his thunderbolt introduction into Fort Worth, Rose was back in New York to assemble a professional staff, hire real chorus girls and entertainers, close *Jumbo*, and, incidentally, try and figure out just what kind of centennial he would produce. He arrived almost hidden under an Amon Carter cowboy hat and flashing a gold-plated sheriff's badge. Billy swaggered bowleggedly into the Hippodrome and said "Hidy" to

Jumbo's cast. Standing on Rosie the elephant's footstool, Billy addressed the company, "My friends, I am now a Texan. I commute between this great city which we have here and Texas, a state they have given me as a plaything."

By mid-April, two thousand men toiled at the centennial site, rushing to meet a June opening date. Flitting among the laborers was the quixotic Rose, shouting, bumming cigarettes, spilling Dr Pepper, directing construction from pencil sketches marked by Albert Johnson back in New York. Rose still had only the slightest notion of what his million dollar show would be.

Billy took a suite in the Worth Hotel, but worked out of an office in the nearby Sinclair Building where he held court and auditions. He installed a wide desk and behind it, an elevated chair that pedestalized him like a minikin magistrate above those who stood before the Rosian bar. Amon's secretary, Katrine Deakins, thought Billy on his lofty throne "looked like a knot on a dead stump."

Newsmen were intrigued by the array of characters flowing through Rose's office:

Four-foot-three-inch John Fox, once Buster Brown for a shoe company. Seven-foot-four-inch Dave Ballard, a schoolboy from Commerce, Texas. Seventy-five-year-old Josie DeMott Robinson, a bareback rider who had worked for P. T. Barnum. A strong woman who bent nails between her fingers. Gozo, the mind-reading dog. Tiny Kline, once arrested in New York for sliding on a wire from a hotel roof to a theater. Joe Peanuts and his Simian Gigolos, a sixteen piece, all-monkey band. There was a man who looked and dressed like Abe Lincoln and a real Russian count who spoke no English, an aviatrix who flew upside down, a parachutist who leaped from balloons, a rancher with a four thousand pound six-foot-two-inch tall steer.

Through the *Star-Telegram*, Rose issued a call for "whittlers, snuff-dippers, crackbox philosophers, old couples, ox-wagons and ox-drivers, town half-wits, the village drunk, etc." to populate Sunset Trail, main street of the frontier section.

A promoter came with a frog circus, and still another peddled a human spine spiked with Indian arrows.

C. J. Maxwell, a Fort Worth man, entered clutching a leather briefcase. He unsnapped the case and dumped onto Billy's desk a live wriggling snake. Rose hopped up on his high chair, screaming, "Get that thing the hell out of here!" The snake, which had two perfectly-formed heads, each of which could be fed separately, was trained to eat from Maxwell's hand and follow him like a loving pet. Despite Rose's initial terror, he recognized a sterling exhibit. He hired the snake.

What had Amon wrought?

Rose was asked to complete in less than two months what Dallas, ten thousand workers and fifteen million dollars were doing in a year. The deadline of June 6 could not be met; Dallas's centennial opened on schedule. But by then Rose knew what he would present and how it would be staged. Not that an absence of final plans blunted publicity. Rose went ahead with propoganda and stunts that had Fort Worthians gape-mouthed.

Rose telegraphed Mrs. Wallis Simpson, called by polite society columnists "friend of King Edward of England." The wire read:

> Would consider it a privilege to present you in person at the Fort Worth Frontier Centennial here in Texas Stop Am prepared to offer you $25,000 a week for four weeks engagement Stop If interested, please cable.

She never answered, but the offer made headlines.

Billy wired Germany to request the airship *Hindenberg* for transportation of one hundred showgirls from

Broadway to Fort Worth. No answer. He offered Ethiopian Emperor Haile Selassie, then fleeing a short-lived palace coup, one hundred thousand dollars to appear "with your lions" in the fiesta. Silence. He messaged Gypsy Rose Lee, promising her "3 G's to perform." The premier stripper wired back, "Strings or Grands."

Billy, shouting irritably, "I don't need a 40 hour week, I need a 40 hour day," hired real Indians — Comanche, Apache, Navajo, Hopi and Sioux — and contracted for a Monkey Mountain. He wrote billboard copy that said nothing, but said it very well:

> BIGGEST ENTERPRISE DEVOTED EXCLUSIVELY TO AMUSEMENT IN THE HISTORY OF THE WORLD . . . Monkey Mountain . . . 92 other attractions of Magnitude and Merit . . . Not Cheap Catch Penny Peep-Shows . . . Take your Entertainment Sitting Down.

Eleven thousand billboards were erected over nine states. They showed near-nude girls gamboling in a western motif, and the slogan: GO ELSEWHERE FOR EDUCATION, COME TO FORT WORTH FOR ENTERTAINMENT. That *ipse dixit*, appearing in various renditions, was the Fiesta's battlecry. The phrase rankled Dallas.

Preachy as ever, the *Star-Telegram* urged Fort Worth's citizens to "get into the Fiesta Spirit," and lectured women on proper dress for shows — "Do not wear freakish costumes like slacks, overalls or beach pajamas." The newspaper, "as a public service for our non-Texas visitors," printed a lexicon of western terms ("Chouse: to stir up cattle more than is good for them"). It reported on reactions beyond its borders: "Fort Worth stole the show last night when WLW, the world's most popular radio station. saluted Texas from Cincinnati. It [Fort Worth] was the first Texas city mentioned and received four mentions to Dallas' two."

Billy Rose, into his final plans, was building a mountain for the *Last Frontier*, his western epic. He said it would incorporate a full rodeo because ". . . rodeo is grand opera on horseback." Billy had never seen a rodeo. Amon suggested that Rose add square dancing to the western plot. Billy agreed, "That's a swell idea."

"What's square dancing?" Billy later asked Bess Stephenson, one of three *Star-Telegram* reporters assigned to write daily stories on the exposition. She escorted Rose to Peacock's Tavern on Fort Worth's north side, where Goober Dixon called a double-L swing while the Rabbit Twisters, a string band, played *Sally Goodin'*.

> Balance all, balance eight, swing yo' pardner like swingin' on a gate.
> Balance all, balance eight, honor yo' pardner and pull yo' brake.

Billy silently sat through the entire performance. The dance completed, Rose whispered in Bess' ear, "Where's the sex in it?"

On the way home, Rose announced, "I'll have 200 dancers."

He had one hundred and thirty-six, and Goober chanting:

> Hurry, girls, and don't get lazy, big fat hogs and lots of gravy,
> *Star-Telegram*, full of news, grab that gal with the high-top shoes.

The Rose-conceived square dance was choreographed by Alexander Oumansky, late of the Diaghileff Russian Ballet Company. Billy was never common.

By mid-June, casts were assembled and in rehearsal. The professional showgirls arrived from New York and immediately asked to see cowboys. One chorine strolled to a nearby drugstore and inquired of a clerk, "Which way's the village?" Indians poured in by the tribesful. Within days, Navajos were feuding with the Sioux, the Hopis with the Apaches and Comanches with everybody. Reporters caught Navajo braves doing the family wash. Local archers beat the Indians in a bow and arrow contest. The Indians struck *The Last Frontier* because the script called for them to enter single file. They could not, they protested, because there were six chiefs among them and each chief had to lead. Rose handed down a Solomon decision: "Make them all chiefs, irrespectable [*sic*] whether they are or not." Every Indian on the grounds was pronounced a chief. Rehearsals continued.

John Murray Anderson arrived to direct the *Casa Manana* show. At fifty, a widower, Anderson was a polished gentleman, a Canadian educated in Europe. He had straight, combed-back hair and a long unsmiling face, and a tongue that blistered. Two men could not have been more ill-matched than the sophisticated Anderson and Bronx-made Rose, but they were perfect for the stage. Rose dreamed; Anderson made dreams real.

Neither especially liked the other. Once Billy big-shotted his wealth at Anderson, shouting, "I have a fistful of money. What do you have?"

"I," replied Anderson quietly, "have one friend."

Erudite and cosmopolitan, as proven by his Ziegfeld extravaganzas on Broadway, Anderson nevertheless had a tinselled beery eye for pomp and pageantry. He knew what sold on stage. His directing style was one of sarcasm and nettled wit. In Fort Worth, he assembled casts to see what he had. Not much, he muttered, and warned, "We have too many of you wretched showgirls and if a single one of you makes a sound, you'll be thrown out."

As rehearsals progressed, fascinated reporters spent leisure hours hanging around the Broadwayites, "watching Anderson yell." "You halfwit with the cigar," Murray lashed at one actor. "Project what little voice you have out here, not into the wings."

"God only knows where that small mind of yours wanders," he hurled at an out-of-step chorine.

Anderson never called cast members or acquaintances by their names but invented chimerical titles for them. His Fort Worth chorus girls were given such aliases as Dry Ice and Child Frightener, Goo-Goo, Fuzzy, The Cobra, Birthday Cake and Eyebrows, Chigger, Cigar and Spaghetti. Anderson's names for Rose were The Mad Emperor and The Mad Hatter. He called Amon — perhaps he sensed Amon's dislike of familiarity from the hired hands — simply and unimaginatively, The Big Chief.

The strange nicknames came from behavioral or physical quirks and none was more obvious or lasting than that for the girl Anderson titled Stuttering Sam — Mary Louise Dowell, the ninteen-year-old daughter of Fort Worth's police chief. Mary Louise first came to Rose seeking a chorus line job for her sister. Rose hired both girls. Mary was six-feet-tall, possessed of perfect legs, a pert face and bright red hair. She had unaffected stage presence and carriage and a smile that beamed even into the nickle seats. She was the model showgirl, except for the stutter.

Stuttering Sam became the focal point of *Casa Manana*, both in 1936 and 1937, then Rose transported her to Broadway as centerpiece for his *Diamond Horseshoe.* Mary Louise Dowell immediately became New York's most celebrated showgirl.

Mary minded her stammer not at all, and her naturalness charmed cynical New Yorkers. James Montgomery Flagg painted her. She dated show business leading men. Columnists Ed Sullivan and Walter Winchell publicized her stuttering quips ("Where did you get that mink coat?" a Stork Club habitue asked Mary Louise. "I found it on the s-s-s-s-subway," replied Stuttering Sam). Once she was introduced to movie titan Jesse Lansky. Trying to say hello, Mary Louise stammered, "Hel-hel-hel-hell, I'm glad to meet you."

Lansky was startled, but answered, "Hell, I'm glad to meet you, too."

Stuttering Sam fascinated Flagg and the columnists and others like Doug Fairbanks Senior and Jack LaRue, with her tales of Texas. "T-T-Texas is God's c-c-country," she would brag, explaining the processes of milking cows, feeding chickens, frying steak and picking pecans. She complained because Toots Shor didn't serve cornbread and buttermilk in his restaurant. Shor affectionately called Sam his "crum-bum doll."

Mary Louise's showgirl career, though, was secondary to her first ambition. She wanted to be a writer. She became a columnist for the *Star-Telegram*, bylined "Stuttering Sam." The columns pattered on about Broadway and its characters, of her adventures in the big city, of other Texans displaced in New York.

Abruptly, in 1942, Stuttering Sam quit show business and took her typewriter to Hollywood, to Warner Brothers where she was hired as a scenarist. There was talk of a film on her life but nothing came of the idea. Two years later, Sam left Hollywood without writing success.

Not everyone was enchanted by the centennial. Albert Johnson entered a cafe for breakfast and a waitress, hearing his accent, asked, "You one of them New York actor people?" He admitted he was. She frowned. The waitress served the meal, and Johnson called after her, "Say, I asked for buttered toast."

"Butter it yourself," snapped the woman, "yore arm ain't broken."

It was not only Texas' natural suspicion of outsiders, but Rose's abrupt manner, and his ideas, which in the end had very little to do with Texas history, that created the problems. A veterans' group complained Rose refused to give them space for their war weapons display. The women, pushed into the background, weren't content with their trash cleanup campaign, sponsorship of Centennial Clubs in schools and the restoration of a log cabin. They publicly condemned the scantily-clad cowgirl symbol on billboards and lamented the absence of a church in the reconstructed frontier town. A Miss Shelton suggested doing away with the saloons and adding Fort Worth's symphony orchestra and an opera "each fortnight."

Preachers, both collectively and singularly, went after Billy Rose's sinful hide. Much of the ensuing debate centered on the centennial's advertising for *Casa Manana*, which depicted bare-breasted but nippleless girls splashing in the theater's lagoon. And mostly it was the Baptists — Southern Baptists are unequalled in their ability to ferret out vice among the masses — who decried the shamefulness of it all.

A committee of Baptist vice-ferreters investigated the fiesta's immorality and reported that all ingredients for public corruption certainly were there — nude advertising with suggestive words and phrases, half-naked showgirls, booze and slot machines. One Baptist minister, S. H. Frazier, told city council members of the "nude women above the water" and asked the tantalizing question, "Are we going to show visitors the old days only as drinking, gambling and carousing?" The Reverend Mister Frazier added, "If I had the money, I would rent a concession stand and preach, morning, noon and night, and distribute religious material out there."

Methodists joined the protest, denouncing Billy Rose from the pulpits. Fort Worth's General Ministers Association voted a resolution condemning the fiesta's advertising and general lack of religious orientation. A delegation was dispatched to confront Rose. Billy later commented, "They were all nice, except one, and he looked like he had 60 yards of rope under his hat to hang me." The meeting changed nothing. Privately, Rose was elated with the preachers' attack. It was better publicity than he could contrive and the ministers' catalog of centennial wickedness showed customers exactly where to look for what they wanted.

Strangely silent during the preacher uprising was that most enthusiastic sin stomper of all — J. Frank Norris. The show's iniquitous facade seemed to have been made in Heaven as a Norris target, but he stayed out of the controversy. In fact, he attended a performance of *Casa Manana* in late Autumn, commenting, "My hat is off to Amon Carter and his associates. They've done a real job." Curious words for a man who once lambasted Sunday picture shows. Norris did not jump on the exposition because he had made a deal with Amon.

Shortly before opening, Amon telephoned the Baptist leader.

"You going out of town this summer?" asked Amon.

"I might. Why do you ask?"

"We've got this centennial show and some nude girls, and we're going to sell liquor. . ."

"I see. Well, I've been intending to hold some revivals. I guess I could start them early," suggested Norris.

"You do that," agreed Amon.

Norris traveled more than twenty-seven thousand miles in distant states saving souls under big tents and did not return to Fort Worth until late September, long after folks discovered the wickedness largely was pulpit-made.

There was of course nudity: thirty-six unadorned breasts in Sally Rand's Nude Ranch. Sally, the fan and bubble dancer, performed in *Casa Manana* but owned and produced the Nude Ranch. *Variety* reported Sally netted a thousand dollars weekly from her nudes. That sin should pay so well provoked Baptist preachers to even more bombastic outrage.

The very Reverend Joe Scheumack commanded that city councilmen "see to it that those girls put on clothes or that the show is closed."

Had he seen the show?

"I have not," he replied indignantly. "I just saw the statues out front. They are an open violation of the law in themselves."

Hitting his stride, Reverend Scheumack said the Nude Ranch "is a contamination of the centennial and flagrant violation of this state's penal code. I think they're about as low as they can get. Such things have a tendency to corrupt the morals of people."

Folks anxious to debauch their morals rushed to see the objects of Scheumack's harangue. The nude business got better.

Sally Rand was one of the most successful strippers in history, though she disdained the term and in fact never undressed on stage — she danced naked but hidden behind fans or balloons and bathed in a baby blue light. Nobody ever saw anything she didn't want them to see, thus her coined wisecrack, "The Rand is quicker than the eye."

Sally was hired at Amon's suggestion. During that horsebacked first press conference, Rose promised his production would have "neither nudity nor smut. Only once had the public responded to smut. We don't need any fans or bubble dances at the Texas Frontier Centennial and we won't have them."

Curious, Amon asked about the smut responded to once by the public.

"At the Century of Progress in Chicago," said Billy. "Sally Rand had a nude act."

"Pulled 'em in, did she?"

"Thousands."

"Let's get her."

Sally's Nude Ranch was billed as the "only educational exhibit on the grounds" and cost two-bits, a bargain. Out front were replicas of classic Greek and Roman statues with bared plaster breasts irking the Reverend Scheumack. Patrons entered through a recreated ranch house front porch, on which sat Adolph, King of the Nudists. He was seventy-four and wore a long black beard. He dressed in a Roman tunic.

Inside were the thirty-six breasts belonging to eighteen pretty girls. They wore cowboy boots and hats, green bandanas, skirtlets and tights. Only breasts showed. Sally branded each girl with a rubber-stamped "SR." The "show" consisted of the girls lounging on swings and beach chairs. Some played with a beach ball. Others shot bows and arrows. One or two sat on horses. A screen wire floor-to-ceiling wall separated breasts from viewers. Jack Gordon, the *Press* entertainment columnist, described the girls as "goona-goona." There was a "kick-off" room to extract another quarter from spectators. Inside was Florence dressed in an organdie gown. A maid helped Florence undress, removing even the black step-ins, and enter her milk bath. Florence bathed in milk twenty-five times a day.

The sinful Nude Ranch was as chaste as those old nudist colony films but fiesta-goers seemed not to mind the innocence of it all.

Sally Rand was never what people thought she was. She arrived driving a chocolate-colored Lincoln touring sedan and done up in a sunbonnet and calico granny dress. For the next three months she was the best publicity campaign of the centennial.

She threw out the first ball opening softball season and speaking to the crowd, removed only her sunbonnet, but promised, "You'll see more of me." She spoke to every service club in town. "I am an exponent of truth in advertising and consequently I stick to the bare facts when selling my merchandise," she told Kiwanis members. "I'm in the same business as you," Sally explained to an advertising club. "Selling white space."

She spoke to PTA groups. She traveled to Dallas and Waco and Wichita Falls, boosting the Fiesta. She bought fifty memberships for the civic music season. She donated time and money to underprivileged kids. In tight shorts, hair braided, Sally gave a pep talk to TCU's Horned Frog football team. She was photographed in the kitchen of her rented home, baking a cake. Sally directed traffic at high noon in downtown Fort Worth. Her grandmother, Mollie Grove, came to visit, and Sally threw a tea party for the old lady. Reporters sat around with show business' best nude act talking of crochet patterns and lemon chiffon pie recipes.

C. L. Richhart was assigned by Jim Record to write an in-depth story on Sally. Rich went to her dressing room, knocked and was summoned inside where he found Sally, naked, lying on her stomach reading the Bible.

Sally stretched, rolled over, and shyly covered her *mons venus* with Psalms 35:17.

Of the seventeen thousand stories appearing around Texas on Fort Worth's centennial, half featured Sally Rand. Her pictures appeared 947 times in Texas newspapers during her ninety-day stay in Fort Worth. Sally was such an accomplished attention-getter that Jack Gordon predicted "when the next city storm sewer opens, there will be a picture of Sally Rand crawling through it."

November 6 was declared Sally Rand Day in Tarrant County. The stripper who dared inflict bare breasts on Fort Worth was cited for her "graciousnesss and consummate artistry" and publicly thanked for bringing "culture and progress to Tarrant County."

June passed. Enter July. Still no Fort Worth Frontier Centennial. Amon was fidgety, anxious for the exposition he had promised. Dallas' centennial show was doing big business. Critics praised the Dallas show, lauding its edifying theses. Visitors said they enjoyed most the General Motors building in which Jan Garber's orchestra played beside a crank shaft spinning seventeen hundred times a minute, and the Chrysler exhibit with its organ and harp concerts. Eddie Barr, a Dallas columnist, sneaked a look at Fort Worth's uncompleted showgrounds and declared, "It probably will be mediocre and cheap."

Fort Worth responded by erecting the world's second largest sign opposite the main entrance of Dallas' exposition. The green and red neon sign was one hundred and thirty feet long, sixty feet high and its message blinked day and night: FORTY-FIVE MINUTES WEST TO WHOOPEE. Fort Worth was spelled out in green neon letters seventeen and one-half feet tall. The sign was second in size only to a chewing gum display overlooking Times Square. Dallas began scurrying around for non-educational exhibits.

Fort Worth concluded its state wide beauty contest to select Texas Sweetheart Number One. Billy Rose revealed that a bright new Hollywood star, Clark Gable, would judge the competition, but as most Rosian announcements, it never happened. Rose, Anderson and Amon culled the entries, awarding the crown to Miss Faye Cotton, a Borger waitress. She was five-foot-six inches tall, weighed one hundred and twenty pounds, had gray eyes and a 35-24½-35 figure. Cotton told reporters she read the Bible each day and had hobbies of dancing and shooting. The *Star-Telegram* commented that the beauty queen had "less personal vanity than a Salvation Army settlement worker." She immediately entered the hospital for a tonsillectomy.

The Dallas *Morning News* chided Fort Worth for not choosing a sweetheart with higher social standing than that of a waitress. The *Star-Telegram* angrily defended the selection with an editorial praising motherhood in West Texas. Meanwhile, Amon searched for celebrities to open the Fiesta. He wanted FDR. The President declined, but promised to furnish his vice president, Cactus Jack Garner. Texas Governor James Allred would come, and Texas Senator Tom Connally, Texas Attorney General Wiliam McGraw, former governor Pat Neff, and American Airlines president C. R. Smith. Elliott Roosevelt agreed to stand in for his father. FDR came to Fort Worth in early July to visit Elliott at his Dutch Branch Ranch west of town. Amon escorted the President on a tour of centennial grounds and suggested a way for Roosevelt to participate in the opening without actually being there.

Rose still was hiring acts. He brought in the Foster Girls, seventeen teenage bareback riders shepherded by Allen K. Foster, who did not allow his cast to date, smoke or drink, enforced a midnight curfew and made them go everywhere, even to meals, as a group. Billy announced he had hired for *Jumbo* the lovely Barbette — "Most breathtaking aerialist in Europe." Daily, Rose issued reports of Barbette's progress towards Fort Worth, of how Barbette was the toast of Paris, of Barbette being wined and dined by crowned heads of Europe. Barbette, newsmen decided, was something special. She was. Rather, *he* was. Barbette was Clyde Vander of Round Rock, Texas, a female impersonator who actually was an aerial star in Europe.

The Fort Worth Frontier Centennial officially opened July 18. Twenty-five thousand spectators crowded the entrance to Sunset Trail where dedication ceremonies were held. Amon entered the grounds driving a Wells Fargo stagecoach. He was dressed in his cowboy costume and whooped and yippeed for *March of Time* newsreel cameras. Amon fired his pistols for the newsreel and admitted, "Yes, Dallas does have something Fort Worth doesn't have — a real city thirty miles away."

FDR was in his yacht, the Sewanna, fishing in the Bay of Funday off Cape Sable, Nova Scotia. At 3:30 p.m., Fort Worth time, he punched a button, sending an electrical impulse to a Maine relay station, which beamed the wave on across the United States to Texas, to Fort Worth, to the entrance of Sunset Trail where it electronically snipped a lasso.

That day Dallas newspapers announced that two million people already had attended the Texas Centennial. Dallas also held a bizarre ceremony, apparently to blunt publicity in Fort Worth. In mid-afternoon, Violet Hilton was married to James Moore, a slide trombone player, on the fifty-yard line of the Cotton Bowl. Five thousand people paid twenty-five cents each to attend the wedding. It was a simple, dignified ceremony. The bride wore white, as did her Siamese twin sister, Daisy.

There was little Dallas could do to lessen Fort Worth fanfare. One thousand newspapermen, including the best-known New York columnists and critics, were present for the opening. Amon had invited them, furnished transportation, food and booze to get them there. Already there was a crashing crescendo of words flowing to the nation.

An American Airlines plane was chartered for the New Yorkers. Billy Rose met the plane, outfitted in one of Amon's cowboy rigs, with spurs, oversized hat and boots. Two guns hung on his hips. Billy quick-drawed his pistols, aimed them at the newspapermen and shouted, "Bang, bang. You're dead." Lucius Beebe, the columnist, wrote that Rose looked like "an East Side kid playing cowboy." The *Star-Telegram* reported that the critics also were greeted by "four pickaninnies in candy-striped suits carrying a banner, 'Welcome Fourth Estate,' while Blackie's Bluejackets struck up 'The Eyes of Texas.'"

That evening Amon primed the writers with champagne and chili at his Shady Oak Farm then sent them to *Casa Manana* for a special press prevue. The prevue was preceded by an hour-long, eighty-five station national broadcast on the NBC network. WBAP originated the broadcast. Its announcers handled microphones, and Harold Hough was anchorman. He lamented that Sally Rand's Nude Ranch would not be presented adequately, adding, "But after all, we do not have television."

Casa Manana's press prevue was an uncompromised success and stories about the centennial blanketed America. Burns Mantle wrote, "For valor, valor touched with profligacy, I give you Fort Worth, even if it suspects all Scotch drinkers are sissys." Robert Garland of the New York *World Telegram*, gushed, "So gargantuan . . . so fantastic . . . so incredible. They have merged the dreams of Buffalo Bill with Broadway Billy. I like the imagination of it, the what-the-hell-do-we-care of its 2 million dollar whoopee." Ward Morehouse, the New York *Sun*'s drama critic, suggested a *Casa Manana* be built in Central Park*. Beebe thought the show was "thrilling . . . a dream come true" but went on to call Texans "scrammy," mostly because a drunken cowboy tried to sell him a twenty-two hundred-acre ranch.

Damon Runyon, writing for the Hearst newspapers, was most expansive: "Broadway and the wild west are jointly producing what probably is the biggest and most original show ever seen in the United States. If you took the Polo Grounds and converted it into a cafe and then added the best Ziegfeld scenic effects, you might get something approximating *Casa Manana.*"

After the show, critics interviewed Billy, who claimed his thousand dollar a day fee was too low. "I'm worth much more than that," he bragged.

"What will you do when you're through here?" he was asked.

"I'll get one of those little Balkan wars and go on tour with it."

Next evening, and for every evening thereafter, at least four thousand people filled *Casa Manana*. The crowd often was mixed tux and overalls, gowns and print dresses, but nobody cared. They came, ate the $1.75 dinner and sighed as Everett Marshall sang to Faye Cotton. Marshall and Cotton were central to the show's

*Billy Rose later opened a *Casa Manana* at 7th Avenue and 50th Street in New York but the cafe/theater was never popular.

plot, so tenuous as to be missed if a patron blinked.

Billy's advertising was not subtle:

> . . . Not only a day but a Decade in Advance of its Time . . . The Largest Theater-Cafe ever Constructed . . . Tables and Chairs for 4,500 Amusement Lovers . . . A Gargantuan-Revolving-Reciprocating Stage . . . Three and a Half Times Larger than that of Radio City Music Hall . . . Two 450 h.p. Motors Required to Operate this Liviathan [sic] of Rostrums, with its 4,264,000 Pounds of Actual Deadweight plus its Lovely Freight of 250 Eye-Bedeviling Coryphees Over a Pool of Limpid Crystal containing 617,000 Gallons of Real Water . . . SPECTACLE and SONG, DANCE, AND COMEDY . . . Past Peradventure, the BIGGEST SHOW EVER PRODUCED.

Beside that modest announcement was an artist's conception of *Casa Manana*, showing ten nude girls splashing in 617,000 gallons of real water.

The Cavalcade of World Fairs was little more than an excuse for huge sets. Marshall and Cotton portrayed a couple who honeymooned at the St. Louis World Fair and liked it so well they went on to fairs in Paris, Chicago and, of course, Fort Worth, wandering among the chorus girls and stars. Ann Pennington danced as Little Egypt (she "cootchied" so violently on opening night, wrote Jack Gordon, that her beads broke and bounced into front row soup bowls). Sally Rand was featured as a "Ballet Divertisement" in the Chicago scenes, alternating her fans and balloons. The latter were five feet in diameter, colored light blue, cost twenty-five dollars each and were made by Goodyear. She lost a couple of them to tacky Texas night breezes and thereafter used the balloons only on perfectly calm evenings.

Marshall sang "The Night Is Young and You're So Beautiful" to Faye Cotton, who wore a five thousand dollar, forty-pound gold lamé gown designed by New York Jewelers, Whiting and Davis. The song, which became the unofficial anthem for the centennial, was dashed off in Billy's Worth Hotel suite by Rose and Dana Suesse, who were stuck for a big number in the St. Louis segment. By early 1937, the melody was high on the hit parade. The Marshall/Cotton scene, Paris' Eiffel Tower glitteringly outlined with five thousand lights, Ann Pennington emerging from a *papier mache* ''100-gallon hat'' — all brought applause. Nothing, however, compared with the final scene when the mammoth stage rolled back. The giant stage, one hundred and thirty feet in diameter and actually only three times the size of that in Radio City, balanced on waters of a blue lagoon*. Each of its revolutions would require a minute and forty-five seconds (front row customers would set their beers on the stage and watch the steins go around). In that final tableau, the entire cast assembled as eighty-five fountains exploded with colored water, the six flags under which Texas served paraded and waved, and Marshall sang ''Lone Star'' as gondoliers poled gondolas across the lagoon. The spectacle was so awesome nobody ever wondered why Venetian-type boatmen appeared in a western scene.

Amon boasted he saw *Casa Manana* sixty times.

Rose's other productions were less popular. Pioneer Palace was a honky-tonk with ten-cent beer, slot machines, pig races on a forty-foot-long bar. Lulu Bates was the star of the show there, singing ''I'm in Love With A Handlebar Mustache,'' a song written by Rose and later appropriated by Amon Carter, who sang it for anyone who would listen, and many who would not. The Palace chorus line was filled by the Rosebuds, a sextet of super-sized girls dressed in ruffled frocks and red hair ribbons; the smallest weighed 215 pounds, the largest, 340. Rose later transferred the Palace decor

*The lagoon proved troublesome. During a final rehearsal, Everett Marshall misstepped backstage and fell into the water. He emerged wet and angry, shouting at Anderson, ''Dammit, Murray, somebody's gonna have an accident and sue you for a million.''

and acts for his most successful dinner theater, The Diamond Horseshoe.

The Last Frontier was Rose's western pageant, staged in an outdoor amphitheater. It was, advertised Rose, the "Vivid, Visual Saga of the March of Civilization . . . THE OLD WEST LIVES AGAIN . . . See Attack of the Hostiles . . . Womanhood in Jeopardy . . . Thank God the Rangers! Battle of Arroyo Grande . . . and The Mail Goes Through."

"Many, many moons ago, the smile of the Great Spirit beamed upon the land of the Red Man. Great herds of shaggy buffalo thundered westward . . ." began the narration, summoning all Indians, a small buffalo herd, the cowboys, a Texas Longhorn herd, a cavalry troop. There were Indian attacks and stage holdups by bandits, a rodeo, trick riders and ropers, those sixty-eight teams of square dancers — all performing incongrously to Broadway music. The New York *Times* reported that on opening night "A berserk bronco catapulted himself and his rider into a 15-foot pool and a Texan, enflamed by the heady goings-on, reached for his .45 and shot out an amber floodlight."

Jumbo was least successful. It was the only inside big show, housed in a bright red building with white castle towers and serrated roof line. Rose didn't know about Texas summer heat. The building was stifling. Eddie Foy Jr., who replaced Durante as Brainy Bowers in the show, threatened to quit. Chorus girls fainted. Three of six pythons died. Temperatures reached 112 degrees on the bandstand. Three days after the opening, Anderson cut *Jumbo* down from two hours and twenty-three minutes to one fast hour.

Dallas, meanwhile, got the message. It opened *Streets of Paris*, a semi-nude show. Gordon reported that the half-nudes were "built like stevedores."

Fort Worth was wide open during the centennial. Illegal liquor was served everywhere because Amon had made a deal with the state's Liquor Control Board, the agency charged with enforcing Texas' harsh drinking laws. Officers agreed to go blind while Fort Worth celebrated. And celebrate it did. Curfews were removed. Clubs stayed open all night. Downtown Fort Worth, usually asleep by nine o'clock, swung until dawn. People danced at *Casa Manana* to Paul Whiteman's music until three a.m., then swarmed into such dine, dance and drink emporiums as the Crown, the State and the Buccaneer. NBC engineers built a complete control room in the Ringside Club from which Whiteman broadcast his weekly coast-to-coast radio program. The band had to maneuver around a craps game that went on for three months without interruption. Musicians from the Whiteman and Joe Venuti bands jammed through breakfast at the State. The Humming Bird, a club in the black neighborhood of Como, played such performers as Fats Waller, and set aside one table for white customers. Dante's Inferno, on the west side, featured female impersonators and was frequented by *Casa Manana*'s male dancers, many of whom were gay. It became the thing to do to go out to the Inferno and "watch the queers dance."

Two million people came to the centennial party. They played through the grounds, ate ten cent banana splits and fifteen cent ham sandwiches, toured the recreated living room of Will Rogers' Santa Monica home. Folks entered the grounds beneath a neon "Howdy Stranger" sign and through a log stockade gate, finding immediately the few educational displays, placed there, said Rose, "so the people can see them and then go have fun." At night, the grounds were bathed in an eerie pink neon light (Rose, anguished by the peculiar color, announced it had been devised purposely to give women a "peaches and cream complexion").

It was a wonderful, eventual, memorable time never before — or since — experienced in Fort Worth. There were multitudes of famous visitors: George White of "Scandals" fame, Jake Schubert and Earl Carroll, the

''Vanities'' producer, came from New York. William Knudsen, president of General Motors, played ''Let Me Call You Sweetheart'' on a xylophone. Patrick J. Hurley, the former Secretary of War, led an endless piffle of politicians. J. Edgar Hoover visited in September, talking about his scheme to fingerprint ''the whole country.'' Amon outpointed Hoover with rifles at the shooting gallery. Ernest Hemingway, driving from Wyoming to Memphis, became intrigued by the billboards and detoured through Fort Worth. Maximilian Adelbert Baer — Max Baer, the fighter, came and sparred for photographers with Barney Oldfield, a pioneer auto racer, who was hired by Amon as the centennial's official greeter.

Amon haunted the shows, mother-henning everything. He often narrated *The Last Frontier*. He strutted in an Indian headress. He sang ''I'm in Love with a Handlebar Mustache'' in the Pioneer Palace. Aubrey Kennedy, explained in the *Star-Telegram* as ''an early silent film producer,'' met with Amon, then announced the pending production of an eight-reel movie to be titled ''To Carter to Davis* to Rose.'' The plot was about a boy wanting to ''build an exposition to bring millions of people to Texas to thrill to the beautiful plains and other scenic loveliness. The elaborate entertainment, including a girl show, causes a strait-laced Texas pioneer father to stand in the way of a romance between his daughter and the boy, but when the father sees the pioneer village street, he is reminded of his youth and allows the boy and girl to marry.'' Kennedy said Hoot Gibson would star. The movie, thankfully, was never made.

Paul Whiteman was declared a Texas colonel and given chaps labeled ''Mr. PW'' by Amon. The orchestra leader bought a white horse named ''Popcorn'' adopted western dress and never again in his life strayed

*John B. Davis, the centennial's general manager.

far from Fort Worth and Amon Carter. Whiteman played host to visiting orchestra leaders, including Wayne King, the Waltz King, whose wife, Dorothy, was born in Fort Worth. King explained his musical title to Gordon: "We are called the Waltz King because we happen to play dreamy music over the radio on the theory that a relaxed mood makes women buy face cream."

Billboard announced that other *Casa Mananas* would be built in Miami, Cleveland, Atlanta and Havana. Chorus girls judged a knock-knock joke contest for the *Press*. John Search-The-Enemy, a seventy-three-year-old Sioux medicine man, died in August. Mrs. Search-The-Enemy, a daughter, Agness Tootoo, and a friend, Bear-Save-Life, accompanied the body to South Dakota for burial. Death was attributed to a gastro-intestinal malfunction brought on by eating raw beef kidneys. Sally Rand's Nude Ranch business was diluted by the opening of "Beauty and the Beasts, featuring Mademoiselle Laurene NeVell, intrepid Eve daring the ferocious onslaught of seven blood lusting Nubian Lions." Three monkeys escaped and pounced on the blood lusting lions, scaring the toothless old cats into several days of non-onslaught with Laurene. The monkeys also rang the bell in the church tower, drank beer in the Pioneer Palace, and dived into Florence's milk bath. A businessman ordered three beers in the Palace, poured each into his upturned straw hat and drank. Gordon reported that a seventy-five-year-old West Texas rancher paid his two-bits and entered the Nude Ranch at 3:30 one August afternoon, and did not emerge until 8:30 that night, apparently none the worst for wear. Three coeds working in the Nude Ranch were recognized and notified by their college they could not return in the fall.

The two-headed snake died August 14, presumedly done in by the heat.

The *Star-Telegram* gorged itself with centennial stories. Even those reporters not assigned to the fiesta were drafted for service. Charlie Boatner, the police beat reporter, had a regular morning duty before beginning to write his stories. A Whiteman musician drank and fought almost every night. If the man was in jail, Boatner had to bail him out. E. Clyde Whitlock, the newspaper's eminent and prim critic, dutifully reviewed every piece of music on the grounds. The Pioneer Palace's melodies were, he wrote, "cabaret style, for those who like that kind of thing. It sounds fast and loud, which are the two requisites for the type." Whitlock reviewed *Casa Manana* and devoted fewer lines to Sally Rand than to her stripping music, a melange of Beethoven, Brahms and DeBussy. For the critic's slight of Sally's bare charms, his reporter colleagues demoted Whitlock to E-Flat Clyde.

It was that way for four months until chilly weather forced a closing on November 15. Billy Rose spent the entire million dollars and more, and investors lost everything. Nobody seemed to care. Fort Worth prospered. Beer sales were up seventy-five percent, soft drinks by thirty percent. Barbers cut forty percent more hair and grocery stores sold thirty percent more food. The Depression that Fort Worth didn't have had been blunted.

For what it was and where it was, Fort Worth's Frontier Centennial may have been the most successful exposition of its type in history, and memorable for everyone. When Damon Runyon reviewed the 1939 New York World Fair, his appraisal was: "No hits, no runs, no Carters."

Billy Rose went on to produce his "Aquacade" in 1937 at Cleveland, then took the show to the New York fair where a highlight was the lavish parade of America's forty-nine flags — one for each state, and Fort Worth's city banner.

The fiesta did not end in 1936 but came back in 1937 when Rose presented a revue of famous books. Dallas, too reopened its grounds, but surrendered after that summer when few customers came. As the Frontier Fiesta, Fort Worth's show continued in 1938 and 1939 with vaudeville acts in *Casa Manana*, featuring such stars as Eddie Cantor, Edgar Bergen and Ray Bolger. Morton Downey was the last entertainer to play on the revolving stage. With war coming, *Casa Manana* — the House of Tomorrow, was shuttered forever.

After 1936, Will Morrissey, a Rose assistant, rhymed his and others feelings about the centennial, the city and Amon Carter:

> I'll miss that Amon Carter, miss his Shady Oaks [sic]
> miss his broth, his Jimmy North,
> miss Mr. Monnig's jokes.
> We are leaving Heaven, going back to earth,
> But gosh, we're going to miss Fort Worth.

The "cowboy" in front of the Shady Oak fireplace.

Amon and Amon, Jr., soon after his recovery in Europe.

Amon with Gary Cooper at Shady Oak.

Left to right, Ruth, Amon, Amon, Jr., Nenetta.

Amon, Harry Truman and Sam Rayburn.

AMON

Amon, Edgar Bergen and Charlie McCarthy, modelling specially made Shady Oak hats.

Amon and New York City Mayor, Fiorella LaGuardia waving one of Amon's hats at the New York City Hall.

Amon and New York City Mayor, Jimmy Walker.

Amon and Eddie Cantor.

Amon Carter.

Amon and Ike.

Sid Richardson with bust (wearing hat) that was a gift from Amon.

Amon and Sid Richardson playing with grandchildren's Christmas toys.

Amon at his desk at the Star-Telegram.

Amon Carter driving a stagecoach down Wall Street.

Amon personally delivering the 1949 Centennial edition of the Star-Telegram.

Chapter 13

The Dallas-Fort Worth rivalry has been overstated. They're both good towns. Fort Worth is progressive and modern. It has outstanding leadership and fine people. Of course, I never go over to the goddamned place.

—Dallas businessman, to James Farley

". . . a bunch of tin-horn bankers and Jews."

—Dallas, according to Amon Carter

My dear sir, how can you talk such nonsense!

—Colleague, to Sigmund Freud

No other city in America has anything approaching such a public citizen as Amon Carter.

—Will Rogers, 1931

13

Given the general expansive nature of mankind, and the unceasing florid babble of Chambers of Commerce, surely Sodomites crowed of orgies more debauching than Gomorrah's. San Francisco and Los Angeles ever nipped at one another's civic hides. It is true a Minnesotan complained that the Bible is a shameful book because it told all about St. Paul and nothing of Minneapolis.

Dilletantes.

Dallas. Fort Worth. Presently, Dallas/Fort Worth, or as it is written on the argument's western end: Fort Worth/Dallas. Note the subtle difference. That awry grammatical device is not a mere virgule. It is a true slash mark, a kind of punctuational skewer symbolic of the towns' obstreperous feuding history. As opponents in the most persistant and clangorous city brawl, Fort Worth and Dallas knew how to fight. They slugged, back-bit and side-swiped, gouged and gutted one another with a gory glee, and with an Olympian skill often expressed with frightening intensity, and absurdity.

They were America's Kilkenny cats trying to eat each other up. Mostly Dallas feasted, Fort Worth got indigestion.

Amon Carter, that immoderate trench-fighter, loved nothing better than going for Dallas' gonads and old Cactus Jack Garner grumbled, "Amon wants the government of the United States to run for the exclusive benefit of Fort Worth and, if possible, to the detriment of Dallas."

Yes, that's precisely what he wanted.

Amon didn't invent the intercity scrimmage, but he made it famous. For any cocked ear, he slandered Dallas, joked about it, verbally lashed it. He stole from the larger city, ignored it, vented his wrath upon its wealthy prominence, schemed against its perpetuity, gawdammed, doomed and condemned it to hell — all without very great harm to Dallas' civic tide and fortune.

They were never twin cities on the North Texas prairie, but a pair of disparate burgs thirty miles and poles apart, rent by the ninety-seventh parallel and all logic. That tight piece of range could not support two big rich cities and Fort Worth early was cast in the lesser role because it played on a barren stage to a destitute West Texas audience while Dallas wooed and won Northern monies and practiced mercantile shrewdness.

For its part, Dallas viewed Fort Worth as Byron Hilton looked on the Bide-A-Wee Tourist Court, slightly bemused and indulgently condescending. Dallas was fat-cat smug, Fort Worth, lean and hungry as a night predator. Dallas grew into a huckster city of contrived haute culture. Fort Worth became a comfortably ambitious town with a high society always one generation removed from flour sack underwear.

Dallas was your Uncle Al who smoked long black cigars and winked at the ladies. Fort Worth was Cousin Clem with a cranky cowlick and boyish faith in the virtue of manure as a sweetener in the recipe of municipal growth. Dallas was skyscraper banks and Neiman-Marcus; Fort Worth, stockyards and Leonard Bros. Department Store where one spat tobacco juice on the floor and shopped for day-old bread and second-hand weenies. Dallas was Eastern; Fort Worth, Western. In Dallas, quipped Damon Runyon, "the women wear high heels, in Fort Worth, the men do."

Dallas author Bill Porterfield looked on the two cities and concluded, "Dallas is softer, shady, an edge of East Texas. Fort Worth has a bigger sky, is a little hotter in the summer, colder in the winter, drier . . . *The West*. We are city; they country. Visitors like them better. We try too hard."

Each city's character was established from the beginning. Dallas opened as a single trading post on the Trinity River. Founding father George Neely Bryan was lonesome there and seven years before the Army built a frontier camp for what would become Fort Worth he rode west thirty miles and asked two families homesteading in the wilderness to join him at his trading post. They gladly moved East to the log cabin civilization. As the towns grew, so did the rivalry. Dallas built a thriving business section, laughing that Fort Worth was unable to muster even one decent saloon. Even Belle Starr, whose refinement was less than blueblood, preferred Dallas' criminal life over Fort Worth's.

Buckley B. Paddock, the *Democrat* editor and ardent Fort Worth chauvinist, stole a flock of Eastern capitalists bound for Dallas. He met the men at Texarkana and talked up his town. He was persuasive. When the financiers arrived in Dallas Paddock chartered a fleet of buggies and led them on to Fort Worth. Dallas' city fathers fumed.

In 1906 a Dallas newspaper noted: "Word has reached here from Fort Worth that two men have drowned in bathtubs in the last six months. It proves that Fort Worth at least has two bathtubs."

The *Uncle Jake Sports News*, a short-lived Texas racing paper, recorded what probably was the first printed Amon/Dallas jibe: "This boy Amon Carter . . . lays awake all night thinkin' up things t' help his town. I figger if th' world wus cumin' t' a end amon wud hav' it cum t' a end in Ft. Worth 'fore it reached Dallas."

Will Rogers later used the crack on his radio program, and, as Amon's close friend, perpetuated the intercity dispute at every opportunity. Rogers and H. L. Mencken, the Baltimore iconoclast, flew into Fort Worth and Rogers quipped, "Had a wonderful trip down here, but I looked for Dallas on the way in. Couldn't find it. It still around here?" A wire to the *Star-Telegram* from Rogers read, "Hello, Amon, I was in Fort Worth this morning. Got gas, a silver cup and a Dallas *News*." When Rogers' radio program was on CBS, he once originated it from KRLD studios in Dallas. Next day, the elated *Star-Telegram* whooped that the humorist mentioned Fort Worth six times on the air and ". . . never once said 'Dallas.'"

The *Star-Telegram* rarely gigged Dallas — gentleman Jimmy North only allowed pettiness when pressed by Amon — though on occasion it taunted the larger city. In 1928, a story told of the arrival of the dirigible *Los Angeles* at Fort Worth's helium plant, pointing out that the airship "overflew Dallas." A mid-1930s editorial observed: "[In the past] we have commented on the special sort of fog which hangs over a certain area situated thirty miles down the Trinity. It produces a peculiar mental effect upon those who are constantly exposed to it."

Al Altwegg of the Dallas *Morning News* probably assessed the two-city bickering correctly, writing, "If Dallas and Fort Worth have a problem, it's primarily

Fort Worth that has the problem.'' It did. No matter what Amon and Fort Worth tried, Dallas continued to prosper and grow, which irritated Amon all the more and he raged in a letter that Dallas ''is run by a bunch of tin-horn bankers and jews.''

One of those Jewish leaders was Stanley Marcus, whose family founded Neiman-Marcus (Fort Worth wags called the famed specialty store, Neiman-Markups). Neiman's had many customers among Fort Worth's society folk but the *Star-Telegram* would accept no advertising from the Dallas emporium. Amon bragged that he bought everything he needed in Fort Worth, and others should, too. That was not quite true. Nenetta kept a Neiman's charge account secret from Amon, and even he was not above sending an envoy to buy special gifts not found anywhere else. It was joked, and may even have been true, that his lady friends removed Neiman Marcus labels from their clothing and replaced them with tags from Fort Worth stores.

Stanley Marcus knew of Nenetta's private account and Amon's clandestine shopping raids but, being a businessman, kept the intelligence to himself. Carter and Marcus finally met at a cocktail party and Amon complained that ad lineage was down.

''Why not let us help you out by advertising in the *Star-Telegram?*'' suggested Marcus.

Amon fixed him with a steely glare and replied, ''The minute you open a store in Fort Worth.''

Amon vs. Dallas stories are legion. Many are pure fiction.

He, everybody said, always carried a sack lunch to Dallas rather than buy a meal there. Amon did that a few times, for a joke. Once, he attended a society ball in the Adolphus Hotel. He made himself the center of attention by leading Freddie Martin's Orchestra and delivering a longish, humorous speech on Dallas. When waiters served dinner, Amon opened a large basket. It was filled with Shady Oak fried chicken.

Another tale has him forced to remain overnight in Dallas and being unshaven rather than patronize a barbershop there. People said he carried a full tote can of Fort Worth gas in his car and refused to use Dallas' service stations. His peach orchard outside Arlington, midway between the cities, spread between Tarrant and Dallas counties. He showed his trees to a visitor and they gathered a basket of peaches in the Dallas County section. Amon insisted they walk back across the county line to eat. Once he told a guest that peaches in the Dallas County zone simply didn't grow as well ". . . in all that hot air." It is true he won a bet of two suits from a Dallas friend but refused to collect because the loser stipulated a Dallas tailor must stitch up the clothes.

Will Stripling was president of Fort Worth's Civic Music Association one year and asked Amon to purchase a season subscription. Amon replied sarcastically, "If there is anything in the world I am crazy about, it is music, and I was especially tickled to think that my membership entitled me to attend, without further penalty, all the concerts to be presented by the Dallas association. It will be a red letter day in my life and a rare privilege to be able to contribute something to Dallas. I will probably go wild over the Spanish dancers November 29th. Those Dallas boys have been feeding us so much bull for the past twenty-five years, that I just cannot keep from having a hankering after Spanish dancers."

Printed cards once appeared in Fort Worth urging, "Please flush twice when you use the washroom! Dallas needs the water!"

Amon was blamed for the cards. He denied it but in a letter to Will Rogers, noted the benefit of Lake Worth "which supplies Dallas with water when we pull the string."

Much of the rivalry was contrived. Amon had fun with the feud. He was friendly with most nationally-known columnists and endlessly fed them items, both imaginary and real, on the intercity quarrel.

He told Inez Robb, the Hearst writer, "It seems we have been in Dallas' hair all our lives. Dallas has the nicest people individually, but collectively, we look upon them with a degree of suspicion as to what they would do if we turned around to spit. Fort Worth is Where the West Begins and Dallas is where the East peters out. I have not been accused of being partisan to Northeast Texas and Dallas and I don't believe you have to live in Fort Worth and West Texas to get to Heaven, although it won't be detrimental in case you get an invite."

He explained to Damon Runyon that Dallas and Fort Worth "have tried to bury the hatchet many times . . . but somebody always leaves the handle sticking out."

Walter Winchell reported on a dinner given Amon by Jim Farley in New York's Ritz Tower. The menu inscription told of Amon's "college yell": "Bring in the liquor/On with the Mirth/To Hell with Dallas/Boost Fort Worth."

During lulls in the bickering, Carter made conciliatory offers to Dallas. He insisted Dallas Chamber of Commerce president John Carpenter join him for groundbreaking ceremonies when the two cities briefly were partners in a joint-use airport. Carpenter and Carter scooped with a double-headed spade, and the publisher joked, "We're here to dig dirt, not sling mud."

Amon uncharacteristically wooed the Dallas establishment during the airport enterprise. Fort Worth needed Dallas in the project.

A busload of Dallas businessmen was invited to the annual stock show rodeo. Amon planned to meet the bus at the Tarrant County line and present each man with one of his costly Shady Oak hats. He instructed Jim Record to provide photographers for the ceremony. Two major highways connected the cities. U.S. 80, the principal road, ran on the south side. Texas 183 was eighteen miles north. JRR told Jack Butler, the night city editor, to have the *Star-Telegram* men on U.S. 80 at seven o'clock.

The reporters and photographers arrived. And waited. No bus. No Carter. At 7:30 Amon telephoned Butler, demanding to know why the newspapermen were not with him as ordered. He was waiting on Highway 183.

Butler explained the mixup, and Carter exploded, roaring that newsmen better gawddamned sure be at Will Rogers Coliseum when the bus arrived there. Butler looked around the office and ordered out every man in sight. The emergency force numbered eight reporters with eight speed graphics and eight dozen flash bulbs. Several cameras had no film but were props for the little drama played out in front of the coliseum.

The bus arrived. A fuming Amon alit, followed by thirty amused Dallasites. Eight flash bulbs exploded as one. George Dolan, then a city desk man with no working knowledge of cameras, said he just fired flash bulbs as fast as he could. "It was like a world premiere," recalled Dolan twenty-five years later. "Everybody shot off all the flash bulbs they had. Blinded all of them. Two passed out from the heat." However exaggerated by Dolan, the ruse succeeded and Amon was mollified.

In another mood of co-existency, Amon hosted Dallas' civic leaders for a hands-across-the-county-line party at Shady Oak. The party began well. Amon stood to speak on the new cooperative spirit of the cities but the longer he spoke, the more he edged into the past, recalling old slights and affronts. He concluded with a strong denouncement of Dallas. His guests were more tickled than offended, and Dallas Mayor R. L. Thornton rose to respond. Thornton held up a paper sack. "This is my dinner," said the mayor. "I brought me a ham sandwich out here from Dallas. I'm not eating anything you got."

Later in the evening, Amon explained to Thornton another facet of the Dallas/Fort Worth rivalry. "It's really a constructive thing. If I want to get something done in Fort Worth, if I want to get some of these people off their asses, all I do is remind them that 'You don't want those Dallas bastards to get ahead of you, do you?' "

Many never understood that piece of the quarrel and every slander of Dallas by Amon brought denunciatory letters from Big D citizens. John Ford, an attorney, chided Amon and his town: "When we get all tense and tired out with the noise and strife of city life, we like to go out in the country for a few hours and relax. And for this purpose we find that Fort Worth is fine — unless the wind is blowing from the north."

After a publisher stole a company from Dallas and boasted loudly of the theft, a woman wrote, "You showed more ignorance than I ever thought any one man could possess. I have heard of some of the dumb things you have done but I never imagined any one man could be so crude and ignorant . . . stay in that hick-town you belong in as you have acted like a real country boy."

Stealing from Dallas was Amon's great raging fever. He coveted every brick and smokestack of its industries and ached to remove all to Fort Worth. As a one-man Chamber of Commerce, he endlessly searched out new businesses for Fort Worth and he especially courted those firms already in the Dallas ledger.

"The great Magnolia skyscraper reaches its steel claws down into bedrock and holds on like grim death when Amon passes by," wrote Tom Gooch, *Times-Herald* editor in 1935.

Amon persuaded Phillips Petroleum to move its Southwest headquarters from Dallas to Fort Worth in 1925 and Frank Phillips wired the publisher, "It pleases us to do this largely because you want us to."

In 1933, Amon visited W. E. Sinclair in the oilman's New York headquarters. Amon inspected a wall map showing Sinclair offices across America. One red pin marked Pierce Oil Company in Dallas.

"That red pin mean you bought Pierce?" asked Amon.

Sinclair nodded.

Amon smiled, extracted the pin from Dallas and punched it into Fort Worth. Soon Pierce Oil moved its offices to Fort Worth.

Those were minor victories. The theft that gave Amon greatest satisfaction, and rankled Dallas the most, came in 1933 when he was successful in moving South West Air Craft Corporation. The company would become American Airlines and Amon was a founder, board member and eventually largest stockholder. Losing South West enraged the Dallas establishment. "Once more," screamed a Dallas *Journal* editorial, "we have been Amon Cartered. We boast that Dallas isn't a one-man town. But in this connection, it is pretty weak boasting."

The Dallas *Morning News* editorialized about "Mahatma Carter . . . who keeps Dallas sitting on everything that isn't nailed down for fear he will move it to Fort Worth."

Beating Dallas, however, was rare. Amon lost more than he won but he never stopped trying. He wrote Nelson Moody, president of Prairie Oil and Gas, when that company was considering a move to Dallas, "We are still anxious to locate the Prairie's Texas office at the most logical point, Fort Worth. We understand that your representative cannot even get a tire fixed on Sunday in your present Texas headquarters [Amarillo]. If you move to Fort Worth, I will have the mayor fix your punctures."

Standard Oil of California bypassed Fort Worth and settled its regional offices in Dallas. Amon sent the company's president, K. R. Kingsbury, a black-bordered sympathy letter, and later complained to Walter Teagle, Standard of New Jersey's chief officer, that the move was ". . . a slap in our face." Losing always was personal to Amon. Everything, in fact, was personal.

In the late 1940s, attorney Berl Godfrey was president of the Fort Worth Chamber of Commerce. He spoke at a Dallas Chamber membership banquet and the *Star-Telegram* assigned Irv Farman to cover the speech. He joined John Rutledge, a Dallas *Morning News* writer at the press table. Godfrey spoke of cooperation between the two cities and, heady with the message's reception, ad-libbed, "After this wonderful hospitality and wonderful meal, I think it would be ridiculous for anyone to bring his sack lunch to Dallas." The audience howled. Only one man brought a sack lunch to Dallas.

Farman wisely ignored the remark. Rutledge did not. He led his story with the quote and implied Godfrey's *bon mot* was a direct slap at Amon.

Farman was summoned to Carter's office. Amon had the *Morning News* spread on his desk.

"Did Godfrey say this?" Carter demanded to know.

"Yes, sir," answered Farman, "but I didn't think it was newsworthy."

Amon studied the story.

"Let me tell you something," he said. "Next time somebody says something bad about me, you write it and let somebody higher up kill it out."

Godfrey already had telephoned to apologize, continued Amon.

"I told him I neither want nor accept his apology. What hurts me is that one thousand of Dallas' leading citizens think someone else is speaking for Fort Worth."

Amon stopped abruptly, stared out the window, then turned again to Farman, with a reddened face, shouting, "By God! I speak for Fort Worth!"

Fighting Dallas was a lifelong crusade for the publisher, and he needed only the slightest provocation to go for the city's jugular. He interrupted an American Airlines board meeting to complain the airline's 1938 brochures did not feature "a picture of the Fort Worth air terminal or Fort Worth itself. Dallas has more mentions although our Southern headquarters is in Fort Worth." He railed to a *Saturday Evening Post* editor, "I wonder how in hell you gave the story a Dallas dateline when Dallas had practically nothing to do with it."

In 1934 the Warm Springs Foundation sponsored fund-raising galas around the nation and afterwards Dallas received praise for its participation. Amon wired FDR: "Dallas only raised $6,500 before expenses. Fort Worth raised $25,000 and no expenses, 1/40th of all the money raised."

During World War II a rougish salesman bought thousands of candles and dyed them black. In Dallas, he sold as many as ten thousand for "real blackout candles that the enemy can't see." Amon whooped and hoorahed over Dallasites' gullibility and spread the story among friends and columnists everywhere.

For all Amon's assaults on Big D (which he often wrote as "Big d"), Dallas remained generally cordial and in 1939 the *Morning News* devoted two pages of pictures and text on the publisher — "Builder of a whole region." He was named an honorary Dallas citizen and the newspaper remarked that he "punches Dallas like cowboys are wont to do slow steers in a shipping chute."

That tribute, strangely, appeared soon after Amon's most insulting rebuff and as Dallas remained in a furious snit over him and football and TCU and the Cotton Bowl, all because he wanted to show his Eastern friends how the cow ate the cabbage.

Amon was never an athlete but he was, wrote columnist Bob Considine, "America's Number One Sports

Fan.'' Grantland Rice, too, conceded the title to Carter, and Damon Runyon. An All-America watcher.

He required the uproar and hubbub of sporting crowds and for most of fifty years he was a World Series fixture, a colorful rooter at ringside of heavyweight boxing championship bouts, a hundred dollar window addict and mint julep veteran for the Kentucky Derby and other racing events. He would don his cowboy costume, strut, holler, jeer, cheer, and jabber happily, making a spectacle of himself.

For the second Dempsey-Tunney fight, Amon invited eighty of his friends, including Will Rogers, and dressed in the famed Shady Oak western hats, carrying Carter's patented bourbon-bearing walking canes, the men marched to ringside with the publisher leading, joshing with the crowd, whoopeeing for Fort Worth and West Texas. Westbrook Pegler viewed the pageant and reported, ''Mr. Amon G. Carter . . . lent a strong intellectual force to the assembly and played a brief solo on a fish horn*. The customers decided the fight was not as loud as the solo. He sat down with the unanimous consent of all present.''

Before it became socially indecorous, Amon would fire off his sixshooters to punctuate the excitement. Promoters loved to have him centerstage and Charles Cominsky furnished annual passes to all Chicago White Sox games, as did John McGraw for the New York Giants. Tex Rickard, the boxing entrepreneur, signed a permanent pass to Madison Square Garden, decreeing: ''This is Amon Carter. Let him through any door, any gate, any time. And don't argue.''

Amon's participatory athletics were limited to a few innings of softball in an early Fort Worth newspaper league and at *Star-Telegram* employee picnics. Briefly, he golfed, but confessed, ''. . . they have improved the

***The Dictionary of American Slang* defines ''fish horn'' as a saxophone [synthetic jazz use] but Amon could not play any instrument. More likely, Pegler's fish horn probably was a cow's horn, which Amon loved to toot.

courses to the extent that it is difficult to find the old balls and eliminated golf as a matter of economy.'' His Shady Oak Farm pond boiled with hungry bass, but he rarely fished. He hunted less than half-a-dozen times in his life and mostly for the companionship, never the wild game. He was not a camper, or hiker or outdoorsman because nature, he decided early, was excessively uncomfortable.

Amon was a batboy for the Bowie baseball team when it played against Henrietta's town nine. Neither team could afford new baseballs and it was Amon's duty to retrieve batted fouls. He went into the crowd to recover a ball and immediately got into a fight with two larger boys. The fight turned into a general fracus halted only when Henrietta's town marshal charged in with drawn pistol. That was George L. Rickard, then called ''Dink'', and he and Amon became close friends. ''Tex'' Rickard later rode his horse to the Yukon where he gathered enough gold for a ranching stake and ultimately became the premier prizefight promoter in America. Amon visited often in New York with Rickard, who regularly had the publisher fire his pistols to start six-day bicycle races.

In 1926, heavyweight champion Jack Dempsey was prodding Rickard to find him a suitable opponent. Dempsey, who had not defended his title in three years, agreed to meet Gene Tunney. The matter was settled by telegram and Dempsey, in California, wanted Rickard to go there for the contract signing. Rickard suggested they meet halfway and, said the promoter, halfway was Amon Carter's office in Fort Worth.

April 21, Rickard and Dempsey sat at Amon's desk as the publisher hovered in the background directing his reporters and photographers. Dempsey, who would lose to Tunney, was euphoric over the anticipated million dollar gate, and unusually chatty with with sports writers, though possibly his banter was more prompted by the water glass of straight gin he drank for breakfast.

Amon, too, was ecstatic and boasted the publicity would increase his city's growing fame. He urged Rickard to stage the bout in Fort Worth where, as in all of Texas, prizefighting was illegal. Amon promised to have the law changed but Rickard wisely chose Philadelphia.

There would have been no need to change the law. Fights were held anyway and Amon was a ringside fixture at all local bouts. Because the fights had no legal status, official decisions could not be rendered. Newspapers named the winners and Flem Hall was the *Star-Telegram* decision maker. For one Saturday night match, an out-of-town boxer showed Hall a clipping-filled scrapbook. The stories glowed with praise. Hall wrote a column touting the fighter as a sure winner.

At fight-time, Amon was front row center, directly across the ring from Hall. The match began and from first bell to last Hall's fighter was whipped soundly by a local boxer. Throughout the bout, Hall could hear his publisher booing the out-of-towner. He glared disgustedly across the ring at Hall.

The moment the fight ended, hardly before the boxers cleared center-ring, Carter slid under the ropes and crawled on hands and knees across the apron toward Hall. Amon thrust his head through the ropes and yelled at the sports writer, "I thought you said that bird could fight."

"He had a scrapbook full of clippings," protested Hall.

"Hell," retorted Amon, "all his gawddamned scrap was in his book."

Amon turned and crawled back across the ring, slipped between the ropes and seated himself, oblivious of the laughter around him.

That was Amon the spectator. He could not remain seated and calm but had to be an involved witness.

He paced football field sidelines, exorting his team to more inspired play, jeering opponents, whooping crowds like a cheerleader. At games of the Fort Worth Cats baseball team, of which he briefly was a part-owner, Amon often came on to the field to discuss a disputed call with umpires, or he would roam the stands collecting bonus money for players' special achievements, such as game-saving catches or propitious home runs.

The Cats of the 1920s perhaps were baseball's best minor league franchise, so popular in Fort Worth that the twelve thousand seat Panther Field could not hold all fans and often as many as a thousand others stood behind the outfield. Managed by John Jacob "Jakie" Atz, the Cats won six consecutive Texas League championships and five of six Dixie Series pennants. Amon doted on his winning Cats and in 1924, even showed off Joe Pate, a thirty-game winning pitcher, and Clarence Kraft, whose fifty-five home runs led all minor league hitters, to Calvin Coolidge. They and Amon, Harold Hough and Silent Cal posed for pictures on the White House lawn.

Amon made the President an honorary Fort Worth citizen. The publisher also handed him a gold key to the liquor-filled vault behind Amon's home but teetotler Cal's response to that Prohibition-era generosity has been lost to history. He called Amon, "Cowboy."

Leaving, Hough said, "Sure am glad you got to meet me, Mr. Coolidge." Cal grimaced politely.

The group traveled on to New York for the World Series, then returned to Fort Worth where Pate and Kraft entertained cronies with tales of the White House and girls on Broadway. Kraft opined, "They sure got some swell Post Office up there."

Amon blustered loudly and long of the Cats and cartoonist Bud Fisher placed his Mutt & Jeff in Fort Worth for a visit. In one comic strip, Jeff told Postmaster Billy Moore that they were the only Republicans in town, while Mutt begged Amon and Will Stripling for a tryout with the Cats, claiming he was better than "Rogers Hornsby ever was." *

The Dixie Series settled the question of the South's minor league champion and was the most important sporting event in the region. For an early series, Amon and the *Star-Telegram* chartered trains to transport fans to Memphis. The idea proved so wildly popular that he continued it for two decades. Later, the trains took fans to Texas Christian University football games and delegates to Democratic political conventions. The *Star-Telegram* even sponsored city-boosting train trips into West Texas for Fort Worth businessmen.

Amon's trains were rolling carnivals. Amon was along, as overseer, as host, as musical director, poker dealer and bartender, always resplendent as the bogus cowboy. *Star-Telegram* reporters wrote mile by mile accounts of the shenanigans and photographers recorded hi-jinks for posterity. There were bands and pep squads, troops of motorcycle cops, occasionally even horses and riders. Whenever the trains paused for water and fuel, Amon unloaded his carnival and staged impromptu parades for startled citizens of stray villages. Not surprisingly, there was hard drinking and baggage cars served as rolling gambling dens where Amon played for dimes or hundred dollar bills and craps games lasted from first chug to last. Flem Hall remembered watching Paul Waggoner, son of old W. T., roll for a $1,500 pot and crap out. When TCU's band was aboard, there were jam sessions and dancing in the aisles and sing-alongs, most often led by Bess Stephenson, who covered many train trips for the *Star-Telegram*.

From three to six hundred baseball fans crushed into the special trains each trip but those remaining behind were not forgotten. Amon related in a Christmas letter of how the *Star-Telegram* broadcast [via WBAP]

*Hornby briefly managed the Cats following his major league career. Fisher was so fond of Amon that he named one of his race horses "Star-Telegram." Star-Telegram, a filly by Shortgrass out of Adele, won few races.

that year's Dixie Series. Thirty-two direct telephone lines were installed in the newspaper office and sixteen operators responded to as many as ten thousand calls a day. Special trains and telephones and baseball teams merely were part of the Amon Carter/*Star-Telegram* public service package for readers.

All baseball trains, to Memphis, New Orleans, to Atlanta, and occasionally a TCU railroad expedition, had to move East through Dallas, a hard fact of geography even Amon could not change. But he was able to extract a certain amount of fun out of the Dallas crossings.

Bill Corum, the Hearst sports columnist, quoted Amon: "Let me tell you, young man, that there's no such place as Dallas. Dallas is a mirage on the Texas plain. When I ride past the wide place in the tracks called Dallas on the train, I get up in the cab with the engineer and ring the bell and blow the whistle, and refuse to let him stop even for water. Which is all you'd get in Dallas, anyway."

He did that, climbed into the engine cab and rang the bell, blasted the steam whistle, hooting at Dallasites. Once he even rode on the cowcatcher, and another time, mounted the engine straddle-legged as though it was a real iron horse, yippeeing and waving his hat to agog onlookers.

Amon's well-publicized trans-Dallas excursions caused this puzzler in the *Dispatch-Journal*:

Q. What is the fastest thing on two wheels?

A. Amon Carter passing through Dallas on a bicycle.

The Carter conundrum was printed as the most bitter Amon vs Big D confrontation was stalemated. It was a vicious little sniping war waged over possession of Texas Christian University's Fightin' Horned Frogs, the 1938 national football champions, undefeated and untied and hardly tested, and completely under the influence of Amon Carter, who had at long last a proper weapon with which to bloody Dallas.

It is proper to criticize Amon's flaccidity for losers. Always busy, he only had time for winners. Before the Cats reached for their first Texas League pennant, he was a lukewarm baseball patron. TCU had been playing football for decades but until it was taken into the Southwest Conference and began winning consistently, Amon was uninterested. When, however, the Frogs neared the winner's circle, they became, as Fort Worth and West Texas, his.

For three decades until World War II, Fort Worth was a prime sports breeding ground. Out of the schools and colleges came Ben Hogan and Byron Nelson, who dominated golf, Rogers Hornsby and Tris Speaker of baseball fame, Sammy Baugh, the legendary quarterback, Wilmer Allison, who won at Wimbledon and was U.S. singles champion in Tennis, Earl Meadows, the 1936 Olympics pole vault gold medalist. Tiny Centre College of Danville, Kentucky, upset mighty Harvard, 6-0, in 1921, and half the team, including the game's hero, Bo McMillin, were from Fort Worth's North Side High School.

If nothing else the city rates an asterisk in sports trivia for producing Francis Schmidt who invented that imperishable locker room declaration: "They put their pants on just as you do, one leg at a time."

Immortality is obtained by such aroused phrasing. Amon's most lasting effort perhaps was "Give 'em hell in the Christian spirit."

That was the pith of a pep rally harangue at which Amon orated long and excitedly about Saturday's game with Southern Methodist University. The Dallas school was the traditional rival of TCU, a Church of Christ institution.

"Give 'em hell, but do it in a good Christian spirit," Amon taunted the students and team members. A school official later spoke and said his definition of Christian spirit probably did not "jibe with Mr. Carter's."

Amon stood instantly, interrupted and defined his conception of Christian football: "Knock 'em down. Pick 'em up, dust 'em off and ask 'em how they feel. If they can answer, knock 'em down again."

Once the winning Horned Frogs were his, Amon became a locker room and pep rally activist, expounding on his theory that losing somehow was detrimental to the future of Fort Worth. He used exotic methods to collect victories for TCU. In 1931, Texas A&M had a standout team. TCU merely was adequate. Neither school could score in the first two quarters and at halftime Amon charged into the locker room. "Men!" he shouted. "If you win, I'll give $1,000 to the athletic fund. If you tie, I'll give $500."

He sweetened the pot: ". . . and I'll give every player a watch!"

Strengthened by Amon's elevating pep talk, TCU knocked off the Aggies 6-0 and each man received his watch. Wee Horned Frogs substituted for numbers around the timepieces' dials.

Shepherding his team to victory after victory, Amon guarded against the players' complacency with lectures stressing the Frogs' vulnerability. "You guys don't want to be like Lot's wife, so proud of your past you've got no future," he once rebuked. He even ordered the *Star-Telegram*'s sports department to write stories "playing up" the Frogs' opponents.

Amon was pleased with his coaching. He gave the teams expensive Shady Oak hats and threw banquets for them. When TCU won its first Southwest Conference football championship in 1929, the hero was a sophomore fullback, Harlos Green, who kicked an extra point to tie SMU. That tie gave TCU a clear conference title and Amon collected Green's magic cleated shoe. He had it bronzed and mounted.

With the impetus of a conference championship, Amon was able to sell the community on supporting construction of a new concrete football stadium, which eventually seated forty thousand fans. The publisher personally sold half a million dollars worth of bonds and the concrete arena was named Amon Carter Stadium.

Amon, said Nenetta, "went crazy" when TCU was winning. He paced and yelled, whooped and stomped his purple and white Justin hand-made boots with Horned Frog designs cut into the heels. And he would lead the band through rousing numbers, sometimes even the "Amon Carter March," written especially for him by director Don Gillis.

TCU's band played swing in the mid-1930s, and Amon's baton led it across the nation. He made sure the band was along for train trips and in each destination city, Amon's mayor friends provided motorcycle escorts and sirening fire engines as the whole entourage marched to its hotel, band out front with the big-hatted cowboy strutting for crowds.

In San Francisco to play Santa Clara University, the team and band and Amon marched down Market Street to the Mark Hopkins where Carter was guest of honor at a welcoming banquet. He joshed, joked and bragged of his TCU Frogs' great football ability until the audience began yelling for him to put his money where his mouth was. He commanded the hotel staff to bring out a "number two washtub, right out front here and you fill it up. I'll cover anything you bet." The galvanized tub overflowed with money — thousands, estimated witnesses — and Amon guaranteed every bet. He won it all on TCU's victory.

The Frogs played Fordham in New York and Damon Runyon trailed the railroaded Texans from depot to City Hall for an Amon-staged pep rally, then on to the Polo Grounds. Runyon wrote that Carter "went in for the yip-yip-yippy business . . . especially in the early stages when Texas Christian whipped a score over on Fordham faster than you could say Wojciechowicz. Between the football halves, Mr. Carter, in person, led the band in a parade about the field and upwards of 25,000 inmates . . . cheered the imposing figure. The field was muddy. Mr. Carter's high heels sank to his fetlocks in the ooze at every step.''

TCU lost, 7-6, and Runyon recorded Amon's reaction when a lady fan asked for his autograph. She inquired, ''Well, how did you like it?''

''I didn't like it, Ma'am.''

''Oh, don't cry about it. It was a wonderful game.''

''I'm not crying, Ma'am. And it was a wonderful game. But you asked me how I liked it and I tell you I didn't like it. I still don't like it. In West Texas, Ma'am, truth always comes first.''

That evening Amon appeared on Robert Ripley's national radio program, extolling TCU's swing band. ''Well, Bob,'' said Amon, reading the script, ''Believe It or Not, we've got the biggest horns of any college in the country and how we can blow them!''

The bass horns were Amon's idea. He wrote TCU's president, Dr. E. M. Waits, ''On the subject of the band, I would like to see about 75 pieces for next season, supplemented by a couple more bass horns. With all the brass SMU has, we are certainly not going to let them get away with six bass horns to our four.''

Dallas again. Always Dallas. Amon led the TCU band one year in a pre-Cotton Bowl game parade and the marshal placed SMU's band out front. Amon was furious and threatened to take his TCU band back to Fort Worth. ''Fort Worth never gets behind Dallas,'' he shouted at a marshal. Amon calmed when told the bands were arranged in alphabetical order.

From the mid-1930s, TCU was dominant in the conference and it, and in fact all SWC teams, became an innovating force in American football. Coached by Leo ''Dutch'' Meyer and starring, first, the inimitable Sammy Baugh, then the miniaturized Davey O'Brien, the Horned Frogs became an aerial show. They threw footballs as no team ever before and Meyer declared in a *Saturday Evening Post* article, ''The Southwest is just now being recognized, footballically speaking.''

TCU was undefeated in 1938. Dallas promoters of the three-year-old Cotton Bowl were joyous. They were confident the Frogs would play there New Year's Day, probably against Texas Tech. It would be an all-Texas contest and they would have the nation's number one bowl game. Well before the season's conclusion, Cotton Bowl promoters were visiting TCU offering, rumors said, fistsful of money and other enticements, including a new automobile for Coach Meyer.

Politely, the Frogs refused all offers. Tempers began rising in Dallas.

Meanwhile, Amon was busy. With two games to play, TCU's name popped into national columns urging it be selected as visiting team in the Rose Bowl against the University of Southern California, the probable host school. Runyon wrote, ''We have half a notion to write those Rose Bowl people . . . and tell them that if they want the greatest show they have ever seen in all their born days they are suckers if they do not invite Senor Amon Carter, the Hidalgo of West Texas, and the Texas Christian University football team to play in the bowl on New Year's Day.''

Backstage, Amon spent $740 of the *Star-Telegram*'s money for more than a hundred telephone calls to California eliciting private support for TCU's appearance in the Rose Bowl. He contacted every sports writer and publisher in the state. At the behest of C. R. Smith, American Airline executives called on Norman Chandler at the Los Angeles *Times* to conscript that prestigious corner. Amon enlisted W. R. Hearst, and the press mogul sent down an order to Frank Barham, publisher of the Los Angeles *Herald Express* to ''help get TCU in the Rose Bowl.'' Carter wired governor Frank Merrian and the USC president, signing without authorization Texas governor W. Lee O'Daniel's name to the telegrams.

Amon's letters to newspapers promised in the beginning, "3 or 4 thousand" Texas fans for the Rose Bowl, brought there on *Star-Telegram* chartered trains. At the end he was estimating "25,000 TCU supporters." "Frankly, we can't blame the Trojans for preferring as soft a spot as possible," he twitted, daring USC to take on the Horned Frogs.

As selection time neared, Amon grew fidgety. Walter Winchell revealed on his radio program Sunday evening that Duke University would go to the Rose Bowl and TCU would play in the Cotton Bowl. Amon angrily telephoned Winchell on the air. Following a commercial break, Winchell admitted to his audience that "nothing is sure yet for the Rose Bowl."

The Rose Bowl selection committee, under siege by Amon's sales blitz, delayed its announcement one day, but in the end, named twice-beaten Duke as USC's opponent. Amon failed. Enraged, he telephoned columnist Bill Corum, who was drinking at Toots Shor's in New York. Corum, who said Amon "had on his sixgun voice," recorded the publisher's tirade.

"It's a shame!!! It's a shame!!! Let me tell you it's a downright outrage, a reflection on the fair name of Texas and an insult to the greatest football team that ever walked in cleats. Our boys will play any two teams in the country on the same afternoon."

Dallasites chortled, and prepared to receive the Horned Frogs on New Year's Day. But suddenly TCU announced it had accepted a bid to play Carnegie Tech in the Sugar Bowl.

Dallas boiled, pointing its trembling finger at the one man it held responsible for the defection.

"The boys just wanted to take a little train ride," alibied Amon.

What followed was the most massive get-Amon crusade ever. Stealing a business was one thing but robbing the Cotton Bowl was high treason, a heinous crime and not just to Dallas but all of Texas.

"The news that Brutus had stabbed Caesar couldn't have been more unbelievable," gasped columnist Eddie Barr. Carter "manipulated the Frogs out of town" and was a "small town poo-bah," Barr raged.

Letters to the editor called for a boycott of Fort Worth, its citizens, its products and especially Amon Carter. He replied, "Sour grapes just naturally grow in the shade of sour dispositions."

Amon was the "publicity-mad Fort Worth publisher" and the *Dispatch-Journal*, most vituperative of the Dallas newspapers, printed a cartoon entitled, "The Bowl Weevil," which depicted Amon's head on a football body. The vicious insect gnawed on a stalk of cotton.

Sports columnists mused that Carter "with money for everything else" should build a stadium of his own and call it "The Stockyards Bowl."

The *Dispatch-Journal* published a page one editorial explaining Amon's great sin: "The spleen against Dallas which Amon Carter has cultivated in his overwhelming devotion to Fort Worth sometimes blinds him to common sense and the opportunity to do something beneficial for the state . . . [this] narrow small-town conduct will live long in the memory of Dallas, we fear."

Amid all the vocal clatter Davey O'Brien won the Heisman Trophy, annually given by the Downtown Athletic Club of New York. Earlier, he had been named recipient of the Washington Touchdown Club trophy and Philadelphia's Maxwell Trophy. All were symbolic of the greatest football player in America. The Heisman is the most prestigious.

O'Brien, the Frogs' minute quarterback, was 145 pounds and five feet and a couple of handshakes, as Amon described him. He was a "pony-built, piano-legged boy" who threw nineteen touchdown passes and led TCU to its undefeated season and ranking as America's number one team. O'Brien and Dutch Meyer were in Amon's office when word came via Associated

Press that the little quarterback had won the 1938 Heisman. Immediately, Amon telephoned the Downtown Athletic Club president. O'Brien and Meyer could hear only Amon's side of the conversation.

"Listen, this is Amon Carter down in Fort Worth. We're bringing our boy, Davey O'Brien, up there to get your award. What kind of thing is this? Is it a little affair? We're not coming if it's something small. (pause) Get Jack Garner. Will LaGuardia be there? (pause) OK. OK. I'll call them. See if the President'll come. (pause) OK, I'll call him, too. What kind of entertainment you having? (pause) That's no good. I'll get Paul Whiteman."

Carter disconnected, called Whiteman and received the bandleader's acceptance, then placed a call to the White House and left word for FDR.

Having fully arranged the Downtown Athletic Club's award program, Amon turned his attention to getting there. He chartered an American Airlines plane for the quarterback, O'Brien's mother and uncle, TCU coaches, the team's captains, Ki Aldrich and I. B. Hale, and Texas lieutenant governor Walter Woodul.

The plane swooped off to New York and landed at Floyd Bennett Field. A Knickerbocker stage coach drawn by six white horses and led by thirty men on horseback [Staten Island Sheriff's Guard members, reported Corum] awaited the Texas entourage.

Amon directed Woodul and Meyer inside the coach. He placed O'Brien beside him, picked up the reins, called to his white steeds, and away they went.

Thousands of usually blasé New Yorkers gawked at the sight of cowboys and a stagecoach in downtown Manhattan. Amon drove down Wall Street, waving his hat, shouting "Hooray for Fort Worth and West Texas," saluting friends along the way. O'Brien sat beside the exuberant Amon, embarrassed.

The alien convoy halted at City Hall where Mayor Fiorello LaGuardia presented keys to the city to every

Texan and posed for photographers with O'Brien and Amon. Then Amon drove the coach on to 21 restaurant where he hosted a luncheon.

Back in Fort Worth the roasting of Amon slowly abated. Texas Tech played in the Cotton Bowl against, and lost to, the Galloping Gaels of St. Mary's University while TCU beat Carnegie Tech, 15-7, in the Sugar Bowl.

Eleven hundred fans filled three *Star-Telegram* trains to New Orleans and the Amon-led Texans paraded on Bourbon Street, danced barefoot in Jackson Square, drank Ramos Gin Fizzes in the Roosevelt Bar, ate at Antoine's and just had themselves a high old time in the Crescent City, courtesy of Amon G. Carter, who loved to lead a band.

Years later, city editor John Ellis sat in the Worth Hotel coffee shop, adjacent to the *Star-Telegram,* awaiting breakfast. Outside, a Shrine circus parade passed on Seventh Street. There were marching clowns and elephants, roaring motorcycle teams, high-stepping majorettes and loud bands.

The waitress, unknowing of the parade, served Ellis' eggs. She heard the noise and wondered aloud, "What's that?"

Without looking up, Ellis muttered, "Just Amon comin' to work."

Chapter 14

Newspapers can be more fun than a quiet girl.

—*A. J. Leibling,* The Press

The wind, she blows. Texas is one great windy lunatic.

—*Socrates Hyacinth,* Overland Monthly, *1869*

Everybody talks about the weather, but only the Star-Telegram *does something about it.*

—*Alf Evans,* Star-Telegram

"God bless us every one," said Tiny Tim.

—*Charles Dickens,* A Christmas Carol

It used to be that the only way to get fired was to shoot the managing editor. But you had to kill him. Wounding wouldn't do it.

—*Cal Sutton, Managing Editor,* Star-Telegram

The Star-Telegram 'family' is somewhat of a homespun affair. Most people grew up on the staff.

—*Amon Carter, July 16, 1943*

14

Early in his life, James R. Record began to harrumph. It was never a constant, predictable mannerism, but he nevertheless practiced a modified Colonel Blimp harrumph. They were in character, those passionate harrumphs, the pained phonics of a shy man. The harrumphs scaled the mountainous boundaries of emotions, being whatever he wished them to be. He issued angry harrumphs and joyful harrumphs and morose harrumphs and frustrated harrumphs, harrumphs for sympathy, harrumphs for enthusiasm, harrumphs that scolded, praised and condemned.

He harrumphed because it was not within his nature to yell or cry or even laugh loudly. He was a gentleman and gentlemen never betrayed their feelings. He was formal and precise and reserved, as aloof as the headmaster of a good prep school. "A kindly school master," said a reporter of JRR.

Record was shy. That was the wellspring of his eccentricities. He kept himself away from his newsmen to maintain a dignified and proper relationship. No one except his immediate family called him anything but "Mister Record." To the family he was "Ferdinand," the gentle bull who enjoyed sitting on the porch of his ranch house near Throckmorton in West Texas to "gaze across the pasture at the cattle and the trees, and to smell the grass and breathe the pure air."

Because he was shy and remote, his reporters learned to communicate with him by lengthy memo. JRR could not abide long involved discussions and refused to entagle himself in detailed conversations. He used an open newspaper to end unnecessary talk. He held the newspaper between himself and the speaker, screening his face. Once a question was asked and answered or a statement made, JRR wanted to be left alone. He snapped the paper as a period to a conversation. If the talker persisted, Record snapped the newspaper again, louder, then louder, slowly swiveling his chair. "A persistent talker ended up talking to Record's back," said an observer of the ritual.

He opened each conversation, whether in person or over the telephone, with "All Right!", accenting the last word. For outsiders who wandered into the office he would greet them with "How do?" They were expected to say their piece and leave.

His punctuality was maddening, and amusing, to newsmen. He arrived exactly at 7 o'clock each morning, deposited his jacket on a coatrack, collected a basket of notes from his office and seated himself in the swivel chair near city desk. At mid-morning he ate an apple. Precisely at 11:15 a.m., he stood, walked briskly to his office, put on his coat and strolled to lunch, often waiting absentmindedly through green signal lights, walking on red.

Each and every morning JRR's first question was "What's the weather?" Weather was his passion, his avocation, a fetish to be served daily. JRR hailed the weather each morning with the piety of a pharoah greeting Ra.

Weather was important, even vital, to the *Star-Telegram* and Record because weather was the most significant factor of life in West Texas. A good weather story was, within the pages of the *Star-Telegram,* more notable and momentous than wars, plagues, the rise and fall of kings, even a juicy rape case. Weather, especially rain, dictated how life was lived out there on the dry plains, and the *Star-Telegram* reported daily on what folks could expect.

West Texas weather was, if nothing else, versatile. The temperature extremes ranged between a —23 to 120 degrees. Tornadoes struck Waco, Lubbock, Wichita Falls, Dallas and hundreds of lesser towns; sightings of twenty tornadoes in a single day was common. There were sand storms — called "Panhandle showers" — that stripped paint off cars, blistered faces and stung eyes, and when combined with rain and wind, formed pellets of mud flung like machine gun bullets. There were "northers," those sweeping winds of sudden cold as intense as the *buran* of the Siberian steppes, and spectacular summer storms of dreadful booming thunder, lightning like doomsday firebolts.

All of that happened on an annual schedule, but without very much rain. As assorted as West Texas weather was, its grabbag of climatology held little precipitation. When rain happened it was an event, an occasion for fanfare, and the *Star-Telegram* celebrated the rare phenomenon with great bold headlines: MILLION DOLLAR RAIN IN WEST TEXAS! and BENEFICIAL RAIN SOAKS RANCHES.

The evil season of rainlessness was, from all accounts, a stranger to the newspaper. By JRR's edict, the word "drought" could not appear in the *Star-Telegram* and, when used to describe West Texas, neither could the adjectives "desolate," "wilderness," "parched" or "barren."

Flem Hall once traveled by train to El Paso for a basketball tournament. Stuck for a column, he wrote of West Texas, of the land, the stark beauty of the desert. Somehow the column slipped by JRR and was printed.

When Hall returned, Record was waiting with the offending column. He confronted his sports editor.

"Where is it?" demanded JRR, thumping his forefinger on the newspaper. "Where is that 'desert'?"

"B-e-e-e-tween Big Spring and El . . . El Paso," stammered Hall.

"There's no desert in Texas! There's no desert in Texas!" declared Record in a frigid voice. "That's West Texas 'ranch land'!"

Because West Texas was not, to JRR, a desert, no droughts could occur out there. The Sahara had droughts. Bir Misaha, Egypt had droughts. Sharangad, Mongolia had droughts, and New Mexico and Arizona, but West Texas had "prolonged dry spells," which was the phrase Record would accept to explain the rainless days of West Texas. Wink, as it did in 1956, could receive only 1.76 inches of rain in 365 days but its predicament was not drought; Wink was having a "prolonged dry spell." Within pages of the *Star-Telegram* the great dustbowl of the 1930s in the American Midwest never blew over the Oklahoma state line into West Texas. Out there, it was nothing more than a tempest in a dusty tea cup.

During that 1930s drought a national magazine published a story picturing a small West Texas town as deserted and blowing away with the sand. *Harrumph.* JRR would not tolerate such ignorance. He immediately dispatched a team of reporters to the town to clear up the misconception that West Texas was a wasteland. The single story multiplied into a year's worth of articles, as each Sunday newsmen found something optimistic to write about this and that dusty hamlet.

Because rain was crucial to West Texas, and thus the *Star-Telegram,* JRR established a network of special rain reporters. Gauges were distributed into the eighty-four counties of West Texas. The rain reporters were expected to monitor precipitation within their gauges and immediately relay the amounts to the newspaper. Gauge readers were paid $1 per report.

In Fort Worth, real reporters were given gauges and told to report rainfall amounts in their city areas. Often, that meant a pre-dawn hike in a heavy downpour. Herb Owens, soaked with an early morning rain, reported poetically:

> As this wretched day was dawning,
> Out I stumbled, stretching, yawning,
> Through the muck and mire that lay without my door.
> Toward a gauge so distant mounted,
> That my steps I never counted,
> For I feared that I would get there, nevermore.
> But I reached my destination,
> Read the o'ernight accumulation,
> And am now reporting, swiftly true,
> .42

West Texas rain did not always fall evenly but often splashed down in a rush, creating havoc on those poor folks who had prayed for help, but not that much. The newspaper, never wanting to be the messenger of bad news, softened deluges into something like gentle spring showers. In 1930, there was a general cloudburst in West Texas and the *Star-Telegram* welcomed it with a bold headline: HEAVY RAINS ARE BENEFICIAL TO TEXAS PASTURES. The story began with news that the rains meant good crops and well-watered cattle and hope for the future. Only persistent readers found deep within the story other aspects of the kindly rains: Water rose 8½ feet into Childress homes, "tore out bridges and left highways impassable". An Amarillo man was washed into the Canadian River. A mail plane crash-landed out of the storm. Rock Island Railroad track was swept away, stranding a train.

Those Pollyanna rain reports caused Alf Evans to compose and thumbtack to the office bulletin board a joke headline: BENEFICIAL RAINS DROWN 7.

Even into his 80th year when the *Star-Telegram* had become less preoccupied with weather and rain, JRR daily had to know the forecast. It was one of the ironies of his life that, drilling for precious water on his Throckmorton ranch, he struck instead, oil.

It was not just weather JRR manipulated for readers. Many subjects affecting Fort Worth and West Texas received a thorough cleansing before publication. JRR disliked bad news, as did Amon Carter. A 1912 editorial explained, "The Star-Telegram has no patience with exhibitions of pessimism." That attitude accounts for why JRR sometime would hold gloomy stories until other media published them. Record didn't want his newspaper to be the first bearer of bad news. It explains, too, why, when the Dallas *Morning News* charged that Fort Worth retail sales were dangerously slow, JRR sent out reporters and photographers to remanufacture the facts. The newsmen went to a department store to refute the Dallas story. "The only thing," recalled Irv Farman, "was that the story was true. We almost had to hire extras to get the people we needed. In fact, we did pose some salesclerks as shoppers, but we got the 'Things are great' story."

The *Star-Telegram* was more than just a newspaper. It was three newspapers. First, there was the hard-core newspaper with a superb reporting staff that could cover a breaking news story as no other in Texas. It was that basic *Star-Telegram,* carefully protected and separated by JRR from its other missions, that uncovered scandals in government, reported every word of the J. Frank Norris murder trial, collected and published first all names of the generation of children killed in the New London school explosion, tracked murderers and thieves and various other criminal types, editorially stumped for mandatory fire escapes on public buildings, public highway safety laws, reform in Austin and Washington. That *Star-Telegram* was a real newspaper, and an excellent one.

The pure-news *Star-Telegram* reported accurately and in depth all that went on around it, from crimes to sports to governmental processes to farm and ranch news. It was a solid newspaper and even Amon Carter kept his hands off. Not once in his lifetime with the newspaper did he even attempt to keep a friend's name out of a hard news story, and his friends often asked it of him.

Its editorial pages, conservative in all matters, were never intellectual, never campaigned for philosophical concepts but more practical things like highways and parks and zoo elephants.

Leafing through the brittle pages of the early *Star-Telegram* reveals an innocence of the era and journalism. There was a wide-eyed, gee-whiz quality in the stories. World events were explained as they related to Fort Worth and West Texas. Whenever possible wire stories were localized with the insertion of a graf providing the Texas angle. "If there was an avalanche in the Swiss Alps," exaggerated a reporter, "we would write a local story saying it couldn't happen here, and why, quoting experts."

However exacting the basic *Star-Telegram,* no yellow and absolutely no by god blue journalism was ever practiced. JRR would have none of either. He protected the delicate sensibilities of readers and, being a gentleman, he never wished to embarrass anyone. He would not permit the word "rape" to enter *Star-Telegram* pages.* The accepted euphemism was "attacked" (or on occasion, "assaulted"), which may have

*JRR's legacies died hard. The word "rape" did not appear in the *Star-Telegram* until 1967. The word did not find a spot in the evening edition headlines until the early 1970s.

puzzled some readers, as in a story of the 1930s: "Miss Mary Smith was held up by two men Tuesday night and robbed and beaten. She suffered a broken jaw and minor bruises. She was not attacked."

The second *Star-Telegram* was Amon's alter ego. It boosted and swaggered and bragged, ever spreading the message of optimism throughout the land. Amon's *Star-Telegram* could post an eight column banner headline on a busy news day: BUSINESS GOOD; MONEY PLENTIFUL; BUILDING AT ITS PEAK IN WEST TEXAS. It could publish as many as 204 columns of type in ten days on the Fort Worth Fat Stock Show, scooting all other legitimate news onto back pages. It published regular pages devoted to "Texas Development" and series on Fort Worth's "Self Made Men" and sections on the city's "Best Houses, Streets and Businesses."

That *StarTelegram* was a Chamber of Commerce publication and Amon used it like a club on those he wished to impress.

In 1928, Fort Worth was host to the West Texas Chamber of Commerce, and the *Star-Telegram* pulsated with pride over the high honor. WEST TEXAS CHAMBER OF COMMERCE IN FORT WORTH MEETING crowed the newspaper on page one as delegates convened. The *Star-Telegram* went on to instruct its rural cousins from the west how to act in the big city. "Visitors who find themselves in trouble through ignorance of local laws will be dealt with lightly," it promised. Under the heading, "Good Things to Remember for Our Auto-Driving Visitors" was published this list of reminders: "Don't drive over a fire hose"; "Don't drive your car down the center of the street"; "Don't allow bicycle riders to hang onto your car", and "Don't argue with the traffic officer — if he has made a mistake, the court will right the wrong."

If delegates minded that condescending lecture, they never complained. Perhaps they were too busy reading about themselves. Throughout the week, the *Star-Telegram* turned over its major columns to reporting all details and every uttered word of the convention. Daily, there were pages of pictures and reprinted speeches and stories on those speeches. The newspaper even grouped West Texas news on two adjoining pages to enable delegates to have a convenient reference to news from home.

Regular readers who cared to learn of important matters in Kansas City, where Republicans were selecting a Presidential nominee that week, had to search among the boosterisms. In Amon's opinion, the West Texas Chamber of Commerce was of far more value to Fort Worth than the GOP, and possibly he was right.

It was within the second *Star-Telegram* that stories were molded to suit Amon Carter's whims of journalism, though admittedly he did not have his finger in each important boosterism article.

JRR, who worshipped Amon and felt he could do no wrong, knew his publisher's mind. Record kept to the party line, which is probably why he filled the bottom of page one with an eight column picture of 108 visiting undertakers. To cram 108 massed faces into eight columns must have been as formidable as stacking a clutch of angels on the head of a pin.

When Amon meddled into editorial business of the second *Star-Telegram* it was with the idea of improving the stories to suit his version of the news. Bell Helicopter Corporation began construction of its new production plant in Fort Worth, and Lawrence Bell, the firm's president, came to speak. Bell orated on the new partnership of his company and Fort Worth, of the bountiful future the pair would share.

Back in the office, the reporter finished his groundbreaking story and passed it to Amon for final approval. Bell was quoted extensively. Amon found a statement with which he did not agree and asked for a copy pencil. "Hell, he didn't mean to say that," Amon said and changed Bell's direct quotes to please himself.

Once Amon was sorting and selecting pictures for a page to memorialize visiting oilmen. JRR was at his elbow. Other editors were near, awaiting the publisher's choices.

Among the final group of pictures to be published were two photos of the same man.

"Mr. Carter, we have a policy against running a person's picture twice on the same page," instructed Charlie Boatner, a city editor.

Amon was amused. "I never heard of such a policy, have you, Mr. Record?" he said.

"No, Mr. Carter," replied JRR, who had made the one-man, one-page rule.

The boosteristic *Star-Telegram*, which could banner during the Scopes Trial such breathless intelligence as WEST TEXAS BUYING POWER TREBLES IN 10 YEARS, often camouflaged the first and real *Star-Telegram* and critics forgot that underneath all that puffery breathed a solid newspaper.

The third *Star-Telegram* was a playful little thing, serious as all get-out but nevertheless a frivolous package slipped between the hard news and squishy chamber of commerce messages.

Because for so long the *Star-Telegram* was the only acceptable reading matter in West Texas and because much of its circulation was out there in the provinces, it became a kind of family album for its western readers, a yearbook and almanac of memories and homemaker hints and livestock advice. Removed from its format, the third *Star-Telegram* would have made a serviceable little weekly newspaper for Muleshoe or Chillicothe.

The *Star-Telegram* went into eighty-four counties of West Texas and beyond — as late as the 1940s, 2,500 papers were delivered daily in Roswell, New Mexico; the home edition of the morning paper was sent two hundred miles beyond El Paso or seven hundred miles from home base. JRR often bragged that the *Star-Telegram* was read in eleven hundred Texas towns, most of them in the west. To service this territory, he organized a network of correspondents, numbering as many as six hundred. Additionally, Record regularly dispatched Fort Worth-based reporters into West Texas where they foraged for news on the prairies. And news out there was not what it was in Fort Worth. International anxiety was meaningless in West Texas. What really was important was: Could Bossy live on mesquite beans and cactus pods, and Will the turkey plague in Cuero spread to San Saba?

Those legions of correspondents were there to report on the notable events of their communities, and the New York *Times* with its Balkan intrigues be damned. Thus, the third *Star-Telegram* was brimming full of such one-inch stories as "Members of the First Baptist Church of Lampasas have completed plans for the building of a parsonage" and "A harvest of Haskell maize has been sold at $35 a ton" and "Plans for the opening of cotton picking season in West Texas are being perfected" and "Twenty-eight rattlesnakes have been killed on a farm less than eight miles from Childress." Of such piddling matters are circulations built and fortunes made.

There were full page layouts headlined HARRY VETCH EXPERIMENT IN RISING STAR and detailed explanations of MELON BLIGHT IN PARKER COUNTY and lists of new teachers in Cooke County, art exhibits in Seagraves, parade reports from Stamford. With neither shame nor favoritism, the third *Star-Telegram* published pictures of grandchildren visiting in Floydada, of "the first Girls' Tomato Club in Comanche County," of a new crematory in Abilene, a rising young store executive in Colorado City, little girls who won dancing contests in Lubbock and every bride between Amarillo and Zavala.

Sophisticated Fort Worthians may have been startled to find in their Sunday *Star-Telegram* a page of

NEWS AND SUGGESTIONS FOR THE HOG BREEDER ("Don't let sows get constipated — see to it their bowels are in kept in good working condition") but without those imperative tidings the newspaper would have been little needed in West Texas.

Such attention to the essentialities of West Texas life was repaid by fawning loyalty. When JRR's newsmen went out there they found themselves hailed as celebrities. Frank Reeves' name was known by every farmer and rancher for five hundred miles. Flem Hall was a more famous sports writer than Damon Runyon. Reporters covering banquets were introduced along with visiting Senators. Silliman Evans once went to Pampa for a story and the town threw him an appreciation dinner.

The third *Star-Telegram*, as trivial and amusing as it seems in retrospect, was substantial stuff to the readership it served. Any newspaper could, as the first *Star-Telegram* often did, change the course of state governments, but only the third *Star-Telegram* and Amon Carter could improve the discomfort of farrowing sows.

Content of the bucolic third *Star-Telegram* was, as much as anything else, a considerable portion of what Amon felt was necessary for newspapers — public service. "A man cannot live off his community. He must live with it," he often said and extended to philosophy to his newspaper.

From the beginning, the *Star-Telegram* burrowed into lives of its readers. In 1909, it editorialized for more and better city parks and at the same time conducted an essay contest among school children on "Why Fort Worth Should Have More Parks."

The newspaper campaigned successfully for a public industrial corporation to finance "practical city building." It sponsored special trains to athletic events and political conventions, was patron for "The Holy City," a mechanized miniature model of Jerusalem, served as godparent for automobile shows, home shows, quilting bees, ranch and farm shows, vacation shows, bird watching tours to the Texas Gulf Coast, and more than two score cooking schools. To promote art, the *Star-Telegram* distributed art appreciation courses and portfolios of Old Masters and undiscovered authors were given their opportunity with Scholastic Writing Awards programs.

JRR was responsible for publicizing each newspaper promotion, and each took valuable news space which he grudgingly gave, but, at the same time, gladly provided because it pleased Amon. At the publisher's request, JRR formed the Fort Worth Zoological Association and served as its president (reporter Bess Stephenson was drafted as secretary). He used *Star-Telegram* pages to obtain animals for the zoo. Through public subscription, giraffes were bought by the inch and foot, elephants by the pound. The zoo became a daily assignment and animal pictures plagued page one for forty years. Through Record, the newspaper sponsored research into diversified farming and agriculture, including production of the "battleship [sized] hog."

Amon initiated the Free Milk and Ice Fund and the Goodfellows Fund in 1912 and the annual Golden Gloves Tournament in 1937 (proceeds of the amateur boxing matches went to charity). Goodfellows began as a Christmas season drive to collect "toys and goodies" for poor children and became the newspaper's most successful promotion. JRR insisted that names of all contributors be published on the front page, a decision that often consumed half of PI in December.

When disaster came, the *Star-Telegram* immediately was there as a convenient community vehicle by which the public could help. In 1949, Fort Worth was inundated by flooding and the newspaper's relief fund gathered $335,000 for victims. It raised $18,000 after the Texas City ship explosion, and $18,000 for Olney, $50,000 for Waco and $37,000 for San Angelo, all of which were struck by tornadoes.

The newspaper fought for more and better highways, almost singlehandedly established Texas Technological College in Lubbock at a time when politicians believed West Texans weren't worth educating. It politicked for state parks and higher crop and beef prices. Amon became president of the association wanting a national park in the Big Bend area of West Texas. He and the newspaper gathered funds to purchase 750,000 acres. Amon and Bascom Timmons delivered the park land deed to FDR on a propitious date — June 6, 1944, waiting while the President monitored reports of the Allied invasion of Europe.

All of that, and hogs, too, the *Star-Telegram* supported and promoted and championed, ingratiating itself with its readers, making itself an indispensable household budget item. West Texans and Fort Worthians had to subscribe; they would miss too much without the *Star-Telegram*.

Because of the area it served, the *Star-Telegram* had no choice but to become more than a newspaper, and its first purpose, that of providing comprehensive news coverage, suffered as other requirements were added. Amon had very little real feel for journalism but he understood that the public service and boosterism necessities of his newspaper greatly harmed its professional reputation. As Jimmy North explained in a letter to publisher Ted Dealey, "He has said in family councils the Dallas *News* is a much better paper than our own." The Dallas *Morning News* could be a newspaper. It had no critical need to elevate the lives of poor dirt farmers and ragtag ranchers or bring hope where none existed.

For most of fifty years the *Star-Telegram* held West Texas as its own, but slowly circulation and influence diminished, which was a predictable result of Amon's ballyhooing. More people came. Good local newspapers flourished. The *Star-Telegram* owned all the rights to the best, most popular syndicate features and press wires in West Texas but gave up its monopoly. Katrine Deakins said Amon "thought it would help," but the act of disenfranchisement was not entirely charitable.

Mostly it was the morning edition which was shipped into West Texas and distances slowed its distribution. As long as readers were isolated they never knew the news was old. But radio, especially development of instantaneous world wide news programs during World War II, revealed to West Texans that their old friend, the *Star-Telegram*, was always late. Bus and train schedules were curtailed with the growing popularity of automobiles and getting the newspaper into West Texas at all, particularly into smaller communities, was increasingly difficult. The pattern of newspaper advertising changed. Large national advertisers began buying single markets.

High school football is a good example of why the *Star-Telegram* moved out of West Texas. Football, considered a test of manhood by *macho* West Texans, was a game with fanatical supporters. Entire towns locked their doors on Friday afternoon to watch the local high school team play football. Using its network of correspondents, the newspaper reported on as many as three hundred high school football games in the Saturday morning edition. At least fifty games were staffed each week. The coverage filled five open pages each Saturday morning.

Then outdoor athletic field lights were developed. High schools began playing football at night. The *Star-Telegram* no longer could provide complete coverage in the Saturday paper. The correspondent network was turned over to the Associated Press and soon every newspaper had what the *Star-Telegram* developed and owned exclusively.

In a sense, West Texas grew up and no longer needed its sponsor, the *Star-Telegram*. Amon had promoted the growth, nurtured it to maturity. West Texas could go it alone, and did.

Jimmy North was a square-shouldered blocky-statured man with a dark, almost Indian face. A contemporary described him as "retiring, but breezy, gregarious, the kind of man who whistles in the morning." North, said another, "could do everything in the office better than anybody else, but rarely did." Without North, Amon declared, "We would be in a hell of a fix."

Jimmy North, as editor, did not often edit. He was overseeer of day to day operations and, with Bert Honea, ran the *Star-Telegram* while Amon fiddled with the world. He, as the others, was a gentleman who began his memos to JRR with "My dear Mr. Record . . ." North rarely interfered with the editorial processes because those were JRR's responsibilities. He had a profound respect for the reporting staffs but confessed to a friend that the reporters were "an unbridled bunch." Mostly, Jimmy did not breach JRR's domain because when he did Record would ask him to fire or discipline someone, and North disliked doing either.

Newspaper offices were never the frantic places portrayed in fiction. There was a sustained intense but leisurely pace to them, a hum not a roar, and brief periods of hubbub, but generally they were just as any other business office. The *Star-Telegram*, with the cast of a Russian novel and plot of The Little Train That Could, had, however, JRR, who was not ordinary, even in the extraordinary world of newspapering. Record ruled over two full staffs, one for each edition, and his eccentricities created an atmosphere of unconformity.

Most reporters and editors came and never left, remaining because there was an excitement to the place, because the newspaper was quality and respected and consequently so were they, and because no one would make them leave. As Jimmy North, that shy peculiar gentleman, JRR, could not dismiss his reporters without provocations that would have meant criminal charges in other businesses. Few of those discharged had to face

JRR; he either foisted the distasteful duty on North or sub-editors. JRR fired Gotcheye, a copyboy thief, with a stern lecture, and a week's pay, but the experience was traumatic and Record moped about the newsroom for weeks. Reporters who deserved firing, and they were very few, were pushed into a corner like stacked cordwood, given the most trivial and onerous assignments, left out of general payraises, and ignored until they understood their predicament and voluntarily quit. The non-firing policy left few openings for new reporters as the older ones stayed on and on. Still, the *Star-Telegram* became known as a newspaper where an itinerant reporter could find "temporary" work because gentle JRR could not deny a job to a man who needed one.

The *Star-Telegram* was not unlike one of those banana republic plantations where a benevolent *padrone* cared for the workers' every need. Amon gave his employees free insurance and bankrolled with $4,500,000 of his own money a generous retirement program. Christmas bonuses came every year. Once, in the 1930s, Amon was in New York when bonus checks were distributed. When he returned he decided the bonus had been too little and he issued another. During the Korean war, employees who went into service were paid the difference between their military pay and the salary they left behind. Amon and Nenetta put $1,425,000 into a special fund which provided emergency assistance to workers. When a disastrous flood hit Fort Worth, many of its victims were *Star-Telegram* employees. The fund paid all of their losses. Often Amon personally took charge of an employee's troubles. One reporter's son was born with a cleft palate. Amon found a doctor and paid for the expensive operation to correct the boy's disfigurement. The *Union Banner*, a local union publication, praised Amon as "perhaps the only employer in the United States who pays the entire cost."

Only the newspaper's backshop was unionized, and Bert Honea handled negotiations. But once Amon came to a contract discussion dressed in a shabby ragged suit and shoes with holes in the soles. The *Star-Telegram* never had a strike nor even a serious labor problem.

In the newsroom, the staffs were considered "family," and treated as such. JRR not only could not fire his people, he was reluctant even to reprimand them. The act of dressing down a wayward reporter distressed him and he rarely did it, but resorted to an assortment of excoriating glares, grimaces and harrumphs which were as punishing as the real scoldings. JRR's pantomimed discipline was as effective as heated words and a disapproving stare from the managing editor usually corrected any situation.

JRR was a strict editor who wanted every detail in every story. Ida Belle Hicks, an amusement writer, was assigned to cover the opening of a new play. During the performance, a mouse unexpectedly ran across the stage. The audience roared. Hicks left the mouse out of her review. Next day, JRR read a review in the *Press* which had an account of the rodent's performance. He called Ida Belle to his desk and lectured her sternly, "Next time, mention the mouse . . ."

E. D. Alexander discovered JRR's penchant for decision-making. Record reveled in a decision. If Alexander wanted to cover a story, he approached JRR with the opinion the event "wasn't worth much and we probably shouldn't do anything with it." JRR always pondered the matter and ordered Alex to do the story.

At various times, the *Star-Telegram* had a policy against reporters accepting freebies. JRR, who hated to deny his "family" anything, handled the policy in his own special way. When a circus press agent brought his wad of free tickets to the office, JRR would explain the newspaper's policy. The press agent would leave the tickets on the corner of Records's desk. JRR would pointedly drop the tickets in his wastebasket, rise and immediately leave the newsroom. A city editor rescued the tickets and distributed them.

JRR's life was filled with little crosses carved by the peculiarities of his staffs. There was George Dolan, given the temporary promotion to assistant city editor, standing atop his desk to hand out daily assignments until harrumphed down by JRR. Dolan later was barred from taking obituary calls because the news unnerved him and he giggled when relatives told of their departed loved ones. And Bert Griffith who, with Ned Record, JRR's brother, decided to welcome a new, sweet and innocent reporter, Bess Stephenson, to the *Star-Telegram* family. They took her to lunch at a nearby whorehouse. Presley Bryant, the state editor often called "The Terrible-Tempered Mr. Fang," would, when irked, stand and slam his chair back against a desk. JRR would rush over to examine the chair and desk for damage, then glare at Bryant. Bryant also wore tennis shoes in defiance of Record's strict dress code and daily vaulted the low fence dividing the newsroom from the elevator lobby. JRR grimaced but never spoke of his grievances against Bryant.

Byron Utecht was the first American reporter to ride with Pancho Villa. He was absent-minded. Utecht lit one cigarette after another until half a dozen burned in ashtrays around the city desk. Record, who refused to smoke in the newsroom, would stub out the offending cigarettes, then stand, harrumphing at Utecht.

Icky Pierce drank. Posted to the courthouse, Icky promptly went off to the nearest saloon and forgot his assignment. Late in the day, he telephoned city desk to report that his absence was caused by the mob trying to spring their criminal friends from county jail. It was a near-riot, exclaimed Icky. The city editor immediately sent Alex Stedman to assist Icky with the big story. Icky urged Stedman into the saloon. Late that evening, Icky returned to the office and was ordered to hurry with his mob story. Icky pecked out two sentences, stood uncertainly, and walked out. Editors read the sentences: "There ain't no mob. I have gone home." Next day, Icky and Stedman were banished to the obituary desk where the latter uttered an immortal line: "The wages of gin is death notices."

It was Icky who, sent to interview J. Frank Norris, stopped first at a bar before confronting the controversial minister who hated liquor.

Norris sniffed Icky, then placed a fatherly hand on the reporter's shoulder.

"You've been drinking," accused Norris.

"No, I never drink," protested Icky.

"Young man, you've been drinking."

"No, honest, I'm a teetotaler."

"Now, Icky . . . aren't you about half-drunk?"

"No, sir, preacher, just like you I never plead guilty to anything."

Frank Reeves, a lean gaunt man, a real cowboy who turned to photography then writing when ranchlife became boring, ranged over West Texas as no other *Star-Telegram* reporter. He had a studied disregard for money and rarely filed expense accounts. He often misplaced his paychecks. The newspaper's accounting office would send frantic notes to JRR, urging him to force Reeves to straighten out his finances. At the end of the year when accountants were trying to close their books, JRR would stand over Reeves while he made out expense accounts, usually totaling thousands of dollars.

JRR, who disliked ostentation of any sort, often was irritated by his music critic, E. Clyde Whitlock. Whitlock, a balding cherub who played his violin for office Christmas parties, was painstakingly methodical and a slow forefinger typist. He sometimes fell asleep while writing a review. Whitlock loved big words as much as JRR hated them and his reviews were bewildering labyrinths in which multi-syllabic words blared like trumpet fanfares. Once when an outdoor concert was rained out, Whitlock wrote that the cancellation was because of "meteorological impediments." He reviewed Margaret Truman's concert in Fort Worth with the observation, "There are vocal faults, lacks and limitations but it is significant that they are amenable to amelioration under understanding guidance." JRR marked that column with a huge "?".

Whitlock wrote his own obit ("to run after my funeral") in which he called himself a "sesquipedantitarian," and added in a shaky hand, "Ave atque vale — hail and farewell."

Bert Griffith, too, wrote his obituary and affixed a note commanding "When I die, say I died — none of that 'passed away' crap." Dolan's obit asked that his creditors be designated pallbearers at his funeral. "They carried me through life," he said. "They may as well finish the job."

Boyce House was a breezy reporter who talked more than he wrote and he was a prolific writer. On a rainy Sunday afternoon he wrote in four hours a book, "I Give You Texas," which sold 225,000 copies. It was filled with all those Texas brags espoused by Amon. House had been editor of a weekly newspaper in Eastland, a small West Texas town, when he broke the story of Old Rip, a horned frog. Rip supposedly was cemented into the cornerstone of a courthouse. Thirty years later, the cornerstone was opened and there was Rip — alive. Rip and House became famous. Rip went on the road, escorted on an eastern tour during which the toad entourage stopped by the White House. Cal Coolidge ignored the nation's business for fifteen minutes to inspect the Texas frog. A few months of fame later Rip really died, was embalmed, stuffed and laid to rest in a tiny red satin-lined casket. House, on the other hand, came to the *Star-Telegram* where he would chatter on until JRR popped his newspaper like a machine gun.

Silliman Evans was without peer as a political writer in Texas, and perhaps the best reporter ever to work for the *Star-Telegram*. But competent though he was, his smart-alecky ways irked everyone. He was jockey-sized and arrogant, uncommonly preoccupied with self, pugnacious, dissolute, petulant and dauntless — the perfect weapon to loose against the political shenanigans of Ma and Pa Ferguson. Because of the Ferguson stories, Evans was drawn close to Amon, and the reporter began to ape the mannerisms of his publisher. He even adopted Amon's brand of cigars. Once in Austin Evans and Bert Honea left a restaurant. Evans scooped up a supply of expensive cigars. Honea, who knew Evans' salary, asked, "You don't put those on your expense account, do you, Silliman?"

"Not as such, Mr. Honea, not as such."

Evans left the newspaper to become public relations director of Texas Air Transport and later American Airlines, then worked for the Democrats. After the 1932 election he was awarded the splendid title of Fourth Assistant Postmaster General. From that post he became president of Maryland Casualty Company, then, using Jesse Jones' money, purchased the bankrupt Nashville *Tennessean*. Within six months the newspaper was making money. Successful as a major publisher, Evans bought a showplace estate and began staging parties for visiting celebrities. He gave expensive gifts and became a major booster of Nashville. He named his son Amon Carter Evans.

And C. L. Richhart, the pattern mold for nonconforming newspapermen.

Rich was gnomic with prankish eyes, the soul of a gypsy. His irregular lifestyle gave him the complexion of a morgue attendant, but there was an infectious laugh, the breezy nervous energy manner, the perpetual motion mind, the eternally optimistic spirit. He was never on time, neither for work or assignments, was endlessly broke, ever happy and always helping others, usually with *Star-Telegram* money. "I always visualize Rich as an elf with the exhausted remnants of a cigar protruding from a plastic cigar holder clamped in his teeth," wrote

Phil Record, who was a copyboy when he first encountered the irrepressible Richhart. "He looked as though he had gone into his closet blindfolded to select the day's wardrobe."

Early on, Rich both irked and bewildered the tidy, systematized JRR, who did something he rarely did. He fired Rich. Amon interceded and Richhart's job was saved. Later, Rich and JRR found an accommodation of friendship. Nobody could remain angry at Richhart.

Rich became a sinecure of sorts for Amon because the diminutive reporter, when not distracted, was competent and, said an observer, "the best public relations man on the staff."

As most everyone else, Amon at first tried to change Richhart. He surveyed the shabby clothes and unkempt appearance and ordered Rich to upgrade his wardrobe. Rich bought a suit off the rack — and charged it to Amon.

It was Richhart to whom Amon turned when he wanted a train stolen. After World War II the French sent thanks for America's help in the form of a Friendship Train which toured the country laden with Gallic exhibits. Fort Worth and Amon had packed boxcars with foodstuffs for European war relief in 1943 — Columnist Drew Pearson reported that Amon delayed the train while he had "Fort Worth — Where the West Begins" stamped on flour sacks. But the French Friendship Train was not routed through Fort Worth. The ingratitude angered Amon and he commanded Rich to go get it. In Austin, Richhart convinced French and Texas officials to bring the train to Fort Worth. Afterwards, promised Rich, the train would be returned to its regular route. The train was delivered and Fort Worthers were gratified. The French asked for their train and Amon said, "To hell with them." They had to come after it.

When not doing little things for Amon, Rich had the usual reporting duties, except that no one ever knew where he was supposed to be. The morning city editor once asked his counterpart on the afternoon newspaper, "Can I borrow Richhart for an assignment?"

"Borrow him? I though he worked for you!"

Richhart, with a bedouin's loathing for permanency, belonged to no man, but flitted hither and yon, disappearing and reappearing with the whim of a playful breeze. Because he was always late for work, Jack Butler wasn't disturbed when Rich telephoned one early morning. "Did you find the stories I left?" asked Richhart.

"Yes," replied Butler.

"Well, I've run into a fellow who wanted me to go to a chuck wagon breakfast."

"OK, but I want you to check out a story and call me."

Long pause. "From Stamford?"

"Stamford!" moaned Butler, visualizing the ranching community two hundred miles west of Fort Worth.

"Well, I told you this fellow wanted me to go to a chuck wagon breakfast."

In the early 1950s the *Star-Telegram* sponsored a community Christmas Tree. Rich was assigned to select the hundred-foot-tall tree from New Mexico forests. He chose a tree and arranged for it to be delivered to Fort Worth. Then Rich met a guy on his way to Seattle. Richhart, having never seen Seattle, went with the man.

Each New Year's Eve Rich celebrated the event with a curious ritual. He ran through the newsroom ringing a cowbell, a practice that disturbed the night city editor, Cal Sutton. One holiday season, Richhart was sent to Mexico City on assignment, and Sutton anticipated a quiet evening.

At midnight, the telephone rang. A deskman answered it, and motioned to Sutton, "It's for you."

"Hello," said Sutton, and over the wires from Mexico City he heard, "Happy New Year! Clang . . . clang . . . clang . . ."

However unpredictable, Rich owned a gentle sweet humanity that spread over everyone. There was the wartime Easter when Jack Butler was drafted into the Navy. His wife, Mary Lou, was left to manage with one small child. She was pregnant with another. Mary Lou and Catherine Gunn, whose husband, Stanley, the *Star-Telegram* Pacific war correspondent, had been killed months earlier, spent the holiday loneliness together. Catherine had two children.

Neither woman was in a festive mood. Until Richhart arrived. He came by taxi, with corsages for the wives and Easter eggs for the children, and of course with the happiest gift of all — himself.

Reporters who learned of his generosity that Easter were sure he charged the taxi ride to the *Star-Telegram*, plus, to be sure, a sizeable tip. C. L. Richhart always went first class on the newspaper's money.

Which brings us to the *Star-Telegram* Employees Association picnic of 1948, not coincidentally the last outing underwritten by the newspaper. The association was formed in 1939 and the newspaper management agreed to fund an annual picnic. The one thousand or so dollars were, believed Amon, money well spent, and the picnic always was a pleasant affair with potato salad and lemonade and softball games.

In 1948, Rich was elected president of the association, thus *maggiordomo* of the annual picnic.

The site he selected on the shores of Lake Worth had a beach and sports facilities and old pavilions. The buildings, he believed, were a little shoddy. He brought in carpenters to spruce them up. A bog of quicksand was found on the grounds. He hired workmen to bridge the dangerous patch. He contracted with a caterer, Walter Jetton (later to be famous as Lyndon Johnson's favorite barbeque chef). Because the *Star-Telegram* operated in shifts, Rich declared the picnic would go on for thirty-six hours. Everybody would be able to attend. And of course the workers needed transportation. A fleet of buses was chartered.

July 18, the picnic opened and for the next day and a half association members marveled at what Rich had wrought.

There were fringed surreys to transport new arrivals over the quicksand bridge, speedboat rides and seaplane flights, a miniature train, goat carts (JRR puckishly drove one for the kids), wagons for hayrides, canoe-tilting contests and horseshoe tournaments, softball games, hourly drawings for door prizes and floor shows by the Flying X Ranchboys, square dancing, free liquor and gambling at a pavilion Rich outfitted as a casino. Bands played for dancing until after midnight.

According to published reports, the picnickers consumed three hundred pounds of barbecued beef, three hundred pounds of ribs, two hundred pounds of ham, seventy-five chickens, five hundred pounds of baked beans, seven hundred loaves of bread and four hundred cases of soft drinks. Not all of the eaters were association members and their families. Employees of other companies holding nearby picnics abandoned their nickel and dime fun to join Rich's extravaganza. Off duty policemen arrived and never left.

Amon was there. He played softball, danced with the ladies and sang, "I'm In Love With The Man With The Handlebar Mustache." He appeared to enjoy himself.

Richhart's surprise came at sunset of the second day. He gathered the picnickers on the lakeshore. Across the water, the twilight exploded with a panorama of fireworks. Rockets soared and burst in sparkling showers, bombs shattered the night, blossoming firey sky missiles spread fingers of reds and greens and blues. A classic fireworks display. But more was coming — Rich's finale.

There, above the water, etched in fire dozens of feet high and, a reporter later wrote, "lighting up the night sky for miles around,'' was the flaming portrait of Amon G. Carter.

Onlookers were stunned and within the silence was the astonished voice of Jimmy North: ''Damn! What next?''

Rich's picnic cost $12,000 to produce and the *Star-Telegram* never again sponsored an employees outing. When the bills were assembled and totaled, a seething Amon summoned Richhart.

''I guess what we oughta do,'' shouted Amon, ''is make you a gawddamned vice president in charge of finances.''

Rich later denied it, but allegedly he answered, ''I dunno. What's it pay?''

Chapter 15

I am the emperor and I want noodles!

—Ferdinand III, 1656

I didn't hire you to tell me I can't. I hired you to tell me I can.

—Amon, to his attorney, Abe Herman

Being God ain't no bed of roses.

—Father Divine

It may be because I despise the publisher I cannot view him in any light but as a menace to the people of Fort Worth.

—Karl Crowley, February 2, 1938

Nobody can be exactly like me. Sometime I have trouble doing it.

—Tallulah Bankhead, actress

Amon Carter is damn fool on many things . . .

—Amarillo Globe, *May 11, 1936*

15

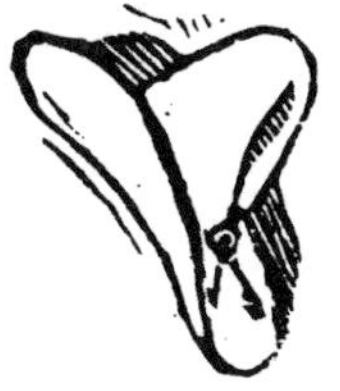

Amon had no rebellion to authority for he, unmistakenly, *was* authority in Fort Worth and West Texas, a unilateral *deus ex machina* whispering *sotto voce* to characters strutting on stage or out there in the spotlight himself as a beacon for all. His way was the right way, the only way, and that was that, unless one was prepared for the blast furnace fury that was sure to come. Amon would brook no interference. "There is only one white hunter on this safari," said a contemporary of Amon's singular role as authoritarian.

Cross Amon, defy him, and one acquired an antagonist with a superb memory for old outrages and a fine aptitude for retribution. There is a tale from his youth illustrative of the keen sense of vengefulness he possessed. In his chicken and bread days at Bowie a Pullman porter on the Rock Island Line barred Amon from peddling his sandwiches. Porters, in those days, trafficked in

Mockingbirds, which were plentiful in North Central Texas and brought a precious price in Chicago. In Bowie Mockingbirds brought a dollar a bird. They were easy to capture and boys made a good business of them. Bluejays, on the other hand, were a cantankerous bird, difficult to trap, worthless in Chicago. After being insulted by the porter Amon spent weeks gathering Bluejays. Finally he gathered five in a hatbox and represented them as Mockingbirds to the porter. With a kindly smile, Amon pocketed his five dollars. In the same space of time, he could have collected twenty-five Mockingbirds, but he lost twenty dollars to take the porter's five. He had the further satisfaction of causing the porter to be known as "Bluejay" for the rest of his working days. Sweet revenge.

With such training in his youth, Amon developed a low tolerance for slights and affronts and what he believed to be ingratitude. He despised ingratitude, toward himself or to others. There was the businessman who one year refused to contribute to Rivercrest Country Club's employee Christmas fund. Amon never forgave the man and thirty years later still ranted about the member's piking ways. Silliman Evans, after becoming a Nashville publisher, was a force within Tennessee's Democratic Party. At the 1936 Democratic Convention Amon still was campaigning for John Nance Garner as President and solicted Evans' help with the Tennessee delegation. Evans, who never wished to displease Amon, agreed to help but privately continued to support FDR. Amon learned of the deceit and gawd-damned Evans for his treasonous act. Evans deeply regretted the loss of Amon's friendship and wrote long fawning letters attempting to repair the damage. Amon was unmoved. "I've got my foot on his neck," he told Katrine Deakins. "I'm just gonna make him squirm."

Amon was incapable of hiding his anger. He confronted whatever or whoever riled him. "It has come to my attention," he wrote a man who gossiped about him around the Fort Worth Club, "that you, as a busy body, have been devoting considerable time to the discussion of my personal affairs."

When a Texas & Pacific Railroad crew accidentally burned a portion of his Arlington peach orchard Amon composed a near-fictional sarcastic letter to J. L. Lancaster, the company's president. It read:

> I am the peaceful owner of a little farm adjoining the Texas & Pacific Railroad between Arlington and Fort Worth. I have lived on this farm for years and several years ago arrived at the age which made it impractical for me to do hard farm labor; so, I decided to plant a peach orchard. Since which time, I have been pruning, nursing and tutoring these trees and about the time I had them in good condition to bear fruit, and give me a sufficient income to take care of my modest requirements, I find the big Texas & Pacific Railroad comes along, carelessly, without thought or consideration for its neighbors, with a motor car and sprayed oil on the grass on your right-a-way and set fire to it. As a result, you have destroyed one hundred and seventy-nine peach trees, leaving only four or five that might live, although it is doubtful.
>
> Now, I have always been considered a fair man and want to do what is right, provided what is right agrees with my idea of what is right.
>
> In conclusion please get your Directors together and study this matter over and let me have a check, as I naturally would prefer to settle a matter in this way than I would to bring it up in the Court House here. In addition, to all of the financial loss, I am heartbroken over having this orchard destroyed. It may be of no consequence to a great railroad like the Texas & Pacific, but it sure is an important matter to me. Now, please give me a personal answer on this and do not send me form letter 8786 which usually denies all responsibility, as I know damn well who burned up my orchard.

That was pure Amon at his angriest. He once again took on the T&P over the matter of a dead hog. The telephone company built a new line across his peach orchard, near which he maintained a hogpen. Workers left a gate open and a sow wandered away to be struck by a freight train. He asked Texas & Pacific for payment, and was offered $12.50. He then went to the telephone company and demanded retribution for its carelessness. He collected $15.00. For years Amon told over and over how he received $27.50 for a $25.00 hog and how the railroad paid for a sow already paid for by the telephone company.

Amon always had troubles with railroads. The Southern Pacific Railroad refused to extend its switching limits to Fort Worth. He told off its president in a three page letter, then sought out and welcomed to town a competing line, the Katy, to freeze out Southern Pacific. He took on the Colorado and Southern for a two year fight. The Interstate Commerce Commission allowed the railroad to lease the Fort Worth and Denver Railway which ran from Dallas to Texline on the Colorado border. Giant Burlington Lines controlled Colorado and Southern Railway and the merger, it stated, would mean a $25,000 annual savings. To Amon, it meant only that Burlington's removal of FW&D's general offices from Fort Worth to Denver and closing of shops at Childress in West Texas would leave 189 employees without jobs. Amon dictated an editorial describing how Ralph Budd, Burlington's president, was attempting to sacrifice "The Fort Worth and Denver Railway on the altar of Burlington front office convenience."

"You, Mr. Budd, have cast the die," concluded the editorial, "with utter contempt for fair and decent treatment of both your faithful employees and old customers."

Amon forced the merger question into public hearings and witnesses credited his testimony with the ICC's decision not to allow transfer of headquarters or closing of the Childress shops. Amon won, but Amon was mad. He wrote to Budd, "As evidence of my sincerity, I am bringing up a boy . . . to carry on for me at the Fort Worth *Star-Telegram*. In my final papers to the young man, I am leaving everything discretionary with one exception, namely: The Burlington blitzkreig against Texas. On this I have asked that he never relent in keeping the good folks of Texas continuously informed (through our newspapers and radio stations) of just HOW MEAN the Burlington has treated us 'country folks.' ''

And still Amon was unsatisfied. He ordered that the *Star-Telegram* stocks of paper no longer be delivered by the Burlington's new subsidiary, the Fort Worth & Denver, a loss of $12,000 monthly to the railroad.

The matter should have ended there but years later Budd came to visit Amon. ''I want to apologize,'' the railroad president said. ''I thought you were just meddling in our business, but after war came along we needed the shops here and in Childress. Without them we would have been in a mess.''

Amon graciously thanked Budd and, watching him leave, muttered to Walter Claer, his oil office manager, ''I still don't like that man.''

Amon's sweet revenge was costly to Burlington. Many who crossed Amon found the experience expensive. Stanley Moore, his black chauffeur, wanted a shed built at his home. Amon agreed to pay for the building and asked Stanley to obtain an estimate from Cameron Lumber Company. Cameron was the firm from which Amon's oil companies purchased large orders of cement amounting to thousands of dollars. Amon agreed to the price and Stanley built his shed. Cameron's final bill, however, was double its estimate. Amon exploded and ordered Walter Claer never to buy cement from Cameron again. Several years passed and one day Amon told Walter, ''You can buy cement from Cameron again. I guess they've been punished enough.''

No affront, to himself or to his city, was too small for his attention. Returning from the airport with a reporter, Amon drove past the new Bell Helicopter plant. A large billboard advertising the Worth Hotel had been erected in front of the new facility, obscuring the view. "We've got to do something about that," he told the newsman. Next day, the sign came down. General Motors' Southwestern parts depot was housed in an old building west of downtown on Seventh Street. Amon passed the shabby building each day on his way to the office. The structure offended him and he especially was disturbed by its sign. Amon, who spoke only to presidents — he knew where the power lay, wrote GM's chief officer, W. S. Knudsen, "That sign on your depot looks like a widow woman's boarding house." He told Knudsen to replace it. An American Airlines sign over an airport counter irritated him. He complained and the sign was lighted and lowered two inches. He also demanded that the airline serve a chicken dinner between Fort Worth and Memphis, and it was done.

Amon could never understand why other men and companies did not support Fort Worth with the same fanaticism he and the *Star-Telegram* felt. Whatever Amon was boosting for the moment always needed money and financing came from Fort Worth's business community. He soaked the companies good — those involuntary contributions became known as the "Amon Carter Taxes." Not all firms participated in the funds subscriptions, which caused Amon to be unhappy. He chewed out the president of Western Union because its Fort Worth branch "never helped in civic projects." He wrote the president of an ink company, "I've been doing business with you for twenty years and I know what's going on in this town. Every time we have a fund-raising campaign you don't give a penny. You're not going to get another dime's worth of my business."

When sufficiently provoked Amon punished all of Fort Worth. In 1953, he and the *Star-Telegram* pushed hard for a city bond issue. Voters turned down the issue. Amon fumed. "To hell with them," he pronounced to a reporter. At that time the newspaper sponsored the annual community Christmas tree and while the voters refused to raise their taxes, C. L. Richhart was in New Mexico searching for the perfect giant pine to place in downtown Burnet Park. Amon telephoned Richhart and summoned the reporter home, treeless. Fort Worth had no Christmas tree that year.

Amon once clashed with entertainer Arthur Godfrey, who came to Fort Worth on behalf of the Air Force Association. He and Amon were introduced at a reception in the home of General Samuel Anderson, commander of the Eighth Air Force. The men, at first, chatted amiably. They began speaking of their famous acquaintances. Godfrey dropped a name. Amon dropped one in return. Godfrey flung out another name. Amon countered with one of his celebrity friends. The name-dropping contest reached shouting proportions, and Godfrey stomped up the stairs. He did not return until Amon left the reception.

When Douglas MacArthur arrived in Fort Worth fresh from being fired by Harry Truman, the general was there to test his political popularity. He was scheduled to speak at Farrington Field, a high school football stadium. MacArthur, sponsored by Scripps-Howard newspapers, including the Fort Worth *Press*, really was off limits to Amon. The publisher, however, never strayed far from a visiting celebrity's side. The general and Mrs. MacArthur entered the stadium riding in a convertible. Amon was on the track at the opposite end of the field. Reporters were astonished to see their publisher sprint across the field, throw open the car door and leap in beside the startled MacArthur. Amon joined the general in waving at the huge crowd. That evening MacArthur was guest of honor at a Fort Worth Club dinner. Amon, of course, was present. For more than an hour the general refused to come to the dinner because he was angry with Amon for the afternoon intrusion.

The *Saturday Evening Post* article on Amon appeared in late autumn, 1938, and it irked the publisher. When Alva Johnston first contacted Amon about the story, Carter, flattered, suggested it be done in two parts "like the one given Mr. Chrysler." Johnston replied that the magazine wanted one story in one issue. Amon sat still for interviews and Johnston sent a first draft. It was riddled with tales of the cowboy and Amon griped to Jimmy North that Johnston's story made him look like a "playboy showman . . . and ballyhoo artist." Amon proposed to Johnston that the story be rewritten with heavier emphasis on Fort Worth's eminence in America. Johnston demurred. On Amon's behalf, North wrote Johnston suggesting that the story idea be abandoned. Amon would pay Johnston for his time and trouble and the article could be done at a later date. Johnston turned down the offer and prepared his story, "Colonel Carter of Cartersville," for publication. At the last minute, Amon wrote the *Post* editor complaining that "Col. Carter is a hell of a name to hang on me." He asked the editor to insert ". . . Where the West Begins" into the title. The *Post* ignored Amon and soon the entire country was laughing at the *divertissements* and capers of the consummate cowboy. Amon fumed and fussed about the injustice of it all — didn't anyone understand that the cowboy was unreal, that he only was a plaything, an imaginary character from childhood dreams? No, apparently no one understood that, and Amon grouched about how he was "unknown for anything else."

Of all Amon's feuds in Fort Worth the most famous was with H. C. Meacham, department store owner and mayor. They were long-time friends who fell out and exactly why they became enemies is unknown. There were several versions of the feud's origin: (1) They bought a ranch together and quarrelled over mineral rights; (2) Meacham reneged on paying his share of the ranch; (3) Amon used more of the land than

Meacham wanted; (4) They argued over favors of a girl; (5) They argued over division of a case of gift liquor, or (6) They argued over payment of a planeload of liquor illegally flown to Fort Worth from Mexico. Probably the real reason was none of those, or a combination of any and all, but for whatever cause or causes the men truly hated one another.

Until the split, Meacham's department store ran at least ten pages of advertising each week in the *Star-Telegram*. Whether by Amon's edict or Meacham's voluntary withdrawal, the ads stopped. That was a loss of more than $100,000 yearly for the newspaper. Meacham's loss was greater. Left only with the small-circulation *Press*, the store underwent a severe decline in sales. Bankruptcy loomed. Probably Meacham kept the advertising away from the *Star-Telegram*. When Meacham first ran for mayor (and won), the newspaper editorialized on its front page against his candidacy. Meacham called his managers together, vowing, "There will never be another ad from Meacham's in the *Star-Telegram* as long as I live." And there was not. Meacham died in December, 1929, and the Monday following the funeral his store's advertisements reappeared in the newspaper, just in time for the Christmas rush.

Meacham's death did not end the matter. Within pages of the *Star-Telegram* the city's airfield was called "Municipal Airport" rather than its correct official name, Meacham Field. That policy continued for eighteen years until 1947 when Amon suddenly, and with some irony, married Minne Meacham Smith, second daughter of his old foe.

Not all of Amon's enemies — and there were more than a few — came to him because of personal confrontations. Several were acquired because of his newspaper, and at least two of them were acquired on a warm afternoon in 1934. That day a pair of motorcycle patrolmen stopped on Highway 114 between Fort Worth and a suburban town, Grapevine. Nearby, they noticed a black

Ford sedan with yellow wire wheels parked on a side road. Inside, the officers could see a man and woman "necking." They strolled to the car. As the patrolmen approached the couple stepped out of the Ford and fired shotguns, killing both officers instantly. A farmer in an adjacent field saw everything. The man and woman jumped into their Ford and sped away.

They were Bonnie Parker and Clyde Barrow, and within an hour, all of North Texas was being searched. The *Star-Telegram* bannered the senseless killing, its headlines telling of the INTENSIVE MAN HUNT FOR CLYDE BARROW AND HIS CIGAR-SMOKING WOMAN COMPANION, BONNIE PARKER . . ." Where Bonnie and Clyde disappeared to was a mystery until Amon heard from them. The outlaw couple drove to Decatur, forty miles north of Fort Worth, and hid out in a tourist court. They bought a *Star-Telegram* to read of their crime and Clyde became angry. He wrote Amon a rambling, almost illegible and illiterate, chatty, threatening note, dropped it by the Post Office at 7:30 p.m. April 3, and then disappeared again with Bonnie. The letter read:

> The postman may not find you at home but you will get this letter just the same. And you better think, decide and make up your mind and not let your Editor make another remark about Bonnie like you did the other day. They called her the cigar-smoking woman. Another remark about my underworld mate and I will end such men as you mighty quick. I know where you and your reporters live. Isn't every girl in Fort Worth cigaret feign [?] and whore they all lie around in cars night after night . . . And those dirty son-of-bitches came out to that by road [to] stop us from fucking. All I regret was that the third cop wasn't there while our guns were hot.* Men and women are out in Dallas every day and night screwing and the department never sends a policeman after them . . . You rich bastards go to church and are dirty rascals same as other robbers. You

*A third patrolman was cruising several hundred yards ahead of the slain officers.

> and your friends take whiskey and Fort Worth girls to Lard's ranch in New Mexico. Bonnie and I are not married and we fuck when we please too. And I am going to take up for her and she will take up for me. We may go back to that farm house near Grapevine [and] pump that family full of lead for reporting us. But we'll drive to the Brazos River near Breckenridge [100 miles west of Fort Worth] tomorrow.
>
> Say boy can't robbers get away fast in cars these days. I'm glad this country is different from what it was when Jessy James lived here.
>
> If old lady Ferguson puts out a reward for us we will steal her out . . . Now and then I do something extra. I cause tragedies by writing to married women and sign some man's name there her husband is acquainted with. Then he does a little shotting vice versa [?] Sometimes make the letter sound very nasty. Men ought to abuse lots of women because they don't respect the men in the city or country either . . . Well, I must stop writing. We'll be seeing you soon, Clyde Barrow.

The letter scared hell out of Amon. It was never mentioned in the *Star-Telegram* but until the couple's ambush and death in Louisiana, Bonnie was never again called a cigar smoker. Police provided protection to Amon and his family until the threat of Bonnie and Clyde had passed.

Clyde's letter was the most menacing Amon ever received, although there were other highly critical messages. Karl Crowley was a Solicitor General of the U.S. Post Office Department who quit his post to run for governor of Texas in 1938. He lost badly, especially in Tarrant County where he received but 690 of 35,936 votes, probably because of a front page editorial in the *Star-Telegram* which in part declared, "Crowley gives the impression in Texas that Washington officially does not go to the outhouse without first asking him."

Crowley jumped on the hate-Amon bandwagon. He wrote a letter to a friend in Washington and a copy of it was sent to Amon. The Crowley letter said, "With reference to this skunk, Amon Carter, I want to say that the rank and file of Democrats are willing to make an open war on him. I consider him the most evil and pernicious influence on public affairs in the state of Texas. I do not think he should be allowed to own a newspaper, much less have a monopoly on radio in Texas."

Amon's temper caused him trouble more than once. When angry he wanted immediate retribution and his reactions were never temperate. There was the incident when he was embroiled in a local political squabble and dictated a letter outlining the many shortcomings of his enemies. Seven hundred copies of the letter were mailed. Sidney Samuels, his attorney, read the letter and declared it libelous. "Those men can sue you for every penny you've got," advised Samuels. Amon telephoned Charlie Boatner, the police reporter, at 9 p.m. and told the newsman to "get those letters back from the post office."

"Mr. Carter, you can't do that," protested Boatner. "You can't get letters back after you've mailed them."

Amon insisted and because he was Amon Carter the Postmaster assisted Boatner. The men searched until 3:30 a.m. to collect all seven hundred letters.

Amon's little disputes did not often erupt into print, and certainly not in Fort Worth. Outside, however, his influence and power diminished with distance and there are a few published criticisms. The Amarillo *Globe News,* for reasons unstated and now forgotten, published an editorial aside titled "Amon Carter: Little Emperor." The anonymous writer claimed he attempted to interview Amon and was refused, and went on to snort indignantly, "As Editor, Politician and Cow Town's official greeter, you have shown an offensive disregard for such human weaknesses as breeding, intelligence and education . . . Vengeance is mine, sayeth Amon Carter!"

At a distance of three hundred and fifty miles the Amarillo newspaper was safe enough. In Fort Worth, Amon was unassailable. Even the opposition *Press* made only light jabs at him. Amon ran a tight ship. He managed the city civically and politically, but rarely out front; his dominion was the smoke-filled back room — usually in the Fort Worth Club — in which major decisions were made.

"What are you going to do about that industrial problem?" a reporter once asked a Chamber of Commerce official.

"I don't know," the man answered ruefully. "Amon Carter hasn't told me yet."

However hidden away his presence there was never any question of who ran Fort Worth. Nothing he did not want printed ever appeared in the *Star-Telegram*, or even the *Press*.

At a small Shady Oak dinner party, Sam Rayburn, speaker of the U.S. House, rose to speak and indicated he wanted his remarks off the record.

"There is no reporter present, I believe," Rayburn said to Amon.

"There is," the publisher replied, "but he and I work for the same newspaper."

Byron Utecht folded his notepaper and tucked his pencil into his pocket.

Shady Oak often was site of political gatherings, at which Amon made the timetable. The bar always closed thirty minutes before dinner. At one affair Amon fired his pistols to signal the bar's closing. A few minutes later Amon noticed that Edgar Deen, Fort Worth's mayor, still was at the bar. Amon summoned James Wood, one of the city policemen always in attendance for Shady Oak dinners. "Officer," Amon ordered, "go over there and tell Edgar that gawddamned bar is closed and unless we need a new mayor, to get the hell over here right now."

Deen actually ran to Amon.

Amon's catalog of men with whom he feuded was a lengthy tome. Many of them were politicians, who had more to do than please Amon. There was Governors Ma and Pa Ferguson, Sterling, Allred and O'Daniel, Congressman Jim Wright, the omnipotent Lyndon Baines

Johnson. Allred, Amon wrote John Nance Garner, was "thoroughly lacking in sincerity, being almost a feather for every wind." W. Lee O'Daniel, believed Amon, "managed his public affairs with a lack of dignity."

The political *sturm und drang* was ever around Amon but never so tumultuous as in 1952 when he bolted the Democratic Party to support his old friend, Dwight Eisenhower, for President. Amon's position was not in that year a revolutionary one. Many prominent Texans campaigned for IKE. But Amon Carter had helped push the former general into the campaign as a Republican, and there were Texans who could not forgive him for that.

One, a Fort Worth attorney, wrote a cordial disapproving letter to Amon. It read:

> You have no doubt aided in throwing Texas to the Republicans, but I feel sure that even you cannot be fully pleased with the tactics used in accomplishing the purpose. I want you to know that the writer will welcome the day when your death is announced and will upon such event feel that Fort Worth at long last has been blessed to rid itself of the worst enemy the city has ever had. I trust that I may soon enjoy this pleasure.

Amon wanted to publish the letter but Jimmy North, with a cooler temper, refused. "Just throw it in the wastebasket," adivsed North.

Amon's backing of Ike also split him from LBJ. The publisher was never an enthusiastic Lyndon supporter. Amon's friend, Sid Richardson, liked and campaigned for LBJ and pushed Carter to help the young Senator from Texas. Curious about Johnson, Amon ordered Boatner and Sam Kinch, the Austin bureau chief, to "check him out." The two reporters researched LBJ for six months and produced a book-sized report. Amon read it and declared, "Nothing there I wouldn't have done."

Amon was instrumental in having his neighbor, Fred Korth, become a Lyndon campaign manager (Korth later was appointed Secretary of the Navy) and he and still another Fort Worth neighbor, John Connally, advised and gave financial assistance to the future President. Shortly before taking his Senate seat in 1948, LBJ wrote Amon:

> You did so much in so many ways that I could never fully express my apprecition. When I steered too close to impetuous and intemporate action, you pulled me back. When a firm hand was needed to steady the ship, you supplied it. . . . I just hope that I can use the opportunity to do as much for Texas — in the same impersonal spirit — as you have done. I will always look to your counsel to keep me pointed in the right direction.

That was, of course, before Amon decided to ride Ike's horse in the 1952 election. LBJ, a confirmed Democrat, stuck with the party, and the britches were split. Lyndon explained his predicament with Amon to Booth Mooney, his administrative aide.

"The Fort Worth *Star-Telegram* always was for me 'till last year," Lyndon said in 1953. "Strongest paper in the state and my best supporter. But when I was committed to [Sam] Rayburn to introduce Adlai Stevenson when he appeared in Texas, Amon Carter called and asked me — no, he didn't; he *told* me — not to do it. I explained about my commitment and said I'd have to live up to it, and I did. Now Old Man Carter won't even accept my telephone calls. He even scratched me off his Christmas list."

Lyndon continued: "I'm gonna keep trying, Booth. First thing tomorrow morning, I want you to write a letter to Amon Carter for my signature. . . . Make it warm and friendly, but sad because of the differences that's come between us. Tell him I'm the same Lyndon Johnson I've always been. Tell him I'm working for Texas just the way he is and we can get a lot more done for the people — and for Fort Worth — if we work together. The way we used to. Really pour it on, Booth, and let's see if we can get through that hard old head of his."

Not a chance. Amon never answered.

And Amon took the feud to his grave. In his last few days of life he called his son and daughter, Sid Richardson and Katrine to his bedside. He discussed his estate and the newspaper and what he expected of his children. And Amon had a footnote: ". . . if the paper ever supports Lyndon Johnson for anything, I'll turn over in my grave."

By the time he broke with LBJ, Amon's political power and influence were waning. He was old and sick, but mostly everything had changed after World War II. Fort Worth was filled by young men unawed of Amon Carter, unwilling to do his bidding merely because he wanted it.

Greatest proof of that new era was a 1954 Congressional election in which Amon's incumbent, Wingate Lucas, was challenged by Jim Wright, the young mayor of Weatherford and a former *Star-Telegram* correspondent. He had ambitions beyond the mayoralty of a small town, and knew Amon could help him. Wright attempted to speak to the publisher at a ceremony honoring General William Hood Simpson, a Weatherford native and war hero. After the speeches, Wright approached Amon, "I'm Jim Wright, Mr. Carter."

Amon, Wright recalled, looked uninterested.

"You don't know it, but I used to work for you," continued Wright.

"Well, that's nice," said Amon, and turned away. Embarrassed, Wright promised himself he would never "risk a second dose of that treatment."

Wright entered the Congressional race against Lucas. The *Star-Telegram* virtually ignored the young politician. He resorted to buying time on Amon's television station (probably the first time a Texas candidate used TV heavily). But no matter what he did, the newspaper would not give equal space to his campaign. He recalled a rally at which a thousand people came to hear him speak. A *Star-Telegram* reporter, Bill Haworth, was present, Wright said, ''but the story was killed. The *Star-Telegram* never printed a line about it [the rally].''

In the final days, the newspaper published an editorial supporting Lucas and criticizing Wright for not offering ''well-defined ideas'' and for not having commented on the farm program, taxation, federal spending or other important issues.

The following day, Wright wrote and paid $974.40 — all he had — for a six column advertisement in the *Star-Telegram.* It was, blurted the headline, an OPEN LETTER TO MR. AMON G. CARTER.

''You have at last met a man, Mr. Carter, who is not afraid of you . . . who will not bow his knee to you . . . and come running like a simpering pup at your beck and call.''

Wright charged that he had taken stands on issues in greater detail ''. . . than your private errand boy congressman'' but the *Star-Telegram* had kept news coverage of his statements ''well concealed.''

''This is a new day,'' wrote Wright. ''New blood and new minds and new thoughts, fresh from the people themselves, are needed . . . it is unhealthy for ANYONE to become TOO powerful . . . TOO influential . . . TOO dominating. It is not good for Democracy. The people are tired of 'One-Man Rule'.''

Perhaps they were. Jim Wright, who would rise to Congress' second most influential leadership position, defeated Lucas.

The old order was dying.

Chapter 16

Of the Corporation of the Goosequill — of the Press . . . of the Fourth Estate. . . . There she is — The Great Engine. . . . She never sleeps. She has her Ambassador in every quarter of the world — her courtiers upon every road. Her officers march along with Armies, and her envoys walk into statesmen's cabinets. They are ubiquitous.

—William Makepeace Thackery

It is well that war is so terrible or we should grow too fond of it.

—Robert E. Lee

War is delightful to those who have had no experience of it.

—Desiderius Erasmas

16

World War II was the exclusive copyrighted property of the *Star-Telegram.* No part of the hostilities could be reproduced or transmitted in any form or by any means without written permission of the publisher. It was Amon Carter's personal war and, oh, what a glorious, quintessential thing it was, for awhile.

Amon and America dealt themselves into the fracas only hours after the Japanese pulled their surprise, and from the beginning, he and his newspaper played like the war was an all-Texas affair. Readers were led to believe Texans — especially Fort Worth and West Texas *Texans* — were the only barriers between the enemy and victory; All others were but spear-carriers in the drama.

Honolulu's ashes still were smoldering when Amon raised high his shield and sword, marshalling his forces. He rushed off a lengthy missive to President Roosevelt, telling FDR how to run the war:

"The disaster at Pearl harbor, as tough as it is, may be a blessing in disguise. It certainly unified the country overnight. [You] . . . silence those goddamned isolationists and America First sons-of-bitches, Lindburgh, Wheeler, Bennett, Clark, Nye and Fish. If they open their mouths again they should be put in concentration camps. From now on, all sabotage of any nature should be answered with a sharp bayonet or a good old Texas forty-five."

To Texas Senator Tom Connally, Amon wrote, "This is the greatest time of crisis since Valley Forge."

Amon was sixty-two, too old for duty in the trenches, so in the beginning he stayed behind to rally the home folks. But he telephoned Washington, pulling strings to have his reporters accredited as war correspondents. Two days after Pearl Harbor, Amon told Jimmy North to select his best men and get them ready to ship out. The reporter warriors were to write only about Texans, he instructed.

There were Texans enough to fill any newspaper. Ten percent of the population, more than any other state, joined the armed services. Texas A&M furnished more officers than any university, including West Point. Seven hundred thousand Texans were Over There, fighting for America's Freedom, the *Star-Telegram,* editorialized, and that was as it should be since everybody knew Texans were the most patriotic, most heroic, the bravest of all Americans, capable of whipping every Jap and German with bare knuckles and a peach orchard switch, and before breakfast.

As self-proclaimed house organ for the Second World War, the *Star-Telegram* played to its readers. Subscribers were urged to bring their used *Star-Telegrams* to the office and have them mailed free to servicemen anywhere in the world. The newspaper paid postage. The *Star-Telegram* even sent a few copies of its rival, the *Press*, because the war, after all, was an emergency and everybody had to pull together. An endless line of mothers appeared in the newsroom with photos of their sons and daughters in service. Carter's newspaper published all pictures, some as many as half-a-dozen times — when he or she was inducted, at the first training station, when they were promoted, when they were assigned overseas, in times of valor and decoration, and sadly, in times of death.

Amon became Texas' largest war bond buyer. The *Star-Telegram* conducted a running campaign to boost sales of bonds among its readers. Its newsboys sold 4,742,016 war savings stamps, more than any group in the state. Amon fronted for every bond rally celebrity troupe visiting Fort Worth.

Rationing came. Food, gasoline, synthetics, tires, booze. *Is This Trip Necessary? Loose Lips Sink Ships. Use It Up, Wear It Out, Make It Last, Do Without.* The newspaper called on Texans to sacrifice luxuries and comforts, even essentials, to support "our boys." Amon bought nylon hose on the black market for special gifts, because, after all, one could sacrifice only so much.

W. Lee O'Daniel, the governor, was at his flour-peddling best. He stumped Texas, ostensibly to arouse patriotic fervor among the masses. Actually, he pumped his own image. Amon was furious that O'Daniel would play politics with the *Star-Telegram*'s war. The governor traveled about in a state limousine and Carter leaped on the Cadillac as a reason to publicly censure O'Daniel.

The governor was making an ". . . abusive use of auto tires," Amon dictated in a lengthy editorial. North refused to print the broadside. Not because of the auto tire issue. The general tone, protested North, was too overwrought, especially the lead paragraph:

"W. Lee O'Daniel is the agent of Hitler in America."

For support, North called in Sidney Samuels. The natty lawyer read Amon's editorial, and smiled. "Mr.

Carter, you can't print this,'' he advised. ''It's libelous.''

''Are you telling me what I can and cannot print in my own newspaper?''

''No, I'm only telling you of the consequences if you do.''

''You write it then,'' ordered Amon, ''and make it legal.''

Samuels' version was legally publishable, but bloodless; Amon wanted blood.

''Do it again,'' the publisher shouted at Samuels, ''and don't be so gawddamned Christian.''

A proper rendition of Amon's charges were never agreed on, and North vetoed any editorial criticism of the governor's four-plies. Angry but undeterred, Amon bought — it is said he paid cash, in hundred dollar bills, banging each one on the desk as he counted — a full-page ad in his own newspaper to say what he wanted to say about O'Daniel. That is, he said what he wanted to say the way Samuels wanted him to say it — bloodlessly.

The war, in the beginning, was going well, Carter thought. He kept up his correspondence with Washington. He wrote the President on behalf of osteopaths, urging that they be accepted for service as other doctors, and soon they were. He asked Texan Jesse Jones, the Secretary of Commerce, to have FDR persuade the Canadian government to send its fliers for training in Texas, as ''. . . they did in the last war.'' The West Texas Chamber of Commerce raised $128,000 in defense bonds, and Amon wired the good news to Roosevelt, adding, ''. . . and there were no Lindbergs [*sic*], pacifists, isolationists or fifth columnists present. They do not thrive in West Texas.'' He pressed Frank Knox, the Navy secretary, to name a ship ''Fort Worth'': ''Of course, I figure Fort Worth rates a battleship. If you find a real strong, tough, high-spirited, fighting craft that will give the enemy Hell and never run up the white flag, name it after Fort Worth.''

FDR sent the publisher pictures of his meeting with Churchill in Casablanca. And the President returned his diamond-studded belt for cleaning and repairs. The President asked that another hole be added, and Amon worried that Roosevelt was working too hard and losing weight. Carter also continued to help run the war. He offered his counsel, by letter and wire, to Eisenhower, to Admirals Chester Nimitz, a fellow Texan, and Bull Halsey. To Hap Arnold, commanding general of the Army Air Corps, Amon suggested that all American Airline pilots and planes be drafted for a massive bombing raid on Tokyo. Arnold replied that he would think it over.

Carter's dream of having a battleship named for Fort Worth, as other sovereign states, was never realized. Lieutenant Johnny Van Dyke, a *Star-Telegram* employee, wrote, however, that he was a bombardier on a B-29 named the "Amon Carter," and had just concluded a raid on Wake Island.

The plane came off the assembly line of Consolidated Aircraft Corporation's Fort Worth facility. *The Bomber Plant.* A whole town grew around the plant as West Texans moved in to work for high wages. It was White Settlement, but called "Liberator Village," a place of ricky-ticky houses and open sewers named for the light bomber put together bolt by bolt in the mile-long windowless factory. Well, a mile and twenty-nine feet. That extra ten yards was Amon's lagniappe to Texanism.

Amon knew war was coming. That, in 1939, was not an astonishing piece of prophecy. Many believed America would be drawn into the fighting. Carter and FDR had discussed the country's entry into war, and Amon had scouted ahead for the President in England during his trip with Pan American Airways. War was inevitable, and the country began putting up its defenses. Among the plans were government-financed aircraft factories, and Amon meant to get one for Fort Worth.

As chairman of a Chamber committee to bring the bomber plant to the city, Amon prepared — actually, the work as usual was done by *Star-Telegram* reporters — a tome of praise to impress the site selection group. Fort Worth offered to Consolidated tax incentives, a waiting, eager work force, an existing seaplane base on Lake Worth and the availability of regular East/West American Airlines flights for easy movement of executives. The site, said Amon, was beside an existing airport and runways easily could be extended for military aircraft.

R. H. Fleet, Consolidated's president, bought Amon's pitch. Major General George Brett, acting Air Force chief, did not. Brett preferred Tulsa. The two men argued by telegram:

> Maj. Gen. George H. Brett
> War Department
> Washington, D.C.
> 13 Dec 1940
>
> Retel if Fort Worth comes through with its promises Stop We prefer it as location.
>
> Cheerio
>
> Consolidated Aircraft Corp.
> R. H. Fleet

> R. H. Fleet
> Consolidated Aircraft Corp.
> San Diego, Calif.
> 17 Dec 1940
>
> Fort Worth not under consideration in present project Stop Please furnish today result of Van Dusens trip to Tulsa Stop It is urgent that action be taken today.
>
> Brett

Maj. Gen. George Brett
17 Dec 1940

Result Van Dusens trip Tulsa unsatisfactory Stop We think Fort Worth site ideal.

Fleet

R. H. Fleet
18 Dec 1940

Request you submit your plans and estimates on Tulsa location at once.

Brett

Maj. Gen. George Brett
19 Dec 1940

Your telegram reminds me of Henry Ford statement that customer could choose any color he desired just so he chose black.

Fleet

R. H. Fleet
19 Dec 1940

Choose any color you wish but you are still going to choose black.

Brett

General Brett announced Tulsa as site of the new bomber plant. An apoplectic Amon beat his fists against the wall and exploded by telegram to FDR that Tulsa did not deserve the factory. Fort Worth had the best offer, best site, climate, size and existing facilities, raged Amon. "It seems almost a crime against national defense to permit the rejection of this site as against Tulsa," he stormed. FDR retreated to the position that Tulsa was an Army decision and he could not interfere.

Amon always was the kind of man who would call on Noah's flood to fill a bathtub, and he inundated Washington with telegrams to congressmen and senators, administration biggies and old drinking buddies. He signed many of the wires with Governor O'Daniel's Name. And Amon went back to the President with a final argument, "Why not allocate to Tulsa the possible additional plant to be built?"

January 3, 1941, Senator Morris Sheppard wired Amon: "War Department announces plants for both Fort Worth and Tulsa."

Next morning, the bi-city selections were made public, and Amon messaged FDR, "Bless your heart. Thanks for your timely and friendly help." He sent another telegram to Sheppard asking assistance in having Captain Elliott Roosevelt — "A clean-cut, double-fisted six-footer" — assigned as military overseer for the plant's construction.

Less than a month later, reported *Time* magazine, Amon was back on FDR's doorstep seeking more federal help. He later boasted to Harold Hough, "Well, I got my extra."

"Extra what?"

"My extra feet. That Tulsa plant was going to be the same size as ours. I couldn't have that."

The plants, and another in Georgia, were to be identical. Amon demanded a change. Army architects added two more support columns and twenty-nine feet to appease the publisher. Fort Worth had the world's largest aircraft factory and the first with a fully automated assembly line. At the height of the war, thirty thousand Fort Worthians — West Texans newly arrived — worked there and Amon bragged that his city had the highest per capita income in America.

The *Star-Telegram* went off to war with other Texans. Phil North, Jimmy's son, became a public relations officer on General MacArthur's staff. At least eight women joined the WACs. The men spread out to all branches of military service. As other businesses, the newspaper soon had a manpower problem, and Jim Record began hiring — reluctantly — women reporters, as many as seven in one month of 1942. Record, with definite ideas about women and their place, which was not a newsroom, had no choice. He needed reporters, whatever their sex. He hired women, and hoped for the best. Soon they were everywhere and JRR would look out on his feminine crew and harrumph morosely. The few remaining men called the new order, "JRR's Harem." To underscore the seraglio theme, women reporters arrived at one office party dressed in harem costumes, complete with diaphanous pantaloons and bare stomachs. JRR blushed. The girls danced as they believed haremites might, and during a lull in the entertainment C. L. Richart played his trump — a black porter dressed in the costume of a palace eunuch and secreted in the morgue. At Richhart's signal, the eunuch roared into the city room on a motorcycle, circled desks — and an harrumphing JRR, and disappeared down the hall.

Christmas parties were traditional, and the one time each year when Record put aside his guardian dignity. He would smoke cigars in public and sip his toddies. JRR financed the third floor bar from his own pocket. Arrival of many women in the newsroom changed the Yule fest. For one thing, the men drank more and more until Record finally banned liquor from future parties. The incident ending the drinking happened at the pencil sharpener after celebrating supposedly was over. JRR strolled to the sharpener to put a new point on his copy pencil. He looked down. At his feet was a comatose male reporter, supine on the floor, the man's head in a wastebasket. *Harrumph!*

"Somebody take care of this," he ordered, wagging his fresh pencil point at the inert headless body.

And sex. . . . There are wonderful legends of quick-groping trysts on back stairs, between file cabinets in the morgue, and at least once on the roof. Exaggerations, probably, and even if true, none seem to have found a logical, satisfactory conclusion anywhere in the building. Mr. Record was not a man who wanted sex mentioned within his hearing. He even refused to explain Bar Mitzvah to a new young girl reporter because it concerned puberty. Martha Morris, a pretty girl who actually had reporting experience, was hired for the morning staff, and a male reporter proposed a little after-hours sparking. Miss Morris retorted, "Get lost!", a devastating 1940s putdown.

The man complained to City Editor Cullum Greene that Martha had been rude to him. Greene told Record. JRR summoned the wayward girl to his desk. Greene, Record scolded, said she was not "being nice" to the reporter. He lectured her on the war, on the shortage of competent male reporters and the necessity of keeping the few who remained, and how other women were out there waiting for jobs on the newspaper. He suggested she be "a little nicer."

More amused than angered, Morris, a very shapely girl, cocked a hip and asked coyly, "Mr. Record, just how nice do you want me to be?"

Suddenly realizing what the conversation was about, Record stood and back-pedaled, blushing, blustering, "You . . . you know Cullum. . . . He's just . . . an . . . an old hen! Don't think anything more about it!"

Later that day, JRR, still in shock from actually discussing sex with a female, reached to file a carbon on the paper spike, a stiff sharpened metal wire mounted on a lead base. He speared his hand clean through, between the thumb and forefinger. Women bewildered JRR.

The heavy cross of girl newsmen wore on Jim Record. One editor had become a heavy drinker, often arriving drunk to work, reeling and thrashing about with a hand over one eye because he could not focus his vision well enough to see with two. With no male replacement for the editor, Record pretended the drunk was not drunk. North could not. He suggested something be done about the man.

JRR reluctantly called the editor to his desk.

"If you don't stop drinking," JRR threatened, "I'll have to fire you."

"No, you won't."

"Won't . . . ! (Harrumph!)"

"You can't find anybody to take my place."

True enough. The man stayed on, one hand over an eye, and Record ignored him.

Star-Telegram employees who went to battle were considered ". . . out of the office." Amon Carter had loaned them to America. He kept them on the Christmas bonus list. Daily, the newspaper was mailed to them. Reporters away at war were expected to file an occasional story about their experiences but especially on other Texans they encountered around the world.

Meanwhile, the real *Star-Telegram* war correspondents beat the battle bushes for Texans. "Any Texans here?", they asked in foxholes and tents, bars, CQs and barracks from Bougainville to Bordeaux. The *Star-Telegram*'s policy of localizing all stories extended to World War II. It wanted coverage of Texans at war, much as it had reported on county fairs in Monahans and baton-twirling contests at Odessa High. North's instructions to his correspondents were (1) "Be careful" and (2) "Write only about Texans."

Before going out to the Pacific, Stanley Gunn spent an evening at the San Francisco Press Club. A local reporter, envious of Gunn's assignment but astounded at the narrowness of it, asked, "You mean you're just going to write about Texans!"

"Who else is worth writing about?" answered Gunn, smiling.

Gunn and Sam Kinch, a courthouse reporter, went to the Pacific. Later, Charles Boatner was out there.

Flem Hall left behind his sports beat and sailed for England. Robert Wear, too, was in England and, following D-Day, France and Germany. Wear moved to the Pacific after V-E Day. All trailed the heaviest action in search of Texans. The *Star-Telegram* had more men — Boatner, Kinch and Wear — on the *Missouri* to witness the Japanese's formal surrender than any newsgathering organization.

Stanley Gunn was not there at the end.

Tall and thin, a quietly-confident pipe-smoker, Gunn was thirty, married to his high school sweetheart, Catherine, and the father of two children. He was late for the war. Gunn had been editor of the Austin *Tribune* when it folded in 1943. Record immediately hired him. Gunn was sent into the Pacific to inquire, "Any Texans here?"

He was dead in four months.

As other *Star-Telegram* war correspondents, Gunn wrote folksy, newsy little stories about Texas boys. The stories told of the soldiers' lives between battles, of their recreations, their hobbies, their thoughts of home. He even found one pair of Texans who had labeled their island foxhole "Shady Oaks [*sic*], Where the West Begins," and had them send pictures of the sign to Amon. The correspondents' stories seem like personal notes to families of Texas servicemen. They wrote, too, real letters to parents, telling of visits to sons and daughters half a world away. After Gunn's death, JRR reminisced in *Junior,* the *Star-Telegram* employee newspaper, that he had seen an eleven-page letter written by Gunn to a mother. She had asked Gunn to find her MIA son. He never wrote a public story of his search. That was a personal matter between him and the anguished mother.

In October, 1944, Gunn went ashore at Leyte with first American troops. He and seven other correspondents took over a house in Tacloban, capital of the Philippine Island. Before dawn one morning, Japanese planes attacked the town. Wing bombs fell into the correspondents' house. Associated Press reporter Asahel Bush was killed instantly. John Terry of the Chicago *Daily News* was mortally wounded. In the quietness after the bombing, Gunn cried out, "I'm hit. Can you help me? Help me out of this hole."

John Walker of *Time* reached for his hand. A flashlight beam played on Gunn. There was no hole.

In shock and pain but awake, Gunn helped wrap his mangled legs in a towel. He was taken to an evacuation hospital. Correspondents and soldiers lined up to donate blood, and General MacArthur, who gave Gunn an exclusive interview two weeks earlier, personally ordered plasma and other medical supplies sent to Leyte for the wounded Texan.

Gunn underwent a four-hour operation. He died.

Arthur Veysey of the Chicago *Tribune* wrote about Gunn's last days. As the *Star-Telegram* correspondent was carried into the operating room, he raised himself on an elbow and looked into the masked faces waiting for him.

"Any Texans here?" he inquired. Then he smiled, and quietly closed his eyes.

One source says Carter wept and said, "Oh, gawddamn . . .", when told of Stanley Gunn's death. Perhaps he did. It would have been like him to cry for the wasting of young Gunn's life, and surely, the loss of the newsman remained Amon that his own son might never return home.

World War II was the lowest period of Amon Carter's life. He had depressions and doubts of his own worth, was uncharacteristically moody, emotional and indecisive. Nenetta, the second wife, said the war years took away, for the first time, his buoyancy, the resolution he held against every obstacle. He was never the same again. The war years changed him. For the remainder of his life there was a delicate bitterness in Amon Carter and it was in this period, from 1943 on, that most of the small, mean memories of him were made.

It was because of the son he worshipped. *Cowboy.* Amon Gary Carter Junior.

Young Carter was twenty-one as war began, a University of Texas student who had graduated in 1938 from Indiana's Culver Military Academy. He was a second lieutenant in the Army Reserve Officers Corps, called into service in May, 1942.

The son had a physical likeness to the father, accented by the same early balding hairline. Both were similiar-sized, squarely built, and energetic. Amon had depthless pride in the youngster and was preparing him to assume the empire's mantle of authority. At ten, the publisher had placed his son on the street selling newspapers. A year later, the boy arose at three a.m. each day to deliver a home route. In summers, he worked as a copy boy, and later, in the photography and advertising departments. The publisher established the Amon Carter Junior Scholarship at Texas Christian University, given annually to the newsboy with highest grades among Fort Worth's graduating high school seniors. On young Carter's eighteenth birthday, Amon wrote a long letter of congratulations, telling of his pride in the boy's accomplishments, of the dream that ". . . you can step into my job." Amon lectured his son: "Courtesy is the cheapest as well as the most valuable assets [*sic*] one can possess."

The new lieutenant was sent to Fort Knox, Kentucky, for training, and the father visited, timing his arrival for the running of the Kentucky Derby. Carter gave young Amon a used pocket knife for which he demanded payment of one cent because of ". . . the old superstition that you must never give away a knife, but sell it."

Late in 1942, the son was ordered to Ireland for advanced training as a field artillery officer. Amon asked Washington for credentials as a war correspondent, ostensibly to review allied morale but realistically to see his son.

By the early 1940s Amon Carter was an internationally famous man. His exploits among the high and mighty had been recorded and reported widely by syndicated newspaper columnists and in national magazines. His cowboy impersonation had been seen, cheered and applauded all over America. The 1936 Frontier Centennial had registered Carter's name as familiar as any Hollywood star or Washington politician. So, when he went off to play war correspondent in Ireland and England, the real war correspondents there reported on him.

The Associated Press noted that he landed safely in Belfast, mid-October, 1942. Amon cabled Katrine Deakins that he and his son were together. They visited only a short time before the soldier resumed training. Amon amused himself by dining with local dignitaries and seeing the countryside. He especially enjoyed viewing the obelisk erected to General Robert Ross at Rostrevor, County Down. Ross, Amon wrote Roosevelt, led British troops in the burning of the Capital in Washington, 1814. He also sent stamps for the President's collection.

Carter traveled on to London in November, settling into the Savoy Hotel where he played celebrity for English newsmen. He told them at a press conference, "Texas being practically three times as large as the British Isles in no way dampens our enthusiasm for the British people."

Putting on his twangy prairie voice, he added, "They're just fine folks, as near Texans as they could be not having been born there."

The British Broadcasting Company, describing Amon as ". . . one of America's leading publishers," had him speak to fellow Americans on a special radio program. Carter told his countrymen that their soldier/sons were "very fit" and eager for action. He praised the British people who "feel that no price is too high to pay for liberty'' and urged deeper understanding between the countries. He compared the United States and England to a ''span of thoroughbred horses . . . they need practice before they can run in double harness.''

Amon ended his broadcast by saying he spoke as a father ''who has a son over here.''

Young Amon was given a ten-day leave and joined his father in London where the two Texans were entertained by Lord Beaverbrook, who later wrote that ''Carter, Junior, is a husky, lively young man . . . ready to go to town against the Germans anytime.''

They visited Sir Dudley Pound, ''Admiral of the Fleet and First Sea Lord of the British Navy.'' Amon presented the admiral with a silver five-shilling piece. The publisher also searched out other Texans, especially men in the ranks, and cabled families that he had seen their sons and they were well.

The two Amons attended at least one swanky party with General Eisenhower, Lord Mountbatten and ''royalty.'' Later Carter would tell of the evening, always chuckling ''. . . and Amon Junior was the only second lieutenant there.''

Before parting, Amon reminded his son of their agreement. *Editor and Publisher,* the newspaper trade magazine, earlier printed details of the deal Amon proposed to his son: ''. . . one hundred dollars each for every dirty Jap, one hundred dollars each for every Damn German and ten dollars for every Italian, plus a bonus of five hundred dollars extra when you get as many as twenty.''

Shortly after Christmas, the publisher returned to Fort Worth. He had written no stories as a correspondent. Belatedly, Amon made an entry in the guestbook in Suite 10-G at the Fort Worth Club:

''10/3/42 . . . AGC . . . leaving for Ireland to see Amon Jr. Told Amon goodbye in Liverpool as he left for Northern Africa. He was all pepped up over getting into action. Good Luck, Cow Boy, from Dad.''

The son had little opportunity to collect the proffered bounties, even the fire sale amount posted for the bargain basement Italians. He was sent to central Tunisia, where Allied Forces were finally boxing in Rommel. North Africa and war, young Amon thought, was somewhat boring. He wrote home, telling of his unit's camp in an old Roman ruin, and how the men passed their time playing blackjack — he collected 2,500 French francs in one game. Their only diversion was "Photo Joe," a German JU 88 observer plane snapping their pictures from on high. His final letter was postmarked February 13, 1943, in which he sent home samples of Tunisian money for his coin collection. Next morning, Valentine's Day, he disappeared.

Amon Carter returned from overseas in a sunny mood. The war surely would be a brief affair, now that his son had joined other Texans, he joked with Katrine. The Lone Star State boys would take care of things mighty quick. Amon was optimistic and happy. Then the letters stopped.

His moods turned darker, at first angered, then dispirited, then hopeless, as the days passed. He became quieter, less active, and he took to staring vacantly at nothing, his eyes filled with tears. Amon spoke often by telephone with Nenetta, who had moved to New York after their 1941 divorce. She remained optimistic; Amon fell into deeper depression.

A War Department telegram reached Fort Worth March 11. It vaguely described a North African battle and stated Amon Junior was presumed ". . . missing in action." The *Star-Telegram* printed the terse announcement as a two-paragraph story on its front page, under a one-column picture of young Amon in uniform. That was the first. For the next two years, *Star-Telegram* readers followed the adventures of Amon Carter and son through a series of letters, stories by wire services and war correspondents, and finally, by the publisher himself, as he invaded Europe to rescue his son from "... those gawddamned Germans." The pair combined to become a kind of Texas-style civilian Red Cross. At all times, young Amon was a symbol for every POW Texan and other parents in a similar plight found sympathetic companionship with the publisher.

Carter, after the momentary shock of the initial telegram, reacted typically. He reached for the Western Union blank and telephone and began contacting friends in high places, seeking more news of his son. He cabled the International Red Cross in Geneva, and a Red Cross field director in Tunisia. Major General James A. Ulio, adjutant of the Army, wired his sympathies and recounted the fighting in which Amon Junior was lost, adding that American forces lost fifty-nine men during seven days, with 170 wounded and 2,006 missing in action.

Amon petitioned the White House for help and on March 26, the President replied that he had made ". . . repeated inquiries, and the absence of definite news does not lessen the possibility that he was taken prisoner." Eleanor Roosevelt sent a note of regret, as did all Texas politicians in Washington and hundreds of Amon's friends. Waiters at the Fort Worth Club signed a sympathy card. William Best, vice president of General Cigar Company, mailed a box of one hundred Robert Burns Panatellas "to be saved for Jr's return*." The Texas House of Representatives unanimously adopted a resolution, which read, in part:

> Whereas, Lieutenant Amon G. Carter Junior, son of a distinguished Texas citizen, was among the first to enter the Armed Service in Defense of Democracy and American Ideals and proved his willingness to undergo any sacrifice to maintain those principles, and . . . he is an outstanding type of young American and Texas

*The cigars were never smoked. When Amon Junior went into service, Carter gave up cigars, vowing not to smoke again until after the war when his son returned. Even with young Carter home, however, Amon never smoked again.

> manhood, upon which depends the future of this country and civilization itself . . . resolved that the Texas Legislature extend to the father . . . its deep sympathy; and at the same time congratulations for the heroic participation of his son in the North African Campaign to drive out the Axis.

Hap Arnold messaged Amon, "Don't give up hope. He is alive."

Carter didn't think so. The despair returned. Katrine arrived at work one morning to find a sealed envelope on her desk. Late the previous evening Amon had scribbled a long letter. He wrote on the envelope "To be opened if we do not hear again from Amon, Jr.", [signed] "A. G. Carter, March 19, 1943." Katrine did not open the letter for several years, long after Amon, Jr. had returned home. It read:

> Dear Katrine:
>
> After talking to Colonel Sumerall this A.M. — I can't help but feel more discouraged regarding sweet Amon, Jr. Some how I can't help but feel we are not going to see him again. God love his sweet soul. He certainly deserved a better fate, still bless his heart, it was just what he wanted to do — and he would not have it otherwise. In fact, while I was in England one of his superior officers told me they might send some of the boys back to this country to help train the new armored divisions and if they did he was going to send Amon, Jr., claiming he was a good officer, etc. I made no comment but later, in conference, I did mention it to Amon, Jr. and he said, 'Oh, Dad, I could not do that'; that he just could not go away and leave his gang — meaning the men and officers in the 91st Field Artillery. In fact, he was complaining about half the Division getting the lucky break in going to Africa with the first contingent for the invasion November 8. In fact, Amon was in London with me at the time. All of these things merely go to show his spirit and of course I was proud of him. In fact, he told me in Louisville before leaving for Fort Dix and Ireland — he said, 'Dad, I think some of the boys that are holding back will be sorry of it before the War is over.' Further, stating, 'I may not get back, but if I do I

> will have the satisfaction of feeling I have done my part.' Well, I was so proud of him I gave him a big hug and said 'That's the stuff, Cowboy', although tears came to my eyes. In fact this statement he made was the cause of my telegram to him April 1, 1942 offering the bonus for each German, Italian and Jap.
>
> Whatever comes I will always have the feeling I did everything possible to make him happy and including making a 10,000 mile trip to see and be with him. In fact I would not have missed the trip for all the money in the world. I have not given up hope but I must confess I am slipping. I guess it is the first time I have ever been a quitter. One thing it has taught me is how to pray, which I do each night. It just seems he is too fine to have to go when they could take me instead. Still I can't help but believe in the Lord and his wisdom in justice to all of us. So, again I am fervertly praying each day and night for this sweet youngster to have a chance and come back to his loved ones. How I wish I could take his place.
>
> It's been fine to find so many friends take such an interest in his case — at least it has given me a chance to find out who my real friends are at a time like this. I am writing this to be sealed and only given to you in the event my premonition should prove to be correct. God grant that I am wrong. While I know you and Carl [Katrine's husband] love and worship him, still it is hard to let you know just how my heart aches. Ruth is an angel. She and Bertice have been a great comfort as you and Carl have been, not to mention other sweet friends.
>
> I hope I am wrong.

May 3, a message from Amon Junior suddenly arrived. He was in Poland, interred as prisoner of war number 1595.

Captain W. Bruce Pirnie was young Carter's commanding officer and in June he wrote Amon explaining the Valentine Day fate of B Battery, 91st Armored Battalion. After weeks of inactivity, Pirnie said, battalion commander Lieutenant Colonel John Waters [George Patton's son-in-law] placed his troops on alert. Germans were approaching. Rommel once again had broken out of an Allied trap. Before dawn, February 14, Pirnie sent young Amon and a sergeant to a nearby mountaintop where they established an observation post. At daybreak, Pirnie was on a rise above his camp, scanning the desert with binoculars. A pair of Mark VI tanks ("they looked like two huge, long-nosed crabs") rose from a distant *wadi* and began shelling the American position. "Their guns made terrible scarlet and white flashes, for all the world like large firecrackers set off in the night," wrote Pirnie. He radioed Amon Junior for a report and the lieutenant replied that a large force of tanks and armored infantry was moving on the battery's left flank. Pirnie gave retreat orders, but forgot to tell Carter and the sergeant!

By the time he remembered the observation post, his phonemen had collected their equipment and moved on. Throughout the day, Amon stayed in his position high above Faid Pass, watching the Americans move away from the approaching Germans. By dark, the running fire fight stopped and sounds of battle passed the mountain, disappearing into the western desert. The lieutenant and sergeant waited another day, then slipped out, hiking east, away from the German-held pass.

They wandered the desert for ten days, escaping the heat by walking in early mornings and evenings. At night they hid in caves and ravines, shivering with the sub-freezing temperatures. For food, they chewed the pulpy insides of cactus, much as Comanches did in early West Texas. Amon Junior split the cactus pods with the one-cent knife given him by his father.

The pair marched on, searching for Allied troops. February 24, early morning. Carter and the sergeant slept in a clump of cactus. Amon was prodded awake. Above him was a bedouin clutching a rusty double-barrelled shotgun. The Americans tried to explain they were soldiers in need of help. The Arabs — thirty in the group, including women — began beating the men with sticks and fists. The women spat on them. The sergeant tried to run but was struck down with a rock. The bedouins beat him into unconsciousness, and continued to strike his senseless body (he suffered permanent brain damage). Young Amon feigned unconsciousness. The Arabs stripped the men of their clothes and even tried to file a gold ring from Amon's finger. Later in the day, the soldiers were sold to a passing German patrol.

Both were transported to Tunis where Carter was loaded onto a German JU-52 (Junker) and flown to Capua, north of Naples. He went into a cattle car with other captured officers and was shipped to Oflag 64 at Szubin, Poland, southwest of Danzig (now Gdansk).

Amon Carter, relieved that his son was alive, once again manned his telephone*, seeking more information about the POW camp. FDR sent aerial maps to Carter and he studied them intently. He wired the President and Senator Tom Connally to order IKE to notify all Allies not to bomb Stalag No. 3-A (American intelligence designation of Oflag 64). He postscripted a lengthy denunciation of the Red Cross' inefficiency. And he began the quasi-clandestine exchange program with his son.

Their's was a lend-lease Texas-style underground. Amon Junior's first letter mentioned names of other Texans in the camp, including John Jones, nephew of Jesse Jones, Amon's capitalist friend and FDR's commerce secretary. The publisher immediately telephoned parents of the men and told them what he had learned. Those who could not be contacted by phone were written long letters. Young Amon said the prisoners were short on food, warm clothing and blankets. Carter dispatched a supply of all to the POW camp.

Excerpts from the lieutenant's letters were printed in the *Star-Telegram* as names of other Texas prisoners

*There is an incredulous, patently false, tale of Carter attempting to telephone Adolph Hitler — more of the moss-backed apocrypha appendaged to the publisher's legends since his death. His friends and family say it never happened. Still, it is intriguing to ponder what would have been Amon's effect on the already-dotty *Fuhrer*.

were ferreted out and passed on by young Carter. He began searching through camp records of all the men, especially seeking Texans. Their names were relayed to his father. Carter personally contacted parents of the men, printed their names in his newspaper and generally acted as clearing house for Texas prisoners in Oflag 64. At one time the senior Carter was corresponding with more than two hundred Texas families. His files bulge with letters from parents, and not only Texans, but Pennsylvanians and Bostonians and Californians, all pleading for news of their sons. Amon Carter's pipeline to Poland was free of governmental red tape and operated much more quickly than the military or Red Cross.

After the war, Orpho Ziegler recalled his capture and imprisonment in Oflag 64. "The first person I saw was Amon Carter, Junior. He was contacting new prisoners, getting the names of the ones from Texas and the names of their parents. Carter would get the names to his father and his father would contact the parents." The Army notified Ziegler's parents, who lived in East Texas, that their son was missing in action, presumedly dead. "It came like a bolt out of the blue when Mr. Carter telephoned them that I was still alive and a POW," remembered Ziegler.

Three months later the Red Cross confirmed Ziegler's imprisonment.

Amon Junior was among the first twenty prisoners in the camp. When he arrived, it still was being converted by Polish laborers from a youth correction institution, and was known as Stalag 21-A. French and British prisoners captured at Dunkirk had been imprisoned in the camp. Amon became parcels officer, and began the Carter-to-Carter pipeline on information and supplies, using at one time an underground group in neutralist Portugal to pass through large packages.

In addition to serving as the Polish branch of the Carter POW business, young Amon also published the camp's confidential and clandestine newspaper. Several times weekly, he was sent to the Szubin railroad station to collect mail and packages. He befriended a Polish girl who worked there. Each night she listened to British broadcasts in the Polish landuage, then wrote the latest war news in German on tiny bits of scrap paper. She left the notes in a waste basket. Amon Junior rescued the news from under gaze of German guards and sneaked it back into camp where the messages were translated and copied on toilet paper. POWs passed the toilet tissue *Star-Telegram* from hand to hand.

German guards, generally benevolent to their officer prisoners, were intrigued by the endless flow of packages to young Carter from his father. One group approached Amon Junior with a request, asking, "Can you get a piano for us? You have a wealthy father."

By January, 1945, the world, including prisoners of Oflag 64, knew war was ending, knew Germany had lost. Still, the POWs were unprepared for the panic caused by approaching Allied armies. One morning, the Russians were in the next valley, and German guards grouped their prisoners, began marching them westward toward Berlin. For more than a week and one hundred miles the POWs were herded in snow and freezing weather toward the German capital. A few Americans escaped, found refuge with Polish families and awaited the pursuing Russians. In a small village near the German border, the guards suddenly deserted. The Americans begged food and wine and were celebrating when a troop of Latvian SS soldiers appeared. Once again, they were prisoners. The SS troops commandeered a train and loaded the POWs into box cars, packing the men so tightly that they could not sit. The train moved into Berlin February 3, and halted on a siding. Amon's feet were frost-bitten. That day Allies sent more than twelve hundred bombers over Berlin as the Americans huddled in their locked box cars and watched bombs fall. Several bombs fell onto the train, killing many officers. Amon's boxcar was untouched.

After the raid, the prisoners were moved once more, taken to Luckenwalde, a suburb twenty-five miles from Berlin, placed in still another POW camp. For almost a month, the Americans had no food but the little they could scrounge from guards and nearby German families. And then the guards were gone, fleeing before the Russian Army. Soviets replaced the German guards and the Americans still were not free from the war.

Amon Carter knew none of this, knew only that the Polish connection had been severed. No letters, no news, nothing. Washington inquiries returned silence. The old sorrows came again to Amon. He feared the worst. By April, he was in Europe.

The opportunity to be in Europe came in the form of a tour sponsored by SHAEF headquarters. General Eisenhower asked for a small group of publishers to "inspect German atrocities, the war damage and *prison camps*." (Italics added.)

Amon already had determined he was going to Europe, come hell or high command and he telephoned his Washington Bureau chief, Bascom Timmons. He told Timmons to get him on the plane. Timmons replied that the request was impossible; the plane was filled. Carter told Timmons to contact General Barney Giles, the Air Force chief coordinating stateside arrangements for the tour. Amon ordered Timmons to force Giles to find a place for him. Reluctantly, Timmons telephoned Giles.

"Amon Carter wants to go on that plane to Europe," Timmons explained.

"Impossible," answered Giles. "The plane is full."

"I told him that. Now, you call and tell him."

"Hell, I can't tell him 'No'. He won't take 'No' for an answer."

Amon and seventeen other American publishers landed in Paris, April 24, 1945.

Nenetta, Katrine and daughter, Ruth, thought his pretense for going to Europe farsical. Each knew Amon. How could the man who blanched at the sight of blood, anguished over sick pets and tonsillectomies, endure the barbarisms of Dachau and Buchenwald? They believed him too old and too despondent for the long trip, but each knew he would not be stopped.

Nenetta, especially, fretted over his pervading depression. Amon paused overnight in New York to see her. Walter Winchell reported April 26 in his syndicated column that Carter had been in the Stork Club and "sent over $100 to pay for 6 blind soldiers' night out because 'My boy is in a Nazi prison camp.'"

Before joining other publishers, Amon deposited ten thousand dollars in a bank account for Ruth, then a student at Sarah Lawrence College in Bronxville.

He told Nenetta, "I'm going to look for Amon Junior. If I don't find him, I'm not coming back."

Shocked, she admonished, "Yes, you are!"

"No," he said, sadly, shaking his head, "I'm not."

The publisher group remained in Paris one night, then flew to Germany to inspect Buchenwald. Amon slipped away.

Beside Carter was Robert Wear, a *Star-Telegram* correspondent, and trailing close behind were half the American reporters in Europe, sniffing at a magnificent human interest story.

Meanwhile, the *Star-Telegram* received an Associated Press bulletin stating that Amon Junior had been seen by two freed American soldiers and was "alive and well."

Carter knew none of this as he and Wear moved across Germany. The pair stopped for days at General Omar Bradley's headquarters before moving to the command post of General William Hood Simpson, commander of the Ninth Army, and a native of Weatherford, twenty miles west of Fort Worth. About May 4, Carter and Wear were in a jeep near the Elbe River. They met Seymour Freidin, a correspondent for the New York *Herald Tribune.* Freidin greeted Wear, whom he knew. When introduced to Amon Carter, the correspondent pulled a handwritten note from his pocket and tossed it to the publisher.

The note was from Amon Junior. He gave it to Freidin earlier that morning. The lieutenant told of the Russian liberation April 22 and said he was remaining at Luckenwalde until Americans arrived. Young Carter asked Freidin to file the news with the *Star-Telegram.*

Carter and Wear drove immediately to the camp. The son was gone.

That day the American Army finally had come to Luchenwalde. Soviets refused to allow the POWs to be taken and US tanks had smashed down the front gate, threatening to fire on the Russians. Trucks came to transport the captive officers to 83rd Division headquarters. Amon Junior joined Frank Conniff, a reporter for International News Service. They drove toward General Simpson's headquarters.

Carter and Wear lunched with Simpson and Brigadier General Robert C. Macon, the 83rd commander. Afterwards, the publisher walked to the division command post and stood, waiting for a jeep. He and Wear were leaving again to search for young Amon.

"Well, Dad, here I am."

The lieutenant arrived with Conniff and parked down the road, from where Amon spotted his father. He slapped his father on the back and they embraced and kissed.

For a week, father and son remained together before the Army again claimed the lieutenant. With Wear and Bess Stephenson, who had left the *Star-Telegram* to become a WAC officer, Carter celebrated V-E Day in Paris. Young Amon was shipped off to America.

His father rejoined the touring publishers, who had completed their atrocity inspections and fallen into sightseeing. Carter even filed several stories to the *Star-Telegram* — so elated was his mood — as the men moved down the continent.

Carter's war was over; his son was safe, going home. The publisher followed two weeks later. Back in New York, he telephoned Katrine to report on the trip. Because of his gratitude for having his cowboy home after two years of imprisonment, Amon issued a generous order.

"I want you to give a thousand dollars to every church in Fort Worth," he said to Katrine.

Pause.

"Even the colored churches?"

Pause.

"They pray, don't they?"

"Yes, I expect they do."

"Well, gawddamnit, pay 'em."

As news of Amon Carter Junior's deliverance from evil Nazi captivity flashed across the *Star-Telegram*'s front pages, and the publisher's European reports arrived, a creaky little old lady made her way to the editorial offices and announced that she, and she alone, effected young Amon's release.

"I asked God to save him, and He did," she said and demanded that the newspaper publish the fact of her providential miracle.

Mary Sears, the women pages editor, dismissed the lady.

"Amon Carter makes his own deals with God," Sears sniffed indignantly.

At home, the publisher provided a practical means of showing Texas involvement in the war. He ordered that all names of Texans killed in the fighting be printed because there should be a public record of the dead. The

Army list alone numbered more than fifteen thousand names and, in agate type, covered six full open pages.

The publisher's post-war European reports mostly were dull accounts of how Texans once again had saved the world for Democracy but in the final story, he noted a sidetrip to Milan. Afterward, he messaged Fort Worth:

"I stood on Mussolini's balcony and gave a loud cheer for West Texas."

Chapter 17

The rich are different from you and me because they have more credit.

—John Leonard

Amon does my talking for me and every time he does, he costs me money.

—Sid Richardson, billionaire

That Mr. Carter is the voice of the Administration in the Southwest, there is no question.

—Lubbock Avalanche, *1934*

Always do anything Amon asks you to do. Just give half as much money as he asks you for because he always asks for twice as much as he expects to get.

—Father's advice, to Web Maddox

Je veux que le dimanche chaque paysan ait sa poule au pot — It is my wish that every peasant have a chicken in the pot on Sunday.

—Henry IV, first Bourbon king, 1608

17

Amon Carter was instinctively, almost compulsively, generous and no one will ever know how much money he gave away. He was the kind of man who never opened his own presents until late Christmas Day because he loved watching his family and friends open gifts he had given them. He gave money and things to everybody, anybody, with a random casualness that defied all reason and any certain documentation. He had fits of philanthropy as spontaneous as they were anonymous.

Amon could be, and often was, the bully of the block but he also was an impulsive compassionate giver without peer. A poor TCU student needed money for a trip home during the holidays. Amon learned of the boy's plight and paid for a train ticket. A family was seriously injured in an automobile accident. The father was hospitalized for a year. Amon read of the family in the *Star-Telegram,* paid all hospital bills and supported the family, and set in motion a newspaper campaign to make safe the intersection at which the accident occurred. Neither the student nor the family ever knew the name of their benefactor.

Two boys were injured in a motorcycle accident. Amon, anonymously, paid their medical expenses. He gave $1,500 to St. Francis Xavier Academy in Denison with the stipulation no one ever know. His contributions to St. Joseph's Hospital included an X-ray machine, blood lab, elevator and parking lot, and as Dr. R. J. White wrote, "They are daily used and enjoyed by hundreds of people who don't know where they come from, but I do." He financed the first beauty shop in Fort Worth and provided seed money for the crippled children's society. He regularly supported an old blind lady who sold the *Press* and the widow of a bank president who died broke. He wrote a monthly check for the expenses of a society widow left penniless by her late husband ("She was a woman of great elegance, but no money," said a friend), and he supported two old black women who had no other source of income. A cement contractor, nearing bankruptcy, would have lost his home, but Amon saved it. The shanty home of a black family burned. Amon repaired the house, gave the family six hundred dollars and had Leonard Bros. Department Store sell them household items at cost. He gave a station wagon to a church federation which operated a children's home. He gave Jewish charities $1,000 each Christmas. He bought the old hotel in Bowie at which he worked as a boy, kept it as a home for Mrs. Jarrott, paid all her expenses, paid for her funeral. Bill Inch, his childhood friend, died and Amon gave the widow oil stock to provide an income for the remainder of her life. Ray Eisele, a Packard dealer, received a note from Amon: "It is Christmas and Our Lady of Victory needs a new car. They will be by to pick it up. Send me the bill." Amon, never a church-going man, gave an all-faith tabernacle for the community of Crafton, his birthplace, and paid $30,000 of $45,000 needed to purchase a rectory for St. John's Episcopal Church. An elderly couple would have lost their small grocery store but Amon bought the mortgage and gave it to them.

At one time, as he grouched in a letter, Amon supported thirteen relatives, several of whom he gave jobs at the *Star-Telegram*. He paid $50 monthly to an elderly uncle, $40 to his grandmother, $60 to his stepmother whom he despised, and $75 to his sister, Addie, a troublesome woman who endlessly asked for more money. He supported her children, gave them educations, marriages and homes.

He gave the county medical society a new building and funded the school library at Montague High School in West Texas. He sold property in Amarillo for less than he paid for it to provide the town with the best site for a Post Office, and he gave a rare book collection to TCU.

Cranky, cantakerous, irascible, grouchy old Amon Carter never missed a birthday of Pappy Waggoner's wife or Mrs. W. S. Stripling, Sr. He always was there, smiling, with a kind word and bouquets of flowers.

While he provided generous benefits to his employees, there was more. *Star-Telegram* photographers were called upon by Amon for special pictures so each Christmas, in addition to the usual company bonus, he slipped them extra cash, always warning, "Now, don't say anthing about this to the others." Jack Butler prepared to buy his first home, a step that required selling his car to make the down payment. Amon learned of Butler's plans and stopped him. First, he had Walter Claer see if Bulter was getting his money's worth. Butler was not, reported Walter. Amon was selling some land to a developer. As part of the deal, Butler was given his choice of a free lot in the new development.

Each Christmas Amon gave a crisp new five dollar bill to each rest home patient and orphan in town. There was one stipulation. The money was to be spent in any way and for any thing the old folks and orphans wanted. It was not for essentials. It was for fun. One Christmas Lena Pope, who operated the city's largest orphanage, used the money for badly needed linoleum. Amon learned what she had done, and was furious. He reprimanded her, then paid for the linoleum and replenished the supply of five dollar bills for her orphans. Orphanage directors and heads of other charitable organizations brought their lists to Amon shortly before Christmas. One Christmas a preacher asked for three hundred dollars. The next December he wanted $350. Amon compared the costs and sent a reporter to find out why the minister needed more money.

"He has ten more orphans," the envoy reported.

"Pay him," ordered Amon, satisfied he was not being cheated.

That was Amon, too. Careful with his money. Though he lived expensively and well, and gave away millions, the pennies were tended like a flock of worrisome sheep. He never passed through the business office and ground-floor advertising department without turning out lights and groaning about the high cost of electricity. A few months before Amon's death, LeRoy Menzing, then oil editor, was assigned to cover a Middle East petroleum conference.

Amon generously told him, "Use my apartment on your way through New York. Throw a party if you want to and put it on my bill — but don't use the telephone. Those birds charge 21¢ a call. Look in the closet. There's a private line hidden in there. Use that one."

Once he escorted Nenetta and two friends to New York for a week. Amon, the superb host, paid for everything — train tickets, meals, Broadway shows, shopping, entertainment. Before leaving his apartment Amon gathered up the empty soda bottles. He brought them back to Fort Worth where he collected a few cents refund on each bottle.

Amon's impetuous generosity could have a comic element. Hospitalized with his first heart attacks in St. Joseph's Hospital, he learned one of the nursing sisters was returning to Ireland for her first visit in years. She was a small woman encased in an old-fashioned lace corset which she tugged at endlessly to ease the discomfort it caused her. Amon instructed Katrine Deakins to buy her a new one.

The sister thanked Amon and confessed the modern stretchy corset was too small. She didn't like to ask, she said, but what she really wanted was long woolen underwear.

Amon supplied the nun's long underwear, and tucked inside enough for the plane ticket to Ireland.

Those were Amon's private charities, known to few or no others. He gave flashy gifts to his celebrity friends and doodads of the moment to his personal friends. And there were the public contributions.

He, for example, bought the stock show's grand champion steer. Acting as auctioneer, he often raised his own bid, or he proffered a money commitment for Sid Richardson.

"Sid Richardson bids $5,000," Amon would shout. "By the way, anybody seen Sid today?"

Richardson was a barrel-bodied, taciturn, plain-spoken man with a face of furrow-like wrinkles, one of the last great wildcatting oilmen. Most often broke, Sid was a fixture around the Fort Worth Club where his bills went unpaid for years. When he finally struck his keystone pool in Far West Texas, its reserves were valued at more than a billion dollars.

"Luck did it," Richardson said of the strike. "I'd rather be lucky than smart 'cause a lot of smart people ain't eatin'."

With his bills paid, Sid, a lifelong bachelor, settled into the Fort Worth Club as Amon's close friend, confidante, political crony and handy reserve fund for the publisher's various projects.

Sid always screamed at the costs, but he paid.

Once Richardson was relaxing on an Atlantic cruise. Amon telephoned him via ship to shore phone and asked for a $37,000 contribution. Sid moaned, began pleading poverty.

"Then I'll just charge this phone call to you," joked Amon.

"Like hell you will! Put me down for the $37,000."

Through Amon's exhortations, Sid paid a thousand dollars each year for suppport of 4H Club members at the annual Stock Show. In 1945, Sid was vacationing at the Westward Ho Guest Ranch near Phoenix when Amon doubled the oilman's annual pledge.

Then Amon wired Richardson the news, adding, "Unless I hear from you in the next five minutes, I will assume it is OK."

Sid's reply telegram was terse: "Looks like you didn't hear from me in five minutes."

Easter was the one time each year when Amon attended church.

He went with Katrine and her husband, Carl, and often towing Sid, who was as lax a churchgoer as Amon. The publisher, however, paid his dues, never dropping less than five hundred dollars into the collection plate. Sid was nicked for a like amount.

That 1945 spring Sid remained at the Arizona guest ranch. Amon again wired his friend that the usual five hundred dollars was expected from the church. Sid replied irritably, "Thought if I was out of Fort Worth during the Stock Show and Easter that I could break even with you and pay my hotel bill but looks like I didn't go far enough."

Another convenient lode to mine was old Pappy Waggoner, Fort Worth's second billionaire and a man having penurious ways with a dollar. Once Waggoner had his shoes polished and handed the shineman a two-bit tip.

The man complained, "... but your boys usually tip five dollars."

"They got a rich daddy and I ain't," snapped Pappy.

The rancher/oilman, always as earthy and plain as the day he came off the West Texas plains to make Fort Worth his home, was tapped by Amon for every purpose, especially political.

The publisher drew ten thousand dollars from Pappy to finance a trip to the 1932 Democratic Convention of the Old Gray Mare Band, a popular musical organization from Brownwood.

Later, Amon went back to Waggoner for another ten thousand with which to pay expenses for the Texas Christian Band to President Roosevelt's inauguration.

"Naw, Amon," said Pappy, "I'm tryin' to quit."

But Amon got the rancher's money. He always did.

When the publisher was raising funds to construct Texas Christian's new football stadium, a finance committee member approached Pappy and secured a thousand dollar pledge.

The man proudly told Amon of the contribution.

Amon snorted, "I'll show you how to raise money."

He telephoned Pappy.

"I'm putting you down for $50,000," Amon told Waggoner. "That'll buy a whole section. Your ranch brand is 3-D. I'll have 3-D put into the concrete in your section."

Pappy paid, not happily, but he paid. A *Star-Telegram* photographer once was assigned to take Waggoner's picture. Pappy pulled a silver dollar from his pocket and held it high.

"Here, take a picture of this," commanded Pappy. "It's one dollar Amon Carter didn't get."

Amon had an audacious respect for money, and could never understand why others did not share his ecstasy. Once when the *Star-Telegram* raised its advertising rates, Amon explained the increase to Leon Gross, president of Washer Bros., one of the newspaper's largest advertisers.

Amon said the rate increase was necessary because of rising costs.

"Yes," said Gross at the end of Amon's presentation. "I can see that. We'll go along with you."

"But, Mr. Gross," Amon began again, ticking off the costs on his fingers. "Everything is going up . . . newsprint . . . labor . . . ink . . ."

"Mr. Carter, I've already told you we'd be willing to accept the increase," broke in Gross. "What else do you want me to do?"

"I want you to be enthusiastic about it," said Amon, cheerfully.

When Amon spoke of raising money, listeners began squirming. They anxiously looked for exits, feigned illnesses, excused themselves to go to the toilet, seeking any escape. But if one lived in Fort Worth and one had money or access to money, Amon came after it.

How much the publisher raised for projects in his city is unknown. No one kept score, a contemporary guessed "four or five million," which surely is a conservative amount.

He raised virtually the entire $450,000 needed for TCU's stadium, and $400,000 for a new YMCA downtown building. Amon, said Jimmy North, individually raised $1,285,000 with which a local corporation purchased Hotel Texas to keep it from Dallas investors. He sold $600,000 of $800,000 in bonds to finance construction of the Fort Worth Club. A hospital project needing $700,000 was stalled until the finance committee turned to Amon. He collected the final $347,000.

Amon was a member of the Democratic Party's national finance committee, and personally contributed so much money to the Demos that Will Rogers announced President Roosevelt would name the publisher Secretary of War to replace Patrick J. Hurley.

Rogers wrote in his January 23, 1933, newspaper column:

> I hear that Amon G. Carter, of Fort Worth, Texas, owner of the biggest newspaper in the Southwest, will take Hurley's place in the Cabinet. Carter, from all I can gather from the 'inside,' will be the man that will draw that splendid Cabinet plum. Amon will make 'em a mighty fine man. He is mighty well liked by all Democrats and 50 percent of the Republicans. (Well, I will say a dozen anyway.) He would handle our army mighty well in peace and put us on a mighty pretty war if the occasion arises. So, while all the other cabinet positions are more or less up in the air from what we can hear, why it's practically clinched that Carter will succeed Hurley, who by the way is a very good friend of his.
>
> Carter has practically retired from active management of his paper, but sometimes has it sent to New York or Washington to read.
>
> He is by far Texas' most public-spirited man. So, with [John Nance] Garner daily inquiring as to the health of our President, and Carter at the head of our military hoardes, why Texas will have received more than her share of the spoils in the late political war. All his old friends in Texas (of which I almost consider myself a native of) . . . hope this new honor will not make him break an old custom of years, and that was to always be in the Capitol, Austin, on all Ferguson inaugurations. This Carter Cabinet hasn't been generally broadcasted, but those who knew say 'it's in the bag.'

In the *Star-Telegram*, Amon tacked an editor's note to Rogers' column:

> Thanks, Will, but your information is all wrong. The publisher of this newspaper never has accepted political

> appointment of any character and has no intention of so doing.

Amon truly did not want a political office, neither elective or appointive. He had more power backstage. Amon always had a pipeline into Washington and generally was believed to be FDR's main man in the Southwest.

He, for example, was able to collect two million dollars in federal highway money after the administration shut off the funds. Amon and Jesse Jones of Houston rustled so much government money for the Lone Star State during the Depression that Washington wags spoke of it as the "star loan state."

Texas' national politicians — it was especially said of Senator Tom Connally — acquired reputations as "Amon Carter's Rubber Stamps." Harold Ickes called Amon "the Horace Greeley of Texas," and not kindly.

Roosevelt was a good friend in addition to being a valuable source of Washington largesse. Secret Service agents had standing instructions that photographs of FDR would be taken in Fort Worth no matter what orders were in other cities. Once when FDR passed through Bowie on a campaign train, Amon boarded and sold the President one of those early-day sandwiches peddled by the Chicken and Bread Boys. Roosevelt dutifully handed over a dime. Amon pocketed it with a polite, "Thank you, sir!"

Amon's strong friendship with Roosevelt grew in spite of the publisher's frantic efforts to make a President out of John Nance Garner. Throughout Roosevelt's three terms Amon openly and continuously campaigned for Cactus Jack's ascension to the Presidency. Of all his political friends, Amon most cherished John Garner.

America has never had another politician like Cactus Jack, whom labor leader John L. Lewis described as a "whiskey-drinking, poker-playing evil old man." Lewis was partially right. Garner, perhaps the most truthful politician ever elected to office, admitted his uselessness as a newcomer to Washington.

"Naturally I didn't amount to anything up there at first," he told a reporter. "For 5 or 6 years I just answered roll calls and played poker."

When he had been in Congress eight years, he was asked what occupied him most. "Staying in office!" he snapped.

With a tuft of graying hair brushed to one side, the waggling Andrew Jackson eyebrows, the bulldog jawline, John Garner was a familiar figure in American politics for forty years.

Washington never changed him. He tucked pieces of cooked venison into his pockets, went to bed each evening at 9 o'clock, kept a dollar watch in the vest of his off-the-rack suits. When the watch inevitably broke, Amon bought him another and passed along the receipt proving the timepiece cost no more than a dollar. Garner hated to dress, was most comfortable in old denims. His wife, Ettie, who as his private secretary worked along side of him as though he was still plowing a field back in Texas, once bought him a sixty dollar suit. Nine years later he grouched that the suit was a cheap one because the pants were wearing out.

As a farm boy turned lawyer Garner went to Washington during Teddy Roosevelt's administration and rose to Speaker of the House of Representatives, an ironic title because John Garner was a man of almost no words. Compared to Cactus Jack, Silent Cal Coolidge was as chatty as a debutante.

Garner made exactly three public speeches in forty years of public life, none at all for the first twenty-five years. Between 1933 and 1941, he spoke three times, the last to members of the United States Chamber of Commerce. Truthful as always, he preceded his speech with, "There isn't a single man living who can quote me on a question of administration policy for the last seven years. I'm telling you this because I'm not going to say a thing tonight that means a damn thing.''

There was one, and only one, radio speech. In 1933 Bernard Baruch, James Farley and Sam Rayburn called on Garner to speak on behalf of the Democrats. Garner replied, ''I never made a speech in my Texas district and I don't intend to start now.'' The men pled with the vice president, but he was adamant.

He bought train tickets for a trip back to Uvalde.

The Democratic trio solicited Amon's help in changing Garner's mind. Amon spoke with his old friend, insisting the radio speech must be made, and finally Garner relented.

Garner angrily told an administrative aide, ''Louis, cancel those damn tickets. Looks like I don't have anything to do with my own affairs anymore.''

Amon sat beside Cactus Jack in the CBS studios throughout the twenty-six page speech. Afterwards, Amon collected the pages and filed them away in his *Star-Telegram* office.

Elected vice president (Garner's mother, asked for comment on her son's new office, said, ''He's a good boy, it won't hurt him any'') Cactus Jack was unchanged. He still nibbled on venison from his pocket storehouse and refused to buy an automobile, left all formal dinners at 9 o'clock.

As Vice President, Garner was visible but uncommunicative — and bored with his job as the ''spare tire of government.'' He only spoke rarely with reporters, once to grumble his now-famous assessment of the vice presidency. The office, he said, ''is not worth a bucketful of warm spit.''*

When Roosevelt sought an unprecedented fourth term, Garner quit in disgust. He attended FDR's fourth inauguration, wearing a top hat too small and borrowed

*Privately, Cactus Jack was a trifle more succinct. ''. . . not worth a bucketful of warm piss,'' was the way he put it.

from Jesse Jones — Garner refused to spend the $1.50 to rent a hat; it fell off three times. On the platform, Roosevelt whispered in his ear, "Goodbye, Jack, I'll miss you. You were the strongest vice president in history."

To reporters, Garner answered all questions with, "No comment." To one, he added, "That's the way I came in, that's the way I'm goin' out."

He went home to Uvalde to sit on his porch and sip Amon's Shady Oak whiskey. Bascom Timmons, the *Star-Telegram*'s Washington bureau chief, wrote Garner's official biography. Much of the research was done by Bess Stephenson, who had gone to work in Washington after the war.

In 1947, Timmons reported a minor event in the life of the man who quit the nation's second most powerful job for a principle. Old Cactus Jack, wrote Timmons, had declined all requests that he write his memoirs. Taciturn to the end, Garner carried his political files of forty years, the letters, memoranda and official papers, to a small rise behind his home, and burned everything.

Amon loved crusty old Cactus Jack. He kept the Vice President supplied with drinking materials, especially cases and cases of the exclusive Shady Oak bourbon. Garner smoked Amon's cigars and wore his hand-tooled belts and a special Shady Oak hat inscribed "Hooray for John Nance Garner and West Texas."

The publisher wrote long folksy letters reporting on Texas politics and sent along jars of homemade pickles and maramalade. In return, when Amon visited Garner in his Washington office the vice president would get a gleam in his eye and roar, "Amon! Let's you and me go into the back room and strike a blow for liberty" — a signal for the pair to nip from the whiskey cache.

Amon had Garner's portrait painted, not once, but three times, and copies were hung in Austin and Washington. Carter hired Electra Waggoner Biggs to sculpt the craggy features in bronze and busts were sent to the two capitols. A third was given to Texas Tech and a fourth resided in Amon's office near the lighted portrait of Will Rogers, proof of the publisher's deeply held respect for the little man from Uvalde.

About the same time the Waggoner granddaughter began work on Garner's bust, Amon commissioned her to sculpt Sid's head. It simply was a gesture of friendship, but one Amon parlayed into a practical joke. Amon asked Biggs for the plaster cast and had Walter Claer sneak it into Sid's office. An engraved plate was attached, reading: From One Old Bastard to Another.

By the late 1940s Amon and Sid were intimately involved in several political conspiracies, though close friends believed the oilman exterted too much influence over Carter. It was Sid who pushed Lyndon Johnson off on Amon, much to the latter's later unhappiness. Together, they pressed Dwight Eisenhower to run for the Presidency, though Amon was not particularly pleased the general selected the Republican Party as a vehicle to the office. Amon's support of Ike in the 1952 election was considered by recidivous Democrats as a treasonable act, but few of them understood the absolute necessity of Eisenhower being President. It was a matter of oil.

Sid met Ike when the latter was a young lieutenant and their friendship grew through the years. Richardson persuaded Amon that Eisenhower was the man to dedicate the long boxed-up statue of Will Rogers and the publisher established a lasting companionship with the future President. A 1950 entry in Suite 10G's logbook recorded Ike's feelings: "With best wishes to Amon in memory of an afternoon when his old friends Sid and Ike chinned with him through the problems of the world and quantities of good scotch."

In the mid-1940s Texas oilmen were in a dither about rights to offshore petroleum deposits. Harry Truman vetoed a tidelands bill in 1946 which would have given Texas and other states ownership of all offshore oil. In April, 1952, Amon wrote Truman urging him to sign a second bill soon to be passed.

"Facts of history make the tidelands matter, insofar as Texas is concerned, a moral as well as a legal matter," said Amon. After Congress passed the bill in May, the publisher again wrote the president asking that he sign the bill or allow it to become law without his signature. In that letter Amon noted Truman's veto in 1946 was being widely criticized still and national defense requirements now justified Texas' retention of tidelands resources.

In Washington, Truman told newsmen he had written a "fellow down in Texas" that school children of other states would be the losers if the tidelands bill became law, but evidently the fellow "wanted all of this money to go to Texas. It is not going there if I can help it." Amon fired off another letter to the President in which he argued that the tidelands bill left to the federal government all lands outside traditional boundaries, "the area which has by far the greater potential production of oil."

Truman vetoed the bill, and Amon wrote still another letter — published in the *Star-Telegram*, it covered 34½ column inches — attacking Truman's reasons for killing the bill and closed with a promise that Texas would continue fighting the issue until it was "settled in accord with the principles of right, justice, and honesty."

Privately, Amon and Sid were priming Ike.

Four months earlier the oilman and George E. Allen, a Democrat and former chairman of the Reconstruction Finance Corporation, sailed to Paris — Katrine Deakins said Amon "made Sid go" — to persuade Ike he had to return by April if he wanted the Republican nomination. They also enlisted the help of Billy Graham, the evangelist then becoming a national figure. Graham said in a 1970s interview that at Sid and Amon's urging he had spoken with Ike in Paris.

Ike came home.

Eisenhower was nominated, and offshore oil ownership became a campaign issue. Ike said he favored allowing states clear title to the lands. Adlai Stevenson took the position that the matter had been settled. Less than a month after Ike's inauguration, reported Columnist Drew Pearson, Amon delivered to the new President a copy of the 1849 Joint Resolution for Annexing Texas to the United States. The document, said Pearson, convinced Eisenhower of Texas' right to the tidelands. In May, 1953, Ike signed the bill conveying those lands to Texas and other states.

With the tidelands issue finally settled, Amon, said a friend, flashed the smile of a spinster who had finally scored.

He and Sid formed a corporation to establish Eisenhower's birthplace in Denison as a state shrine.

Locally, Amon never actually groomed and boosted into office any politician but there were men he supported heavily, both with money and newspaper space. Anyone who ran for office solicited his approval. Those who did not obtain his support attacked those who did as "Amon Carter's puppets."

Internally, the political climate around Amon spawned at least three* candidates for state offices from among members of the *Star-Telegram* family. Boyce House quit to run — *sans* Amon's support — a losing race for lieutenant governor. Hough ran for Governor, but never seriously. There was, however, W. Lee O'Daniel, said to have been "one of Hough's politicians." Amon hated the man.

O'Daniel was a flour peddler who emceed a daily WBAP show featuring the popular Light Crust Doughboys, a hillbilly band. Hough urged O'Daniel to test his political popularity and one morning the flour salesman

*While publisher of the *Star-Telegram* Louis Wortham served several terms in the Texas Legislature.

asked casually, ''What do you think I ought to do about the politicians who have this state hogtied? How would you like me to run for governor?'' Listeners liked the idea. Sixty thousand letters of support arrived at the station.

O'Daniel became a candidate for governor.

He campaigned with the radio show band, which changed its name to the Hillbilly Boys, and Texas Rose, a weeping-voiced torch singer, and a sound truck. For each rally, he passed flour sacks among the crowd for donations and reportedly made a profit on his electioneering.

It was a good show. O'Daniel sang religious songs, read his poems (''A mother is a mother/wherever you find her/Be she a queen/or an organ grinder'') and shouted his slogan of ''Less Johnson Grass and Politicians.''

His platform was ''the Golden Rule and the Ten Commandments,'' and a promise, if elected, to provide a thirty dollar a month pension for old folks.

Despite critics pointing out that O'Daniel had not paid his $1.75 poll tax, and thus not voted, in five years, he beat twelve opponents in the Democratic primary, largely with left-over Ma and Pa Ferguson vest pocket voters who knew a good demagogue when they heard one. Amon and the *Star-Telegram* supported Ernest Thompson, a West Texan.

In early 1938, W. Lee O'Daniel, the flour peddler, took possession of the Texas governor's mansion. Hough's politician inspected the home's screened-in porch, and exclaimed loudly to reporters, ''Boy, I can sure do some trick and fancy sleeping in here.''

The legislature, of course, refused to pass his pension plan. O'Daniel muddled around for two years and, to Amon's consternation, was re-elected in 1940, still promising old people a monthly income.

In Fort Worth, Amon smokescreened his sponsorship of a string of mayors and council members. He allowed them few ceremonial duties, especially in the field of groundbreaking.

Amon was Fort Worth's groundbreaking expert, using nothing but special chrome plated shovels, each of which were engraved for the occasion. "Amon was born with a silver shovel in his mouth," said Alf Evans of his publisher's groundbreaking mania. Dirt for any Fort Worth project could not be turned without the exuberant Amon to wield one of his silvery shovels — his office, his home and Shady Oak were jammed with the engraved spades.

He, as was his wont, dominated all ceremonies. Late in his life, Amon gave money for construction of a nurses home at St. Joseph's Hospital, and dignitaries, including Amon, assembled to break ground. Amon's silver shovel had not been delivered. He was fussy about the delay. Starting time arrived and departed. Everybody waited. Amon would not begin without his special spade.

Meanwhile, a group of Catholic hierarchy, headed by auxiliary bishop A. Danglymayr of Dallas, waited inside the main hospital building with a coterie of nuns, priests and altar boys. The bishop was weary of waiting. He marched his entourage to the groundbreaking site, following a church-prescribed procedure. The auxiliary bishop sprinkled holy water on the ground, said prayers in Latin. An altar boy handed him a dime story shovel painted with gold paint. A red ribbon was tied to the handle. The bishop scooped up dirt. He motioned to Amon to perform next. Amon hesitated. He glanced over his shoulder, searching for the tardy silver shovel. Finally, he turned and accepted the gaudy spade. Amon scooped, but clearly his heart wasn't in it.

Later, a reporter went to Amon's home for approval of the groundbreaking story. The publisher was livid. He described in detail, according to the reporter, "what kind of dumb SOB the bishop was." Amon gawddamned the churchman for turning first dirt and not waiting for the shiny special shovel.

As a final indignity to the bishop, Amon ordered the reporter to write that he [Carter] turned the first spadeful of dirt.

Amon also was the city's master of ceremonies for all grand events, dinners and celebrations. He was a splendid speaker with an uncanny memory for names and details, but too often preachy and windy. As he grew older he spoke too long, bringing out tales of his deprived youth and singing them loudly on far too many occasions, or bragging of his successes and accomplishments, an old man cataloging his past.

Time magazine told of his introduction that was so long the speaker had no time remaining. Amon often joked about when he introduced William Jennings Bryan and left the great orator only three minutes of speech time.

Amon emceed dinners and events all over America, but delivered only a single formal prepared speech in his life — to an oil convention. As emcee, he had a smooth, stammerless delivery and an apparently limitless stock of appropriate stories and inspirational aphorisms with which to spread the gospel of Fort Worth and Texas.

He called himself a "peptimist," explained as a cross between an optimist and a pessimist — "A peptimist looks on the bright side of life, but always with a flashlight handy."

"There's a lot of difference between people and folks," he would tell audiences, adding, "It's a long way from cornbread to caviar but just a short way back."

Among his favorite speech brighteners were: "You can't fill a sack that's full of holes"; and "Eggs want to be smarter than hens"; and "Step off the curb and watch yourself go by and see what you think"; and "Be polite to your customers because the only fellow who ever made a success in business by driving his customers away was a taxi driver,'' and ''Abe Lincoln was not a great man because he lived in a log cabin but because he was able to get out of it.''

Somehow Amon was able to associate those little homilies with the magnificence of Fort Worth.

And if his friends were unable to stop him, especially in his later years, he applied the adages to himself, his bootstrap lifting abilities and, after 1949, how he sold all those advertisements for the *Star-Telegram*'s centennial edition.

In that year Fort Worth became a century old and Amon believed the occasion perfect for a memorial edition of his newspaper. The result was a 480 page behemoth printed on 1,578,000 pounds of paper, a plumed worded Brobdingnagia so immense that folding and inserting were done in the Pioneer Palace, by then a derelict structure rotting on the old 1936 Frontier Fiesta grounds.

The October 30, 1949, centennial edition was a record, in terms of number of pages, for Texas, and contained the most advertising lineage — 61,811 column inches — of any single newspaper ever published in the United States.

Amon Carter, then seventy years old, personally sold 220 of 271 full page advertisements.

Characteristically, Amon sold his ads with the same subtle approach with which he collected cash for other pet projects. He telephoned friends and announced, ''I'm putting you down for a full page ad.''

Around town, businessmen jokingly asked one another, ''Have you joined Amon's Full Page Club?''

At least once, Amon's direct method brought double revenue for the *Star-Telegram*. A bank's advertising manager scheduled and budgeted a full page in the centennial edition. Amon did not speak to advertising managers. He spoke only to presidents. He telephoned the bank's president and ''put him down'' for an advertisement. The bank had *two* full page ads in the special newspaper.

While Amon could speak only to presidents, they and other friends spoke only to him. Those men of the Carter circle never bothered with the *Star-Telegram* circulation department when their newspapers were delayed or missing from their lawns. They called Amon. Amon relayed the messages to the circulation department.

Publication of the gargantuan centennial edition provided Amon with an excuse to take revenge for all those late night and early morning telephone calls. The newspaper's front page was finally clamped around other sections about 3 o'clock that Sunday morning, and Amon was waiting. He shanghaied George Dolan, then a night rewrite man, and a photographer to drive him about the city.

As they moved through the darkened deserted town, Amon sat in the back seat dwarfed by stacks of the huge papers, chuckling to himself.

When the trio arrived at the designated houses, Carter would hop out, trot to the door and knock loudly. As the occupant sleepily opened the door, Amon shoved the mammoth newspaper into his arms while the photographer recorded the event. "Here's your newspaper!" Amon shouted. "Don't call me about it not being delivered!" Then he would lope back across the lawn to the waiting auto, laughing gleefully.

At a final stop shortly before sunrise, Amon ran to a door and yelled loudly for the man inside. Minutes later, the door opened cautiously to reveal a figure in a long white nightgown. He carried a shotgun.

"You old sonofabitch!" Amon cried.

"Amon!" shouted the astonished man. "*You* old sonofabitch!"

They fell into each other's arms, giggling like schoolgirls.

If there ever was a man conspicuous with his money, it was Amon. He was as flashy with it as a racetrack lout. He was a lavish tipper, an easy touch for a handout or loan, a sure thing for a charity fund collector. Not that the money he gave away was always his own. Mason Lankford, the Tarrant County Firefighters Association president, visited with Amon and asked, somewhat hesitantly, for a one hundred dollar donation. Amon peeled off a hundred dollar bill and passed it to Lankford. Then he had Katrine telephone twenty-two business firms. Lankford walked out with $2,200 for his association.

Amon kept his cash in fifties and hundred, even thousand dollar bills, all folded into a metal clip he called his "money brassiere." He was forever sending Katrine to the bank for a fresh supply of money, especially hundred dollar bills, which he favored.

Once he carried around for months a ten thousand dollar bill which he would haul out to impress friends and passing strangers.

Amon's gaudy theatrical way with cash was a personality trait of the cowboy. The cowboy flashed and lavished Amon's money on the world with the wastrel appetite of a small boy before a candy counter.

The cowboy, in fact, kept Amon broke most of his life.

Stony broke. Busted as a sharecropper. The cowboy treated Amon shamefully.

Except what he could borrow, Amon had little cash to call his own. He was borrowed ahead on his *Star-Telegram* salary. His newspaper stock was heavily mortgaged. He often was months behind on his grocery bills, payments lagged on automobiles, his country club debts mounted, Fort Worth Club charges went unpaid as other members grumbled.

The cowboy, that eternal prodigal playboy, was a classic spendthrift. Amon ran most of his life to stay ahead of the cowboy's creditors.

By 1916, when he and Louis Wortham owned controlling interest in the *Star-Telegram*, Amon had established a fiscal policy of borrowing from Peter to pay Paul, also Tom, Dick and Harry. That year he borrowed $25,000 to pay "personal loans." Two years later when the note fell due, Amon borrowed from another bank to pay the debt. The dollar relay was a never-ending race against insolvency.

Wortham retired in 1922 to write his excellent four volume history of Texas. Amon became publisher and majority and eventually owning, according to columnist Dorothy Killgallen, 66 2/3 percent of the newspaper corporation. Remainder of the stock was spread principally among Jimmy North, Bert Honea, Al Shuman, Harold Hough and JRR.

The newspaper supported Amon's lifestyle, his cowboy extravagances, the civic and charitable contributions, and it was a treadmill that frazzled the nerves of penny-conscious Bert Honea.

Honea, said Alf Evans, seemed to have a peculiar theory about money: "It was fine to make, and bank at six percent interest, compounded, but a mortal sin to spend."

Honea's genius for figuring out ways to beat the cowboy kept the *Star-Telegram* afloat.

A lack of liquidity was one reason (a minor one, however) Amon did not buy the Washington *Post*. He never expanded his Fort Worth empire, though he was offered newspapers in Lubbock and Amarillo and Dallas. He never felt the need to be a publisher in any other city — until the Washington *Post* went on the auction block. Amon wanted a voice in Washington. In 1933 the *Post* was bankrupt, housed in what Honea called "a little ole building" with a "worn down press" as its only real asset. Honea and North spent ten days in Washington inspecting the newspaper's books and assessing its value. Honea decided it was worth half a million dollars. Amon wanted to buy it. He told Honea, "You and Jimmy'll have to go up there and run it."

"That's when the deal fell through," recalled Honea, who had no intention of leaving Fort Worth, leaving the *Star-Telegram* cashbox in charge of the cowboy.

Not that Amon would have used any of the money for himself. He only borrowed money for important things, like paying his income tax, and giving it away. Often he mortgaged stock or land to pay for his load of Christmas gifts — as much as $30,000 one Christmas, said Walter Claer.

At times the money squeeze became almost unbearable. In the mid-1930s Amon frantically telephoned Honea from New York, where the publisher had gone to renew several past-due bank notes. Instead, Amon called in a panic, the banks were threatening to foreclose on the *Star-Telegram*. Ten thousand dollars was needed that day. Honea somehow got blood from Fort Worth turnips and saved the newspaper.

In the 1930s, too, Amon's marriage to Nenetta was dead. She asked for a divorce, and a settlement. Panic again. Had she insisted, Honea recalled, the newspaper would have had to have been sold, or forced into bankruptcy. Amon had mortgaged all his stock, all stock of Honea, North, Hough and Shuman. He had borrowed to his personal limit at every bank in Fort Worth, and several in New York. Katrine had been forced to guarantee several of his notes. The grocer pressed for payment.

Nenetta agreed to wait. She moved to New York.

As everyone else, she was waiting for Amon to strike oil. He, after all, had only been looking for it twenty years. His luck had to change.

Oil wildcatting was a big craps game and Amon loved the gamble of it.

As all wildcatters, there was very little science to Amon's oil ventures. He was a hunch player trusting to luck, and his mostly was bad. In 1920, he and Nenetta's father, W. C. Burton, drilled for water on property owned by Pappy Waggoner. They struck oil in what became known as the Wilbarger Pool. Amon immediately sold his interest for $100,000, gave a portion of it to his first wife, Zetta, and with the remainder, paid his debts, as far as it went.

From that moment on, Amon was consumed by his quest for oil. But, now aiming for oil he, however, struck only water, or dust. He continued to drill in New Mexico and West Texas and became something of a novelty in the oil business. Once he was introduced as "the only big oil producer who has never produced."

Word passed that Amon was unlucky and other oil men refused to participate with him in wildcatting ventures. After ninety dry holes — surely a record — Amon struck again in the New Mexico Mattix Pool.

His hopes were raised and the strike gave him operating money for more wells in Gaines and Yoakum counties. Oil remained a phantom. His crews worked around the clock. Days became weeks as he awaited word from the men. While Amon waited, the crew, living at a well-site on the Wassom Ranch, sought diversion from long work hours. They shot rabbits and stole corn from a nearby field. They roasted the corn and bunnies over open fires.

The ranch foreman ordered the crew away from the corn patch and threatened to call the law about the rabbits. In the future, he told them, they could pay fifty cents a dozen for the roasting ears and fifty cents each for rabbits.

The foreman's tightfisted manners enraged Amon. He settled the matter by buying the ranch of several thousand acres. Amon told the men to eat all the corn and rabbits they wanted.

They rewarded their boss's generosity by bringing in the discovery well of the Wasson Pool in June, 1937.

Amon sold his holding in the pool to Shell Oil Company for $16,500,000 — to that time, the largest oil transaction in Texas history. Nenetta, for waiting, received forty percent. They were divorced in 1941.

Amon was out of debt forever. Even the cowboy could not spend all that money.

Honea, who said, "If Amon hadn't found oil, we would have been hurt, but he found it, we all knew he would," breathed easier. No longer was it necessary for Amon to rifle the *Star-Telegram* cash drawer for pocket money.

The practice rankled Honea more than anything else. At the end of the day, Honea would find the petty cash short. He could not balance his books. He reminded Amon of the troublesome practice a dozen times, then the two men had a shouting argument.

"It's your money!" hollered Honea. "You can take it if you want to. But leave me a marker saying how much you took. My books never balance. Just leave me a chit, that's all."

"Alright, alright!" shouted Amon. "I'll leave you a gawddamned chit."

That afternoon Amon again raided the petty cash drawer, and true to his word, he left a chit.

Honea read it:

Dear Bert:
I took it all.
Amon

Chapter 18

Mr. Carter never made a mistake. I always thought of him as the infallible man.

—James R. Record

He was the last of the empire builders . . .

—Billy Rose

Amon was the most human man I ever saw.

—Nenetta Burton Carter

In a land of giants, he dwarfed them all.

—Congressman Jim Wright, June 27, 1955

His death closes a chapter in our history . . .

—Lyndon Baines Johnson

Thou'lt come no more,
Never, never, never, never, never . . .

—William Shakespeare, King Lear

18

As the Indian lodges of early America, the Amon G. Carter Museum of Western Art faces the rising sun on ground sloping away to the east, toward the river and Fort Worth's tiered skyline, dominating a place now designated Amon Carter Square. Beside it, to the north, is Camp Bowie Boulevard, down which Amon daily drove to the *Star-Telegram*, always in second gear, always recklessly. Opposite and slightly to the right are the Will Rogers Coliseum and Auditorium and the bronze statue of the Oklahoma humorist astride Soapsuds. Humorist and horse look west over Amon's museum to each sunset. South are the Fort Worth Art Museum and Museum of Science and History. In front, beyond a manicured grassy terrace and three decidedly unwestern impressionistic sculpture pieces by Britisher Henry Moore, is the Kimbell Art Museum, a repository of classical art mandated and endowed by another Fort

Worth millionaire. Amon Carter Square is flush with culture, an irony for those who felt Amon had none when he lived.

The museum, a ruggedly handsome, limestone-faced structure, houses Amon's — no, it is the cowboy's — incomparable hoard of paintings and sculpture pieces by Charles Russell and Frederick Remington.

Amon's will dictated the museum as a legacy to Fort Worth:

> I desire that this Museum be operated as a nonprofit artistic enterprise for the benefit of the public and to aid in the promotion of cultural spirit in the City of Fort Worth and vicinity, and particularly, to stimulate the artistic imagination among young people residing there.

Amon specifically directed that there never be an admission charge to enter his museum. Even in death, the publisher intended to pay the freight.

The collection is a superb representation of life in *The West*, one which old Lan Twohig would have understood and appreciated. There is, in fact, a highly apocryphal tale of a real cowboy brousing in Amon's museum. He, the story is told, stopped before a Remington painting depicting a buffalo kill by a Plains Indian riding a spirited horse.

A middleaged matron stood nearby, also studying the painting.

She gushed, "Ah! The noble savage!"

The ranch hand eyed her coolly.

"I wouldn't say that, ma'am," he drawled, "but he's riding a dang good horse."

One suspects that Amon Carter would have taken that truthless tale and made an impromptu speech subject of it, savoring its westernality, the validity of its message. The museum does attract the remnants of *The West*, especially each year during the stock show when

West Texans come to town. They drive in from the plains in their Cadillacs and pickups and many roam the museum gallery communing with the real west of Remington and Russell, and Amon. They are like brontosaurus, out of time and space, leftover props from a synthetic drama of long ago.

The cowboy began assembling his artworks before Amon could afford such effete tomfoolery. In 1928, Bertram M. Newhouse, a New York art dealer, showed the publisher six water colors and an oil by Russell. All reminded Carter of the Texas of his imagination. He promptly signed a $7,500 note, paying for his new treasures in two yearly installments. He continued buying western paintings by Russell and in 1935 acquired his first Remington oil. He could have made a profit immediately on that painting, titled "His First Lesson." The oil cost $5,000 and he hung it on his office wall.

Will Rogers saw the painting and offered $10,000. The cowboy refused to sell.

By 1952, as noted in *Time* magazine, the cowboy's appetite for art — and Amon's bank account — was much larger.

"He cast an envious eye on a big bunch of Russells, then housed cozily in a fine, old Great Falls, Montana, saloon called the Mint," explained *Time*.

In Montana, a state where a young Amon once foiled a light opera presentation by jubilantly firing off his pistols, the Mint collection, said the magazine, was called ". . . the big one that got away."

After the death of Sid Willis, Russell's old friend who owned the saloon and art collection, the paintings were sold to Ken Egan, a native Montanan who intended keeping them in the state. Montana appointed an official board with the mission of purchasing the artworks. Little money was available and the commission marked time.

Egan died in a hunting accident and almost overnight, there was the cowboy, money in hand, to purchase the paintings from Egan's family. His raid was credited with stirring Montana into a public fundraising campaign to hold Russell's works in the state. The public clamor came too late. The cowboy had vamoosed with the goods.

The cowboy's museum holds 293 art specimens, including forty-eight oils, sixty-seven water colors, and thirty-three pen drawings by Russell, and ninety-eight art objects by Remington. It is *the* definitive representation of western America, displayed in a superlative museum, just as Amon directed in his will.

Amon's will is a model document of philosophical and practical humanity, so perfect in its phrasing and execution that hundreds of copies were requested by others with a philanthropic bent. The will's thesis was written by Sidney Samuels, Amon's frail scholarly attorney — ''Sidney had just enough body to hold up his intellect,'' remembered Nenetta. Samuels produced a piece of literature in Amon's name:

> I [Amon] have learned while climbing the steep path of fortune, and I have come to realize that they who acquire wealth are more or less stewards in the application of that wealth to others of the human family who are less fortunate than themselves.
>
> Year in and year out, it has been borne in upon me that money alone, nor broad acres, nor newspapers, nor stock, nor bonds, nor flocks and herds, nor estates of oil and gas hidden in the recesses of this planet can, of themselves, bear testimony to the fine quality of man or woman.
>
> As a youth, I was denied the advantages which go with the possession of money; and, therefore, I am endeavoring to give those who have not such advantages but who aspire to the higher and finer attributes of life those opportunities which were denied me. I am a part of the heritage of Texas. Its pioneer spirit that peopled the wide

> spaces and laid the foundation of a happy future comes down to me in the strain of blood, and I wish to share it with others who would make Texas their home and their inspiration.
>
> The grave is a democracy for all human kind. There is no rank in death — the pauper laid away in an unlettered grave carries with him as much of worldly goods as the rich man whose body is clad in silken shroud. Neither the winding sheet nor the shroud is lined with purse or pocket. The hand that in life grips with a miser's clutch and the ear that refuses to heed the pleading voice of humanity, forfeits the most precious of all gifts of Earth and Heaven — the happiness within the heart that comes from doing good to others.

The thirty-two page document is a blueprint of benevolence. Writing about the will, the *Press* commented:

> The hand of Amon Carter reached out in bounteous generosity from the grave to bestow $800,000 on friends and associates in many walks of life — with bequests to 117 people, including a Negro washerwoman and a newsboy who sells the late publisher's papers on the streets.

Dated August 11, 1954, the will made principal bequests to Amon Carter, Jr., and daughter, Ruth [Mrs. J. Lee Johnson III] of $100,000 each. Mrs. Minnie Meacham Smith Carter, Amon's third wife, received $24,000 annually, free of all taxes. Katrine Deakins, his secretary of more than thirty years, was left $50,000, as was Roy E. Carter of Kermit, Amon's half-brother. Nancy Crouse, a blind *Press* vendor, was bequeathed $1,000. Nannie Moore, a black employee, and Monroe Odom, still peddling the *Star-Telegram* from his pinewood box, each were given $250. The Fort Worth Fireman's Fund and Fort Worth Police Association were granted $10,000 each. personal servants were left $500 apiece and eleven employees of the Fort Worth Club received amounts ranging from $100 to $1,000. *Star-*

Telegram carriers were given $10 each at Christmas and Thanksgiving until the total amounts equaled $25,000 and $6,000 respectively.

In specific directives, Carter gave $50,000 to be spent within a period of ten years at Amon G. Carter Riverside High School for scholarships, assistance for the needy, and recreational facilities. Amon also directed that a tract of land owned by his foundation on Lake Worth be developed for camping, athletic and other recreational facilities for students of Fort Worth schools.

His grandchildren received $25,000 each, and his osteopath physician, Dr. Phil Russell, was bequeathed $5,000, and the children of his sister, Addie, were given amounts from $500 to $20,000, and his friend and attorney Abe Herman, who succeeded Samuels, was granted $2,500, and Herman's two sons, $500 each.

Amon's will scattered money with the same cheerful nonchalance he practiced in life.

There were bequests for children of friends and employees, $100 for "Mammy" Korth, the "colored nurse" of Fred Korth's children, and $25,000 for the city of Bowie, and $500 each for surviving Chicken and Bread Boys, and $500 to $1,000 for sixteen *Star-Telegram* employees, (none of them reporters or editors), and $250 for Sid Richardson's driver, and $200 for a St. Joseph's Hospital X-ray technician, and $1,000 for a cousin, and $250 for the "colored" aunt of Stanley Moore, Amon's chauffeur, to be paid in monthly installments of $25.

Almost a year passed before Amon's net worth was announced. The estate totaled $10,252,294.51, from which there was to be deducted outstanding miscellaneous debts, including $500,000 for management and division of bequests, $250,000 in attorney fees and $70,000 for repayment of a loan to Sid Richardson.

Even then, no one knew exactly how much money Amon had amassed in his lifetime. Much of his wealth had been assigned to his children and other family members before his death. The estate's balance — $7,285,990.22 — was handed over to the Amon G. Carter Foundation. He and Nenetta endowed the foundation with seed money totaling $8,500,000 at its conception, June 13, 1945.*

The foundation continued Amon's scattershot system of benevolence in Fort Worth. It contributed, among other things, a hall of science and electric football scoreboard to Texas Christian University, established the non-profit Carter Blood Center, spent $600,000 in building Camp Carter, a YMCA facility on Lake Worth. Within its first fifteen years, the foundation built a $50,000 James R. Record Aquarium, gave $37,000 to Texas Tech and $25,000 to Texas Wesleyan College, provided $200,000 for the Tarrant County Society Academy of Medicine, $127,000 for the Panther Boys Club, $300,000 for the Greater Fort Worth Hospital Fund, $135,000 to the Fort Worth Crippled Children's Society, $11,000 for the Lighthouse for the Blind, and $500,000 for construction of a Hall of Medicine Wing at the Fort Worth Children's Museum (now Museum of Science and History).

Amon, in death, was as obvious and shepherding to Fort Worth as he was in life.

In the late 1940s, Amon, then a wealthy aging patrician, put away the cowboy forever. He had outgrown the boots and chaps and blazing guns ritual, and other western paraphernalia which had by then become a movie and novel cliche of Texas.

He settled in to live out his days as a dignified man of means, a fawning grandfather, and generous husband to Minnie. She was a beautiful slender woman with delicate features perfect for the jewels he lavished on her. They took long ocean cruises and entertained

*By the mid-1970s, Amon's foundation, fueled by his oil holdings, had escalated to a worth of $74,000,000, which ranked it as Texas' sixth largest, immediately behind the Sid Richardson Foundation.

at home, becoming socialites of the first order in a Fort Worth society finally growing beyond its cowchip origins.

In 1953, at seventy-three, Amon still was a vigorous, active man, having very little to do with operations of the newspaper, radio and television stations, but tending to his oil business. In that year, he had the first of his heart attacks — "A doozy of a coronary," said Ruth.

He was at home and immediately Minnie rushed him to St. Joseph's hospital. On the way, they were stopped by police at a driver license checkpoint. Minnie had no license, and for whatever reason, the police were not told of Amon's heart attack and the emergency of the trip. Amon drove himself to the hospital, undoubtedly in second gear.

Amon was an abominable patient. He lay in the hospital bed for two months, grouchy and demanding, anxious to be up and about, but fearful of the consequences of his heart attack. He alternated between despair and buoyancy. Once reporter Irv Farman visited with Amon for the publisher to read and approve the story dedicating his new airport. Before he would look at the story Amon read his get-well cards to Farman. The last he read slowly and with deep feeling, with tears in his eyes, ". . . and it's signed 'Ike.'"

He was a borderline hypochondriac all of his life. There were those three weekly osteopathic treatments in his home by Dr. Phil Russell which, he once wrote a friend, were all that "saved my life" for so many years. Always squeamish and queasy with sicknesses and illnesses of others, Amon was doubly uneasy with his own malconditions though he was unusually robust and healthy until his heart attacks.

His most serious medical problem had been hemorrhoids, which he had removed, forever calling his operation a "Beatonectomy" for the Dr. Beaton who performed the routine surgery.

Once Amon's legs became inflamed and painful and he was fearful he had contracted some terminal blood-clotting or circulatory malady. His doctor diagnosed the dreaded disease as "too-tight garters."

Amon finally was furloughed from the hospital with instructions he must never again exert himself or become excited. His children and family and Sid Richardson escorted him home. They had a surprise. During his hospitalization an elevator had been installed in his home because doctors said he no longer could use stairs.

Amon grumbled about the uselessness of an elevator and the expense.

"But, Amon," explained Sid helpfully, "look how much easier it'll be to bring your body down."

Amon of course dismissed his doctors' orders from his mind and after a period of further convalescence did much as he pleased. And soon there was another heart attack. Between attacks, Amon was impossible for doctors and family to control. He, said Katrine, "bucked and pitched" until allowed to attend an American Airlines board meeting and a newspaper publisher convention.

Though frail and weak, there were moments when he flashed the old angers, as when he crossed Taylor Street from the *Star-Telegram* to the Fort Worth Club and nearly was struck by an automobile driven by teen-age boys. He stood in the street, shaking his fist at the speeding automobile, and yelling, "You gawddamned sonsofbitches . . ."

Mostly confined to bed, Amon would watch television — "Gunsmoke" was his favorite program — until after midnight, then telephone friends and associates. Harold Hough finally took his phone off the hook. Amon switched to Jim Byron, WBAP-TV's news director. Amon wanted to discuss the station's operations, especially why it "runs so much Dallas news." Byron tried to explain that television was unlike newspapers. Newspaper circulation could be controlled; TV signals sprayed everywhere, including Dallas.

Doctors finally limited Amon to one telephone call a day. He obeyed them, but would talk for hours on his one phone call.

He presided over opening night of the Stock Show Rodeo in 1953 and later in the spring attended a special ceremony at the YMCA's Camp Carter. Bundled in the light-colored camel hair coat, Amon sat in freezing weather while speakers paid tribute to his generosity. He was presented with a bound book of about one hundred letters from youngsters expressing their appreciation for Camp Carter.

Later, Jim Vachule carried the Camp Carter story to Amon for approval. Amon wasn't interested in the story. He insisted Vachule eat dinner — hot dogs and ice tea — with him, then opened the scrapbook and began reading the children's letters aloud to the reporter. Amon kept Vachule so long the newsman missed his deadline.

W. L. Redus, an editorial writer, visited Amon at home and had a similar experience. Amon was excited when Redus arrived, babbling on about two books — a Fulton Ousler inspirational tome and Douglas Southall's *Lee's Lieutenants*. Those were, Amon revealed, the first books he had read in thirty years. Redus said Amon "was agog by what he found in them."

With Redus, Amon soon turned, as he did with most visitors, to the past, reviewing his life. In those last months, he went into his memories again and again. Depending on his mood, the retelling of his life was either as the Book of Job or as lighthearted as a fairy tale. He spoke of his accomplishments and honors, of the companies he had lured into Fort Worth, of his famous friends.

He remembered being one of only three living men — Charles Lindbergh was another — to have a Pullman sleeping car named for him. Amon's name replaced

Henry W. Longfellow, who only was a poet, not a cowboy. "I'm just happy it's not a baggage car," Amon said at the time.

He reminisced about the bomber plant and the public health hospital and Chicago Pneumatic Tool Company which he sold on building a $4,500,000 plant in Fort Worth, and the regional headquarters of Continental, Pure and Sinclair oil companies he dragged into town, and once there, how he tended to their business. Sinclair regional officers declared they were moving their headquarters to Houston but Amon stopped that silly notion by telephoning his personal friend, Harry Sinclair. Gulf did move its regional offices from Fort Worth to Wichita Falls. Amon insisted Gulf return, and it did, though the lesson was an expensive one for the oil company.

He spoke of his honorary doctorate from Texas Tech, the first given by that prairie college, and of another from Texas Christian University, and most proudly of having his name on a school — "It's sorta nice to have your name on a high school when you never had the opportunity to go through one." One sultry late May evening in 1951, Amon, with other Amon Carter Riverside High School graduating seniors, received his high school diploma. Sid, seated beside Amon during ceremonies, whispered in his ear, "You ole bastard, if you ever graduate from high school again, you can do it in the winter or count me out."

He recalled the plaque at Meacham Field dedicating the air facility in his name: "The Matchless Texan — Amon Carter — Range Rider of the Air." And "The West Texan," a thirty-eight foot twin-motored cruiser friends had given him. And that the Texas Legislature had declared him "Ambassador of Good Will" because, said House Speaker Homer Leonard, "If Texas had a press agent, you are it." And of the appreciation dinner given him by members of the Fort Worth Club, an honor he had delayed by one ruse or another for thirteen years until the dinner was given anyway against his wishes. Among the gifts for him that evening was an oil portrait which he professed to like, but did not.

In December, 1954, Amon came to the *Star-Telegram* to sign Christmas bonus checks, but he was too weak to finish and Katrine, who could sign his name as well as any good forger, had to continue for him. Nenetta saw him there and they spoke a long time, of their children, and, again, of the past. He attempted to dictate several letters to Katrine but his mind wandered and he stopped. He was frail and weak and never again was seen in public.

By early June even Amon knew he soon would die and he called Amon Junior and Ruth, Katrine and Sid, to his bedside to discuss the estate, the museum he wanted built, personal matters. It was then he declared, "If the paper ever supports Lyndon Johnson for anything, I'll turn over in my grave."

An evening or two later, about ten o'clock, Amon went into a coma. On June 19, Father's Day, he briefly awoke to ask, "Am I still here?", then lapsed again into unconsciousness. Four days later, forty minutes before the morning *Star-Telegram*'s two-star deadline, Herb Schultz received the telephone call.

He turned to others around the city desk and announced:

"He's dead."

"I doubt whether there are any leading people on the American scene and very few on the international scene who did not know him," said Lyndon Johnson the following day on the floor of the United States Senate. "Amon Carter was a man who stood in the main stream of the history of our times. He walked with cattle men and kings, with crop farmers and with Presidents. He had the common touch that kept him close to all humanity and the uncommon qualities which made him a leader. He left behind him monuments that will endure for years to come and such men are rare."

Republican floor leader Senator William F. Knowland of California followed Johnson, saying Amon was "a great Texan . . . one of the outstanding newspaper publishers of our time." Senator Alben Barkley of Kentucky said, "My friend, Amon Carter. . . contributed profoundly to the thinking of the people." J. Edgar Hoover commented that day, "It is the loss of a cherished friend." Senator Stuart Symington of Missouri commented, ". . . no citizen was more interested in maintenance of air superiority by the United States." Former Texas Senator Tom Connally said, "We shall not see his like again." Herbert Hoover told reporters, "Amon Carter was a unique and distinguished figure in public life."

In the U.S. House of Representatives, Congressman Jim Wright, who had fought Amon for his job there, eulogized, "His death leaves a void which no other person can quite fill. Fort Worth and all of Texas were the beneficiaries of his life; all are losers in his death."

As news of Amon's death spread across the country, telegrams and messages of condolence filled the *Star-Telegram* office. Ike messaged, "Terribly shocked and distressed to hear of Amon's death." Texas Governor Allan Shivers said, "I will miss him as a close personal friend . . . his benevolent and charitable heart knew no bounds." U.S. House Speaker Sam Rayburn said, "He was my friend for thirty years." Washington columnist David Lawrence wired, "He made an indelible impression on those of us who were fortunate to know him throughout the years."

Bernard Baruch said, "He was the best type of not alone Mr. Texas but USA."

Other messages came from Arthur Hays Sulzberger, publisher of the New York *Times*; Harold Talbott, secretary of the Air Force; Sherman Billingsley, owner of the Stork Club; Ben Fairless, board chairman of U.S.

Steel; Winthrop Aldrich, U.S. Ambassador to Great Britain; boxers Jack Dempsey and Gene Tunney; Eddie Rickenbacker and Samuel Goldwyn; Gene Autry, who once sang on Amon's radio station; Nelson Rockefeller and Henry Luce, the *Time* and *Life* publisher; Theodore Hesburgh, president of the University of Notre Dame, and comedians Bob Hope and Edgar Bergen.

Eddie Cantor wired, "He gave so much of his heart, he had nothing left for himself." And Billy Rose messaged, "He was the last of the empire builders, and Fort Worth is his monument."

All of the messages were, no doubt, sincere, but none conveyed the yippee and whoopee of Amon Carter's cowboy. In death few remembered the cowboy.

Amon's, of course, was the largest funeral in Fort Worth history, especially at the grave site where fifteen thousand people came to pay last respects.

The funeral was at four o'clock because the cowboy said he wanted to be buried in the late afternoon, near sundown. All of Fort Worth noted the services. Downtown stores closed. Flags were at half-mast. Forest Park Zoo and the James R. Record Aquarium closed from four to five o'clock, as did the sheriff's office.

Reverend James K. Thompson, a Presbyterian and long time friend was in charge of services which by Amon's instructions were kept brief. Reverend Thompson was there because Amon once said he wanted the minister "when my time comes. I know he will be generous to the subject." Services were held in the First Methodist Church because it had the largest auditorium in town, and its pastor, Reverend Gastoon Foote, a *Star-Telegram* Sunday columnist, participated in the eulogies, characterizing Amon as a man "who shaped the skyline of our city with the deftness of an artist's hands."

Reverend Foote concluded, "His name was chiseled in marble and his likeness etched in bronze, but there is much more to remind us of his presence. Though he lies down to a well-earned rest, his spirit is yet among us. No man left more of himself behind than Amon Carter."

Amon lay in a gray casket banked by flowers, including Billy Rose's floral tribute in the shape of a Shady Oak Stetson. All of the auditorium was filled and speakers had been set up in an adjoining banquet hall. Outside, many people stood on the sidewalk listening through open windows. Governor Shivers sat in the front row, and Patrick Hurley, former secretary of war, was nearby, as were American Airlines president C. R. Smity, and Harlow Curtice, General Motors president, and Delos Rentzel, former chairman of the Civil Aeronautics Board, and Monroe Odom, who left his pinewood crate in front of the Worth Hotel to attend his boss's last public moment.

Reporters who covered the funeral viewed the body before the casket was closed, and noted Amon was dressed in a dark suit and somber red tie. Nenetta saw a few soup stains on the tie.

The newsmen seemed genuinely disappointed Amon did not go to his grave with pearl-handled six-shooters strapped on, dressed in the familiar polo-coat and Stetson. They saw the dark suit and one purportedly commented, "It seems so undignified."

Another reporter said he was sure Amon intended to have the flowers arranged to spell out "Welcome to Fort Worth — Where the West Begins."

Four vans were needed to transport flowers to Amon's grave. Thirty motorcycle mounted policemen led the procession from the church to Greenwood Memorial Cemetery on the west side.

Graveside services were brief. Pallbearers were too old and infirm to lift the heavy bronze coffin and eight policemen actually bore Amon Carter to his grave. The deed done, one briefly touched his cap in silent tribute.

Soon the fifteen thousand left the cowboy and gravediggers spread dirt over the casket. One grave worker, by some quirk of circumstance that would have pleased Amon, was one of those tens of thousands of displaced West Texans; the man had fled his barren little prairie hamlet for better things in the town that the cowboy built.

Even later, the cowboy was alone among the thicket of oak trees to savor that final sundown. It was, they say, a glorious sunset.

Epilogue

The *Star-Telegram* was as one of those high hidden valley villages of the Andes where all men lived to great old age.

Many — most, in fact — of the reporters and editors there in the very earliest plum days were still around in the mid-1970s. Flem Hall, E. D. Alexander, Ida Belle Hicks, Bess Stephenson, James Byron, Frank Mills, DeWitt Reddick. They were in their sixties, seventies and eighties, as was the indomitable C. L. Richhart. Bearded, balding, blithe as an imp, forever irrepressible, he remained a wondrous little man. For his golden wedding anniversary, Rich persuaded his wife to put on trunks and boxing gloves. They sparred for photographers. She cold-cocked him.

Others have passed on. Frank Reeves died February 4, 1975, in bed. Heart attack. He refused to retire. After the newspaper pensioned him off, Reeves returned to the office and continued writing. Editors gave up and let him do as he wished. Characteristically, Frank forgot to cash his pension checks. The morning after his death, editors found in his typewriter the beginnings of a story memorializing the horse in development of West Texas. He was ninety. E. Clyde Whitlock died May 10, 1970. Heart attack. He had refused to retire and continued to write his multisyllabic reviews, often falling asleep in mid-sentence. He was eighty-four. *Ave atque vale.* Alf Evans died May 14, 1975. Heart attack. He, though on pension, had not retired. He remained to edit religious news and prowl the hallways long before dawn in search of someone with whom to talk, to entertain with that wry way he had. In one of the last pre-dawn conversations we had, he philosophized, "The trouble with life is it's too damn constant." He was sixty-nine.

Most of Amon's old friends and colleagues are dead and gone. James Farley died a few months after I spoke with him of his experiences with Amon. Silliman Evans came to Amon's funeral. That night, in Suite 10G of the Fort Worth Club, he died in his sleep. Heart attack. He was sixty-one. Al Shuman died September 12, 1955, following Amon by a few months but fulfilling his vow to the publisher. Shuman retired in 1932. Amon, who did not believe in retirements, chided him, and Shuman said, "I'll outlive you." Heart attack. He was eighty-three. Harold Hough died January 4, 1967 after a half a century with the *Star-Telegram* empire. Heart attack. Jimmy North died during a business trip to New York, October 16, 1956. Heart attack. He was seventy. JRR died July 1, 1973, in his sixty-sixth year at the newspaper. Heart attack. He would not retire, but lived to see the newspaper he helped create become modern with computers and phototype and reporters hunched over typewriters that hummed with an electric energy not their own. For his funeral, at which he was described as "a man who had no enemies," JRR's last day was clear and cloudless and hot with a twelve mile an hour southwesternly wind. There was no rain. He was eighty-seven.

I spoke with Pauline Naylor of her memories of Amon less than a month before she died. She was a puckish little woman wearing diamonds and surrounded by cats and her late husband's superb collection of rare books. As she spoke of the publisher and the cowboy and the *Star-Telegram*, she paused thoughtfully, and said with a smile, "I'll bet Amon Carter was mad when he died because he wouldn't know how everything turned out."

There is truth in that. Amon, the neurotic perfectionist, liked neat endings. Some of what happened would have provoked him into a spate of gawddamns. The newspaper did support Lyndon Johnson, several times, in fact, but in 1955 no one had any notion LBJ would become President. A native Texan in the White House had to be applauded and supported, if for no other reason than state chauvinism. The *Star-Telegram* pulled away from West Texas, abdicating the plains kingdom to concentrate on a metropolitan circulation. The empire itself was broken up in the face of a governmental order about monopolization of a communications market. The television station went to LIN Broadcasting Incorporated. The newspapers and radio stations were sold to Capital Communications Incorporated of New York. The undisclosed sale price was said to have been in excess of one hundred million dollars. The *Star-Telegram* alone brought more than seventy million dollars, to that time the largest price ever paid for an American newspaper. Not bad for a dream begun over a pile of burning cow chips.

Bert Honea still was there after seventy years on the job, daily checking the computer's accounting accuracy against the detailed, meticulous ledgers he continued. Capital Communications offered Honea a lifetime contract. He refused, explaining, "I don't intend to spend the rest of my life at this place.'' He was ninety-three.

Amon Carter rested in a marble and granite mausoleum on a grassy knoll surrounded by trees. It was not boot hill but it was a pleasant place to be. He was moved to the crypt two years after his death. Amon bequeathed himself the mausoleum. In his will — but never reported in the *Star-Telegram* — he set aside $100,000 for the mausoleum and instructed it to be enscribed suitably ''to attest the love I hold for my fellowman and my devotion to the cause of the weak and the underprivileged.''

Above the crypt's door are these words: His Life Made Charity As Real As Hope Itself.

Amon Carter needs neither apologist nor protector of his memory. There were too many of both. He was a piquant man with a generous hand and heart, but one of angers and vanities, onerousness, ever immoderate and amazing. He was not a journalist but he raised Texas journalism to a public service perfection, and in the process, raised Texas journalism.

His cowboy, a parody of real Texans like old Lan Twohig, still is with us, always will be a personality famous for its whoopees and yippees. Whatever else Amon Carter may have left behind, he consigned forever to the world that big-hatted, booted, six-gunning, swaggering, blustering satire of a cowboy. Even Amon's death was in the celluloid tradition of his cowboy. Amon, the man who raised professional Texanism to a grand art and made all western cliches seem irreducible truth, died as the sun sank slowly in the west, the town ridded of bad guys, the gun notched and cleaned, the girl won and left to stand alone in the dusty street. Dissolve, fade out. Cut. Print it.

He left behind a widow, two ex-wives, two children, two radio stations, a television station, a newspaper, a passel of oil wells, innumerable legacies, several lies, many legends and a whoopee-ing cowboy.

It fell to Alf Evans to pronounce the most telling epitaph for the cowboy. Paraphrasing humorist Frank Sullivan's thoughts on a dead friend, Alf said, "I don't know where Amon Carter is today, but wherever it is, the people there are having a good time."

And that's the way it was a long time ago . . . Where the West Begins.

Index

C

D

E

F

G

H

I

J

K

L

M

R

S

T

U

V

W

X

Y

Z